By the Same Author

Creationism
(published by Classroom Resources)

They are People Too!- a course in international citizenship
(published by Classroom Resources)

The Peaceweaver
(published by Raider International Publishing)

Let the Stones Talk

*Glimpses of English History
through the People of the Moor*

Christopher Steed

authorHOUSE®

AuthorHouse™ UK Ltd.
500 Avebury Boulevard
Central Milton Keynes, MK9 2BE
www.authorhouse.co.uk
Phone: 08001974150

© 2011 Christopher Steed. All rights reserved.

No part of this book may be reproduced, stored in a retrieval system, or transmitted by any means without the written permission of the author.

First published by AuthorHouse   4/14/2011

ISBN: 978-1-4567-7687-9 (sc)

Any people depicted in stock imagery provided by Thinkstock are models, and such images are being used for illustrative purposes only.
Certain stock imagery © Thinkstock.

This book is printed on acid-free paper.

Because of the dynamic nature of the Internet, any web addresses or links contained in this book may have changed since publication and may no longer be valid. The views expressed in this work are solely those of the author and do not necessarily reflect the views of the publisher, and the publisher hereby disclaims any responsibility for them.

Dedication

This book is affectionately dedicated as parting gift to the people of Yatton Moor where I had the privelige of accompanying them on their continuing journey for fifty four happy months.

The cover picture shows cottages on the glebelands adjoining Yatton Parish Church, sketched in 1851 by the aunt of the then Vicar, Henry Barnard. Every effort has been made through the Yatton History Society to ascertain the source of this picture but without success.

Back cover shows Artist's impression of an iron-age hillfort as at Cadbury-Congresbury. © English Heritage Photo Library.

Contents

Introduction	Time and Change in a North Somerset Parish	xv
Part 1	**Sixty Generations on the Moor**	**1**
Chapter 1	Land of the Dobunni	3
Chapter 2	The Hill – Fort People	19
Chapter 3	One day they saw ships	31
Chapter 4	Lords and the Lives of the Miserable	41
Chapter 5	An Ecclesiastical Building Spree	59
Chapter 6	Armageddon and the 44th generation	69
Chapter 7	A Tale of False Accusation	75
Chapter 8	A Position in Society	89
Chapter 9	The People of the Village	97
Chapter 10	Religion-shock	117
Chapter 11	A Sea of Troubles	133
Chapter 12	The Bite of a Mad Dog	151
Chapter 13	Social Transformation on Wheels	165
Chapter 14	On a Street Corner in Yatton	179
Chapter 15	The Day Before Yesterday	205
Chapter 16	The Great Yatton Feast	227
Part 2	**The Mid- Victorian Generation**	**231**
Chapter 17	The Undeserving Poor	233
Chapter 18	Society in Layers	245

| Chapter 19 | Educating the Rural Poor (and other stories) | 263 |
| Chapter 20 | Like Losing a Father | 281 |

Part 3	**On Reflection**	**297**
Chapter 21	The Significance of Significance	299
Chapter 22	A Useful Lens?	311

| Appendix 1 | The Eight Manors of Yatton Moor | 327 |
| Appendix 2 | Census Data 1841 compared with 1881 | 331 |

Bibliography specifically relating to Cadbury-Congresbury Hillfort	333
General References	337
Index	361

List of Maps

The Moor in Roman times	4
The Moor in Medieval times	42
Yatton in 1840	166

List of Illustrations

Mosaic pavement in Wemberham Villa	13
Lay-out of Cadbury-Congresbury Hill-fort, Henley Temple and 'the Spirit-Road'	16
Norman font in Kingston Seymour Church	61
Norman tower in Kenn Church	62
Robert Gyene and Egelina de Wyck	83
Sir John Newton and Isabel	93
The Newton tombs	96
A house fit for the Prebend of Yatton c1495	102
A completed church (minus the spire) – St Mary's Yatton	116
Elizabeth Kenn, who married John Poulett in 1614	139
Yatton Railway Station c1920	174
Driving sheep to market c1910	176
Isaac Joules the gypsy	200
High Street Yatton	210
approaching the station in pony and trap c1920	210
Mr Travis with his portable hardware store	211
Basket weaving at Church of England National School c1935	217
Kingston Seymour Manor House c1840	251
The Bell Inn Yatton c1880	253
Buckler's drawing of Holy Trinity Church, Cleeve c1841	284
Church Hall & Institute, mid-19th century Yatton	290

List of Tables

Counting the people of the Moor- population in 1840/1880	248
Church-going on the Moor in 1851	286
Employment on the Moor – comparing the Census data	331

A Word About Sources

This book had its genesis in visits I made to the present generation on the Moor while I was serving on the clergy team there between 2006 -2010. Older members of the village were enthusiastic about telling me of their experiences growing up here. I quickly realised these were worth recording as valuable social history. To add to the living history, I only had to look around me and let the stones talk to realise that the whole district was set amidst a tremendous story reaching back to Roman times.

As I began to consider writing, several things began to happen which underlined that here was a rich story to be told in a consecutive way. I was given access to some remarkable new work that has been done through the Yatton, Cleeve and Congresbury Archaeological Team (YCCART) on Cadbury-Congresbury Hillfort stimulated by County Archaeologist Vince Russett. People pressed information into my hands that was just too juicy to resist; diaries came down from attics. I was given regular briefings before he died by Nicholas Deas, a researcher whose accuracy and thoroughness has become legendary round here. And there was enough material through 19th century newspapers to convince me that there was fresh material that could be used to weave a narrative about time and change in a rural commununity.

To all these friends and contributors, my heart-felt thanks for their generosity. I especially want to thank Alan Denny and colleagues at the Yatton History Society for assistance and advice. Mary Campbell did sterling work on information needed for the sketch maps that demarcate the three main periods covered by this book. To them all and Andrew Bryden who took on the task of preparing the maps, I am so very grateful. Roger Lawrence was of inestimable help scaning all the images used.

Chris Short & Brian Bradbury from YCCART were generous with help and comment.

I benefited from expert assistance from staff at Somerset Heritage Centre. I acknowledge kind permission of the Somerset Archaeological and Natural History Society to reproduce sketches of Yatton Parish and Holy Trinity Parish Churches, effigies there and at Kingston together with the Prebendal house in Yatton- all by Buckler for the Smyth-Piggot collection housed in the Somerset Heritage Centre. Dave Batson of Yatton allowed me to use his photos for the 1920's pictures here. English heritage kindly allowed me to use the artist's impression on the back cover.

As far as possible, I have avoided using the fascinating material that continues to be published by the Yatton History Society under the title of Yatton Yesterdays. The same applies to Marion Barraclough's expert 'History of Yatton' which provided me with a very helpful framework when I needed it. I hope no one will feel that I am pinching the best bits of research; there is still plenty to go round and bring out!

I want to acknowledge too the enthusiasm provided by those who contributed to the file I opened under the general heading of the "Yatton Moor Oral History Project." Ray Naish, Bob Ford and Viv Wathen were extremely helpful- to name but three!

Thanks lastly to the Claverham Society of Friends for permission to use the Eliza Clarke diaries, to the estate of Mrs W.J. Court for 2nd World War diaries, to Dr Viki Coakin for sight of the William Derham papers and descendants of Isaac Joules who showed me their family archives and generously allowed me to draw from them.

To all these friends and sources responding to my requests, I say a huge thanks!

The Moor in 1791

Kenn... "is a small parifh, fituated at the very northern extremity of the hundred and on the confines of that of Portbury. The country is flat and marfy and there is a large moor called Kenn-Moor, adjoining to that of Nailfea, towards the north, in which there is a decoy pond, thefe levels being frequented by great numbers of acquatic fowl. A river, rifing at Midglitt pits in the parifh of Chelvey traverfes this parifh in its course towards the fea, and contains eels, fandabe and plaice........ The Church is a small fabrick of the place, having a turret at the weft end in which hangs one seal..."

"Yatton is a large village lying about a mile north from Congefbury, two fouth from Kenn, the fame diftance foufweft from Brockley and thirteen from Briftol. Its most ancient name was Jatone which fignifies the Town-port, from the Saxon Iace, janua, and Ton, oppidum, this place in early ages having formed an entrance or paffage, as it were, to the Channel, at what time its waters overfpread the valley. The parish contains a great variety of furface; the north, weft and part of the fouth, being a fine level country of rich paftures; but on the eaft and foufeasft it rifes into hills and craggy rocks, interfperfed with combes and dingles. One of the eminences is called Cleve-Toot and has a very picturefque appearance, being a large copped and conical mountain, rearing its naked head to a great height above the level of the plain. On the foufweft fide is Cadbury- Hill, the third of that name in this county, which is not however deeply intrenched like the others, but ftill retains veftiges of ancient fortifications, and being naturally frtong was no doubt occupied by our military anceftors. To the foufeaft is Kingswood, a large tract of coppice with fome timber. In this panfh are two frpings called Bishop's-Well and Holwell, fituated near each other, about a quarter of a mile eaft ward from the village of Yatton and both formerly accounted efficacious in confumptive maladies. Thefe fprings form rivulets which fall into the river Yow.

The village of Yatton is very neat and has a refpectable appearance. It confifts of one very long ftreet, through which runs an excellent road, continued hither from Brockley......

To the northeaft of Yatton is Claverham, which at the Conqueft was written Cliveham and was then held by Geffrey Bifhop of Coutances.

xiii

The tithing and hamlet of Cleve is fituated eafteward from Court de Wick and in the road from Congrefbury to Brockley."

"Westward from Brockley but divided from it by the hundred of Winterftoke is Kingston –Seymour, lying in the laft fubdivifion of the Hundred and contiguous with the Bristol Channel. It is a fmall frtaggling place, confifting of forty-two houfes, arable land and very rich, being worth on average thirty-four fillings an acre throughout the parifh. Two rivers here difcharge themselfes into the sea....the land feperated by ditches more than hedges, there is little wood and elm the principal. There are many large orchards....

Collinson, (Revd). *The History and Antiquities of the County of Somerset* (Bath, 1791), Vol III p592, 616-7. Also Vol II p172

Introduction

TIME AND CHANGE IN A NORTH SOMERSET PARISH

"*It is an odd thing*", reports Gerald in his journey through Wales in 1188, that in a rock by the sea, not far from Cardiff, there is a small crack. "*If you press your ear to it, you can hear a noise like that of blacksmiths at work, the blowing of bellows, the strokes of hammers and the harsh grinding of files on metal*". [1]

The landscape of the Moor is like that. If you press your ear to it with imagination, you might hear a noise like that of blacksmiths at work, the harsh grinding of farmers and labourers wrestling with the land, peasants and lords inhabiting a structured cosmos and the steady, slow - motion lives of the villagers across sixty generations.

Time: the capacity to stand outside yourself, above yourself and move quickly and backwards through a ménage of memory. Time: a stream meandering from the past towards the other country that is the future. Strangely immersed in its secret flow, we are caught, inexorably held in the living current of history for a while; prisoners to a movement that rushes us forward, ever forward. Those who dwelt in the strange land of the past did not realise they lived in history. They were inhabitants of the Now. For we are, let it be said, an older version of our younger self; unfolding chronology of time and experience cautions us from telling a story from perspective of journey's end. The people of the Moor had no idea they were living in the Middle Ages.

Experiences of the past and expectations of the future are knit together into a linear progression. Time moulds the human continuity. It provides inner coherence and identity, enabling yourself to rise above yourself and write a narrative that integrates times past with times present. This mental task we call history. The narrative in front of us is such a history, the unfolding biography of a community, a largely rural parish in North Somerset – or two parishes to be precise as they are now demarcated. This area, with five village communities offers a lens on wider currents in English history.

Former inhabitants of our communities played out their lives as the latest new creation, the generation of the present. They were born, lived and had children like their fathers and mothers did before them. Then came the studied realisation that there were more miles behind them than in front of them and that they would yield to the next generation to take forward the stream of life. The location of the human subject is set firmly within the territory of the living yet with the ability to imagine.

The time is two thousand years of living history, some of it clear to us, some of it obscure but all of it vivid in the lived experience of those that moved across farm and field, Manor and church. Some sixty generations have arisen, stood to attention to live out their days on the Moor or were associated with it. History is embedded within the everyday life of its people. It is also bound by place as well as time.

Place: a location where the inhabitants of time live, the stage where they come to play out the scripts they are handed. Until the 19th century, the villagers will rarely venture more than ten miles from their community. It will become part of their identity. They will be someone's son, someone's daughter. But they will also be someone from the Moor. Until the day before yesterday when greater mobility bequeathed alternative futures, place fixed their identity and gave them roots. In 1841, the first bookend in our glance at the mid-Victorian generation, very few inhabitants were born outside the village. By 1881, when most will have played out their lives, only a quarter of the inhabitants counted in the Census were born within Yatton.

The place is a rectangular piece of land about six miles by three. This living theatre bordered by some 20 miles offers a stage of some 5,400 acres, marked by a river to the south, the river Yeo, meandering from Congresbury to the sea at the Bristol Channel some three miles distant. The River Kenn drains the northern part of the peat moors. On the soft, marshy alluvial clay in the north, centre and west around Kingston, Kenn and Yatton itself there is high quality land. In addition to coastal resources and access to the western seaways, the North Somerset Levels here provide summer grazing, wildfowl and fish. Cleeve-Toot and wooded hills towards the east yield fuel and timber. To the south-west of the benefice lies Cadbury Hill – known to archaeology as 'Cadbury-Congresbury.' It looms large in the early part of this narrative as a hill-fort and possibly religious shrine or elite community. It is a misnomer to call this varied landscape 'the Moor;' which is merely convenient shorthand for the district whose biography we are unfolding.

I am not trying to describe anything other than the normal crimes, rivalries and passions of small town or village society in which some will swim and others will sink. The Moor is not especially unusual except that a wealth of historical documents locate it amidst major events in our history – the so-called 'dark- ages', Domesday and the tales of medieval landowners, the churchwarden accounts that reveal late medieval life and the impact of Reform movements in the 16th century and the rich tapestry of documents and newspapers that highlight mid - Victorian social history.

Towards the end of this narrative, in the years between about 1760 and 1830, the combination of population growth, enclosures of rural land, urbanisation and industrialisation force a dramatic transformation in the landscape of old England. During the last two hundred years, everyday life has been transformed. From a village- based farming community, Britain is now an industrial one. Other villages on the Moor remained part of a rural world but Yatton became an industrialised village. Railways came and brought prominence, access, movement; above all, fresh possibilities. The old society began to break down. Children no longer followed in the footsteps of parents. Old assumptions no longer governed the way life would unfold.

Superimposed further upon the physical landscape of these North Somerset Levels has been the sacred geography that covered every square inch of England. For a thousand years, people have been coming to these parish churches to pray and to congregate; to weep and to give thanks. Concern about the parish church provided a focus for community life, for merry- making and the abrasive contrast of triumph and tragedy that marked the lives of its villagers. Religion was not just what people did on Sundays or festival days. It shaped rites of passage; the steady drum-beat roll-call of births, marriages and deaths. The Parish moulded work, leisure and superstition. It provided the rhythm for the unfolding year, a rhythm dominated by seed-time, harvest and constant battles against the sea. The requirements of faith transformed any nature religion into a sacred cycle; festivals, of Advent and Christmas, of Candlemass and Lent, of Easter and Pentecost. That was special time, marked by the colours of the church and of priest. Then comes six months of ordinary time. It was a cyclical move forward much like a wheel comes back to its start on its journey.

Modern Christianity has been pushed to the margins of social, political and scientific life. The Church is conscious that the world can do without it. Through its parish organisation, the Church has played a crucial role in the history of local communities. Even now, Church and community come together for a village event which is the way it always was but no longer true of larger towns. Few aspects of daily experience were exempt. How buildings have grown and been altered in their decoration, furnishings and structure; how the services, liturgy and ritual have been modified at different times and how parishioners lives have been affected by Church, schools and tithes is vital to the journey of a North Somerset Parish through time and place.

The size is impressive. In our secular age, religious categories are much less employed to make sense of the world. It is intriguing to image a society where towers rise above the fields. No part of the Moor would have been out of eyesight of one of the five churches that dot the landscape. Everyone would have heard the bells calling them to pray and to look up. Societies lacking in heavy moving and lifting equipment and living close to the soil spent much time and wealth on the construction of these buildings. The parish churches of the Moor remain the largest and most impressive buildings amongst its five villages. They are a constant reminder of the role that the church played in the life of the communities over time.

There are many elements here that are not necessarily new but which deserve to be brought to wider attention.

- The finds on Cadbury Hill that shed new light on the dark ages
- The medieval landowners of the Moor
- How churchwarden accounts powerfully illustrate late medieval church life
- The 19th century social life of the villages through contemporary lives as told by newspapers of the time and family history
- The Yatton Oral History archive.

Part One of this book takes us through the march of the generations who lived on the Moor for two thousand years of its history. After the medieval period, life chances begin to improve. Hence the life of a generation I raise to about forty years rather than the thirty hitherto. Part Two is an in-depth look at the mid-Victorian generation, a social history for those who want to go into more detail about how the life of a group of village communities worked. The period 1840-1880 has been chosen for this because it offers analysis of high-quality Census data.

Part Three attempts some social analysis in line with a theory of human action I am developing. In effect, I postulate that the life experience of people and groups is shaped by the value society places upon them and ask if that idea is sustainable on an historical canvas.

There lie many stones across the surface of the Moor. The story of the churches and their use is vital to the understanding of a journey of a community through time. But there are stones that lie under the surface of a Roman villa, stones that lie on Cadbury hill-fort and sketches of stones to do with houses and dwellings. The stones provide a microcosm of the journey we now make across sixty generations. If stones could talk, what stories could they tell?

The biography of this community over twenty centuries is heavy with the proceeds of the soil. Yet the North Somerset Levels here are not only rich in arable land, they are rich in history. Many toilers have worked in this field. Listen to the sound of sixty generations as they have played out their lives on the landscapes of the Moor. Look through the lens they provide of the changing face of England and its history, where the people of the Moor worked and worshipped.

Part 1

SIXTY GENERATIONS ON THE MOOR

Chapter 1

LAND OF THE DOBUNNI

ROMAN SITES IN THE PARISH OF YATTON

HAWKINS BRIDGE

LITTLE RIVER

HORSECASTLE

WEMBERHAM VILLA

RIVER YEO

CADBURY FARM

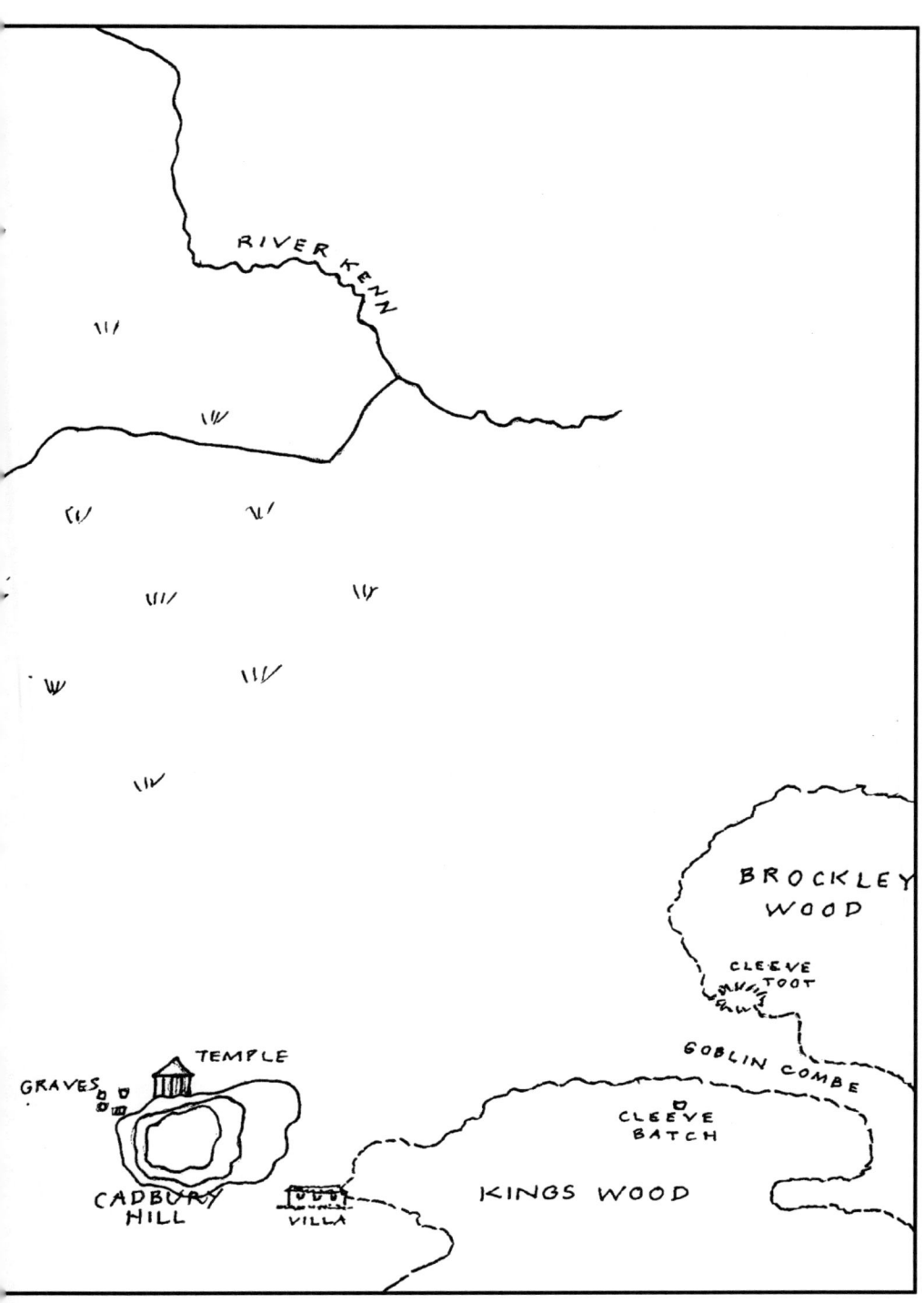

From the sky-line of the Mendip hills they descend, remorselessly subduing any opposition. Any tribe that puts up a show of defiance to the Roman Army is conquered and defeated. The commander of the western wing of the Roman invasion is Vespasian, the future emperor. He has under him a crack unit, the Second Legion, the renowned Legio II Augusta. Before being ordered to Britannia, the Second Legion had been based at Strasburg. With this highly efficient war machine, Vespasian moves systematically north and west, beginning with his capture of the Isle of Wight. The green hills of Dorset and Wiltshire fall to him.

The year is 43AD. The generation that faced the Roman onslaught is the first of sixty that will play out their lives on the Moor. This generation, the last of the pre-Roman iron- age Dobunni tribes - people must have some inkling of what is coming.

The picture of what led to Roman occupation is changing. To show his status as conqueror and hero in the footsteps of Julius Caesar, the Emperor Claudius took charge of four legions, 45,000 men, at Richborough, Kent in order to subdue Britannia. There probably had been rather more contact between Britain and Gaul than used to be thought. Julius Caesar made a reconnaissance in 55/54 BC.[2] The interval between that and the full-scale invasion by Claudius was not a complete blank as far as activity by the Romans across the water in Gaul were concerned. It may well be that they were trading and even settling in south eastern Britain by the time that Claudius decided to inflate his prestige by occupation of this troublesome island. Concerned with their own righteousness, the Romans usually sought some provocation before military intervention. The tribes of southern Britain are creating alliances under the growing threat from Rome. In Roman eyes, that makes the situation look unstable.[3] So a little easy glory, a sixteen day stay and the British expedition now becomes the personal venture of the Emperor Claudius rather than Aulus Plautius, whom he instructs to subjugate the rest of the troublesome country.

At any rate, Vespasian, military commander in the West, moves quickly. Suetonius, the Roman historian, tells us that the future Emperor was unashamed of his humble origins. He had already seen military service in Thrace, Crete and North Africa. Now, entrusted with the command of a legion, he captures the Isle of Wight (or Vectis), fights thirty battles, conquers two warlike tribes and captures twenty strongholds. That was just the initial campaign. A biographer records that he and his brother undertook dangerous reconaisance missions, even going behind enemy lines. Sweating no doubt under their armour, the heavy Roman infantry stormed the hillforts, the oppida, one by one. The enormous earthworks of Maiden Castle at Dorchester fell to them despite copious ammunition dumps in the form of thousands of stones at the disposal of the slingers inside.[4] South Cadbury was captured but continued to function as a small town.

Vespasian keeps coming, marching in at the head of the Second Legion to claim yet another area for Rome. It is hard-going in places. Battle-hardened formations faced hordes of painted Britons: male and female warriors defending their homes and their land. The Romans always found de-centralised societies harder to conquer than unified groups or States. They have to fight them piece-meal and not always in pitched battle on grounds of their choosing.[5] Roman conquest of Somerset was slow but relentless.[6] How long the initial thrust takes is not clear. By 47AD, it is clear that Fosse Way has been constructed by the Legion across Somerset as a way to project imperial power, connect a series of forts and serve as a supply route for continuing operations to the north.[7] A road from Old Sarum to Charterhouse on the Mendips has also been suggested as being Roman.[8] It was typically straight. By 49AD, the Romans build a fort at Ham Hill and at Ilchester in Somerset; to become a regional centre for their initial occupation.

Amongst their other invasion goals, the Romans were after lead. The existence of local lead pigs dating from about 49AD shows that within five or six years of the campaign, the Romans knew about the lead. It was quickly exploited. Mendip lead contained a special prize, 0.4% silver, which was extracted on site. Compared with lead from Spain, Mendip lead could be gained by opencast mining. It had a competitive edge.[9] All resources must be colonised for the benefit of Rome. Mining entailed the stationing of a permanent garrison at Charterhouse- Roman Iscalis - together with a settlement the size of a small town, a fort and an amphitheatre.[10] From inscriptions on the lead pig, the settlement was probably called 'Vebriacum'.[11] The pattern of conquest was for captives to be used for the mining. Prisoners from the Moor could well have been amongst the labour force.

Once, on the Moor, there were inhabitants of another world. There are few traces of them today. The Dobunni tribe were not the first peoples to settle the rich agricultural lands of the North Somerset levels. From about 12,000 years ago, conditions improved when the last ice had receded. The stage set for the unbroken settlement of Somerset. Some of our ancestors occupied the limestone caves at nearby Cheddar and Wookey Hole. Limestone gravels have washed down from the Mendip Hills and helped to shape the landscape of the Moor. [12]

Six thousand years ago, neolithic farmers came to grow crops and breed cattle. What these strangers were like, how they saw the world or what they wore during their short lives can only be conjectured from finds elsewhere.By the Bronze Age, around 1500BC, there is a more settled existence. Neolithic axes have turned up. A hundred fragments of flint scrapers from this period have been unearthed at Bickley facing the south-eastern side of Cadbury Hill.

The Moor was well settled in the Iron Age. Iron Age people betray themselves locally by various Celtic fields. Agriculture provided the way of life for most pre-Roman people in Somerset and this would have been especially true of the rich alluvial planes on the Moor. Somerset is well endowed with one prominent feature on the landscape of Iron Age settlement- the hillfort- of which there are some fifty examples. Some of these were small enclosures. Others were on the scale of Ham Hill, South Cadbury and Brent Knoll.

The most prominent iron-age site locally is Cadbury Hill (known archeologically as Cadbury-Congresbury). It is a strongly defended hilltop enclosure, about eighty acres in size. There are stronger defences towards the north-east, where access is easier. An inner rampart is complemented by a steep slope into a ditch, the outer rampart and a bank. The hill-fort looked westwards over the North Somerset Levels to the coast of the Bristol Channel. Though set at some eighty meters above the sea, from here, the coast of South Wales is visible. Hillforts were like medieval castles. Not all were occupied and settled as permanent communities. Some were symbolic or had religious value. They reflected the status of the tribal community and of its Chief.

The known story of this hill-fort begins in the late Neolithic period, perhaps 2500BC, when hunter-gatherers left scatters of stone tools on the hill tops, recovered during the excavations of the hill fort and the temple. Apart from some later Bronze Age flints, and a number of Beaker period (c2000BC) pottery sherds from Henley Hill, nothing further is known at the site until excavation showed Iron Age occupation and activity on both hills. The earliest dated finds on the hill were Neolithic flints. But then came some spectacular late Iron Age finds — some pottery, at least one brooch, a Dobunnic coin, and a remarkable bronze figurine. If the dating is correct, that implies religious activity began on the site in pre-Roman times. Fragments of human skulls dating from c790-390BC have been found in a layer of rubble. [13] In 1968, excavations will reveal that Iron Age ramparts on the eastern side of Cadbury-Congresbury hillfort conceal some eight hundred and thirty stones for slings. It is likely that, as a fortified settlement, the hillfort went out of use in the third century BC. Cadbury seems to have declined before the Romans arrived, to the point where talk of the site being abandoned is not out place.[14] The later history of the Moor is very rich in records. In pre-Roman times, except for Cadbury-Congresbuty, the record is sparse. Few farmsteads were there to watch anxiously the Roman arrival.

Somerset did not exist as an entity until medieval times. In the second century AD, the geographer Ptolemy identified a number of tribes that had dwelt in Britannia. The Dumnonnii controlled Cornwall, Devon and Somerset as far as the River Parrett. Then there were the Durotrige peoples, the tribal area that gave the Romans most trouble. They inhabited south Somerset, as well as Dorset and Wiltshire. The Romans also recognised a third tribal entity - the Dobunni - whose zone of influence was North Somerset, the Mendips and well into the Cotswalds. In his account of the invasion of AD43, Cassius Dio calls them the 'Bodunni' but this is a scribal error. This three-way split in tribal identity originated much earlier, possibly as far back as the first millennium BCE.[15] But as often happens, occupying powers are blind to the way that their presence has helped to define those that are opposed to them. The very act of Rome recognising a political configuration called the Dobunni helped to sharpen tribal identities out of regional cultural divides.[16] Although it is not a simple matter to equate coin distribution with political territories and social identity, evidence of pre-Roman coinage suggests a region for the Dobunni from North Somerset to Gloucestershire.

From the mid-first century BC, coins begin to be minted by local tribes.[17] The coins suggest that the Moor was occupied by the Dobunni. This tribe probably capitulated early on to the Romans, unlike the Durotriges to the south which rose up against the Romans later in the AD 70's - only to face a massacre at South Cadbury. Vespasian's forces seem to have captured the area without too much trouble. It is possible that the fort on Cadbury

Hill was a last stand for some local groups as its continued occupation by the Dobunni will not be tolerated by the Romans.[18] There is though no evidence of a battle or the storming of Cadbury-Congresbury Hill. If there had been resistance, the hillfort was no match for a professional army, especially one commanded by Vespasian who wants to control the mouth of rivers.

By definition, tribes build themselves up from smaller units and tend to lack a centralised authority.[19] Whatever there was of an old tribal aristocracy can stay on as clients of Rome and even granted access to the wider community that was the Roman world- as long as they accepted the new order.[20] The generation that lived in a broad political entity calling itself the Dobunni found that they were taken over by Roman legal administrators.[21] It was in the interests of the Romans to promote a hierarchical structure amongst the old tribal areas. Roman policy was to recruit local elites, called decurions, drawn from the old aristocracy and local chieftains, to maintain control after the Legions moved on. The 'Civitate', roughly equivalent to a county, was administered by elite councils, called the 'Ordo', drawn from these decurions. The Moor lay within the Civitate governed at Cirencester or Durocornovium Corinium.[22] The Roman occupation is similar to the Norman Conquest a thousand years in the future. Decapitation possibly of the head people if they gave trouble and Romanisation of the remainder- this was the pattern. They are not taking over as an alien army of occupation; tribal life continues. There are many instances of Romanised wealth and status in the district, amongst them wealthy estates belonging to Romano-British aristocrats.

The Second Legion stays in the south-west to build a fortress at Exeter around AD55, though units of auxillary troops drawn from the Empire helped to garrison forts such as at Charterhouse. By about 66 or 67AD, the Second Legion is being posted north to Gloucester. The South West is largely pacified. Tantalising glimpses remain of a Roman presence on the Moor. How far these reflect settlers of Italian origin, auxillary troops or native peoples settling down under the occupation cannot be determined. They participate in the wider Roman world, visiting the springs at Aqueas Sula- Bath- and mixing with legionnaires who came to recharge or retire. Some of them live to a ripe old age. At the fortress of Caerleon in Wales,

Julius Valens, a Second Legion veteran, is commemorated by his wife on his death after attaining his personal century.

On the Moor, it is now the third century. Some two hundred years have gone by. Seven generations have lived and died in a Roman world. By now, the time before the Second Legion came is distant folk memory, stories told by your grandfather who heard them from his grandfather's grandfather. Local people are no longer smarting from defeat. Ethnic Britons are granted Roman citizenship. They have settled down. The pattern of agriculture is largely unchanged. The countryside is dominated by an elite, usually from tribal origins, collecting rent from the many small homesteads and farms that went back to the Iron Age settlers. By the middle of the second century, however, large villas are beginning to dot the landscape of Roman Britain. The eighth generation on the Moor since Roman times will be aware of one of these.

In the year 1884, two discoveries will come to light that reveal the Roman presence on the Moor. 800 coins are found. The coins were from the 3rd century. Every time there was a new Emperor, a fresh batch of coins was minted. These bear the marks of the Emperor Gallenius (253-268), Postumus (267-272, the Tetrici (276- 282), Claudio Gothicus (269-270), Victorinus the elder (265-267) and Salonius (268).

Roman coins were used to pay for labour and economic activity so the district was economically active, commercial and probably prosperous. It could be that the North Somerset Levels were drained in part in Roman times by rich and powerful people so as to re-claim excellent alluvial land for agriculture. Those working the land in the vicinity have long had to do battle with the encroaching sea. There does not seem to have been any extensive sea flooding in the Roman period.[23]

And then, two miles away across the Moors, the remains of a villa were found. A labourer was laying drain pipes. His work was prevented by some stonework set in mortar. He found he was cutting into a piece of Roman pavement. Excavations followed. Local memory is that of recalling the progress of the excavations and seeing the fine pavement as it was gradually exposed. The lines of two rather thick walls came into view, one of which penetrated into the bank of the River Yeo, some 50 feet distant. The inference was that the course of the river had been diverted. Before the villa could be embarked upon, its designers would need to ensure it would not get inundated. At any rate, these two walls evidently formed a canal leading to an offloading stage. The occupants of the villa could have easily reached the open sea.

Further into the villa was a chamber for storing fuel and stores perhaps and then a boiler house, a hypocaust. A flue passed round the apse and continued into the villa. It brought the particular form of under-floor heating that characterises Roman villas in Britannia. Charcoal would have been burnt here. It was an efficient fuel. The apse itself, one end semi-circular, was probably covered with a dome and had an entrance with two columns. Such entrances in places like Pompeii have indicated that this was where the statue of a god was placed.

First one room was found, then another. One was paved with white stone, then came one with paving of much finer quality; the mosaic being smooth or even polished with border patterns, ornamental scrolls and blue stone. Various other rooms were uncovered; ten in all, including a kitchen forge. Then a room was revealed with a wonderful pavement area coloured in blue and white mosaic and cubes of red earthenware.

Mosaic pavement in Wemberham Villa

The excavator was intrigued by the presence of a cross in the centre of this room, which was nearly four metres square. He supposed that the Villa was occupied by a Christian. But the cross is not the usual shape with the cross-bar higher on one side. It intersects itself exactly. This room seems to have been the dining room, or open area where the owner received guests. It is heated by the hypocaust. Another room was thought to have been a women's area; bones that could have been hair pins were found. A vestibule or entrance area completed the picture, leading to a possible staircase to personal quarters.

Wemberham villa was one of many country properties erected in Britannia in the 2nd to the 4th centuries. The Romans introduced towns into Britannia but most people lived in the countryside. The economy was a villa, or farm-based, economy. Lands and estates were concentrated around these villas. It reflects growing wealth but also inequality. Many slaves serve the owners of the villa and farm the countryside.

The burden of taxation by head of population (or caput) fell on to the smaller holders of freehold farms. Wemberham was hardly a house of significant size for a magnate.

The fact that the villa was on the estuary of the River Yeo could suggest that though Uphill was the local Roman port of choice, a villa here could be a boat house or a frontier post to watch over the Channel. It does have access to the hinterland. What makes Wemberham Villa unusual is that it is a villa of some importance very near the coast. There are only a handful of villas at sea-level around the shore-line of old Britannia. The proximity to the sea suggests that the Villa is either a Customs house or residence for some kind of official controlling movement of people and goods. The River Yeo is after all tidal here up to the village of Congesbury.

We might imagine life at the villa in the third century. Messengers have come by sea or by road from the provincial capital, Durocornovium Corinium. They will be served by slaves at the villa, perhaps relaxing in the warm baths. Sandals may needed as the mosaic floor of the dining room can be very hot to walk on in winter if the heating is on, courtesy of the charcoal-burning furnace and the hypocaust. For dinner, the guests will participate in a three-course meal. To judge from discoveries there of shells, the people who lived at this villa dined often on oysters. Other shellfish, fish, salad and mushrooms might be served as the appetiser. For the main course, fish would be on the menu since the villa was close to the sea but there would also be game and poultry. Sauces and vegetables accompanied the meal. Fattened dormice were a special delicacy at that time. After the main course, the table would be cleared away and in would come the 'secunda mensa', laden with honey cakes, fruit, nuts and honey cakes. The meal was concluded with wine sweetened with honey.

All this was a far cry from either slaves or common people who had very little of their own and of whom we know nothing. They grew what food they could on rented land for their families or for sale. Many slaves served a villa like this, slaves with titles such as the *focarius* (to keep fires and ovens alight), a *paedogogus* (teacher and tutor), a *calamistera* (hairdresser), a *cellarious* (in charge of cellars and pantries), a *cesterix* (housemaid), *scissor* (kitchen slave working with carved meats), a *tonsor* (barber) a *praegustator* (food taster and cook) and a *silentarious* (to ensure slaves were silent in the master's presence). If the owner of Wemberham villa was of some standing, he will have had also a *scurra,* whose task it was to flatter the guests.

Guests at the villa will notice a new sight on the skyline in the third century.

In the Tracks of the Spirit-Road

A Temple is being constructed at Henley Wood, on a prominent spur, adjacent to the hill-fort of Cadbury Hill, also a religious site by now. Hill-forts were considerably affected by Roman occupation. Wherever the defences of hill-forts have been examined elsewhere, the Roman period suggests decay and collapse. If there was a return here to the social organisation of Iron Age times afterwards, this may indicate that Cadbury-Congresbury continued to function throughout the Roman era.[24] The rulers were fully aware that the hill-fort area was of enormous significance as a repository of folk memory, tribal identity and religious ideology. It was all the more important to bring it into the Roman system.[25]

Very likely, it is religious ideology that provides the connecting thread at Cadbury-Congresbury between the pre-Roman period all the way through to post-Roman times. In the third century, a series of temples is springing up across Somerset, probably to strengthen the life of its communities in the area. A British deity may have been incorporated into the pantheon.[26] At nearby Brean Down and Brent Knoll, much later dedications of churches are to St Bridget- a rare event. This may derive from attempts to Christianise a pagan site ('Briga' means 'high place'[27]). The temple at Henley would certainly have qualified as a high place. The Romans tended to synthesise pre-Roman deities and their own religious icons; witness the way the cult of a pre-Roman deity at Bath became dedicated to Minerva.

At any rate, to the south of the Henley Temple is a shallow gulley close to the line of the present parish boundary and separating the site from the hillfort of Cadbury Congresbury. Today this track provides the easiest access to both sites; it could have done so in the Roman period and later as a kind of 'spirit-road'. Although the view is to the West, entrance to the temples was on the east side. A ditch - or temenos- marked the eastern boundary of the Temple precinct.[28]

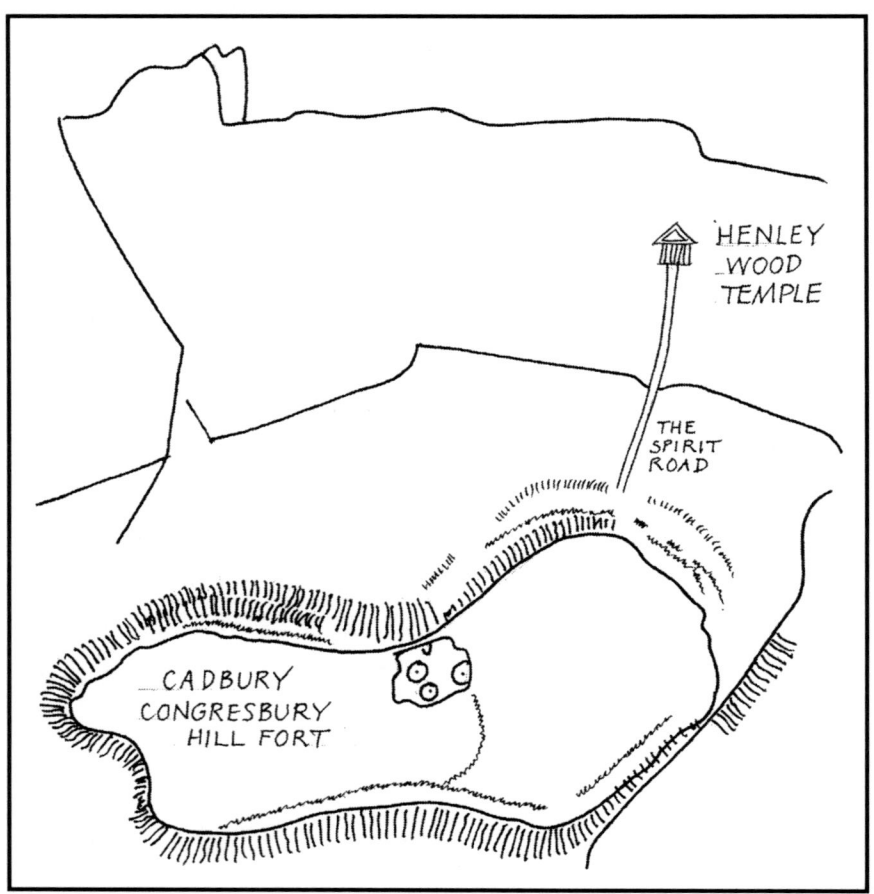

Lay-out of Cadbury-Congresbury Hill-fort, Henley Temple and 'the Spirit-Road'

The Temple is of a conventional Roman-Celtic type, nothing special about it. Three times it will be re-built.[29] Discovery of coins there suggests a period of use for the 1st phase from AD 225-50. It may be close to another villa at Henley Wood.[30] Scattered Roman coins and pottery from Cadbury Hill show some Roman settlement, although these may relate to no more than leisure activities. The Temple had accommodation for its many devotees. It is tempting to imagine religious processions passing along the spirit-road there, from Cadbury Hill to the Temple, with its commanding views over the Moor. An observer standing inside the hill fort and looking along the causeway would be looking directly at the site of the temple and burials on Henley Hill. Some cemeteries in Roman Somerset suggest a Christian presence at such places though the evidence is not conclusive.[31]

The Romans had a considerable stake in North Somerset. The nearest major site to settlements around Cadbury-Congresbury is the puzzling walled town of Gatcombe. Elsewhere, there is prolific activity, both secular and religious. There is evidence for another villa on the Cleeve side of Cadbury Hill. The Moor and the Congresbury Yeo were probably not the main routes for the export of lead.[32] But products made from mining would have been increasingly available locally. Stone moulds for the casting of pewter have been found at nearby Chew Valley and at Camerton, At the appropriately named Venus Street in nearby Congresbury, there is a Roman kiln, churning out large quantities of pottery. On Kenn Moor and Yatton Moor, remains of Roman industrial activity and arable farming have come to light. At least three settlements have been recorded from building debris churned up by scatterings of the plough. A local inhabitant relates that Roman remains were found on the farm in Kingston Seymour and that Roman pottery was found at the nearby sea wall. The implication of the finds was that this may have been a site of a cremation.[33]

What was life like for the ordinary Briton here in Roman times? The Moor was an area that saw summer grazing, wildfowl and fishing. There was high quality land for farming and upland grazing for animals in the hills beyond Cleeve and Wrington. The area is agriculturally rich; it was an agrarian economy in Roman times. Further south, at Bradley Hill at Somerton, the economy in the 4th century was based on sheep and this may have been true of Cadbury Hill. The little meat consumed was mutton. It would have been of poor quality since the animals were grown primarily for their wool. In the various farmsteads dotted around the landscape that continues into medieval times[34], two small dwellings accommodated perhaps eight adults and four children. The social organisation was based on the extended family. Life was harsh. A cemetery has been analysed at a

4th century farmstead on Bradley Hill. Two children in three died before the age of four. The average life expectancy for a male was 42 years. A woman could expect to live to only 31 on average.[35]

By now, the people of the Moor have been Roman for three hundred years. Its inhabitants may have been dotted around various farmsteads that were a continuation of the iron- age society several hundred years before. But they were solidly Roman. Since the third century, all freeborn provincials were deemed to be citizens. For this reason, to imagine an occupying force, keeping at bay sullen and resentful natives is wide of the mark. The ordinary folk have been incorporated into the Roman world. They looked to Durocornovium Corinium in the first instance, as their regional centre. But beyond that, they looked to Rome. They were Romans.

"To contrast 'Britons' with 'Romans' in the fourth century is as meaningless as to contrast modern Kentishmen with Englishmen".[36]

The Moor was a quiet and relatively prosperous part of the Roman British world and remained that way until the end of the fourth century. Then the world collapses.

Chapter 2

THE HILL – FORT PEOPLE

A hundred or so years pass. During the next 150 years, five more generations are about to be born and live out their lives. Twelve generations have come and gone since the Roman Legio Augusta first descended from the sky-line. It is now 400AD. The land is mute witness to drastic events.

A profound shock is coming over the Roman British settlements on the Moor. The world that the 13th generation is plugged into is disintegrating. It is the end of Empire.

Yet evidence from that time also shows that, on the Moor, Cadbury-Congresbury hill-fort produced a society, Christian in religion, capable of converting pre-Roman hill-forts back into occupation centres and trading with the rest of the then known world.[37]

None of that could have been predicted at the beginning of the 5th century. The economy has been ailing for some time. Ordered Roman life has been breaking up. Soldiers and officials are no longer being paid. Britain is ceasing to be part of the Roman Empire in the West. It used to be thought that in the year 410AD, the Legions depart. This was not the case. Auxillary or local troops had defended Britannia for a while. What happened was that the Emperor Honorius turned down a British request for men and money to defend the frontiers against encroaching Germanic tribes. The Imperial Government was simply not in a position to help. The situation was meant to be temporary. With Alaric the Hun at the gates, however, the Empire was having problems of its own. On 24th August 410, Rome is compelled to open its gates to the Hun leader.

Britannia is on its own. For a while, it has been administered through its Provinces, which now become the local authority. The hypothesis that Iron Age tribal divisions persisted into the Late Roman period as *civitates*, which in turn survived into the post-Roman centuries as self-governing British polities, is much debated.[38] Left to its own devices, Civitas Dubonnorum is in danger of becoming a failed State. Taxes are no longer being collected in coinage. The money economy collapses; barter is the means of exchange. Local administration fails.[39] Safe assumptions are no more. The veneer of civilisation began to erode. It will take centuries for the political vacuum to be filled; longer still to catch up with the technology of Roman times.

Those with money begin to bury it. Elsewhere, although the Empire is disintegrating, hoards of gold at this time are rare. In the south-west of Britain it is a different story. Hoards of gold and precious metals are far more common; one fifth of all hoards found in Britain are in Somerset.[40]

Two old place-names on the Polden Hills are suggestive- 'goldhord'. Anyone with wealth is clearly hoarding gold rather than use it.

Yet burial of treasure is only one sign of what is happening in the social dislocation. Villas have been falling on hard times for a while. Their owners can no longer afford to pay for the upkeep. Now they are downsizing from stone to smaller, wood dwellings. At nearby Camerton, squatters live in the villas for a while but then settlement ceases altogether.[41] This may have been the case at Wemberham villa. Their markets gone, landowners are ceasing to grow grain and turning instead to animal husbandry. Towns are also in rapid decline. The countryside is rapidly returning to subsistence.

There are those that are waiting for the opportunity. After the Romans depart, substantial numbers of Germanic peoples begin to cross the North Sea and settle in Britannia. Some of the settlements they initiated or took over grew into larger units. These are well-known from the names of English counties today- the South Saxons, West Saxons, East Saxons and the land of East Angles. In the Western part of the British Isles, the Celtic people groups who had experienced Roman occupation and had become Roman-British, resist the Saxon encroachment. They neither trade nor mix with them. Instead they fight. It is the background to the legend of King Arthur.

The traditional 'dark age quickly' scenario saw the ending of the military occupation leading quickly to what would in the 1980s have been hailed as 'systems collapse.' With towns and villas being deserted by the last half of the fourth century AD, the loss of the monetary economy is followed by social and economic chaos. An economy based on villas disintegrates into local subsistence farming. Provincial capitals like Corinium Durocornovium are gradually abandoned.[42]

There is another model, more evolutionary and less apocalyptic, that sees England as gradually yielding to a Saxon society. Historians no longer talk of the Dark Ages; it implies that post-Roman times were a catastrophic mystery.[43] It is too polarising to see the emerging pattern as Celts (Old English) v Saxons. This is misleading. As Norman Davies observes, *"this pseudo-racial stereoptype simply does not fit the facts"*.[44] Both fought amongst themselves. There were shifting alliances and no single homogenous 'Saxon' grouping. Over time, Germanic- based tribes disputed England (not now a political unity) with native Romano-British (Old English) 'Celts'- and won.

Looking at social life in terms of systems is becoming more common. To see an individual as part of a web of relationships, such as a family constellation is profoundly illuminating. History can also be studied through systems. Yatton Moor is not an isolated entity and should not be studied that way. What today we call the Celtic fringe is and remains part of the Roman Empire, except that power has moved east. Archaeological digs on Cadbury-Congresbury throw light on this process. The South-West of England is engaging in long-term trade with the Eastern end of the Roman Empire, Byzantium. Although it is not a centralised entity, the South-West is plugged in to the new Roman authority.[45] It should not be seen on its own but as part of a European and North African system, an economic system based on trade.

By contrast, after Britannia is left to fend for itself, the Germanic end of England is not part of the Roman world. That is the case in the 5th and 6th centuries until Pope Gregory sends Augustine in the year 597 to bring Saxon tribes back into the fold.

Two different societies were growing in post-Roman Britain. They have little to do with each other. Few items of Anglo-Saxon origin made before AD570 turn up in Western Britain. No 6th century pottery made in the West found its way into the Germanic east. The East does not seem to trade with the Latin and Frankish world and it was only in the 590's that contact between Kent and what is now France begins to develop. In the West, it was a different story. Post-Roman Britain traded with the rest of the continent. Direct shipping links with Bordeaux and Spain were common.

Locally, the territory of the old Dobunni tribe including the Moor came to be incorporated into a regional entity based on Cadbury's namesake-South Cadbury. The 'Wansdyke', the post-Roman bank and ditch running from Maes Knoll in the west to Bath in the east, may represent the political boundary between the Old Welsh Somerset and the new Saxon English groups forming to the north. It is some kind of treaty line, rather than a line of defence.[46] At any rate, Somerset is probably British until the mid 6th century.

The place of Cadbury-Congresbury in the post-Roman landscape is unclear. What is clear is that the hill-fort is being re-occupied. But why is it in use again? The re-emergence of patterns of settlement typical of Celtic times needs explaining.[47] The evidence from the site from a dig in 1959 showed an extremely well-preserved archaeology. For the first time, Mediterranean amphorae, of a type only recently recognised as being from post-Roman times, were found. It was as a result of this work that larger, open plan excavations happened ten years later. The results from this work and more recent analysis are intriguing.

Here is a community in post-Roman times using a range of buildings, eating large quantities of meat and acquiring pottery that was both local and foreign.[48] Large scale excavations revealed several unexpected facets of the archaeology of the hill, not least connections to the Eastern Mediterranean and North Africa.

This was clearly not the Dark Ages. A report summarised the findings.[49] The hill-top of Cadbury Congresbury was frequented in Neolithic and Bronze Age times. Substantial defences were built at that time when the site became a hillfort. But now, 60 or 70 years after the legions left, the hill-fort is re-occupied. New earthworks are being built, including a bank dividing the hillfort into two parts with a linking entrance..

The presence of imported exotic pottery and high quality metalwork at Cadbury- Congresbury points to an economic importance. Does that mean the hill-fort people also had a social and political importance? YCCCART, a local archaeological group,[50] has discovered a series of 12 penannular stone walled enclosures containing huts, the nearest only 500 metres from Cadbury-Congresbury's eastern entrance. These farmsteads in the form of roundhouses for people and animals are possibly dependent on Cadbury-Congresbury. On the hill-fort itself, eight buildings of late or post-Roman date were defined. The structures are of circular and rectangular design. There is evidence of a large timber building, fit for a Chief. Within the ramparts, a wide variety of other features, including pits, post-holes and timber-slots have been found. There were cairns with a central pit filled with votive offerings, which turned out to be paralleled in remote parts of Ireland. Under a cairn of stones there was another discovery. It was the remains of a human skull![51]

The evidence is intriguing. Somewhere, possibly around 475-500, there is a Chieftain who has the power, influence and money to persuade a group of people to re-populate the old-fort. He persuades them to be involved in regional endeavours to keep the encroaching Saxons at bay for a hundred years by participating in construction of the Wansdyke. The Chieftain is also sufficiently geo-politically aware to allow trade to flourish with the Byzantine Empire, trade which relied on long-haul deep sea vessels. Who were these hill-fort people?

The group who initiated these works was of high-status. They patronised craft-workers, and with access to glass and ceramics in a way that demonstrated international trade links. The new finds at Cadbury show that distinctively exotic tableware from North Africa is being imported along with fine plates from Byzantium, glass work and metal work. The elite on Cadbury Hill were importing wine from southern Greece, and olive-oil containers from southern Turkey. The evidence for a strong Mediterranean influence at this time is clearest both at Cadbury- Congresbury and at Tintagel. Pottery from the eastern Mediterranean was uncovered at South Cadbury. At Tintagel, slate tablets have been found, showing the kind of crosses more common to the Mediterranean than to Britain. The Tintagel burial feast suggests that Mediterranean people were arriving as well as Mediterranean goods being traded.[52]

This was not how the Dark Ages were supposed to be. Why would the Byzantine Empire want to have dealings with the Chief on Cadbury Hill? There are two ways to read the trade that clearly went on. One is to see it as a series of one-offs following a commercial instinct to deal in luxury and high-status goods for high-status people.

The other interpretation is to see it as part of a trading entity which places Cadbury-Congresbury and indeed the south-west, within the economic and maybe political orbit of the East Roman Empire. Fast forward the tape another couple of generations and the motives of the Byzantine Empire to have dealings with the Chief on Cadbury- Congresbury could become clearer. It is likely that Justinian in Byzantium, determined to reclaim the lost Roman Empire to its former glory saw Western Britain as a natural part of the Roman sphere of influence, part of the Empire.[53] At any rate, Byzantine diplomatic interests seem to be involved. This is State-sponsored trade.[54]

The flurry of media interest in autumn 2009 in the discovery of Saxon gold shows a continuing understanding of our knowledge of this time. The dark ages are less dark. 650 items of gold weighing more than 5kg and 530 silver objects weighing more than 1kg- almost all of them martial- were recovered from a Staffordshire field. Large issues are raised by such a discovery- the fall and rise of early kingdoms, the expression of regional identities, the conduct of war and how these societies went about the production of fine metal are all illuminated by the discoveries. So too is the transition from paganism to Christianity; a few Christian crosses are amongst the finds.[55] While less dramatic either than metal from some corner of a Staffordshire field, or the Sutton Hoo discoveries in 1939, the

Cadbury-Congresbury finds can claim to bring strong definition to an earlier, post-Roman world in the British West.

There is something else. This new centre of power was almost certainly Christian.

A sherd of North African pottery with a reconstructable Christian cross upon it was amongst the finds on Cadbury Hill made by Keith Gardener. It raises the tantalising possibility of links with the legendary saint, the priest Cyngar after whom the local village of Congresbury was named.[56] At Henley Wood, a cemetery has been discovered have been discovered on the site of the old temple building. The cemetery, originally containing approximately 90 graves, was of individuals of both sexes and all ages. They were mostly orientated west to east (heads to west) with few if any grave goods.[57] Radiocarbon tests suggest that the cemetery was in use between the 5th and 7th centuries AD. The cemetery is close enough to be linked with the settlement on Cadbury Hill a few hundred metres away. The existence of a possible 'Spirit Road' to the site of the old Roman Temple could mean that a pagan site is being taken over by a Christian site. Not only are those that live there wanting to Christianise Cadbury, it seems likely that the Temple burial site is continuing to be used, a holy site recruited by a very different belief system.[58] At the same time, a remarkable bronze figurine dating from the late Iron Age was discovered. The site had fertility symbols and may well have been the centre of religious cult.

By now, Christianity was spreading throughout the old Roman Somerset. Celtic missionaries saw to that. How early on it is impossible to say. At a time when the early church was struggling to hammer out basic Christianity, 4th century churches were being formed in Somerset. Roman centres such as Bath and Illchester may well have been early sites of Christian churches. But now the society that is taking shape in the five generations after the Romans left is largely Christian. It is mistaken to assume that this kind of grave is Christian just because there are no burial items and because of the orientation.[59] Yet with recent finds from the site, the balance of evidence points to a Christian use for it by the sixth century.[60]

All this raises intriguing possibilities about the continuity from Roman times as the old villas slowly developed into Saxon manors and Christian parishes.[61] When Christianity came to Somerset and indeed Britain is unknown. The Glastonbury legends relate how the Christian faith was brought to Somerset in AD63 by Joseph of Arimathea at the request of the Apostle Philip. What he was supposed to have brought with him then became the stuff of legend and myth to this day- the Holy Grail. As related by the 12th century writer Geoffrey of Monmouth, the Grail legend was linked with the story of King Arthur and the Knights who went in search of it.

Legends and the lives of the saints provide one reference point for early Christianity. The story of Cyngar the Priest is one of these, associated with the foundation of a Bishopric for Somerset. This too is debateable: the Celtic missionaries went from place to place, calling people to the faith wherever they went and it was not the usual pattern to have a seat in the way that Saxon and Norman Bishops did later on.[62]

St Andrew's church in Congresbury is reputedly the site of St Congar's foundation. It is a Celtic dedication (although such an association cannot be demonstrated before the 10th–11th century). Congresbury was the site of a Saxon minster, probably on the same spot that was given by Alfred to Asser. Could Cyngar have been here as a Welsh saint or even a Byzantine nobleman (as one theory has it), living on the hill and going down to found Congresbury? This does rather depend on the unproven assumption that the hill-fort itself was once called Congresbury.[63] At any rate, there is now wider acceptance of the role of Christianity in North Somerset in those uncertain times between when the Roman presence had withered and the arrival of Saxon influence in the 7th century.

The question is, what led to the disappearance of the society on Cadbury Hill? If it occupied a key position in the Celtic British world of its time, why did it cease to have much significance subsequently? Between 550 and the end of the sixth century, the area was taken over by the Saxons. Saxons had extended their reach into the west of the country, taking over the south midlands, Dorset and the borders of what came to be the separate land of Wales. By 577, Bath had fallen. Around that time, Cadbury/Congresbury would have been submerged in the tide. Some time during the second half of the 6th century, the site became deserted. The apparent lack of any medieval settlement seems to imply a wholly agricultural role for the hill from here on. So is the decline of the community on Cadbury Hill due to the major changes initiated by Anglo-Saxon military, political and ecclesiastical domination?

There may be another factor. This factor may help to explain why the south west was gravely weakened. It was a major systems collapse. 536AD has been the postulated date for a catastrophic event, the 'year without a summer'. The case has been made based on tree-rings that there was a major event such as a comet in that period.[64] Social and political consequences such as crop failure, economic collapse, famine and disease and anarchy have been projected from the environmental record. Needless to say, it has proved controversial from historians who dislike the determinism implicit in single events.[65]

Then there is plague. For around 547, the terrible plague that had devastated the Mediterranean had arrived in Britain. We associate Bubonic plague with the terrible years of the Black Death 800 years later. But in the early 540's, Yersinia Pestis devastates the Roman Byzantium world. It has been proposed that unusual climatic turbulence experienced throughout the known world in the 530's created the right conditions for plague.[66] Plague arrived in Alexandria, devastated Antioch in Syria, then reduced Constantinople from a city of half a million to a 100,000 inhabitants.

Britain was plugged into that world- no more so than Cadbury Hill. A proposal into the effect of the plague on Britain and Europe suggested that two locations in particular stand out as the most likely points of entry for the plague. Tintagel on the north Cornwall coast was one of these. The other was Cadbury/ Congresbury. Both were in direct contact with ships bound for and coming from the Mediterranean. Yet by the second half of the 6th century, Tintagel was deserted. This was at the same time as Cadbury-Congresbury. Its close ties with Byzantium had proved to be both its success and its undoing. The relatively sophisticated society in the British West of the country found that their on-going trade links with the Roman Byzantine world came at great cost. In time, ships laden with goods were transformed into plague ships. The means of such terrifying conversion was the Black Rat.

We can imagine the devastation. The plague struck the western part of the country. With what result we do not know. The 14th century Black Death is much better recorded. Plague pits are non-existent. Yet the evidence from excavations at the former Roman city at Wroxeter points to a major reduction of population at this time- perhaps up to 60%.[67] If there is anything to this plague narrative, Western Britain, including the area around Cadbury- Congresbury was gravely weakened.

This, rather than immediate post-Roman times, may well be the era when the South-West, including the Moor and its environs experienced a major systems collapse in the late 530's and 540's. It has not received the archaeological attention it deserves. Nevertheless, a picture is building up. Even the thinnest layer of top-soil, investigated by a local archaeology group[68] has thrown up the possibility of a religious centre rather than a secular society, an elite society capable of trading with Byzantium and North Africa, a society who buried their dead in an apparently Christian manner and were capable of refurbishing an old site as a centre of power.

Against this backcloth, the 13th to the 17th generation to live on the Moor since the Roman invasion play out their lives. The 13th generation see huge changes as Britannia slowly disintegrates; their great-great grandchildren in the 17th generation will be strongly affected by cataclysmic change once again. The Old English environment now yields to Germanic tribes who have been lying in wait for this time.

Chapter 3

ONE DAY THEY SAW SHIPS

The next five hundred years, down to 1066 are misty with obscurity. For five hundred years, as far back then as looking back to the early 16th century would be to us, some 17 generations rose up, unfolded their lives and were then quietly engulfed in the passage of time. The 18th to the 34th generations are those we know least about. A quarter of the story of a community on its journey through time is in the Anglo-Saxon era that in turn yielded to Viking insurgency.

Around 550, a few homesteads dotted the landscape of the North Somerset Moors surrounding the intriguing society of the hill –fort people. Gradually, however, the old pattern of Romano-British villa estates evolves into Saxon Manors. In time, these centralise into the outline of a village. Roman and post-Roman buildings crumbled away. Peasants move from homesteads and isolated farms into villages. By the end of these misty five hundred years, before the Norman Conquest, Yatton is a definite community with a Saxon name, a defined land allocation, boundaries of field and parish and also a church. The Celtic or Old Welsh society that lived here faded away together with their buildings. They have adopted the language of the newcomers.

The battle of Dyrham in 577 is claimed to have settled the fate of North Somerset.[69] Three local 'kings' feature in the Anglo-Saxon Chronicle; their capture is supposed to leave the whole area open to the Saxons. This is open to question.[70] The Chronicle itself records that North Somerset fell to the Saxons at the battle of Penselwood in AD658. Why did they not take Somerset for 80 years? Were they kept out by the Wansdyke, the rampart erected along the Avon to keep Somerset safe?[71] It may well be that the battle of Dyrham was of symbolic importance rather than a turning point.

Whether by gift, conquest or default, landlords arose in control of the new estates that had succeeded the Roman villa economy. It was under one of the Kings of Wessex, King Ine, that the Saxons colonised the Moor. Kings of Wessex were Christians from the time of Ine, who ruled from 688 to 726AD. The Laws of King Ine show that the Old Welsh society went hand in hand with their new English landlords. For the most part, the Saxon conquest allowed for an assimilation of the old into the new order. It was not a war of extermination. In fact, Saxon encroachment was probably migration and gradual settlement rather than an elite take-over. King Ine's laws were the seeds of what evolved into 'land in exchange for service' - though it was the Normans that brought the fully-developed feudal model.

How far the fields on the Moor may have changed is an open question. Open strips of fields, that were the hallmark of Saxon and then Norman estates, can still be identified on the maps. They are curvy strips, quite unlike the straight fields that came 1200 years later through the Parliamentary enclosures. Throughout Somerset, the new occupiers found and developed the old Roman estates. Some Saxon estates were based on the earlier Old Welsh or Celtic boundaries. The new rulers took the best estates for themselves and distributed others to their nobles and warriors. Then, with the transfer of land complete, grants to the church could begin.[72] The Anglo-Saxon Chronicle records the internal politics by which the West Saxons sought to build a stable, hierarchical society from the confederacy of chieftains that preceded it. The new religion, Christianity, brought the Saxon world into contact with continental models of kingship and the State that characterised the feudal age.

Saxons found Christians in Somerset. The surviving charters of West Saxon kings show a Christian influence. Grants of land were made by King Ine to the Abbey of Glastonbury around the year 681. Muchelney and Frome (funded by Adhelm of Malmesbury Abbey who became Bishop of Wessex) were also monastic sites granted by the King. Not far away, Bath and the area north of the Avon was part of the kingdom of Mercia. The earliest authentic foundation charter for Bath Abbey dates from the second half of the 8th century as a grant of land from Kings of Mercia.[73]

It was the King who left his mark. The contours of the landscape had been shaped by the Old Welsh society, and further back, the Romans. But the pattern of the estates, the parish system and the growth of the church shows the effect of Saxon royal administration, creating the political and sacred geography we know today.

The Moor was West Saxon. Place names betray the Saxon influence. The name 'Somerset' is of Saxon origin.[74] Somerset means 'land of summer people' as Somerton means 'settlement of the summer people' The Welsh still call it Gwlad yr haf, Land of Summer, i.e the land that emerges in their view in the summer. 'Yatton' is believed to be a corruption of the Anglo-Saxon JATONE which is derived from JANUA for a passage and TUN for a settlement or village, hence "the village on the passage around the hill". In his history of Somerset published in 1791, Collinson suggests that the most ancient meaning of 'Jatone' was a town-port from the words 'janua' and 'ton'. He thought the derivation signified that here was an entrance to the Bristol Channel when its waters overflowed. "Jatone" may have been a journey's end during winter for a mission priest as he spread the Christian message to the settlers on the high ground. An alternative version is that Yatton means water-enclosure, from the Old English *ea* + *tun* - the water being the Congresbury Yeo.[75] 'The village on the passage around the hill' is more likely though and will be adopted here.

The Old English spelling of our word 'church' was 'cirice' or 'circe'. Middle English spoken in medieval times altered that to 'chirche' and then 'church'. The 'circe' was instrumental in civilising and governing the people. Priests and monks formed communities known as Minsters (from the Latin Monasterium) as centres of influence from which missionaries could baptise and teach the faith. North Somerset ecclesiastical life was shaped by these Minsters.[76] Bedminster and Wells were not far away. Cheddar, site of a royal palace, was another Minster close to Yatton (to judge by a phrase in King Alfred's will which speaks of a community there.[77]) Churches were then built in the surrounding villages and countryside, becoming daughter churches of mother Minster. Very likely, nearby Congresbury and Banwell had monastic communities which were Old Welsh, or Celtic - Congresbury Parish Church has a Celtic dedication to do with Cyngar the Priest who, according to the legend we noted, founded Congresbury. The Christian society on Cadbury-Congresbury probably evolved into a hermit site.[78] We can imagine Christian people going up the hill to meet with a solitary sage. In time, this may have become a small monastery.[79]

A prayer cross or crude shelter would have been erected for the mission priest from the Minster. This eventually became the first church at Yatton, probably made with wood and wattle. Yatton itself may have been a Minster - the Domesday Book refers to the church with its hide of land. How long Yatton Parish church had existed cannot be said with any certainty. A Saxon Church was there somewhere- but where? Evidence of a pre-Saxon church lies in churchyards that are circular, or at least curvilinear. Circumstantial evidence is that Church St around the north side of the present day church in Yatton has clues to offer. On ancient maps, the street is oval. It may not have been re-aligned just because a new stone church was constructed later on in the 13th century. An oval or circular shape might imply that here was a burial ground around a Saxon or even a pre-Saxon church. All this may mean that people have been worshipping in Yatton before the middle of the seventh century. From there it is only a hundred years back to a possible Christian society on Cadbury Hill before the Kings of Wessex brought Saxon life and culture to the area.

Pope Gregory had instructed Augustine to take over the pagan temples, destroy the idols and then have "*holy water sprinkled into the temples, altars built and relics set there. So the people will have no need to change their places of concourse. And where of old they were wont to sacrifice oxen to demons, in this matter also there should be some substitution of solemnity*".[80] If conjecture about a Christian group of the Old Welsh/British society on Cadbury Hill is correct, this would pre-date Pope Gregory's instruction. They were part of the Celtic Church, not the Roman system.

As generations came and went, the size and scale of rural settlements grows. The story that used to be told is that shortly after the arrival of the Saxons, the countryside was populated with rural communities that led to such villages being formed and that it was the Normans who re-organised the rural landscape into feudalism, Manors and open fields. The picture is more complex. The English village as we know it only began in the tenth century when peasant houses, their fields and their buildings were packed together more efficiently. Scattered farms are clustererd round a central focal point with church and aristocratic holdings of land and buildings.[81] Yatton is firmly within the central area of England where nuclear settlements rather than single farms are the norm.[82] There was a rationale for this.

Grouping the peasants together so that their surplus labour and grain could be exploited more productively meant that they were tied to the owner of the estate. The depression of status means that dependence on superiors has begun to be a way of life. Landlords pressed their tenants hard for greater returns. New field systems and strips of land were larger than individual holdings. They required ox plough teams.

In Saxon times, 'Jatone' had a row of houses along a central track with open fields cultivated by a few hundred inhabitants to the rear. The village was probably built at the conjunction of two ancient track-ways. One led south-north down the existing High St down to the Moors. The other track came from the east, skirting around or directly over Cadbury Hill towards village and sea. 'Waimora', referred to in the Domesday Book may represent '*waeg*' = 'way, path' or even '*waegn*' = 'waggon' (adding 'hamme'): the pasture is at the end of a long track, reached by waggons. This trackway would have connected the old Roman villa with the Temple on the Hill.

In the year 909, the church in Yatton came under a new bishopric. The people of Somerset had been granted their own bishop, Athelm. His seat, 'cathedra' was at the Minster in Wells.

By then, the sacred geography of the parish system was being superimposed upon the landscape. Every square inch of England was covered. It marked the transition from the minster model of a few central churches to local churches rooted in each community. Landowners began to be buried in their local church. Minsters went into relative decline except where they became cathedrals. By the tenth century, the Hundred with its court was the fundamental unit of local Government. But it was the village as a self-contained community and hub of local manors dominated by thegns of Saxon England that became the new social unit of the countryside. It demanded its own ecclesiastical structure. The parish system was the result of this process.

The years pass. The slow movement of the agricultural year succeeds to each passing phase. Eleven generations come and go on the Moor. Then, one day, someone saw the long-ships.

An Icon of Terror

The distinctive shape and sail of the Vikings was to represent an image of terror for that generation and their sons and daughters. Viking raiders took up residence on Steepholm and Flatholm, two islands off the coast of North Somerset highly visible from the surrounding area and Cadbury Hill. Steepholm rises up some eighty metres out of the sea. It is where the Mendip Hills finally expire. Now it is a nature reserve and has the distinction of issuing its own postage stamps. Romans, hermits and monks came to Steepholm.

The island became a base and winter residence for the terrifying sea-peoples that erupt out of Scandinavia from the 790s onwards; the first recorded timing of the movement of pirates from the north who were set on pillaging and who left a trail of destruction everywhere. It was on 8 January 793 that the *"the harrowing inroads of heathen men made lamentable havoc in the church of God in Holy-island"* as the Anglo-Saxon Chronicle records.[83] At the cost of his life, the Sheriff of Dorset had already encountered a few years before *"three ships of the Northmen from the land of the robbers"*. During the decades that followed, most coastal areas of Britain and Ireland saw longships. The church in Yatton no doubt prayed to be delivered from the fury of the Norsemen. The Vikings seemed as terrorists to contemporaries. The reality is that they proved as eager to settle as to ransack, as prone to trade as to plunder.[84] They sent home for their wives as waves of immigrants have done since.

How the life and death struggle for England affected the Moor we have no way of knowing. From their base on nearby Steepholm and Flatholm, the Vikings were unmistakeable and a source of anxious insecurity. They were too close not to have been frequent visitors, whether through trade or plunder. Very likely, the people of the Moor were subject to violent raids, being sold into slavery or subjection to a new lord. Across Somerset, the struggles of King Alfred against the similar sea-peoples known to history as the Danes, resulted in the Peace of Wedmore in 878 and a line drawn across England. The Moor lay firmly on the part of the country ruled by the Kings of Wessex. It was far from the area of Danelaw. Nevertheless, proximity to a Viking base would have meant Yatton was subject to violent infiltration.

English and Dane will live together and fight against each other for a long time to come. Five generations will come and go before King Cnut unites the kingdom in the year 1016. He adopts the policy of the former Archbishop of Canterbury, Dunstan, endeavouring to enforce a stricter discipline upon a lax church. Clerics in Yatton will have felt the growing pressure towards celibacy and the revival of the monastic ideal.

In the years leading up to the Norman Conquest, the manors of North Somerset were held for King Edwards and then Harold by the mix of Dane, Viking and English that was emerging from the melting pot.[85] Concerning Yatton, the Domesday book of 1086 records that *"John the Dane held it in the time of King Edward, and gelded it for twenty hides."*

John the Dane was therefore the boss of Yatton when the Normans took over. Who John was we do know except that he was a Dane who became dispossessed and, according to the Somerset historian Collinson, '*left a progeny in these parts.*'[86]

'King Edward' is Edward the Confessor. He appointed Giso of Lorraine as Bishop of Wells in the year 1061. More efficient methods of government were in the air. Bishop Giso brought with him some of the ideas for reforming the church current on the continent. He had the support of an archdeacon and lesser clergy who would have the title of Canons since they lived by a rule. The estates owned by Bishop Giso were to form the core of the Episcopal holdings through the medieval period. Some estates were obtained during his episcopate for the endowments of the canons at Wells. Yatton was acquired by Bishop Giso. This was the position at the end of

1065 when King Edward wore his crown at the Christmas festival for the last time. In his dying breath, he bequeathed the throne to Harold.

The stage was set for the dramatic events of 1066. The 35th generation is now alive.

Chapter 4

LORDS AND THE LIVES OF THE MISERABLE

KENN
KENN COURT

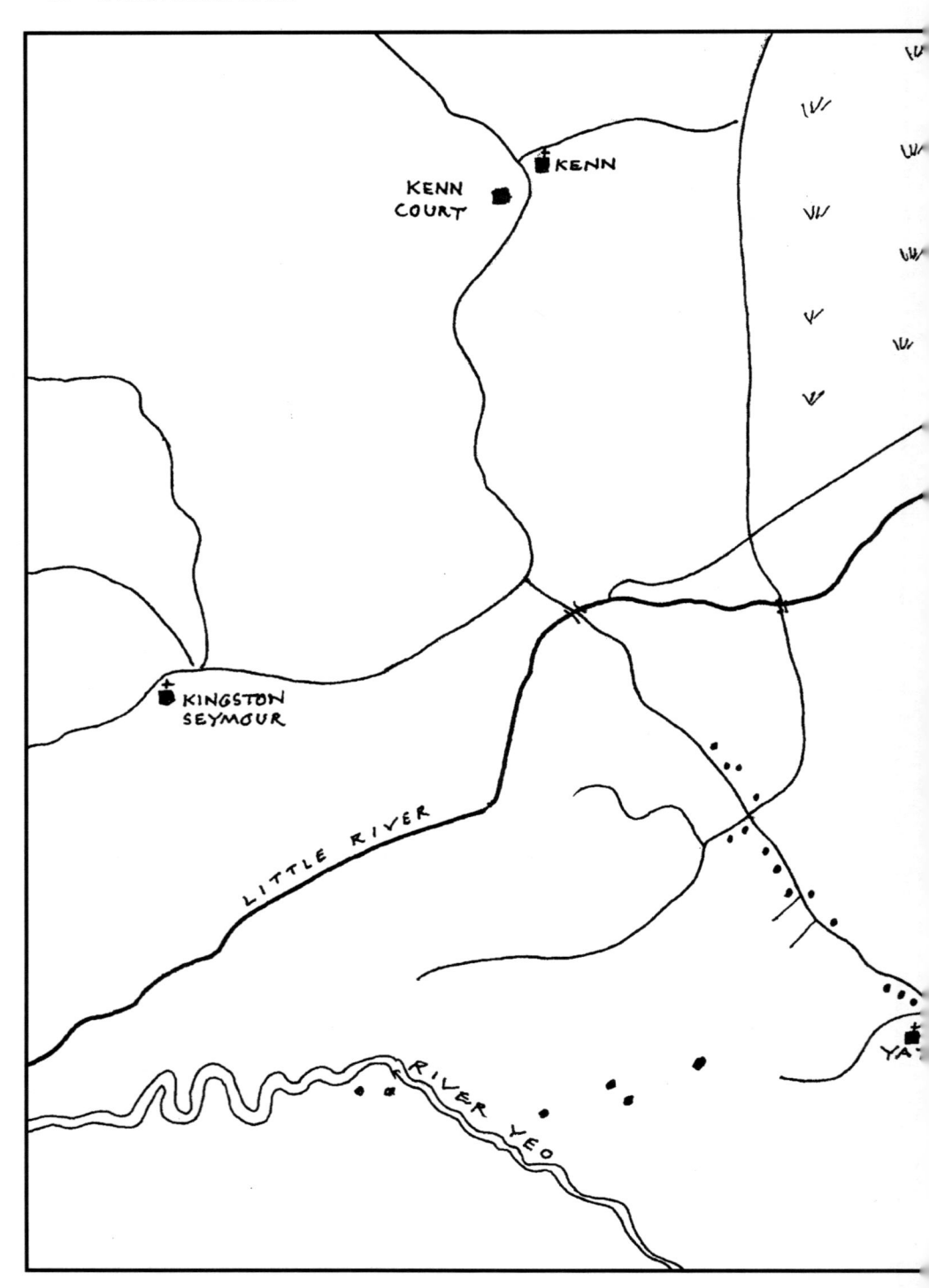

KINGSTON SEYMOUR

LITTLE RIVER

RIVER YEO

YA

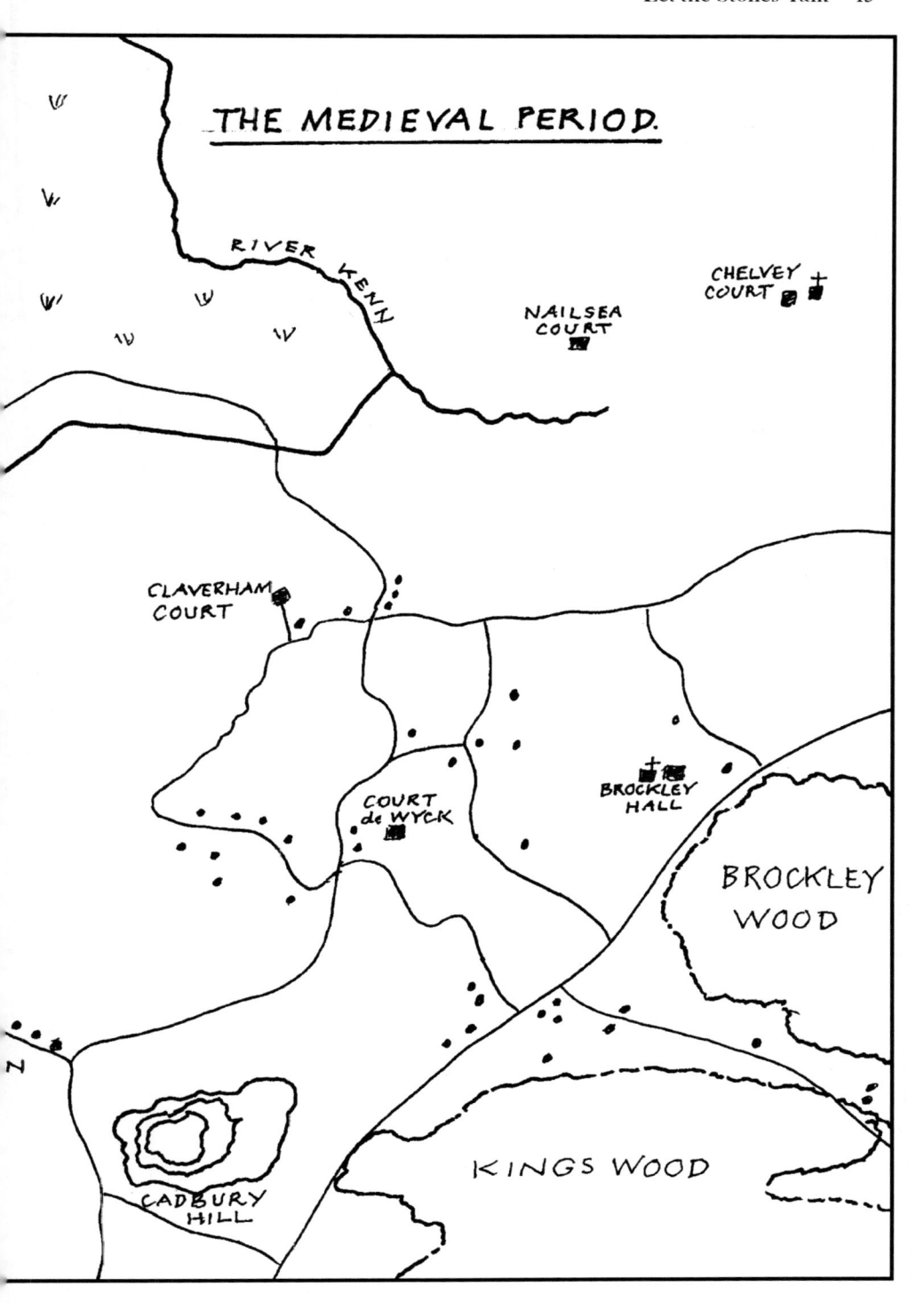

THE MEDIEVAL PERIOD.

RIVER KENN

CHELVEY COURT

NAILSEA COURT

CLAVERHAM COURT

COURT de WYCK

BROCKLEY HALL

BROCKLEY WOOD

CADBURY HILL

KINGS WOOD

It is the end of the year 1066.

We cannot know how quickly the shock news reached the people of the Moor that an Army from Normandy under the command of Duke William had won a dramatic victory at Hastings. 34 generations have lived and died since the Romans came. Over the next three centuries, some ten generations will appear for a while in the living theatre that is the Moor. But the 35th to the 44th generations will live under the shadow of different rulers. The land is mute witness to a conquest by the relentless descendants of the Vikings who had settled in France, the Norse-men.

A popular narrative, fostered by the legends of Robin Hood, was that social inequality and oppression began with the hated Normans. This is a myth. It is true that England was torn apart. The popular name given to the greatest national survey that had ever been attempted in England- the Domesday Book - testifies to the apocalyptic atmosphere. Yet the Normans inherited a very structured social system marked by hierarchy and the exploitation of economic power. The Norman Conquest was a take- over in which they inserted themselves into the top ranks.[87] The grass-roots or indeed the every - day life of the million and a half peasants of England was hardly affected. They merely had new landlords.

The power of local lords flourished as never before. "*The years between 1066 and 1086 witnessed the largest transfer of property ever seen in English history.*"[88] It was akin to the French or Russian revolution in its effects on the forcing the upper classes from their property. What King William and his commanders did not grab as their reward, the families of the former Saxon thegns were forced to redeem. Although peasants may not have resented foreign domination from their new landlords (they were used to it), they did resent this additional taxation. A high level of profits from the Manors was considered a natural return.

Yatton is very well described in the Domesday survey of the shires of England.[89] Indeed most of the 13,000 places described there survive as villages and towns today.[90] Yatton appears in the Domesday Book as an estate of twenty hides- some 2400 acres - belonging to Giso of Lorraine, Bishop of Wells. In the days of Edward the Confessor, the Manor of Yatton and with it right of presentation to the church belonged to John the Dane. William the Conqueror gave both to the Bishop in 1068 in part compensation for some possessions belonging to the See of Wells which in the Confessor's time Harold had seized, and gave to Gloucester Abbey. Harold had seized both Congresbury and Banwell from the Bishop of

Bath and Wells. After the Conquest the Bishop asked William for their return, but the King had learnt of the good hunting to be had on the hill at Congresbury! So although he returned Banwell he gave the Bishop the Manor of Yatton and kept Congresbury for himself. The wooded hill above the village is still known as Kingswood.

Back then, the Norman State had three aims in commissioning their survey, which was an ambitious project beyond the State machinery of other countries in Europe. The Domesday Book was a record of landed estates so that if they came into the King's possession by death or confiscation, it would be clear how much their estates were worth. The Book was also intended to act as a land registry so disputes could be settled. The third aim was to provide a survey so tax could be assessed.[91] At least that is the usual narrative. The reality behind the greatest national survey that had ever been attempted in England was more brutal. The Commissioners wished to legitimise the Norman land-grab, to record that power and wealth are now solidly consolidated into the new era.

The Domesday reference for Yatton reads like this. Describing the estates of Bishop Giso, Bishop of Bath and Wells,

"The same Bishop holds Jatune. John the Dane held it in the time of King Edward, and gelded it for twenty hides. The arable is twenty two carucates. Thereof six hides are in demesne and there are two carucates and three servants and ten villanes and fourteen cottages, with six ploughs. There are thirty two acres of meadow. Wood one mile long and two furlongs broad. Moor one mile in length and breadth. It is worth to the Bishop six pounds. Of the land of this Manor, Fastrade holds of the Bishop five hides, Idelbert four hides. In demesne, there are three carucates and four servants and eigthteen villeins and twenty three cottagers with eleven ploughs. Among them it is worth nine pounds."

This needs some translation. John the Dane is the boss in Yatton before 1066. It is not totally clear how large a hide was. The quantity varied across the country. The usual reckoning is 120 acres. Bishop Giso's holding is 20 hides (around 2400 acres) which required tax. This was land for 22 ploughs or carucates. The ten villeins are rent-paying villagers. 11 cows and 15 pigs grazed on the land. There are 11 plough teams, essentially a horse or ox pulling a small plough.

The Domesday book speaks of the church, held by Benzelin, the Archdeacon. Yatton church had one hide of land around it. *"The Church of this Manor, with one hide, Benthelm holds of the Bishop. It is worth twenty shillings".*[92]

In the same entry, there is a direct reference to a pasture under the name of Waimora, a Manor in west Yatton that in 1086, Waimora belonged to Bishop Giso, the Bishop of Wells. The Latin word 'Pastura' seems to have the modern meaning of the word 'pasture': a grassland for grazing animals, unlikely to be cultivated or used for hay. ("Una pastura Waimora dicta ibidem est, quae tempus rex Edwardi pertinet ad Congresberie, manerum regis" - *"There is one pasture called Waimora, which in the time of King Edward belonged to Congresbury, the King's Manor."*[93])

There are two versions of the Domesday Book. Complicating things when it comes to Kingston Seymour is that in one of these, the standard (Winchester) version, there are two entries. The first refers to a William of Monceaux paying tax on 4 ½ hides. There were 9 villagers and 1 slave. The second (Exeter version) entry speaks of the Bishop's land held by his appointee, William of Monceaux, also amounting to 4 ½ hides (clearly the same landholding). The second entry proceeds to name four thanes, smallholders, who held the land jointly as one Manor under William's authority- Siward, 1 hide, Alvaric the priest, 2 hides, Saeric 1 hide and Saewulf ½ hide.

Alvaric was therefore a farmer-priest. This was not an unusual sight in those days. Most parish priests were farmers of their glebe. In lieu of stipend, the priest farmed the land granted to him by Aldred, last of the Saxon lords. Payment was in kind. In return, the priest served the Manor church. This encapsulates the relationship that grew between the lord of the Manor presenting someone for appointment by the church, giving him the glebe lands which supported the church. In 1066, Alvaric probably ministered in a rude wooden church with little beauty or architecture to commend it.

The Domesday book recorded the dispossession of the English elite biggest take-over of land the country has ever seen and.[94] What happened to John the Dane in Yatton or Aldred at Kingston we simply have no idea. It is highly significant that the starting point in all these entries is who held the land at the time of King Edward the Confessor. This is what the Commissioners went around asking. King Harold does not get a look in. He was regarded as a usurper. As King Edward was claimed to have awarded England to William, there is a straight line being drawn to 1086.

The additional reference for Kingston Seymour in the standard (Winchester) version goes on to add: "*William of Monceaux holds Kingston from the Bishop. Aldred held it before 1066; it paid tax for 1 hide. Land for 17 ploughs. In lordship 3 ploughs and 1 virgate, with 1 slave, 18 villagers and 4 smallholders with 11 ploughs and 3 virgates. Pasture, 40 acres. 20 cattle, 31 pigs; 120 sheep. The value was and is £6.*"

The implication is that there were two different Manors. It is further complicated by there being two different Bishops on the scene. Entries for Yatton come under the holdings of the Bishop of Wells (before he became the Bishop of Bath and Wells). Entries for Kingston and Kenn on the other hand are under the colourful character of Geofrey Mowbray, warrior Bishop of Coutances. Who was this redoubtable prelate?

The Warrior Priest – A Study in Power[95]

After 1066, Claverham Manor was given to Geoffrey de Montbrai (Mowbray), the Bishop of Coutances. Geoffrey was a warrior prelate, administrator and right-hand man to William the Conqueror. When only a young man, he had been nominated to the see of St Lo in Normandy. As part of the mighty Mowbray family, that was down to his brother's influence. Geoffrey elicited funds from his fellow nobles with spoils from their invasion of Sicily. With such donations, he was able to build his Catheral at Coutances. The Bishop knew how to follow the lines of power. He became invaluable to Duke William and accompanied him on the invasion of England. At Hastings, the Bishop could be seen rallying the troops, urging them to victory against the Saxon thegns. It was Geoffrey de Mowbray who, on Christmas Day 1066 at Westminster, led the cry for the Norman conquerors to acclaim their Duke as King of England. Geoffrey was suitably rewarded. His fiefdom was spread over no less than 12 counties mainly in the West.

Geoffrey de Mowbray was certainly energetic. When the men of Somerset rose up (taking advantage of the disturbance caused by the capture of York by the Danes in September 1069) and attacked the Count of Mortain's castle of Montacute, the Bishop commanded the troops that put down the rebellion. Most of the rebels were slain or put to flight. A proportion of the captives were mutilated.[96] He was military leader as well as landowner and cleric.[97] The historian Orderic Vitalis, describes Geoffrey as a man of noble birth, devoted more to knightly than to clerical activities, better able to instruct knights in fighting than teaching clerics to sing psalms![98]

Always at William's side, the Bishop of Coutances took the field in 1075, leading with another warrior prelate Odo, a large army against the Revolt of the Earls. Geoffrey's forces captured their stronghold, Norwich. Given important judicial functions, whuch included admistering law and order in Northumberland, there is evidence that the Bishop of Coutances was one of the Domesday Commissioners. Two years later, he attended the Conqueror's funeral. Fierce loyalty to William did not extend to his son.

The Domesday Book had recorded a total of 265 estates owned by the Bishop of Coutances though Orderic states that Bishop Geoffrey held 280 Manors in England. This immense 'honour' was made up of two main groups of estates, each divided into a number of subsidiary groups. The larger of the two groups was in the West of England- 97 estates in Devon, 10 in Gloucester, eight in Wiltshire, two in Dorset and 76 in Somerset. These Manors included Claverham Manor, Kenn and Kingston. The Bishop of Coutances' land at Kenn amounted to ½ Hide. One slave worked the land, which was valued at five shillings.[99] Lastly, he also holds Claverham Manor - written as Cliveham Manor. The Domesday Book entry read as follows: *"Folcheran holds of the Bishop [ie, Geoffrey, Bishop of Coutances], Cliveham. Gonnil held it in the time of King Edward and gelded it for two hides. The arable is three carucates. In demesne is one carucate with one servant and three villeins and twelve cottagers with two ploughs. There are seven acres of meadow. Wood one furlong long and as broad. Brish wood half a mile long as much broad. It was worth twenty shillings and now thirty shillings."*

The four and a half hides of Kingston amounted to about 540 acres with an additional 40-60 in the other holding. Taking the lands at Kenn into account, probably both entries for Kingston plus that of Claverham to the east, the Bishop of Coutances was the ultimate landowner of eight Hides across the Moor compared with 20 for Bishop Gizo. The average hide has been reckoned to support a family of five.[100] Yet adding up the population in the Domesday Book suggests about 90 villeins and smallholders plus about nine serfs, or bonded labourers. And of course the families of either villeins or smallholders are not taken into account. The Claverham reference speaks of a dozen 'cottagers.' All together, there must have been about 400 people of the Moor in 1086.

The spring of 1088 found the Bishop of Coutances joining in a general revolt against William Rufus, leading, alongside his nephew, Robert, the

Earl of Northumberland, the insurrection in the West of England. The Earl of Northumberland used Bristol, where Geoffrey already held an official position as Castellan, as a base for a series of destructive raids, burning Bath and ravaging the surrounding countryside. It is not clear from the accounts if Geoffrey already held Bristol while the Earl of Northumberland led raiding parties as the chronicler Florence of Worcester states, or whether both together led the raids as reported by the Peterborough Chronicle and William of Malmesbury. The fate of the rising was settled further east. As soon as they realised that Bishop Odo and Duke Robert were unlikely to succeed, Bishop Geoffrey and the Earl of Northumberland quickly made their peace with William Rufus. Geoffrey somehow obtained his pardon early enough to take part in proceedings against the Bishop of Durham.[101]

The whole of these vast estates across England were regarded as personal to Bishop Geoffrey. When he died in February 1093, it was passed on to his nephew, the Earl of Northumberland, who forfeited them only two years later in a rebellion against William Rufus and lingered 34 years in Windsor Castle for his pains.

We know also about another figure named in the Domesday Book, a wealthy farmer called Fastrad. Fastrad had an illustrious son.

The Son of Fastrad

Fastrad is a tenant farmer of substance, who holds five hides of land from the Bishop on Yatton Moor. His son will enjoy a priveliged education.

Fastrad is thought to have come from Lorraine and settled in Somerset during the era of reform and development at Wells under Bishop Giso. The spelling of Fastrad suggests that it is more likely to have been an Old German name rather than Old English.[102] In 1086, at the time of the Domesday Survey of Somerset, Fastrad is one of the 269,000 individuals listed by name. He held directly from Giso Bishop of Wells eight hides of land in Wells, and one hide in Banwell as well as the five hides in Yatton.[103] He was probably the predecessor of the de Wyke family at Yatton who held from the bishops of Bath and Wells land worth two knights' fees (the unit of military taxation then) in Wyke and Milton from 1166 onwards.[104] Wyke is derived from the Old English 'wic' meaning 'a dwelling, a building or collection of buildings for special purposes, a farm, a dairy farm;' in the plural 'hamlet, village'.[105] The use of the word Wick in the sense of a dairy farm was very common in the 13th and 14th centuries.

Fastrad's illustrious son Adelard (or Athelard) was born about 1080. He is best known for his translations of scholarly works from Arabic into Latin and for his prominent role in introducing Arab science to Europe.[106]

In 1088, when Adelard was about eight years old, the city of Bath was burnt during the uprising led by Geoffrey. The rebellion was led by Geoffrey de Mowbray in an attempt to place Robert of Normandy on the throne instead of William Rufus. John of Tours, the newly appointed Bishop of Wells, was granted by William Rufus the right to purchase the city of Bath from the Crown and to move the seat of the diocese from Wells to Bath where the Roman spa was being redeveloped and would have attracted doctors and scholars. Bishop John was also able to become abbot as well as bishop; the monastery became a cathedral priory. Adelard was probably in residence at this time, certainly during the latter part of John's episcopate. The first documentary reference to Adelard is in 1106 when Athelard, the son of Fastrad [Athelardus, filius Fastradi] witnessed a document for Bishop John. Bishop John will live until 1122.

The influence he will exert on his young protégé is enormous. Bishop John encouraged Adelard to go to Tours, his native city. After studying at Tours from about 1100, Adelard went to teach at a school in Laon where the sons and nephews of several of Henry I's key administrators were students. Having dismissed his students, Adelard departed for a seven-year period of travel. He went to Spain and then to Salerno. But the East beckons. Disguised, Adelard learns Arabic and studies Arab science. He translates many works of Arabic scholarship into Latin. Then comes his big triumph- the translation of 'Euclid's Elements'. Most of the original Greek text had been lost. Adelard reintroduces to Europe the full corpus of Euclid's geometry as a logical deductive method. He provides the West with additional information about sines and trigonometry that the Arabs had adapted from Hindu astronomy. One of the first texts which Adelard translated explains Hindu arithmetic and the use of the enigmatic zero, previously considered an exotic addition of no practical value. Adelard is one of those credited with helping to introduce Arabic numerals to Europe.

Adelard was a polymath was with numerous interests. As well as translating other people's work, he was an author in his own right. After the outbreak of the civil war between Stephen and Matilda in 1139, he returned to Bath and wrote a treatise on the astrolabe. This he dedicated to Henry Plantagenet (Matilda's son, later Henry II) who is known to have spent part of his boyhood at that time in Bristol Castle with his uncle Earl Robert of Gloucester. He paused to pen a treatise on the care of falcons – *De avibis* - the earliest known manuscript on the subject, in which he urged the handler not to associate with prostitutes lest he infect the bird with vermin.

Adelard of Bath, son of Fastrad of Yatton is truly the first English scientist.

The Norman Lords

For the three hundred years and ten generations covered in this chapter, the countries of Western Europe were organised in roughly the same way in what became known as feudalism. It was profoundly hierarchical, the ultimate example of society distinguishing between high and low value people. At the apex of the pyramid, the King divided his lands amongst his nobles, who did homage to him and promised to fight for him. In turn, each noble parcelled out land to knights who did him homage and promised to rally to the cause when needed. A Knight coming of age or someone being worthy of the honour and then Knighted, received some land with peasants, farmsteads and villages. These Manors were the basis of the medieval economy. The economy was 'bottom-up'; social rank was 'top-down'.

For the first part of the years of Norman rule, up to about 1150, England was a subsistence economy. On each farmstead, each estate, each nodule of production as it were, people produced their own food. The bulk of any surplus going could be sold to the lords of the Manor who had noble status. Very little was sold elsewhere as barter for other goods.[107] From 1150, a market system begins to take shape. Population and productivity are increasing. The growth of towns involved artisans who bought the surplus and exchanged it for their own goods. It was the growth of a merchant (middle) class. After paying their dues to the landlords, those on the rung above them, better-off peasants were able to sell on the open market. Trade such as there was tended to be in luxury items. It was when long-distance trade involved bulk goods such as wheat and wood that a capitalist economy began to emerge.[108]

As lynchpins of the local ruling class, lords of the Manor were the basis of this growing prosperity. Where the Roman economy was based on villas, the unit of production in the medieval economy was centred on Manors. The local Manors of the Moor were landed estates held by a lord and worked by villeins or tenant farmers who had rights to work some strips of land. The lord of the Manor was entitled to hold a court. The powers of the Manor court varied. Sometimes the lord dealt only with villeins, at other times with free men as well. Manor courts were mainly concerned with the administration of common land and they arbitrated disputes which arose between individuals from time to time. More serious crimes were handled by a leet court, though gradually leet courts and Manorial courts merged. To help the smooth running of the Manor, various officials were appointed. The most important was the Reeve, the business manager and bailiff of the lord of the Manor. But there were also Pontreeves –in charge of bridges and roads – bread weighers, ale tasters, swineherds and tythingsmen to collect taxes due to the church.[109]

In a survey of 1279 called the Hundred Rolls, two thirds of Manors were small - 500 acres or less.[110] A later survey of the land subsidy of 1334, shows that estates in Yatton probably yielded between £10-19 per square mile.[111]

How many Knights there were on the Moor we cannot say. At the time of King John, 4,500 men in England had Knight status. But then the title began to be restricted to a wealthy minority and about a thousand were dubbed knights. Thousands of lesser landowners did not have a specific title. But most of them held land in exchange for military service- in fee as it was called.[112] The Knight's Fee became a unit of taxation. Officially, all those with income over £40 a year could be dubbed Knights but some landowners chose not to bear this honour. It was not the wealth but the implications that troubled them. The Knights were expected to perform ceremonial functions and official duties, such as the county grand jury with its roll of twelve Knights.[113] At time of war, Knights were expected to turn out in full body armour, obtain weapons and buy a war horse. War horses did not come cheap – around 1280, the going rate was £20.[114] The Treasury didn't mind as long as they got the Knight's Fee tax. Early on, the estates had to produce a mounted knight. The Knight's Fee lasts until the 17th century. But long since, it had been easier to raise a professional army. The world is changing.

Manor and village do not coincide on the Moor. There were eight Manors in all, some of them owned by wealthy Bishops who were major landowners in medieval England. They range from the main 'Yatton Manor' to the 'Manor of Yatton Rectory' worth 12 ½ Knight's Fees and two Knight's Fees respectively. The idea was that Manors that made up the parish of Yatton met their military quota of knights and supporting troops. The Manors are detailed in Appendix One. In medieval times, three of these Manors have Manor Houses. They all had tenant farmers and open fields. The Kenn family was resident but the other medieval landowners live elsewhere. These were of varying sizes. Yatton Manor - the main Manor held by the Bishop - was the largest.

By the end of the 11th century, as Crusading was getting under way, there is a new owner of Claverham Manor.

Rufus gifted the estates owned by the Bishop of Coutances to Robert Fitzhamon, Lord of Creully in Calvados, Normandy. Fitzhamon – the name 'Fitz' means 'son of'- was the Norman Hammer of Glamorgan and the Welsh borders during an offensive in South Wales in 1093.[115] How he conquered Glamorgan is a mystery but it may have been by a sea-borne expedition across from Bristol as well as land invasion. The invasion brought about the collapse of the Welsh kingdom of Morgannwg.[116] By right of conquest, Fitzhamon and his successors ruled what became the lordship of Glamorgan.[117]

At the siege of Falaise in 1105, Robert Fitzhamon suffered a brain injury which deprived him of his reason and ended his career. He died in March 1107 and was buried in Tewkesbury Abbey. His heir was his daughter Mabel. Fitzhamon's possessions were held in Royal Custody until she was given in marriage to Robert, favourite illegitimate son of Henry 1, by now King of England.

The Le Sors were of ancient pedigree in Somerset. A Peter le Soure was amongst twelve Knights who were leading figures in that Norman conquest of Glamorgan. These 12 Knights became in effect, tenants-in-chief of many of Fitzhamon's estates.[118] He was rewarded with the 'castell and Manor at Peterton, of one knight's fee.[119] In 1102, Robert Le Sor is recorded as witnessing a charter relating to Bassaleg issued by a tenant of Robert Fitzhamon,[120] Odo Le Sor supported Fitzhamon. When Fitzhamon died, his considerable inheritance passed by marriage of his daughter Mabel to the illegitimate son of Henry 1 who was created the Earl of Gloucester and who built the keep of Bristol Castle.[121] The Le Sors were well rewarded. The

Earl of Gloucester was ultimate landowner of the Manor of Claverham. He entrusted to the Le Sors the fee of St Fagans, two Knight's Fees in Gloucestershire and 12 more in Somerset, including Claverham. In the 13th century, William and John Le Sor are described as lords of Backwell and Claverham.[122]

The last male Le Sor, John was a wealthy man. In 1290, he was obtaining rights to weekly markets and the annual fair at Backwell.[123] By 1295, he is Assessor and Tax Collector in Gloucestershire, where he happens to have three Manors. The Registration of 1303 recording the Knight's Fees for the purpose of taxation shows that the property of Le Sor has been split between his five daughters who are sharing Manorial rights and lands.[124] In his history of Somerset, Collinson says that the Manor of Claverham was passed from the Le Sors to the Rodney families.[125] This is a family we shall meet in Chapter 21 for they were descendants of serfs, those near the bottom rung of the ladder. The life of serfs was a very different experience to that of the Norman lords.

Life at the Bottom

We have met two of the Nobles who were landowners on the Moor, if absent much of the time. Three others will come to our attention. But what can we re-construct of the life of those lower down the social hierarchy, the People of the Moor at the bottom of the pile?

The lives ordinary people lived is beset by poverty, not just material poverty but poverty of records. As anyone writing about that period is compelled to face, the "silence of the poor" is deafening.[126] Of the peasants we know very little. We have virtually no access to the lives, the names, the tragedies and the triumphs of the ten generations of the common people who lived out their lives on the Moor between 1066 and the late medieval period some three hundred years later. Historians pay scant attention to the lives of the peasants for they left few records. For the most part, they are people lost to history. Surviving records deal with wills and inheritance of the medieval landowners. There are few fragments of the meanings by which the the people of the Moor articulated their lives.

Most people in medieval England lived in villages. The communities of the Moor were fairly typical. Each village tended to have three large fields, divided into strips, which the lords of the various Manors allowed the villagers to farm. The villeins paid rent but at the bottom of the pile, bonded labourers, the serfs, paid by working for the lord of the Manor when needed and by giving him some of the food they produced. The villeins account for about 40% of the rural population. They hold about three oxen each and yardlands of 30 acres (called a virgate) or half yardland. Some 60% of the population was servile.[127] That left only a tiny elite at the top and small tenants with small holdings who nevertheless performed important service in the community, the craftsmen, the village blacksmith and millars.

The peasants did not own their land; they 'held' it in exchange for services rendered. Each peasant ploughed and harvested his own holding of land. They knew the land intimately, even assigning names to their furlong or so. Land was in strips, divided into two blocks. Half was cultivated each year. It was a two-field system; barley or wheat one year, then half of the arable land lying fallow the next. The common rules for strip farming meant that everyone on the Moor could work some of the best and some of the worst of the land. In a subsistence economy, the peasants had an equal chance of starving or harvesting. Local sheep were kept for their wool rather than their meat. Most of them were killed as mature adults; mutton was common. Close to Yatton, King's Wood would have been carefully managed. Growing demand from towns meant careful cultivation of a valuable fuel; wood remains the source of power for many centuries.

The Reeves and other officials at the Manors tended to be drawn from the prosperous villains. Sometimes, these posts became hereditary. Medieval wills in Yatton show that local tenant farmers could accrue something to leave behind them. William Saunders left 23 hundred weight of wool to Thomas Waile, a steer to Richard Waile, a cow to John Erolle, 20 wethers to Thomas, a son or brother. The list of Exchequer lay subsidies, effectively tax payers, for Yatton for the year 1327 shows 30 villagers who were villeins. People such as Richard atte Croys (down for 2 shillings), Rogero Sourdogh (also paying 2 shillings) and Alicia Godman (assessed at 13d) paid tax. There were only 3 women; all had surnames.[128] Landlords had the right to appropriate goods and chattels of dead tenants. Widows if they were lucky might receive one-third of their value. Even small holdings descended within the family. Usually this was the oldest son but some provision might be made for children other than the heir. John Hickes of Yatton left £5 to his younger son, the holding itself while the husbandry went to his oldest son.[129]

These are the richer peasants, the villeins. The lived experience of the serfs who are invisible to history would have been rather different. In the French tale Merlin Merlot, a serf protests, *"Alas what will become of me who has never had a single day's rest? I do not think I shall ever know respose or ease....I, unhappy one, I am like a rooster soaked in the rain, head hanging and bedraggled, or like a beaten dog."*[130]

Some peasant laments that have come down to us bemoan their lot in equivalent terms, resentful of the ardous toil that was their lot in life because they are not free.

The truth is, we simply do not know how the serfs saw the world. The serfs provided a labour force for the lord of the Manor to draw on. Typically, they work two or three days a week for him - more at Harvest time. Often, tenants were required to do more labour. The archives of church landlords show that in Somerset, Manors were more successful than Manors in the north and east of England in forcing peasants into heavy work duties. The serfs provided plough teams, heavy instruments drawn by a team of oxen or horses.[131] We may imagine medieval plough teams in action across the Moor. The ploughman and his boy walk wearily up and down the narrow strips from sunrise to when the workload for that day had been fulfilled by early afternoon. Then came sowing and reaping. All this had to be fulfilled on the demesne estates of the lord of the Manor in addition to your own holding. The inevitability of toil was incessant, monotonous and wearying.

There were some advantages. Serfs could get cheaper justice in the lord's manorial court than freehold farmers in the royal courts. And the villeins, the tenants on the estates of the powerful lords, enjoyed a security from brigands and royal officials.

Peasants on the Moor would not have constructed their own houses. They had specialist help, especially with carpentry to make the timber frame. By the 13th century, stone foundations were coming in. Straw or reeds would be used for thatch and clay and dung were used to daub the wattled walls. Straw or reeds made for a thatched roof. A typical peasant dwelling with a hall and a bedroom could cost 40 shillings to construct. Outhouses were often needed for animals; the poorer farmers had their animal living under the same roof. Bars and shutters marked the small windows. There was no privacy. Hedges or ditches surrounded the property. Peasants guarded their precious few belongings, their clothing and their sheets and towels were locked away in sturdy chests in the inner chamber.[132]

It was a way of life that hardly changed over the centuries and very labour intensive. Two dozen people laboured where one person with a machine now works.

Food was uncertain and mainly of low quality. On the Moor, there is a pigeon pie factory.[133] Pigeons were a very useful food supply. A dovecote with 500 nesting holes could produce 200 young every week. The Normans were great pigeon handlers, decreeing that no one but the landlord could have a dovecote. The lord of the Manor could have pigeon pie anytime. But a peasant on the Moor is in serious trouble if they snare and kill any pigeons feeding on his plot of land. Feudal laws, maintained for centuries, ensured that the common people could only look on.

In Chaucer's 'Nun's Priest Tale', the poor widow has only 'milk and brown bread, broiled bacon and sometimes an egg or two'. Bread was the staple. Any rabbits or birds you can catch and eat is extra. After Michaelmas at the end of September, comes the sowing of wheat and rye. November is the blood month when livestock is killed for the winter so there will be meat. Christmas was the great holiday period. The people of the Moor had three weeks off. From mid-December to Plough Monday, just after Twelfth Night, the peasants could rest a bit, eat where they could afford it and drink whatever ale was going. Ploughs were blessed, songs were sung and a religious atmosphere seemed to make sense of life.

The backwardness of agricultural practice and the poverty of much of the peasantry were especially noticeable in the south-west. The Domesday Book here records the highest proportion of servile tenants in the country. Somerset had over 2,000 in this class. This was no doubt related to the large demesnes on major ecclesiastical estates such as on the Moor.[134] Not too far away, though at a later time, a survey of the estates of the Bishop of Worcester in 1299 has indicated that a typical tenant farmer held half a virgate of some 16 acres. Based on yields of three to four times the amount of seed used and average prices then prevailing, grain sales would be insufficient to cover his expenses. Yearly rent alone was some five shillings.[135] The lord of the Manor and the church took up to half the output of the peasant's produce in services, rent and tithe.[136] It was a hand to mouth existence, precariously dependent on seasons and weather. 'Give us this day our daily bread' was their regular cry.

Chapter 5

An Ecclesiastical Building Spree

The change of rulers known to history as the Norman Conquest brings an ecclesiastical building spree that was not repeated until the 19th century. Over the next 150 years the Normans built and re-built thousands of parish churches and many enormous Cathedrals.

On the Moor, the Normans built three churches. There is fragmentary evidence of Norman period in the east window at Kingston Seymour. In Kenn, the early Norman tower still stands, constructed on the site of an earlier Saxon church. In Yatton itself, although the pre-Domesday Book Anglo-Saxon church may have been replaced with a stone building during the Norman period after 1066, nothing now exists of earlier churches. The only evidence of there being a Norman church at Yatton is a drawing of "the Norman Font at Yatton Church". This drawing depicts a font that disappeared over two hundred years ago. Both the Anglo Saxon church and the Norman church were probably located on a circular site to the north west of the present building. A similar drawing of a Norman font at Kingston Seymour is shown below.

Norman font in Kingston Seymour Church

Norman tower in Kenn Church

Most of the present day church in Yatton itself dates from a major 15th century enlargement of a 13th century church. A significant amount of this earlier construction still exists.[137] Somewhere about 1220, work began on the Tower. At the high altar, the Chancel followed about 30 years later, the Nave in 1272, and finally Transepts from about 1280. This church was cruciform-the shape of a cross with the Nave much shorter and lower than the present one.[138]

The size and scale of Yatton church is a puzzle. Who commissioned it and why?

Bearing in mind that nearby Congresbury Parish Church was consecrated in 1215 and is once again in the hands of local clergy under the auspices of the Bishop of Bath and Wells, why is Yatton Parish Church on so grand a scale? It is a quarter- Cathedral size. There is now no need for competition with the King, who had held Congresbury personally, to see who can out - do each other in prestige. The King after all had access to nearby Kingswood, subject to forest law for the benefit of the Normans, who were passionate about hunting. The simple truth may be that the Bishop of Wells regarded Yatton Manor and Church as one the wealthiest of his holdings. The source of its wealth is clear enough. The land on the North Somerset levels must have been rich agricultural land- as long as they keep it from flooding!

Organising the Church

England was an ecclesiastical society- an integrated system of Church and State such as Europe had not experienced before or since. What the boundaries were was disputed as the Middle Ages unfold and the secular State asserted itself. The biography of the communities on the Moor tell us about how society was organised will be explored in subsequent chapters. But what about the church?

Ultimately there was the Pope at Rome. The villagers belonged to an international entity that looked to the Bishop of Rome, a vast empire of faith whose spiritual authority was universally accepted. There was no divide into church and state; the whole of Western Europe lived in the framework of a religious internationalism they called Christendom. The two hundred years from 1050 to 1250 were years of the Papal Monarchy, the nadir of its fortunes.[139] After that, despite inflation in its claims, States pay it less attention. Nevertheless, the papal court did *"lay down rules and conditions for all the main occasions and areas of the Christian life- baptism, confirmation, communion, penance, marriage, religious instruction and religious duties, alms, usury, last wills and testaments, the last rites, burial, graveyards and prayers for the dead."*[140]

Within this framework for the High Middle Ages, people lived and died. The medieval Papacy, huge organisation that it was, was called upon to make a judgement on the Rectorship of Kingston Seymour in 1311.[141] Papal machinery could be invoked if needs be; here was superior justice available to any prepared to take the trouble and pay the expense. There are otherwise very few references in the Yatton records to this higher authority under which the Diocese of Bath and Wells was governed. Until the establishment of the Papacy at Avignon in 1309 and the Great Schism in 1378 Popes enjoyed unchallenged spiritual authority as well as power that mushroomed. They sat as Princes of Europe. Papal monarchy was absolute (in theory at least).

In England, there was a Papal Legate, a Cardinal, and Archbishop of Canterbury; these could be the same. Then there were the Bishops. The Diocese of Wells went on to become Bath and Wells, a position of enormous power and prestige in medieval England. Local records in Kingston Seymour and Yatton demonstrate that this was the primary religious authority which featured in their lives.

Medieval Bishops were important landowners. The Bishop of Bath and Wells had 20 or so Manors in Somerset including Yatton, with others in Gloucestershire and Hampshire and a house in London. An account roll survives from 1337-8. The last months of 1337 and the first few months of 1338 are covered in the document. A Bishop on the move called for items from his estate in Yatton, a plumb part of his properties.[142] The Bishop would often stay and conduct business at nearby Banwell. There is a local tradition that his staff would watch out for smoke signals from over the hills at Wells to indicate if he was needed quickly.

Many Bishops of Bath and Wells were also Government officials. John Drokensford (Bishop from 1309-1329) and Ralph of Shrewsbury (from 1329-1363) were all active in the State as well as Diocese.[143] It was not all inductions and appointments. Occasionally, the faithful were warned to shun someone as a heathen. The Bishop's Register for John Drokensford records a public notice that John ate Churchstyle of Wells, having persevered in hardness of heart, is still excommunicate.[144]

The Diocese was further divided. In Bishop Giso's time Benzelin was the only Archdeacon in the diocese and he continued in office for a while under the next bishop of Wells, John of Tours. After him there were three Archdeacons, the usual number under Norman Bishops. Benzelin, was shown in the Domesday Survey as holding from the bishop the church of the Manor of Yatton with a single hide of land. Later this became known as the Manor of Yatton Rectory. The 15th century former prebendal house (now the Old Rectory) was built for the representative of the prebendary, or Rector, who resided at Wells and appointed a local vicar to serve the village. This was an absentee position that became a source of great injustice.

The clergy who, according to the ideas of the time, should have been living and functioning in the Cathedral at Wells had to be lodged instead with people in the town. Outside the present Cathedral at Wells is an area where poor people beg. At the time of the Norman Conquest, some clergy would have been obliged to join them for their daily needs. The church at Wells was considered too small for a proper Cathedral so after Bishop Giso's death, the new Bishop, John de Villula, moved the headquarters to Bath, rebuilt its abbey and became in effect, Abbot of Bath. One of his successors Robert of Lewes (1136-66) set about organising the Canons at

Wells so they should have a more permanent income stream at a time when the new Cathedral at Wells was being re-built.[145] In 1136, Bishop Robert endowed the Canons of Wells with the church of Yatton along with some land.[146]

Yatton was a wealthy parish. The land was called a prebend. The Prebendary became an honorary position awarded to an important member of the clergy. Each Prebendary shared the leadership of the Cathedral and its various estates as well as the running of the services. The Prebendary, nearly always a non-resident of the parish, received 90% of the tithes. The parish priest received the remaining 10%. Not surprisingly *"the Prebendship was fiercely contested for its position and wealth and both princes and prelates challenged the claim to the presentation"*.[147] The Prebend at Wells had the richer pickings; his local Vicar had to get by somehow. It was not until a claim was made in 1327 that the Vicar and his successors are assigned a house and garden. The Prebendship of Yatton was a 14th century battle-ground for conflict between Church and King. The Register of Bishop Drokensford, Bishop of Bath and Wells, records that he instituted his nephew as Prebend: *"Andrew, son of Philip de Drockensford, Acolyte, collated to the stall of Yatton 12 April 1321"*[148]

Andrew Drokensford was then only an acolyte. As he was studying at university at the time, his uncle arranged for three Canons to pay some dues that had arisen in the vacancy. Barely two years later, the Prebendship had to be awarded to Richard de Thistelden, son of a Knight, who had obtained Papal provision for a canonry at Wells with reservation of a vacant prebend.[149] As if invoking the Pope's authority wasn't enough, only eight months later, the King issued a writ requiring the installation of Robert de Baldock, Archdeacon of Middlesex and Chancellor of England as Prebend of Yatton. It was all political. King Edward IInd was now satisfied that he had recovered the right to this Presentation.[150]

The other parish on the Moor at that time was Kingston Seymour. In 1218, Bath Priory acknowledged the right of Milo de Sancto Mauro and his family to present a candidate - the advowsan as it was called – as Rector of Chingstone (as Kingston had become with the Sancto Mauro family connection). The first Rector of whom we have any record is a Peter de Hermere in 1279 when Edward IIIrd was King. When Peter de Hemere died in April 1290, the living was valued at 33 marks per year. There was then litigation about the next presentation, which was not sorted out until

1291.¹⁵¹ Ostensibly, the living remained vacant until 1293; the date of the next recorded Rector, Henry de Rolling, who died at Christmas 1306.

Here is a fascinating glimpse of the interconnectedness of medieval society. In the Ecclesiastical Court, there was a case brought after his death and the names of those who had presented the name of Henry de Rolling were listed. There was a John de Wengham (Guardian of a local family, John Kenn and Joan de Wengham who are betroathed, though under age). John and Alice de Wyke of Court de Wyke in Claverham are co - presenters.¹⁵² John de Wengham had these local connections but was also the Rector in the Diocese of Lincoln as well as a number of others. To allow him to hold a cluster of Rectorships to the value of 60 Marks had required permission from the ultimate religious authority - the Pope at Rome.

The Bishop's solution was Hugh de Pentris, who held an office known as Succentor of Wells, the value of which was eight marks.¹⁵³ That was low by comparison with Kingston Seymour, by then valued at 20 marks. Nevertheless, Hugh de Prentris had combined that with a Prebendaryship which carried with it the role of bursar. He must have continued with those offices when instituted as Rector. The Papal Registers mention that Hugh de Prentris was not resident at Kingston Seymour.¹⁵⁴

Between Benzelin in 1086 and the Black Death, there are very few Vicars recorded on the Parish registers of St Mary's with which Yatton Manor was associated- an Ameline in 1247, Walter Morel in 1327 and Richard Trellick in 1341, who had to cope with the crisis and possibly perished. However, in the Episcopal Acts for Bath and Wells there is a reference to William of Yatton dated June 1174. He is very likely to be Vicar. The document refers to his church in Yatton and restoration of a virgate of land which ought to belong to the church.¹⁵⁵ We know too of a John Odeline, a Prebendary of Yatton 1260 serving at Wells who evidently encloses a medieval deer park. This may well be the origin of Park Farm in Yatton. There is also a John de Yatton, who features in the Bishop's Register, initially as deacon: - *"Mem to John de Yatton Deac for Priest's Orders. Archdeacon of Taunton to induct March 27 1310"*¹⁵⁶

A notice in the register of the Bishop of Bath and Wells for 1326 concerns a small church on Claverham Manor. From his Manorial estate at Banwell in December of that year, Bishop Drockenford is authorising John Yoley of nearby Blagdon to take charge of William de Sor, Rector of Claverham, being blind and aged, as well as the benefice. The Vicar of Yatton was to stand surety; in effect, oversee the Church.¹⁵⁷

In a separate ruling six months later in July 1327, the Vicar of Yatton is complaining that there is insufficient funding to serve the ministry. The Prebendaries of Yatton nominated the Vicar to the Bishop but they creamed off the tithes due to the Rector. The Rectory of Yatton was rated at 100 marks. The Vicar had to make do with the lesser tithes- the smaller items brought to the church. He pleads poverty. The vicarage of Yatton was worth 12 marks but that had to support two chaplains. The Rector was getting too much. From his estate at Banwell, Bishop Drokensford ruled that the Vicar was to have the manse, Church oblations, fees for anniversaries, requests, legacies, small tithes such as mills, honey and the grain of the prebendal demesne. Provision was made for the beasts in the Rector's pastures, one horse in the Rector's pastures and 10 shillings rent from the priest at Claverham. The Rector at Wells is to have all else and to share honoraria with the Vicar. The Vicar is charged with the cure of souls and with all services in Church and its two chapels.[158] The vacancy lasts for a year. *8th August 1328- Bishop to Robt de Stratford Pr, collating him to Yatton Stall and investing him by his Biretta.*[159]

It may be that the background to this plea of poverty was famine and some dismal harvests that had brought great distress already in the wretched 14th century. The terrible pestilence that brought the equivalent of nuclear Armageddon to Europe was but the climax of 40 years of woe that halved the population. Food supply only just kept pace with demand. If anything changes, the delicate balance is upset.

It was the next Bishop, Bishop Ralph of Shrewsbury who had to deal with the national emergency as Somerset came under attack from Yersinia Pestis.

Chapter Six

ARMAGEDDON AND THE 44TH GENERATION

In January 1349, the vicar of Yatton, Sir Richard Trellick, received a letter by courier from Bishop Ralph. It was apocalyptic; the same effect as if Somerset had just experienced nuclear attack. The communication from Bishop Ralph is a marker to the emergency faced by the 44th generation to live on the Moor since the Roman times. But this is upheaval of a very different sort; invasion not by iron-helmeted legionaiires but by microbes.

"The contagious pestilence of the present day, which is spreading far and wide, has left many parish churches and other livings in our diocese without parson or priest to care for their parishioners........we therefore enjoin and command... that you should at once publicly command and persuade all men, in particular those who are now sick or or should fall sick in the future, that, if they are on the point of death, then they should make confession to each other...whether to a layman or, if no man is present, to a woman".

Richard Trellick would have been even more astonished to read that *"the sacrament of the Eucharist, when no priest is available, may be administered by a deacon. If, however, there is no priest to administer the Sacrament of Extreme Unction, then, as in other matters, faith must suffice."*[160]

The authority to hear confession had been regarded as the preserve of the church. To throw it open to laymen and even to women revealed a situation of extreme emergency. As Philip Ziegler observes in his history of these terrible times, *"it was a confession on the part of the Church that the crisis was out of control and that the normal machinery no longer able to cope with it."*[161]

What Richard Trellick made of the alien entity that had taken the country over is not recorded. He and the villagers could have no way of knowing they were being mown down by Yersinia Pestis.

From the continent and ultimately from the East, plague had spread across England remorselessly. One of the main entry points was Dorset. On August 17th, the Bishop of Bath and Wells ordered processions to take place every Friday to pray for protection from the disease which had come from the East into France, *'the neighbouring kingdom'*.[162] By October 1348, Dorset and subsequently Somerset were overwhelmed with the terrible suffering. The great and the good shut themselves off in their rural Manors and hoped for the best - though the King himself decided to be public and be visible.

We have no access to the effect on the villagers as they faced extinction. If death rates were much as elsewhere, between 1/3rd and 40% of the 44th generation were wiped out. Possibly around three hundred souls perished in terrifyingly short order. The effect on the people of the Moor can only be conjectured. Something was overwhelming them of such ferocity that a man or woman might be fit and strong at breakfast and dead by lunch as the bulboes appeared, unbidden, under their armpits. For instant horror, nothing will surpass these months in 1348-9. 'Who will be next to go?' 'Which of us will still be alive at next Sunday's Mass?'

What we do know is that the villages of Yatton and Claverham, Kenn and Kingston survived. In nearby Wrington and Wick St Lawrence, lime was spread over layers of the dead, thought to be from Black Death. This was to seal the plague in.

In the Diocese of Bath and Wells, the institution of clergy went on and inevitably increased. Bishop Ralph has been criticised for trying to isolate himself from the plague by staying alive in his Manor at Wiveliscombe. Generally though, clergy did not lock themselves away. Visiting their flock to give the last rites, they were easy casualties. The evidence is of a rapid succession of priests in the plague years. The average number of institutions to benifices in Somerset in the 1340s was about 9 per month. At the height of the plague, the figures in the Diocese of Bath and Wells are:

> November 1348- 9
> December 1348- 32
> January 1349- 47
> February 1349 – 43
> March 1349 – 36
> April 1349- 40
> May 1349 – 21
> June 1349- 7[163]

In the first six months of the year then, new priests were needed at a rate three times higher than normal. About a quarter of the steady stream of new institutions seem to have been occasioned by the resignation of the previous incumbent rather than his death. But the question then arises, what caused the resignation? Was it a reluctance to take the terrifying risk from visiting their flock? It is unclear what happened to Richard Trellick in Yatton or his opposite number in Kingston Seymour.

Plague was to return in frequent bouts. In the anxious years of the late twentieth century, Government planning and films explored the impact of nuclear holocaust on a country. The surprising factor is that in the 14th century equivalent, social control did not crumble away entirely. People still buried their dead. Law and order was maintained for the most part. It took a century for population levels to recover. As well as devastating countless lives, however, Bubonic plague was to change forever the conditions of life for the peasants of the Moor.

In the immediate aftermath of the Plague, when it seemed that King Death stalked the land, landlords such as owners of the Manorial estates on the Moor were forced to make some concessions. Vacant land was abundant; labour in short supply. Looking back, the Chronicler of Leicester Abbey, Henry Knighton, spoke of a time when *"the great men of the land, and other lesser lords who had tenants remitted the payment of their tenants, lest their tenants should go away on account of the scarcity of servants and the high price of things- some half their rents, some more, some less, some for one, two or three years, according as they could come to an agreement with them".*[164]

As Knighton records, *"the following autumn, no one could get a reaper for less than eightpence with food, or a mower for less than twelvepence with food. For this reason, many crops perished in the fields for lack of harvesters".*

While the plague was still raging, it was not safe for Parliament to meet. Edward first postponed the Parliament on January 1st until after Easter, then on 10th March 1349, he cancelled it until further notice. It was the Royal Council that issued an Ordinance recognising the problems that would arise because of the lack of labourers and especially ploughmen. The Ordinance of Labourers restricted the payment of wages higher than levels for 1346/7- itself a depression year when wages were low. In short, Edward's answer was for the labourers to remain on the land and work for the same wages as before the plague. It led to many Manors collapsing as labourers worked only the most viable acres.

A mobile workforce was only possible if men broke their feudal bonds and left the Manors where they were tied. The bailiffs of Yatton Manors may have lost a third of their workforce, only to discover that the rest were threatening to leave unless their wages were doubled. Their animals had no one to milk or shear them. For many peasants, it was the end of chronic unemployment. There was as much work as they wished. They could choose where and when they worked and negotiate better terms. Gradually, peasants became more truculent, refusing to take up holdings unless on their own terms.[165]

A chronic shortage of labourers explains why wages carried on rising throughout the 14th and much of the 15th.[166] The result was wage inflation. In the new atmosphere, lords were forced to lease part of their estates (demesnes) to tenants and in effect partition them. The Ordinance of Labourers remained in force until 1378 when it was finally enshrined as an Act of Parliament.[167] The peasants found they were much freer. Escape from serfdom was facilitated by the willingness of landlords, desperate for labour, to receive peasants migrating from other estates- no questions asked. The trouble was that on the death of a peasant, adult sons were reluctant to come forward to claim succession. To do so would make them serfs again. If they fell ill, peasants were not likely to receive charity if they were regarded as strangers.[168]

In spite of greater freedom, the 1370s were a time of mounting social tension culminating in the Peasant's Revolt of 1381. It was not just England. Similar revolts boiled over across Europe. For the English peasants, however, the dreaded poll tax was the last straw. They demanded the abolition of serfdom and servile tenure, the removal of service beyond simple cash rent and the curtailing of the judicial powers of landlords in their manorial courts.[169]. The Revolt did not involve Somerset though peasants could not fail to have been stirred by the news and then the disappointment as, amidst the duplicity of Richard IInd, the Peasant's Revolt was crushed.

Serfdom took a long time to die. As late as 1533, Glastonbury Abbey had 215 families of bondmen on its estates. Few manumissions can be detected in the 15th century and unfree status continues until the time of James I.[170] But in the aftermath of those terrible years the writing was on the wall for the old feudal system.

The generations that lived in the 14th century had a miserable time. Men of fighting age were caught up in a war that lasted a hundred years - England's forlorn attempt to retain dominion over French lands. Villagers faced famine and pestilence on a scale that had been unimaginable. The generation that is born around 1370, the 45th to live on the Moor, have heard from their parents of the terror that evoked the shudder of trauma. But their offspring conceive of a dramatic building project, the effects of which can still be seen. It was a visible expression of hope for the future.

Chapter Seven

A Tale of False Accusation

A Formidable Family[171]

The year after Black Death has scythed the population of England, two wealthy people meet and marry. One is a widow of a local landowner and lord of the Manor in Claverham, Egelina de Wyck. The other is Mayor of Bristol, Robert Gyene, whose wife was lost to bubonic plague. They have been aware of each other. Egelina's husband, Sir John de Wyck, had led a contingent of soldiers from the Moor to take part in the expedition that culminated in the siege of Calais.

Egelina de Hautville, as she was before marrying Sir John de Wyck, was from a formidable family. The De Hautvilles were descendants of the Norman barons who had conquered Sicily just before their Norman conquest.

Her husband has also come from an aristocratic family. In the 12th century, estates and Manors could be subject to a rather arbitrary form of taxation when the King needed money. One such 'feudal aid' as it was called, took place when a dowry was needed to enable the daughter of Henry IInd to marry the Duke of Saxony. The first record of the de Wyke family appears in the Baron's Charters (*Cartae Baronum*) of 1166 in which Thomas de Wicha is returned as holding two Knights' fees in the County of Somerset of Robert, Bishop of Bath[172] – the tiny manor of Wyck and its residence. In short, Court de Wyck was created during the 12th century by the Bishops of Bath and Wells to ensure that the five other Manors that made up the parish of Yatton met their military quota of knights and supporting troops.[173] At any rate, Thomas de Wicha is succeeded in the reign of King John by John de Wyke. One of his descendants, also named John, was a commander in the army of Edward 1st against the Scots. A later noble, John de Wyke of Ninehead, becomes owner of the Manor of Court de Wyck in Claverham. His choice for marriage was Egelina de Hautville.

Knighted, Sir John de Wyck may have been responsible for organising the military contingent from the Parish of Yatton as part of a large force of men required by King Edward III for an expedition to France during the early part of the Hundred Year War. This is where he came across Robert Gyene, who had just completed his first stint as Mayor of Bristol. Robert Gyene is commissioned to fit out 13 ships of 80 tons, each with gangways and the means of transporting horses and men to Normandy for the Battle of Crecy and subsequent capture of Calais.[174] The process of Knights and archers across the Moor to embarkation in Bristol must have been a stirring sight. Pennants fluttering in the breeze and Knights on horseback no doubt fortified the spirits of the inexperienced soldiers marching to war.

Sir John de Wyck died, probably in 1346. The St George's Roll for the Siege of Calais (1345-1348) lists a Sir John de Wyck being slain there. After he dies, his widow, Egelina holds the estate. Quickly, however, she marries. At this point, her new husband, Robert Gyene, enters our story.

A Bristol Merchant

In all, the 14th century Bristol merchant, Robert Gyene was Mayor of Bristol three times.[175] Robert Gyene came from a family of small landowners in North Curry, Somerset, descended in fact from a serf. The records of the Dean and Chapter of Wells indicate that his family was descended from William Gyan of North Curry. William Gyan received manumission in August 1264, being released 'from servile condition.'[176] With his freedom came a grant of land worth 12 shillings and eight pence as yearly rent. The Dean and Chapter were allowed to enclose moors and pastures as long as they saved sufficient common land for William and his heirs.[177] The Dean and Chapter apparently sold the custody of these lands that had been held by William's wife, to Robert, William Gyan's son and heir. Robert, who died in either 1325 or 1326, was father to the future Bristol merchant and Mayor of Bristol.[178] The Calendar of Ancient Deeds record a Deed between Robert's widow, Maud and Joan Gyene, her daughter, in the 19th year of the reign of Edward IInd.[179]

Trade, rather than manufacturing, is the engine of wealth creation in late medieval England. Yatton shares in this growing prosperity. Along with Norwich, the centre of East Anglian cloth manufacture, Bristol was the largest provincial city and the most important West of England port. Gascony had been Bristol's main market. Since the time of King John, the demand for wine drove the import traffic. In the other direction flowed English cloth. Large convoys, numbering 50 or more English ships sailed into Bordeaux in time for the new vintage every autumn. Merchants abounded, amongst them Bristol businessmen such as Robert Gyene.

Robert Gyan - the family name is sometimes spelt as Gyene or Gyan- seizes business opportunities presented by the lucrative trade. He comes to the notice of Edward's IInd widow, Queen Isabella.[180] This was for services rendered to her husband Edward IInd. She grants him her interest in the Bailiwick of the Seashore of Bristol. To modern ears, this is a typically quaint - sounding title. But it was a role that had substance. He had to ensure that merchant ships were properly escorted to port and watch for evasions of Royal Fines, the custom dues and taxes of the day. The grant was as laden with irony as Robert Gyene's ships were laden with wine. It was Queen Isabella who had conspired against the unfortunate Edward and connived at his recent 'retirement'.

A writ issued November 14th 1330 allows Robert Gyene to collect two shillings in the tun on wines imported by foreign merchants in the ports of Chepstow, Gloucester and Bristol.[181] The role was that of Chief Butler. Restricted the next year to Bristol only, it was nevertheless a position of real influence, especially as Robert Gyene was also appointed as a Commissioner to levy subsidies on wools and hides in Gloucester. No doubt operating through a staff, he is in effect a chief tax collector for Edward 111rd. It is interesting to note that the main area of south-western France adjacent to Gascony and Bordeaux where the wine was imported from was called Guinenne. The English king laid claim to this foothold in France since the marriage of Eleanor of Acquitaine to Henry 11nd and it happened to be the greatest wine-producing region in the world.

Economic historians point to a transition to a low interest rate regime as being crucial to answer an historical puzzle. Was the European industrial miracle in the 18th and 19th centuries down to an accident or was the fact that Europe developed differently as a result of factors that were present long before?[182] Adam Smith was later to state that interest rates in Europe, especially Britain, were significantly lower than in the East- 3 – 4.5% was normal compared with 12% at least in Asia.[183]

For it was cheap money that oiled the wheels of trade. Collecting import taxes on the lucrative wine trade and re-lending it made Robert Gyene a wealthy man. Not that business always ran smoothly. In 1331, the Patent Rolls of Edward 111rd set out a complaint made by Robert Gyene. The good ship *La Mariote* freighted by Robert and other merchants at Bordeaux was stranded on the coast of Monmouth across the Bristol Channel. The crew escaped but the cargo washed ashore where it was carried away by a group of clergy no less- a monk and two parsons.[184] This was a 'Whisky Galore' story. The good ship La Mariote was laden with wine and other merchandise.

Another document ten years later instructs the Constable of Bristol Castle to sell eight tuns of wine. The King has been informed that *"the said wine is become so feeble it cannot be kept longer without putrefaction"*[185]

A licence is granted for December 5th 1335 for a chaplain to celebrate divine service daily in the church of All Saints Bristol to pray for the souls of Robert and members of his family including Margaret, his wife. It cost them 60 shillings for the privilege.[186]

Both of Robert's nephews were in trouble with the ecclesiastical authorities at some stage. One of them, another Robert had fallen foul of the Dean and Chapter of Wells. In the year 1337, the year that war starts with France, he had cut down their trees in their lands in North Curry. Not only that, he had beaten their servant, Robert Coppe, and, to add insult to injury, poached on their land. Ecclesiastical sentence was pronounced upon him. Robert had no defence to offer. Having taken an oath to recognise the rights of Dean and Chapter of Wells Cathedral, he was ordered to restore to them the timber he had stolen. The servant he had assaulted was paid 40 shillings in compensation. Because John Coppe was a servant of the Dean, Robert Gyene's nephew had to be whipped round the church (in an act of flagellation) for six Sundays as well as making an offering of a wax candle. For poaching on ecclesiastical land, he had to go through the same discipline for a further six Sundays, pay eight marks, agree not to enter the property of the Dean and Chapter without permission and pay £20 as a bond. He was ordered to appear as a penitent in the Cathedral and consent that a sentence of excommunication be pronounced if he re-offended.[187]

However, the Dean and Chapter were obliged to issue a mandate to the Vicar of North Curry to cite four men and show why sentence of excommunication should not be pronounced upon them. Their crime had been to coming with certain accomplices and *"laying violent hands upon Robert Gyan, clerk and wounding him to the shedding of blood."*[188] Robert Gyene's nephew is described as a clerk. The offence was *"in contempt of God, the church, yea even of humanity and to the peril of their souls through excommunication pronounced by a canon on the occasion"*. The offenders were cited to appear before the Dean and Chapter on a day to be appointed.[189] Evidently, this was in retaliation for Robert's crimes. The family spelling varies a bit- in the 'Little Red Book' of Bristol Mayors and town records, Gyene is styled 'Robertas Çyene'.[190] Shortly afterwards, Robert Gyene indulged his nephew with considerable property in North Curry; a windmill, moor and tenements.

The integration of church and society runs through the documents. In 1337, Robert and his mother Maud are recorded as holding jointly land in Long Sutton, Somerset, acquired by them for life from the Abbot of

Athelney. Three years later, Robert is giving some land in the suburbs of Bristol to the Master and brethren of the House of St Mark. Then in 1344, the Prior and Convent of Bath are giving him the Manor of Olveston though not the advowsan (the right to present the priest).[191]

By the time of Robert Gyene's death, he had broadened his horizons further still. In the town of Oxford, he held in fee a shop and a vacant plot of land worth 13s 4d a year, together with two acres of meadow. This may well have been the result of some trading connections. It enables him to act as Member of Parliament for Bristol. Robery Gyene also held land in Wolverton, Hampshire[192] mentioned in the Feudal Aids for 1346, on the eve of the Black Death, as owned previously by one Johanis de Wolferton.[193] Then there was his house in Bristol, a Norman hall-house that backed on to the Guildhall in Broad Street. It was only demolised in the 1960's.

England was now at war with France. On its outbreak in 1337, one of Robert Gyene's ships, the Labonan, had to be escorted by the Royal Navy to combat the threat to shipping. As we saw, Robert Gyene is closely involved with fitting out the English expedition of 1346. Then comes a much greater national emergency.

Holding the King's licence, Robert Gyene was Mayor of Bristol three times, 1345-6 and then 1347-48 and 1349-50.[194] This meant he was Mayor at the time of the plague. Plague laid waste to the city. Knighton, the chronicler of the catastrophe was exaggerating only a little when he said that *"there died, suddenly overwhelmed by death, almost the whole strength of the town, for few were sick more than three days, or two days, or even half a day."*[195] Of ten thousand or so inhabitants, between 35-40% perished.[196] In the Little Red Book of the town Council for 1349, 15 of the 52 members are struck off. As head of the Council, Robert Gyene had to cope somehow with what seemed like the end of the world, raging to such an extent that the living were scarcely able to bury the dead. How he tried to keep the city going in the face of extraordinary disruption to ordinary life can only be imagined. The mental strain will have been enormous. Then the ferocity of the plague came close to home.

In 1348, he lost his wife Margaret to the dreaded Black Death. It may be as a result of this devastating loss both of city and wife that in 1348, Robert Gyene obtained letters patent to enable him to endow a chantry in the collegiate Church of the House of St Mark for divine service to pray for his soul and that of King Edward, Queen Philippa and members of his own family. For this, Robert had arranged to leave 12 pounds of his will.[197] Evidently, he did not proceed with this foundation at Bristol.

He then married Egelina. Where and how they met would be interesting to know. Robert has high standing as Mayor of Bristol and is extremely prosperous. But Egelina brings to the marriage the Manor of Norton Hautville and the de Wyck Manor at Claverham. Egelina had held this in dower as widow of John de Wyke.[198]

Egelina has also been active in the year of the pestilence. In May 1349, she, owner of one of the Manors on the Moor, is presenting William de Darthynton as priest to the vicarage of her other estate at Norton Hautville near Wiveliscombe in Somerset. Ralph of Shrewsbury, Bishop of Bath and Wells, who had spent the previous winter riding out the plague at Wiveliscombe, duly instituted the new priest. By November of the same year, he is back, admitting a new priest, Richard Cunde thanks to Egelina de Wycke.[199]

We have no way of knowing whether the couple lived at the Manor House. Described by the Somerset historian Collinson in the year 1791, something of its former glory shines through.

> "A little southward from Claverham is the ancient manfion of Court de Wick......An avenue of noble trees led to a large gateway, formed by two Dorrick columns... an opening to a grand court, on the left fide of which ftood the great hall running backwards towards the gardens...Beyond this was the great parlour..the chimney piece is quite perfect and has on its traverfe feveral compartments of grotefque figures, with fcrolls, and round the walls are infcribed moral and religious fentences.
>
> The chapel occupies the northweft angle of the court; the entrance into it is under a beautiful Gothick arch, and in the walls of the porch are receptacles for holy water, pixes and other devotional preparatives. The chapel is fmall and has only one large and lofty window to light it from the court. Over the entrance is a fmall window looking into the chapel for the purpofe of hearing and feeing mafs, and on the north side a gallery.....
>
> In this court are the foundations of an old crofs. The ftables belonging to the manfin are very large and grand."[200]

This was the centre of the estates Robert took hold of. It is tempting to think of the Manor House being a glittering social centre. But it gave him something more that he coveted- an enhanced position in County affairs. Robert was knighted. There is a presumed direct connection with the Yatton area rather than Robert and Egelina being absentee landlords because effigies in the Parish Church are very likely to represent their wall tombs. The effigy of the female is presumed to be Lady Egelina de Wyck; that of the male is most likely her second husband Robert Gyene.

Robert Gyene and Egelina de Wyck

By then, Edward lllrd had been on the throne for 25 years. He was at the height of his powers. Crecy and the re-positioning of England as perhaps the foremost military power in Europe- a position won by peasants fighting armed knights- all this was behind him. Yet his self-confidence had been shaken by the plague that had carried off his daughter Joan, many of his friends and over a third of London. It was at this time, having already created the Order of the Garter at the height of the Black Death, that Edward set about more permanent creations that would bring him lasting legacy.

Amongst these was Windsor Castle, St Stephen's Chapel in the medieval palace of Westminster, Queensborough and Nottingham Castle; all this plus many royal residences to boot such as Sheen, Henley and Rotherhithe.

This programme of building works was hugely expensive. £1000 pounds a year was spent completing the Palace at Westminster, Eltham and Sheen cost over £2000 each, Nottingham Castle over £1000 to re-build. But it was Windsor Castle that chewed up the funds. The eight Welsh castles began by Edward 1st, Edward's grandfather cost about £12,000 each to secure English rule there.[201] But Windsor Castle alone cost over £50,000. Throughout the 1350's, expenditure ran at £5,000 per annum. Edward needed money. He turns to the businessman Robert Gyene, Egelina's husband.

The money Robert lent to King Edward was the largest sum lent to the King by any single person in England at that time. It amounted to 500 marks. A receipt is available dated August 29th 1351.[202] Cash was tight. Robert's stock was riding high.

But there was trouble ahead. Less than a year later, in March 1352, the following order appears in the archives. *"Commission, to John de Codyngton, King's Clerk, to survey the goods of Robert de Gyene at Bristol, which for certain causes have been taken into the King's hands."* On the same day, a similar instruction was sent to the Kings's Serjeant-at Arms in Gloucester to do the same for Robert's properties there.[203] What had gone wrong?

Robert Gyene was accused of embezzlement, alleged to be withholding money that belonged to the king. He was tried and found guilty. The amount was £20,000, a King's ransom in those days.[204] The money that had been withheld had belonged to Hugh Despenser and Robert de Baldock, Chancellor of England, described in the archives as 'enemies to the king'.[205] The King was not the present monarch, Edward IIIrd but his father, the unfortunate Edward IInd. Was Egelina's husband guilty of fraud?

Edward II was the first English King to be deposed. What is commonly known about Edward is that he was queer and that he was murdered by having a red-hot poker inserted through his anus. Almost certainly, neither is true.[206] His miserable reign was overshadowed by powerful Barons, especially Hugh Despenser and his arch-rival, Roger Mortimer. Hugh Despenser was from an ancient baronial family of England, son of the Earl of Winchester. He had risen to high office under Edward IInd. The King had entrusted Despenser with much authority but which resulted in actions that were widely resented, actions that united other barons in the north, the south west and the Marches against Despenser and against Edward. The result had been a mini-civil war in the form of a baronial revolt. Edward IInds' position crumbled. In the year 1326, Hugh Despenser was executed. Dragged through the streets of Hereford, and with verses from the Bible inscribed on his body, he was hung on gallows fifty feet high. Before Despenser died, he was taken down whereupon his heart was cut out and his penis cut off. Both were unceremoniously chucked into a fire.[207] Roger Mortimer, the Earl of March and Despenser's arch rival was now in the ascendancy. Together with his lover, Queen Isabella herself, he forced the abdication of Edward IInd.

Released from captivity, Robert de Baldock had died a year later, the year of Edward's disappearance and supposed strangulation at Berkeley Castle. He too had connections with Yatton as Robert de Gyene had later. Robert was not only Chancellor of England, in May 1325 he had been appointed Prebendary of Yatton.[208] (His arms were enshrined in the south transept of St Mary's Church.) This did not imply he lived or served there- only that Yatton was considered a notable parish.

The debt had remained unclaimed ever since. This is a curious oversight on the part of the new King's Treasury unless, as seems likely, the wealthy Bristol merchant and seven times Mayor of Bristol Robert Turtle had received permission to hold on to the money as an investment. Roger Turtle had died in 1347.[209] His good friend Robert de Gyene was his executor and heir. All Robert's possessions were seized for the King. His gold, silver and other jewels were confiscated. A chaplain, William Poterne, successfully claimed some of them were his, having left with Robert Gyene 12 silver spoons, four pieces of silver and a piece of silver worth £4- 6 shillings - 8d before making a journey to the city of Rome.[210]

In 1355, a statement appears in the documents that shed light on this episode. A John Spicer, Mayor of Bristol in 1351/2, was indicted before the Justices. The charge was of having conspired with others that Robert Gyene should be accused of embezzling the King's money.[211] A group of Bristol merchants acting as a cabal had forged a case against him.

Robert was taken, tried though subsequently acquitted.[212] November 1351 finds him obtaining further letters patent to allow transfer of the endowment to the prior and convent of the Cathedral Church of Bath "to support three chaplains to celebrate divine service daily."[213]

By 1353, Robert Gyene was dead. The archives record this taking place at Fulham on the Thursday before the conversion of St Paul; that is on the 23rd January. A writ was issued noting that the Manor of Wycke had been held by Robert and Egelina as her dower from *"the whole free tenement of John de Wycke, her first husband, of the Bishop of Bath by Knight's Service."*[214]

The Manor of Court de Wyck reverted to Egelina. Her son had to go up to London to give his agreement because she had sold it off to a John of Egerton, no doubt to raise funds. For a fee, Egelina later recovered the Manor of Court de Wyck shortly after Robert's arrest. An order was made to the Sheriff of Somerset to release the Manor to her after taking sufficient security for the payment of 50 pounds.

"Grant to Egelina, wife of Robert de Gyene, who has been taken and arrested by process in the King's Court of the Manors of Wyck and Norton Hautville in Somerset which she holds in dower and for life, as is said, and which are taken into the King's hand by reason of the said process, to hold in aid of her sustenance for the life of the said Robert, or until the King make order otherwise for her estate during the life of the said Robert".[215]

The order went on to note the sale of goods in the two Manors taken into the King's hands which were valued at 76 pounds, 12s and 6d. The King agreed that 20 pounds, 13 shillings and 4d be allowed to her for sustenance from the first week of Lent to Michaelmass (31 weeks). Egelina could also have 119 shillings 4d for petty expenses. Clearly, with her husband's estates seized by the Crown for withholding money from the King, she was in a difficult position. Robert's goods were sold by John de Haddon, the King's Serjeant-at-arms. John Spicer, Mayor of Bristol, was told to supervise the sales and send to the Exchequer his rolls testifying what John de Haddon had been able to sell.

Egelina was devout. It is surprising that the request of a lady of the Manor in Claverham would involve the Papacy but the Papal Registers show permission being given for her to choose a confessor. At the hour of her death, he would give her plenary remission of her sins.[216] She renewed this request in November 1352, with Robert's death imminent.

There is a post-script to the Gyene story. Archives of the year 1465, during the reign of Edward IV refer to a commitment to a William Harwell esquire by John Smythe, a Coventry 'gentilman' and Thomas Frebody, a Warwickshire'gentilman.' The commitment was for the keeping of four acres of land and 2 acres of pasture in Knolle in Somerset. The land was recorded as having been seized from Robert after he became debtor of Edward IIIrd for various sums of money he owed. The lands are still in the King's hands and were likely to remain so for the foreseeable future.[217]

A century after Robert Gyene had died, English defeat in the Hundred Years War slowed right down the lucrative trade in which he had made his fortune. Imports of wine were cut in half; the cloth trade was reduced by

40%.[218] Even though other markets in Portugal and the Iberian peninsular held up, a new mode of commercial thinking was forced upon the merchants of Bristol. They began to engage in exploration. Intended initially to tap the resources of the mysterious East and to find new markets for the cloth trade, the impetus towards exploration took on a life of its own. The stage was set for John Cabot and discovery of a new found land in 1497.

The Manor of Wyck went on to be sold in 1356 to the brother of Bishop of Winchester. After 1405, it came into the possession of the Cheddar family. It was through Isabel de Cheddar that the Newton family are about to enter the story of the people of the Moor.

Chapter Eight

A Position in Society

The Newtons of Court de Wyck[219]

William Worcestre, the late medieval Bristol town surveyor, describes a slipway at the end of Christmas St in Bristol leading to the river for the washing of clothing, linen or woollens. This slipway is referred to in the lease of a ruined tenement in Christmas St which Sir John Newton and his wife Isabel proposed to re-build at great expense.[220] A lease of 1500 refers to the tenement of Thomas Pavy, merchant, in Christmas St, lying to the north of the tenement lately of Sir John Newton.[221]

Sir John Newton and his family have an important connection with Yatton. He is buried in Yatton Church along with his wife Lady Isabel de Cheddar. So were his parents- or at least their effigies. Sometime in the late 1470's, Sir John Newton had the alabaster chest tomb erected in the north transept of St Mary's at Yatton in memory of his father, Sir Richard Newton, and his second wife, Emmota Harvey.

Sir Richard (Cradock) Newton, had been born about the year 1370. He started his legal career as an itinerant justice in Pembrokeshire and ended up as Chief Justice of the Common Pleas from 1439 until his death in 1448.[222] Sir Richard Newton's great-uncle was Sir David Cradock who died in 1390.[223] We know this because the Cradock coat of arms based on heraldic glass in the south transept of Nantwich Parish Church (where Sir David is buried) are identical to the Newton arms in Yatton.

Sir David had a colourful career. He had been Lieutenant Seneschal of the Rouerque region of Gascony from 1365 to 1370 and went on to become Justiciar of North and South Wales.[224] He ended up as Mayor of Bordeaux between 1382-1386.[225] Sir David died of plague at Nantwich in the hot summer of 1390. Richard Newton's first wife Emma, had been daughter of Sir Thomas Perrot and sister to Margaret, 2nd wife of one Gruffyd ap Nicholas, a high ranking Welsh family. His second wife Emmota Harvey, however, was from Bristol. That was where the Newton family had moved in 1430, where Sir Richard eventually became Chief Justice of the Common Pleas, a senior judge in the West Country. That is why Sir Richard's effigy in Yatton Parish Church features a red gown with the collar of SS's (Sanctus Spiritus); there is a Serjeant's Coif on his head and by his side a wallet containing his Seal for sealing someone's fate. His position as Chief Justice of the Common Pleas was a post for life. In his later years, Sir Richard Newton moved to Walton near Clevedon where he died in 1448 aged 78. Being much younger, Emmotta died 28 years later in 1476.[226]

There were major events on the national stage at this time, in particular the Wars of the Roses, a bitter civil war between two rival branches of the Plantagenet line of rulers. All this seems to have had little impact on Yatton. In the parish church with effigies of its wealthy benefactors, the Newton family, that of Sir Richard Newton shows both York and Lancastrian symbols. Sir Richard wears a Lancastrian collar – the collar of 'esses' - yet there is something else. The white rose of York is also clearly on display. Perhaps, amidst shifting power alliances, he was hedging his bets.

Richard Newton's son Sir John and Isabel Newton had at least five children – four sons and a daughter, all born during the 1450's and 60's. They may have lost others in childhood as two funeral torches are bought at Yatton church in 1454, 1465 and again four years later. The Yatton churchwarden accounts refer to:

1469 –"Received of my mastras (the Newtons) for berynyng
    of the torges   xid"
"Received of my lady Newton for berynyng of the torgs
    (burning of the torches)   xid."

Isabel de Cheddar's sister Joan died in 1464 and is buried in Wells Cathedral. Joan's husband died in the tail-end of the French wars in Aquitaine in 1453. Her only son Thomas, Isabel's nephew, perished in the last battle in England between two private armies.

John Newton, son and heir to Sir Richard, would have been the most important church member in Yatton. He had just married Isabel de Cheddar of East Harptree, a rich heiress. Marriage to Isabel brought him the Manor of Court de Wyck in Claverham where Egelina and Robert Gyene had lived. Along with Lady Isabel, he now took up a position as lord of the Manor of Court de Wyck.

Sir John was elected MP for Somerset in 1453 at the age of 28. A "Knight of the Shire", Sir John was keen to show off his social status. This is how Yatton Parish Church came to boast one of the most decorated south porches for miles around. The shields indicate that it was built for Lady Newton and her husband. His future was assured. What better way to show off his wealth and position in society than a magnificent south porch of a significant parish church!

Sir John Newton and Isabel

And then there was his Manor. We saw in Chapter Seven that in the high Middle Ages, this ancient Manor was owned by the de Wyke family. Later the estate came into the possession of the Cheddar family. Isabel de Cheddar brought it with her into the marriage with John Newton. The Manor had its own chapel. Priests were hired to pray for the souls of family members. Only a wall remains now. The Manor house became a ruin due to a fire in 1815 and was demolished four years later. Three hundred and fifty years before, the Manor, though small, would have demonstrated that Sir John and Lady Isabel had arrived. Without it being on the level of one of the stately homes of England, it was a suitable setting for Sir John and Isabel.

Sir John was also active as any landowner of the time would have been, holding the right of presenting a new Vicar or Rector to other family estates. The Register of Bishops of Bath and Wells for 1460 show the institution of John Thornton as Rector of the church of Angersleigh, near Taunton on the presentation of John Newton esq.[227] The previous incumbent was experiencing 'bodily weakness'. In order to *"prevent his being compelled to beg for the necessities of life"*, the Bishop granted him a yearly pension of 20 shillings. Nine years later, John Newton was presenting the next Rector. In the meantime, in 1467, his mother Dame Emmota, widow of Sir Richard

Newton, was presenting a successor at Walton in Gordano where she has been living.[228]

The Church Warden accounts show him as both active and influential locally. *"1483- payde to Nycholas Ket, Scryvener, on Alhalow day in the presence of Syr John Newton, Knt. 40 shillings."*

The Scrivener's job was that of a Ledger. This book, prepared under the authority of Sir John Newton recorded Deeds of Appropriation of the Rectory, the endowment of a Vicarage, the establishment of 2 Manorial chapels and that in the Churchyard. It is costly legal work. The Scrivener is paid a further 45 shillings in 1483.

Sir John will have celebrated Christmas that year with some satisfaction. He had just been appointed Joint Commissioner of Peace for Somerset and is mentioned in a commission dated August 1483 along with a Giles Dawbeney, Knight, *"to assess subsidies from aliens and to appoint collectors of the same"*[229] The next year saw his final appointment, Joint Commissioner of Arrays for Somerset. That was an important role. Sir John's function was to choose knights and foot soldiers from the muster roll of every Manor to fight for the king when he summoned the Feudal Host (Call to Arms). Sir John Newton's tomb in Yatton church shows him wearing armour. Presumably he knew about soldiering. If and where he saw service is unknown.

This was the year before Bosworth. But former allegiances did not count against the family. Three years later, in 1488, Sir John is dead. He was 63.[230]

His family do well. His son, another Richard Newton, was a royal servant both to Richard 3rd and, until his death in September 1500, Squire to King Henry 7th.[231] His first wife Eleanor was the daughter of one of Henry VII's chief counsellors. Having as his second wife Elizabeth St.John, a baron's daughter, made him a relative of the King himself. Sir John and Isabel's son Thomas married a widow Joan Choke but he died in 1496 while his mother was still churchwarden.[232] Thomas is buried in what became known as the Newton chapel. His brother Walter gained a Bachelor of Law at Oxford and went into the priesthood. Another brother Nicholas became a lawyer at London's Inner Temple while sister Elizabeth married John Kenn of Kenn Court, an ancient family on the Moor. She lived 24 more years.

Most Senior People

The office of churchwarden had been around for at least two hundred years. The wardens of a parish occupied a significant position in church and community that commanded respect. They were the most senior lay people, generally drawn from the same social background as the most powerful and mighty.

Yatton churchwarden's accounts are particularly rich, amongst the best documented of any church in the country.[233] St Michael's Bath, begun in 1349, is the earliest but the churchwarden accounts for Yatton hold a fascinating mirror to the years 1445-1560.[234] They were both published in 1891 along with three other country parishes in Somerset, (Croscombe, Pilton, Tintinhull) and one village parish in Devon, that of Morebath which was to be involved with the prayer-book rebellion against the Reformation in 1549. "Somerset & Dorset Notes and Queries" for 1891 hails the documents as *"one of the most important contributions to the History of Pre-Reformation Church Life in England that has ever issued from the press."*[235]

It was in February 1496 that Lady Isabel was elected to be one of the Yatton churchwardens for the year. By now she is an old woman. Although the Newton's were very wealthy, churchwardens' accounts show very little income coming from them. Sir John himself did not leave very much:

1489 – receipts *"of my lady Newton of bequest*
         of Maister Newton   *x marks"* (£5-12)

Although highly unusual, women could become Wardens. This was the case in Yatton. Lady Isabel Newton, who held the office in 1496, is one of the earliest examples of a female churchwarden in this part of the country - no doubt arising from her position in society. Her duties were many and varied. Along with John Bulbeke, she would have been responsible for administering the endowments of the church, recording all payments and expenses, purchasing and looking after the utensils, ornaments and church furniture. Linen and vestments for the Mass had to be kept clean and in good repair.

There was enough to fund jointly with the parish the construction of a chantry chapel between 1491-95 on the north east corner of St Mary's Church, the Chapel of St John. After the Newton wall tomb was added in the early 1500's, the Chapel of St John has become known as the *"Chapel of my Lady Newton"*.

The Newton tombs

After Lady Isabel died in 1498 she had left the Manor of Wyke to her son Richard who only had the estate for two years.[236] The Estate was worth some £20 and 11 shillings. The Manor of Wyke eventually passed to a Nottinghamshire landowner who married Richard's great-granddaughter, Mary, who also happened to be third cousin to Christopher Kenn, from an ancient family on the Moor.[237] He was to buy Court de Wyck Manor in 1574. Significantly, Mary and her sons were staunch Catholics at a time when the Elizabethan Reformation was well-established and to be Catholic was suspect. The Manors had to be sold.

All this was to come for the people of the Moor.

Chapter Nine

The People of the Village

The year is 1445. Richard Bishop is Vicar of Yatton. Two more generations have played out their lives on the living theatre of the North Somerset levels. Two more are about to appear. The villagers have been embarking upon the construction of a magnificent three-dimensional structure that encapsulates their faith and their hope. The building of this church, out of all proportion to the size of the village, will be recorded in ancient records that have survived across the centuries. In these documents, the life of the village seeps out into financial accounts by the churchwardens. Amidst their ambitious building project, what the churchwardens pay out for allow a fascinating picture of late medieval life to emerge.

The 45th and 46th generations will witness the steady drum-beat of progress and prosperity amidst turbulent State policy as the Wars of the Roses and strife of barons ensue. In 1485, Henry Tudor and his heirs will hold the levers of State power.

That lay in the future. For now, the country has recovered from Armageddon; the ravages of the terrible plague. That had been a century before, though vivid in folk memory and reinforced by recurrent episodes of Black Death. England prospers once more, thanks to the production and export of wool and the import of wine. The Moor participated in the growing wealth of neighbouring Bristol. Fortunately for the villagers, no major battles of the Wars of the Roses were fought in the area; the nearest being Tewkesbury in 1471. It would also have helped that none of the great magnates who were especially involved in the fighting had a power base in this area. In the churchwardens records, it is the Bishop who is cited as the great landowner rather than Barons caught up in political rivalry.

Religion is alive and well. There was no decline in belief or practice, neither was zeal abating. Here was another great age of church building. There are some 10,000 medieval churches still standing today in Britain. Between a third and a half were re-built or extended during the 14th, 15th and early 16th centuries. This sacred building programme was complemented by a strong lay piety. Enormous sums of money were raised from poor parishes. In Yatton as elsewhere, re-building or enlargement of a Parish Church was testimony to the enthusiasm and generosity of a whole community. The common people came together to restore their church; communities outdid each other in their zeal. The building project in their parish church was to involve the whole community over three generations. The peasants began a labour of love that stands across the years in mute testimony to their devotion and vision.

St Mary's Church had remained unaltered for a hundred years. Around 1390, the parish decide on a building programme. First the chancel is enlarged. Thirty years later, the rest of St Mary's is to be radically altered. It will take time, a long time. Most of the generation embarking on the project will not live to see the outcome. This in itself requires a certain mind-set, an attitude to time far removed from the speed society of modern times. Then, patience really was a virtue: a patience borne of necessity.

Rebuilding work is accredited to John Stonehouse, Master- Mason of Glastonbury Lodge, working under the instruction of the Bishop of Bath and Wells. The builders who re-built the church left mason's marks as a tribute to their labour. It was rumoured in later times that their names were also engraved behind a fireplace in the village pub.

The architects work to a grand design. Ecclesiastical architecture reflected the influence of the Gothic Perpendicular Period. Churches were larger, loftier and lighter. The three bay nave built two hundred years before was demolished, larger foundations were put in and the arcade extended to five bays. This new nave had doubled in height. This required an aisle to be built on either side to take the downward and outward forces. Large windows were made into the aisle walls and the magnificent west window installed to fill the church with light. Openings were made into the transepts from the aisles to allow access into the side chapels.[238]

The Green Man

You can still see heads and faces carved on the roof supports high up in the Nave and lower in the North Aisle. Although some of these heads are probably the Pope, the reigning monarch and his queen, others were said to be Yatton villagers whom the stonemason decided to copy. In the North West corner of the North Aisle, there is a man with toothache. On the north column nearest the altar there is also the ubiquitous Green Man. The term was only coined in the 1930's but the medieval image of a face sprouting foliage is a face that commands instant recognition in an ecologically-minded generation. The Green Man followed a long cast of characters that featured in the annual May celebrations along with Robin Hood and May Queens. It was not until the Reformation heralded the virtual collapse of visual Christian culture that the Green Man began to perish as an ornament in churches. A sign of fertility and growth very probably but exactly what this quirky face signifies has been much debated. At one time, it was regarded as a pagan left-over, to do with tree worship perhaps.[239] The imagery is difficult to interpret. On one hand, investigations of pre-Christian religion have failed to turn up Green Men. On the other hand, Church art involved a good deal of figures associated with foliage. Besides, medieval villagers were devoutly Christian, not defiantly pagan. The patrons of the church were God-fearing folk and had no wish to sponsor subversive craftsmen. The Green Man probably reflects an ambiguous attitude to nature that goes back to Genesis where the Tree of Life jostles with the woods as a place of temptation and moral struggle.[240] This is, however, another aspect of Merry England. By Elizabethan times, decorating parish churches with greenery was on its way out.

By 1455 to 1458, it is the turn of the tower to be extensively altered. The original square tower was raised by an additional level and a very tall and slender octagonal stone spire put on top. Most Somerset churches at that time have flat towers. Yatton is an exception. It has a spire, a spire that will stretch a mighty 170 feet into the sky.

Yatton Parish church is not the only church building in the district. There is what is known as the 'free chapel of Claverham'. This chapel was in Claverham Court Farm but beyond that not much is known. Styled as a 'free chapel', that could mean it is not tied to a particular Manor and is a chantry chapel to pray for the souls of the founders. Bishop's Registers refer to institutions of priests to serve there. The Chapel is subservient to the main parish church - it is not a separate entity. As the English Reformation was taking off, the Register of Bishop Knyght, the Bishop of Bath and Wells from 1541-1547 who had to manage the transition records: *"The like of Simon Cretynge alias Porter, in the person of Thomas Hoper, his proctor, to the free chapel of Claverham, vacant by the resignation of the last incumbent, on the presentation of Henry Capell, Knight."*[241] A survey of Somerset Chantries on their closure in 1548 documents lands, rents and tithes pertaining to the Free Chapel of Claverham totalling 58 shillings. Of this, 10 shillings was paid to the Vicar of Yatton in rent or pension. Symon Porter, a scholar of the age of 18 was the incumbent. It was not for long![242]

The villagers of Kenn continue to worship in their church with its distinctive Norman tower. Kingston Seymour has its own Parish Church which is also being extended. The main part dates to around 1470. Edward the Fourth is on the throne- only just as he is compelled to leave the country that year until circumstances are right for a triumphant return the following year after the battle of Towton. In the next few years, a Manor house is going up in Kingston Seymour. The Manor was divided but there was a resident lord who built the house, one of the Kenn family, "*one of the best and most ancient families of Somerset*".[243]

Nearly five hundred years later, a 19th century observer will call this "*one of the most perfect and interesting specimens in the county of Somerset.*"[244] By then, the Manor had passed from the Kenn family and was the property of John Hugh Smyth Piggott, the landowner of Brockley Hall. Fifteen years later, around 1850, the Manor house was destroyed by fire. The present house on the site, called 'The Old Manor' is a Victorian rectory. At the back, parts of the medieval house remain. It was a good looking residence with a south facing show front. The south west gable carried Edward 4th's favourite badge- a rose en soleil he adopted immediately after his success in battle at Mortimer's Cross in the year 1461.[245]

The old Rectory in Yatton was also built in the 15th century, Now a private residence, this is the large building that stands back on the south east side of the churchyard. It was constructed by the Prebendary or Rector of Yatton for his bailiff. This is where villager brought the controversial tithes to support the church. It is of grand design, the oldest house in the village.

A house fit for the Prebend of Yatton c1495

A Distant Mirror

What kind of distant mirror do the churchwarden accounts hold up to life on the Moor five hundred years ago in what has traditionally been seen as Merry England?

The parish was divided into three to make administration easier. The east and the west areas, roughly equal to present day Claverham and Cleeve, were committed to the care of two sub-wardens called 'Lightmen'. They brought offerings, intended to keep the lamp of faith and religion open in the churches, to the main wardens. Central Yatton paid its offerings direct to the wardens.

Most of the accounts are in English although there are still a few passages in Latin. Throughout much of the Middle Ages, churchmen would have been virtually the only people able to read and write and they would do so in the international language of the time. Yet in these documents, we are witnessing the increased use of the vernacular, which was driving out Latin. Latin was still be used in worship. This would continue until the religious upheavals of the Reformation period in the next century. By then, in these extracts, Latin has almost entirely disappeared. Sometimes, there is mixture of Latin and English in one entry! The switch to Latin indicates that some wardens were educated in Latin and others were not. Where there is no Latin equivalent available, the writer has to use an English word.

What strikes the reader is the huge range of matters in which the churchwardens became involved. There was no distinction at this time between civil and ecclesiastical and civil parishes. This would continue until the nineteenth century. The church and its officers would have responsibilities for the whole community. There is a reference in 1528 to the need to repair a sluice. This must always have been a major and recurring problem for Yatton and the surrounding area.

Throughout the Warden's records, construction is going on. In 1446, 40 pence is paid to Welyam Stonhowse for making a door in a winding staircase for the bell tower. Perhaps it was for this that an oak is felled at nearby Brockley at a cost of five shillings. Shaping it and bringing it back to Yatton on a carriage will cost a further three shillings and five pence. The belltower is being added to that year- Jon Smythe of Congresbury is being paid seven shillings and seven pence for *'makyng of al maner of eyreen werke for the bellys'*. In 1449, ten marks is spent on the table of the high altar. Cloths will be needed at around 20d a time. There is a special cloth, made of striped silk. One wonders where that originated.

Medieval churches had a grand wooden structure separating the nave of the church from the chancel where the Mass was celebrated. It was called the Rood Screen. In Yatton, the 13th century Rood Screen and the Rood beam had an open walk way along the top, the Rood Loft. In 1447 the churchwardens decided to replace this Rood Loft with a much grander affair along its front (nave) edge.

The Rood Loft, removed at the Reformation, must have been a splendid sight. It was carved, gilded, painted and decked with 69 images. The Carpenter's Account alone was £31. In 1448, three church representatives were paid three pence to ride to "Eastun" (Easton in Gordano) to view the rood loft there. They wanted one of these at Yatton. A payment was made for taking down the old loft. Then in 1449 John Crosse, a carpenter from Claverham, was given the task of building the new Rood loft. John Crosse was rather elusive. There is that same year an intriguing entry to 1d for trying to locate John Crosse at Backwell. He is searching for the best timber to use in the construction of the rood screen. Four times he was missing when needed; a man had to be sent to fetch him. It is also recorded that *"two and half pence was spent on ale given to Crosse in certain times in his work to make him well willed."*!!

In 1449, he will be paid 7 marks and 12 shillings. In 1450, he will receive £5 7d. But it is not clear what the craft status of John Crosse would have been to have earned these sums. In those days, craftsmen operated in guilds. Although usually based in towns, skilled artisans would often be part of communities that travelled in search of work. Local people would do the sawing and preparing the timber but working with wood required expertise. In 1455-6, the old loft is ready to be taken down. It will cost 11d. The next year, John Crosse finished the Rood loft. It has taken nine years of his skilled labour. 1458-9 saw final works taking place........*"pentyng the Rodlofte"* - £3......*"to William Hyll, for ye batylmente of V panys (bays) – xxxv shillings.*

At any rate, the greatly enlarged St Mary's was reopened in 1460. It was a remarkable achievement for the peasants and yeoman who formed the generation of the first half of the 15th century. There were wealthy benefactors, especially the Newton family. But by no means did they fund the whole project. The parish did not retain livestock for income; it boasted of no endowment of land. Neither did it receive financial assistance from the principal landowner, the Bishop of Bath and Wells nor from its tithe-owner, the Prebend of Yatton at Wells. The income raised by the peasants and yeoman farmers is striking. There was always a balance to be handed over to incoming churchwardens that was enough to meet the year's outlay. It was a strong and surviving testimony to their faith.

In that year of 1445, Thomas Thurbane and Thomas Kyngth were wardens. They received income from parishioners of £15-15 shillings and 5d. There were eight listed benefactors and five bequests, including some bushels of wheat to be sold.

"*Item received of the bequest of Walter Modswyne and Egolyn his wife 2 boshells of wete, the prysce of the 2 boshells were 1 shilling.*"

But there was expenditure to be laid out too that year. John Marriott and Thomas Clerke needed paying for their work on the new church house. A cloth was needed for the chalice to cover the communion wine. One penny should be enough. Oil for the lamp will come to twice that.

Building works continue as the parishioners lovingly care for the church that holds so much meaning for their lives. In the next generation, further construction will take place on the chancel, the church cross and the repair and pointing of the spire. In 1485, the year of Bosworth and the formation of Tudor England, the churchyard was enlarged. It cost £3 6s. 8d. The following year, it will be consecrated at a cost of £1.13 shillings.

The new spire will require considerable investment. The Warden Accounts for 1491 offer a window on the kind of expense involved. Stone had to be hauled and sorted. "*for chesyng of the stonys to the masyner (choosing of stones for the mason) 5d.*" The accounts for 1493-4 mention the name of the mason as Fysscher.

Stone had to be brought from nearby Dundry, a much-used local quarry:
"*for xiii lode of frestonys*"   25s 7d"
"*For dykng of stonys (stacking them)*"   20d"

Labourers were needed to haul these stones to Yatton
"*For 27 weynys to cary home stonys and cole, in mete and drink   5s 7d*"

When they arrived, money had to be paid for supporting the chancel to start the work
"*For poyntng of the spyre, of iij pynnaclys, and batylment
of the tower*   - 5 s 7d"

Evidently some kind of wynch was involved
"For the crane setting up   - 2 s 6d"*

"For making a shote (casting metal in a mould) and for hewing of 6 shydes (shroud-wool for fuel), and for warke on ye chaunselle for a carnocke (measure) of lyme and for bryngng home. For many loads of Felton stone, for ryddyng ye ground to ye Crosse and shrydng of ye trees... for stone to ye hede of ye Crosse.... to J Hort ye fre Mason for rydng to Bath to se ye stonys....to halfe a hundred of brymbylls..." and so it goes on. Brambles helped to thatch the stone against frost. Scaffolding will be required for the work.

The Cost of Devotion

The fact that there was a great deal of rivalry between churches to out-do each other to beautify their church in order to demonstrate devotion to God does not detract from that devotion. Much fund-raising comes from village fairs and fetes called 'Ales.' The nave is the responsibility of the parishioners while the upkeep of the chancel was that of Rector or Patron. At Yatton, where the Patron was one of Prebendaries of Bath and Wells, churchwardens' accounts show very large sums of money being raised by parishioners to re-build and beautify the nave. By contrast, the chancel remains small and out of scale compared with the size of the church.

The conclusion seems clear enough. The common people loved their church and were prepared to invest time and money to expand it and keep it in good order. This was not an age of religious decline. That stands out too in the large sums that were spent on religious items, such as vestments and cope for the priests- the huge sum of £25 in 1481 Considerable outlays were required for their repair.

1507-8 "Payd for mendyng ye red vestment, and ye blak cope, and for dyeng of ye old red vestment   *40 shillings"*

In the lobby to Yatton Parish Church are two vestments called Dalmatics or Tunicles that were worn by assistant priests or deacons for reading the Gospel and the Epistle. These vestments date from around 1500 and are two of the few remaining examples of Pre-Reformation needlework.The groundwork is of 15th century blue velvet, down which runs two bands of embroidered panels showing various Saints and Prophets, and is embroidered with "Water Flowers".[246]

All the vestments, portable items and even a stone slab were taken to the Bishop for his blessing. New saints were celebrated. St Katharine, St Thomas, St George, St Nicholas and St Christopher were acclaimed

1467 – "*peynter to peynt the Cystofer*"   *xx shillings.*
1468 – "*for peyntng the crystofer*   *xxii shillings v d*
1479 – "*for making of Seynt Kateryn wex*   *iiid*"
1480 – "*for setting over of the baner of Seynt Kateryn*   *11pence*"
1502 – "*in mete and drynk for bryngyng of Seynt Kateryne*   *vd*"
    " *to ye mason for making of Seynt Kateryne Awter*   *6 s*"
    "*for ye awter stone of Seynt Kateryne*   *8d*"
    "*for ye angell that Seynt Kateryn stonds on*   *8d*"
1515 – "*Payd for mendyng ye tabullment and Seynt Keteryne*   *3s 5d*"
    "*Payd for a prefekt to set afore Seynt Keteryne*   *4d*"
1515 – "*Payd to Thomas Avery for setting up Seynt Thomas*   *12d*"

There were some surprising entries relating to objects of devotion, an image of a saint venerated in West Somerset.
1490 – "*payd for Sint Sunday*   *11 shillings 9d*"

Running through church life was devotion to Mary.
1467 – "*to the peyntng of the Mary*   *1d*
    "*peynter to peynt owre Lady*   *£3*

Villagers expressed their devotion in other ways. 5 shillings and nine pence was passed on by the old wardens in 1456-7 '*for the pascall tapyr*'- a great deal of money for the Paschal candle.
1459-60 – "*for making of the stolys*" *13d*
1490 – "*Payd for a copyll of cruets, selver*   *30 shillings*"
1495 – *frankincense (frongkynsens)*   *1d*
1496 – "*For 6 ells (lengths of cloth) and a halfe of lynnyn (linen)*
    for a surplesse   *3s 4d*"
1500 – "*Payd for making of 2 surpleyce to ye bokbynder*   *3 s*"
    Payd to ye seyd bokbynder for making of a nobe (alb)   *6 d*"

The Ancestor of the Pub

In those days, the church was the only public building in most communities. Then in 1445, the wardens in Yatton embarked upon the construction of a church house. This is to be an expression of communal solidarity. A donation is received from a Jone Thurba towards its timber. The church house probably came under the Bishop as lord of the Manor. At any rate, it provides a village hall. On a Sunday afternoon, villagers gather there. Tubs of beer were brewed using borrowed brewing equipment. It was mainly women who worked in the brewing of ale. This was a village trade that could be found everywhere. In Yatton, many if most women would have brewed ale for sale- after their own household needs were met.[247]

Now the Church is in a position to make its own beer for sale at "Ale Fairs." Such fund-raising will be crucial for fitting out the inside of the newly rebuilt nave and aisles. Revels and Ales could be held here several times a year instead of from the villagers going from house to house as had been the case previously. In 1471 either the church house was extended or a new one built, as it appears to have been made much larger. The brewing room was fitted out with new equipment. An entertainment room was added; a "chamber" frequently hired out for family celebrations. The church house became a place of entertainment, vital to the social life of the village. An organ and clock were kept there to help the entertainment along. Parochial feasting needs safeguarding. In 1446, 6d is paid to make keys to make the church house it secure.

As it could be hired out, the church house provided a source of income. But it will need constant maintenance. *'Repairs to the Church House'* are a common thread in the accounts.

1473 – "J Hyllman for the Cherche howse   xid"
   "for other small articles of furniture and plant,
     for entertainment in the Church House...   1 shilling 7d

In 1492, the year the world changed, the year of Columbus, an inventory is made. Important in this centre of village life is great crockery, lesser crockery, brand-iron for carrying the burning logs on the hearth, troughs, shallow tubs, cloths and *"nine barellys."* The stock of items at the church house such as cups and bowls are frequently replenished. The Parish has to pay out for table cloths, bowls, trenchers and a ladle

*1512 – "Payd for 10 yardys of clothe and a halfe to make tabul
    clothys to ye church house   3 shillings and 11d"
1516 – "Payd for 10 yerds of crest clothe to make 2 mete clothes
    to ye churche howse   2 shillings and 6 d"*

The church house is the ancestor of the pub. It provided the link between church and village pub which to this day characterises most rural communities in England. Church ales that were held there were the main source of income for the church. This was a parish gathering at which food and drink were supplied by the Church Wardens. Ales were accompanied by sports, dancing and general merry-making.

They cost to set up – in 1454, the cost of setting up the first day of the Ale that Whitsun was 1 shilling 6d. But the cost was more than compensated by the large sums of money raised at such events. On the Wednesday of Whitsun week in 1451, the money raised at the Ale that year was 40 shillings.

*1446-47 "Received of the Wardenys of the ale making at
    Whytteson day"   £3 15d*
Seven Ales at Yatton in the year 1464 raised 9 shillings and 3d.

In fact the church seemed never to have been in debt. Church ales were clearly an important social event. Wardens attend those for other neighbouring parishes. They were to be later much criticised although always popular among ordinary folk.

In the 14th century, the Bishop tried to put a stop to fairs being held either in church or just outside. In time, the feeling grew that churches were sacred places and the social events of the parish were held outside the church. After 16th century Reform movements enthusiasm for raising money waned. Increasingly, the church ale house was rented out as a residence.

For now, the popularity of these events spread. Yatton's Wardens went to Kenn and Kingston as well as Wrington and Congresbury to invite people to the Ales. No doubt the offer would have been reciprocated. This was Merry England in full throttle.[248]

Yatton churchwarden records show that Ales were held at Whistun, St James' Day on the second Monday and Tuesday after Easter Sunday and celebrated at Hocktide. Hocktide was a medieval festival that recalled the massacre of the Danes in England on the death of Harthacanute in the 11th century. Traditionally the festivities involved the men of the parish tying up the women and demanding a kiss for their release. The next day it would be the other way round. The women would tie up the men and demand a payment before setting them free. Such games of rough humour carried on until Elizabethan times. May Day remained though as a revel.

This was an opportunity for fund-raising. There were always items to be paid for.

1476-7 – "the caryage of the Altar-table from Wellys id"

Evidently the altar table, a stone slab protable on horseback, was taken to Wells for the benediction of the Bishop. In 1498, another chalice has been made. It too has to be taken to Wells for the blessing of the Bishop before it can be authorised for use. This is an official stamp.

"Payd for halowyng of the chalice..... xi d
"Payd for 3 men and 3 horse to bring said chalice to Wells xd

That year, the wardens have to pay out for *"sekyng of the chych goods."* Evidently, there were several items stolen by a man called Davy Gybbes. But the case was problematic. Three lawyers had to be involved- Masters Rodney, Fitzjames (a future Chief Justice) and Malet. The case cost some £10 to manage which was about the total of church income that year. As this was clearly an expensive action, they may well have wondered if it had been worthwhile. The case was heard at Wells where Ecclesiastical Courts were often involved in pursuit of justice.

Of Minstrels and Marriage

Ten years after the enlarged nave had been built, the South porch was added to the construction. It took two years, between 1455 and 1457. Nikolaus Pevsner, the celebrated church travel writer, described it as the most decorated porch in Somerset.[249] Sir John Newton paid for much of the work to show off his position in society as MP. But it was more than decorative. The Church had not boasted a South Porch before. It was important for major rites of passage in late medieval life.

It was here that business deals were done; sealed at the church door to make it binding. At the South Porch, late medieval salesmen would gather to peddle their goods. In 1469 Chapman the Pedlar paid six pence to be able to stand here on a feast day and sell his wares.

1479 – "received of a chapman to ston (stand) in the porche"

At the South Porch, village plays were performed- Robin Hood or the Everyman saga.[250] Minstrels too would gather, especially at Whitsun. Wardens accounts show regular payments to minstrels who played in the church. Festivities were a part of church and village life. There was little divide between the two spheres and it seemed quite normal for merry making to take place in and around a Parish Church.

The priest met new parents at the porch. The ceiling inside the porch has a vault with moulded bosses. Amongst them is the Green Man, probably because the South Porch also formed an important part of a late Medieval wedding ceremony. Much of the Marriage ceremony took place at the porch. Chaucer writes of his Wife of Bath- *"She'd had five husbands, all at the church door."*

At Yatton Parish Church, on the right hand side of the South Porch, there is a worn Mass dial on which numbers and the centre hole (gnomon) can still be seen. The numbers shown and reading down from the top are - 6, 7, 8, and 9. Although the Mass is held at 9 a.m. throughout the year, the sun will be at a different height at that time depending on the season. So the 6 may be the time of the Mass in Winter when the sun is low, (Christmas), the 7 may be at Easter, the 8 at Ascension and the 9 during the Summer months. The priest would place a small stick known as a "gnomon" into the hole in the middle of the scratch dial to indicate that there was to be a Mass that day and at a time when the sun's shadow reached the next "Mass mark". At the end of the service he would remove the gnomon. Mass was over.[251]

Where Heaven Touches Earth

At the centre of the communities on the Moor is sacred ground, where the divine realm invades common ground, where God is accessible. The interaction between heaven and earth is played out every Sunday when the village gathered to worship. What would have been it like to worship at the Parish Church in late medieval times?

It is the year 1460. Richard Hankyn is Vicar, known in the style of those days as Sir Richard. John Wellyng and William Avery are churchwardens. The church is open for all to see the building work that is now complete. Late medieval churches are colourful places. Traces of what may well be original colours of Yatton Parish Church are to be found - blues and reds. Painted screens, images, some stained glass and embroidery such as is seen to this day adorn the magnificent surroundings. This is in considerable contrast to living conditions for the villagers and peasant farmers.

In most churches, a lytch-gate (lytch means 'body'), marks an area of sacred geography. Here, bodies of the dead lie, waiting to be buried. The Western tower of a parish was the Gate of Heaven. Yatton has neither a lytch gate nor a Western tower. The plan of the church is that of a mini-Cathedral. It is a similcrum, a model of New Jerusalem. The worshippers go through the west door where, despite the lack of a tower, their eyes are nevertheless drawn upwards. Through the nave they are moving, moving down the aisle to their goal. *"The aisle that draws you to the altar....is a ship carrying worshippers towards the holy heart of the building, contained in a separated sacred space"*.[252]

There is a step up towards the chancel, beyond the wooden rood screen where the priests function, restricted to ordinary folk. At the high altar, there are further steps up; up to where God himself is waiting to receive people and the miracle of Christ's sacrifice on the cross is repeated every Sunday.

There is a dread alternative. Amongst those who had died, the blessed were led by smiling angels to the north side. The damned were led to hell's mouth. Behind the statue of Christ on the cross, it was customary to paint the Doom behind the Rood screen. It was a vision of last judgement. The need to escape from hell and secure entrance to heaven was re-inforced amidst the shortness of life here on Earth.

St Mary's Yatton, in common probably with St John's in the village of Kenn and All Saints at Kingston Seymour has three services each Sunday which you are expected to attend. There is also daily Mass in the week. Sunday mornings you have Matins and the Mass. Evensong takes place at 3 in the afternoon. The main service is Sunday Mass. The other two services are sparsely attended. Sundays and feast days are the main time when people could relax. There is a reluctance to spend all Sunday in church. In the week, Daily Mass is often said by the priest alone.

There are no seats or benches in the nave of the church. You have to stand. Either that or you kneel on the ground. The floor of the church was earth over which straw was sometimes laid at the entrance- over the threshold as it was known. 'Carrying your wife over the threshold' is a saying that orginates from this context.

A typical service features no hymns and no sermon. Though it is some ten years since Johannes Gutenberg made his first printing press, if there are any books reproduced by loving hands, few can read them. There is little for the ordinary people to pay attention to. Rather than focussing on what the priest is doing, they wander about. The nave - that part of sacred space which belongs to them - is full of villagers talking with each other, young people giving each other (in the words of one writer) the 'glad eye'.[253] It is not easy to follow the service. The liturgy is conducted in Latin. This adds to the sense of transcendence, the aura of what is going on though not an aid to comprehension. The faithful have long since learnt the Paternoster (the 'Our Father' prayer), Ave Maria and the Creed by heart. It is quite a noisy atmosphere. And it is long. Matins and Sunday Mass together can take three hours.

Generally, the people of the village were happy with their priest. Remarkably few complain that priests are neglecting their duties. In Lincoln Diocese, complaints that priests are not adequately ministering to their religious needs are made by less than 5% of the churches surveyed.[254] In any case, Sir Richard has help. He is not alone.

The chantry was an area in the church designated as a chapel to pray for the soul of a dead benefactor. Fear of purgatory and intercession for the dead was vital to late medieval church life. The Church taught that the souls of the dead could be redeemed by prayers, hence the proliferation of Chantry Chapels, a small chapel in parish church with its own altar and priest. The extra priests helped out on a Sunday.

Now it was no longer needed as a village hall, the body of the parish church could acquire pews. With preaching becoming more common, pulpits were needed. The general level of education of priests is higher than supposed. Around a quarter of priests left books in their wills.[255] Priests were trained in the dominant philosophy known as nominalism. There are no universals, only particulars; the focus is not so much on humanity as individuals, not so much on the loaf as pieces of bread. This was a critique of the earlier metaphysical system taught by Thomas Aquinas where you ascend from the general to the particular. There is no sign, however, of a pulpit in early modern times in any of the churches on the Moor.

Private pews became popular in 15th century. It suited the church. There was extra income. It also suited the parishioners who could be buried 'afore my seat', near to where they worshipped. Church is divided into areas separate from each other. To divide the nave from the chancel where the priest did his work, Rood screens were erected made of wood. Through the Rood Screen is where the Mass takes place.

Church is at the heart of village life and the Mass is the centre-piece of church life. It comes as a surprise to realise that the ordinary villagers did not go up to the high altar to receive communion. This was the task of the priests in the two Chantry chapels either side of the nave. The priests took communion in both bread and wine. It was laid down that the laity took communion three times a year- but only bread. Villagers could only glance through the Rood Screen at the Rector enacting the mass, this re-enactment of Jesus' sacrifice on the cross, out of reach to most. Their access to the holy mysteries was through the chapels at the side. The priests here were also watching the main event. There were slits in the wall called squints that enabled these assistants to replicate what was going on. They mirrored every action, raising the chalice as the main priest gave them the cue, bowing where needed and saying the liturgy until the miracle of transubstantiation was complete. Then the villagers walked up to the side chapels to receive.

Bidding prayers are said for the dead and departed. Once a year, the entire list would be read out. Sacred space is "*the repository of the collective memory of the community*"[256] The villagers constantly move amongs their dead family members. Ancestors were real to them; certainly for a couple of generations. The tenure on a grave was about 25 to 30 years up to late medieval times. The dead are living.

This brings us full circle to the churchyard where people entered. Churchyards were busy places even after the service. There were all sorts of games and recreations- archery, wrestling and the game of 'fives'. Religion is colourful. As well as Sundays, there are the Great feasts to celebrate plus festivals to commemorate local saints. Six times a year, a dramatic vibrant procession stirred and delighted the villagers.

Palm Sunday 1460

It is Palm Sunday in Yatton in the year 1460, the beginning of Holy Week. The main procession of the church is about to take place. The extended Church has just been consecrated. It is ready to be used. Branches have been sprinkled with holy water and distributed- branches of yew, box and willow. The entire village is making its way to the stone cross in the churchyard. They are ranked according to where they stand in social hierarchy. At the churchyard, they are met by the church procession. The priests carry relics and the sacramental Host, the body of Christ. The story of Jesus' entry into Jerusalem is read. When the procession reaches the east end of the Lady Chapel, a chorister dressed as an OT prophet stands and sings Ecce Rex tuus venit (Behold thy King cometh). The choir breaks into what is to become a classic Palm Sunday hymn, "all Glory Laud and Honour." That was the signal for everyone to kneel. The two processions now merge and make their way to the south side of the church. With musicians playing and the choir singing in niches in the west wall that open to the outside, it is very colourful, very atmospheric. The sacrament has been carried round the village by four yeomen in a blue silk canopy. As it returns to the church, it was showered with flowers and unconsecrated wafers.

The procession has reached the west door. It is opened by the priest knocking there with the foot of the processional cross. The relics and the Host are lifted high in a way that allows the procession to pass under into the church. As the sacrament makes its way, the covering over the Rood screen is withdrawn.

As year succeeds to year and Palm Sunday processions roll on in glory, laud and honour, the cycles of church life seems unchanging. Amidst an endless stream of baptisms, marriages and deaths, the years pass and the generations subtly change.

In 1509, the Wardens received from the St James Ale alone the figure of £2 17 shillings and 6 pence. Church appointments often ran in families. A reference in August that year is to a grant from John Buenio, Doctor of Arts and of Medicine, acting with his son, current Rector and Prebend of Yatton (albeit residing at Wells), giving to the Bishop of Worcester as well as John Collet, Dean of St Paul's Cathedral in London, the right of presentation to the vicarage of Yatton. John Buenio was Chief Physician to Henry VII and a friend of Erasmus. The Dean of St Paul's was a vital figure in church circles, underlining the significance of Yatton as a parish. Three months later, William Middleton resigns his position and another Vicar of Yatton is needed.[257] His name is Thomas Gryffyths; he will be there until 1520.

But this is 1509 and a new King sits on the throne. He will bring in the most far –reaching changes that the people of the Moor have ever experienced. There is no indication whatever that the life with the church at its heart was anything less than secure. It is true that John Colett, who now holds the advowsan for Yatton, will the very next year preach against clergy being guilty of pride of life and lust of the flesh. But this was a clarion call for reform - not the Reformation that followed.

In Yatton in 1512, Hock-day was celebrated with a Church Ale. The amount received from J. Bek for his tavern on that occasion was 36 shillings 8 shillings. Church life went on as usual and seemed secure. Henry had no plans to nationalise the church.

A completed church (minus the spire) – St Mary's Yatton

Chapter Ten

RELIGION-SHOCK

It is now 1520. The villagers prepare to receive a new Vicar, Robert Batty. Did they but know it, the earthquake had already begun.

Three years before, Martin Luther had nailed 95 points for debate on the door of a German church. Luther had not set out on a radical attempt to challenge the edifice of power of Christendom. His theological theses sought to debate the theology and thinking behind abuses and practices that were unhealthy to the Christian soul. But when it became clear that there was an institutional problem, the spiritual authority of the Papacy came into sharp focus.

All this was not inevitable in the English Church and would have seemed to any informed villagers in Yatton to be abstruse theology. Indeed, King Henry, in attacking Luther was to receive the title 'Defender of the Faith', which placed him on the same level as 'the most Christian' King of France.

In what is known as the Reformation, old certainties will be replaced. The 49th and the 50th generations will witness a different religious universe coming into being. Colourful processions into a noisy church, comforting sacrament and saints you can see and pray to are about to be replaced by an emphasis on faith that alone justifies the sinning man along with sermons and Bible reading that stress the Word of God.

For these next two generations that came to articulate the meaning of their lives as a worshipping community, Church will begin to have a very different feel to it. It will be violent revolution. Out have gone images, icons and the magnificent Rood Screen that separated the chancel where the priest celebrated mass, from the main body of the church, the nave. The colourful walls have gone; the church has been whitewashed. The changes are not just external. Prayers for the Dead will go. Communion with the dead will be seen as superstition. The old Chantry Chapels that made communion with the dead such a reality were now illegal. The mass has gone, being replaced by the Orders for Holy Communion in the Book of Common Prayer. It is now a memorial and transmitter of grace, not a sacrifice. A great Bible is now in the church, accessible to all; and a pulpit is in place to explain it! *"Gone the mystique of the mass, the glowing vestments and the awesome moment of elevation. Gone the ancient altar vessels and the shrines decked with the generosity of the ages."*[258]

In the years between 1520 and 1540, the rumbling of distant thunder could be heard far-off. Gradually, the thunder grew nearer. It was often trumpeted by supporters of the Reformation that the medieval period was one of decline, a slippery slope down to an all-time religious low before God raised up Martin Luther as a complete new start. In this narrative, the recovery of a new emphasis on biblical Christianity in the Reformation was preceded by centuries of superstition, laxity and a corrupt Church.

That narrative cannot be sustained. Historians tend to look for a pre-Reformation sense of crisis, looking for evidence that contemporaries felt the church to be corrupt, hopelessly worldly and in dire need of sweeping reform. Yet as this story shows, religious life continued in a parish like Yatton. Indeed, the late medieval era was one of an increasing sense of devotion. In 1547, as the English reform movement had hardly begun to bite in Yatton, there were 500 villagers who received communion. That was practically everyone in the village except for the children.[259]

There were no surveys in Tudor England to assess how villagers felt about the church. Yet the people of the Moor still support their parish unstintingly. In 1525, they build a churchyard cross, six steps with a large base. This cross was intended to be a market cross. Dealers would shake hands on the steps here as a reminder that God expected honesty in their dealings. Dozens of wagon loads of stone quarried nearby at Felton trundled down into Yatton. The head of the cross was carved from the finest Bathstone. John Hort, Master Mason at Yatton church personally rode over to Bath to view the finished stones before accepting them. During its first winter the head had to be thatched with brambles to protect it from the frost whilst it weathered.

In 1529, the parishioners pay out for a bell to be taken to Bristol and replaced. The 'belle maker' will charge 19 shillings and 6d. Ten years later, bell repair is needed:

1539 – "Payd to Thomas Carpynter for a hole wekes worke
and hys man Nycholas   *6s"*

and in 1534:
"Payd for a hole sewte of vestments with a Coope   *£30"*

The neighbouring parish of Congresbury seems to have bought a suit of vestments as well. The arrival of the vestments was greeted at a combined Church Ale given by one Thomas Prewetts. Thomas Tucker of Congresbury was paid 1d for bringing them home in 1534, just before the changes in the

Reform movement. The following year, at the Bishop's residence in Banwell, they are dedicated. The charge is 7d.

The warden accounts testify to the devotion of the villagers.

1538 – "bequest from a poore woman   4d"
1538 – " expenses on Schere Thurssday (Maunday Thursday)   4d"

In 1527 wardens pay 9 s and 7d for wax for St James Day. A minstrel is hired to play at the festival. The next year, payments are recorded for gilding of the images.

"Payd for gyltyng of Saynt James as well as of 'owre Lady'   13s 5d and 6s."

When a villager died, their loved ones would arrange for their bodies to be brought to the 'lyche reste' before burial. The church marked the end of life, rites of passage.

"1515 – "Reyvyd for Water Knyth lying yn ye Church   6s 8d"

This is the first use of the phrase *"lying yn ye Church."* A body lies in the Church before burial in a grave beneath the pavement.

1519 – "Resyvd of John Avery for his wyfes lynng in ye churche   6s 7d"
1520 – "J Cradocke for his wyfs lynge in the Chur ch   6s 7d"
    "J. Thurban for his moder lynge in the Church   6s 7d"
    "Matthew Toore for his sisters lynge in ye church   6s 7d"

By 1536, John Avery himself is dead. He leaves 6 s 8d to Yatton Church.

In 1524, the three local ales yield the large sum of £23. In the year 1526, church income reached the princely sum of £51, due in no small measure to the collections at the Ales where the people were assembled. In 1531, the three ales are still very fruitful, bringing £17 8s and 4d into church coffers. Minstrels are still playing along.

1521 – "Payd to a mynnsytrelle   12d"

An entry for the year 1530 simply reads:
"*Payd to a mynstrell at Wytonsunday* 2 s 8d"

Amounts vary. For 1532, the minstrel receives 6 shillings for his troubles; in 1533/4, 8 shillings and 4d is the fee. In 1540, 6 shillings and nine pence is paid out for 2 minstrels. This continued through the Reformation. An entry for 1557 simply read, "*to the Mynstrell.*" Ten years before, a minstrel was named, one R.Wylimet.

Services are by now accompanied by music. Small bells for hand-ringing are prominent in the services. Yatton boasts of an early organ. Organs feature increasingly in the warden accounts. For 1526, they record:

"Payd to ye organ maker £12
Payd for making a fote to ye organs 4 s
Payd in expenses for ye organ maker and for his company that gefe attendance with hym 8s
Payd to ye organ player 21d"

To judge by the entry the next year, the organ maker is based in Bristol. He continues to be paid throughout 1527 and receives the occasional gratuity. At some point that year, the organ is ready. A man called John Felyps (Phillips) played the organ in those days.

"Payd in expenses for bryngyng home ye organs and
to seyd halyard (haulier) 7s"

All this did not mean that religion was inconsequential. It was rather the context in which people lived their lives. The church was at the centre of the community. The villagers remember the church in their wills. The membrane between the business of God and the business of the village was wafer thin. But it was a devotional life that increasingly involved literacy.

1537 – "Payd to buckebyndar 6s 8d"
1537 – "Payd to Syr Harry (a priest) for a bucke 8d"

Literacy was spreading. The printing Press found an appetite for all kinds of liturgical books. Now there were Books of Hours for the ordinary folk to use and Books of Psalms. It was all in Latin. There was a fear of books in the vernacular because of the radical movement known as Lollardy. Though affecting certain parts of Somerset and three Bristol parishes then in the Diocese, it did not seem to trouble Yatton. St Mary Redcliffe, associated with people in the cloth trade, had become a centre of Lollard activity in the last century. Informed villagers would have been aware of it.

Now another Reform movement was upon them.

The Violence of Reform

Although they end up in much the same place, there is no straight line between the actions of Martin Luther and the huge changes that came over the life of the villagers on the Moor in the 1540's. They would have been startled if they thought they were part of a Europe-wide movement. But perhaps the truth is that they were not, at least directly. It was not until the next generation that the English State embarks upon the full bodied Reform movement that was in full throttle on the Continent.

Henry has imbibed unremitting Catholicism. He has also imbibed something else; a desire to ensure Crown control of the English Church. He nationalises faith and devotion because he is nationalistic. The movement he instigates is not the same as developments in Europe though there were many points of contact.

Between 1533 and 1542, the break with Rome had been sealed. King Henry was now the Supreme Governor of the Church of England. Gradually, clergy became subservient to the English crown rather than the Pope at Rome. In 1537, further seismic shock to the social landscape comes when the monasteries are dissolved. Not content with a unilateral declaration of independence from Rome, the Tudor State had closed down the religious houses. The one did not follow from the other; Henry had embarked on a landgrab. You would not know that from the churchwarden accounts. Religious houses were based elsewhere- at Woodspring priory which, according to legend, was built for the Carthusians as an act of penance by Henry IInd for the murder of Thomas Becket. Cistercians founded Cleeve Abbey in 1198. There were Fransciscans in Bridgwater by 1245 and Dominicans in Illchester by 1261. Dissolution of monasteries did not touch the Moor directly. Yet the fall of monasticism which in earlier times had done so much to inspire and preserve a high and noble ideal of Christian life cannot have been greeted with barely a yawn.

Life goes on. Each year, there are three Church Ales, Minstrels, sports and revels. Merry England was undeterred. The fact that Rome was now out of the picture and the Pope no longer the ultimate jurisdiction is not mentioned by wardens except as the sound of distant thunder. The Reformation is as much about villagers across Europe such as on the Moor as it is about the actions of Luther or Latimer. It may have been much more a movement of town than countryside, more radical urban life than the conservatism of the people of the village. The first change the villagers would have been aware of is that Henry VIII ordered a Great Bible to be placed in their Church.

It was in the summer of 1537 that Archbishop Cranmer had won an argument with the King. He pointed out that it was illogical to say that doctrine was to be judged with reference to scripture rather than the Catholic magisterium if an English Bible was not readily available to the Christians of England.[260] He caught the King in generous mood since the pregnancy was nearing its supposed happy conclusion for Jane Seymour – herself descended from the St Maurs of Kingston Seymour. Cranmer was beside himself with joy. *"The authorisation of the Great Bible 'shall so redound to your honour, that besides God's reward, you shall obtain perpetual memory for the same within this realm."* It is debatable whether the inhabitants of the Moor agreed with this sentiment. They would have been startled too by a change the King ordered about the same time, the production of a Bishop's Book. This was a collection of official sermons designed to guide the beliefs of the nation.

A decree of 1538 declared each parish must purchase a Bible, extinguish all lights apart from those on the altar, in the rood loft and before the Easter sepulchre; and remove any images that had been 'abused with pilgrimages or offerings'.[261] The snuffing out of candles and lamps that burned before the saints was a major change. In the wave of Henry's Reform that year, this was accompanied by many minor holy days being cancelled. As Eamon Duffy shows, it caused considerable resentment.[262]

With the strong backing of Thomas Cromwell, the Great Bible appeared on Easter Day, 6th April 1539 from the press of its enthusiastically evangelical publishers. *'The Byble in Englyshe'* showed on its front cover, two estates, clerical and lay, receiving the Word of God from a generous Christian monarch. This was the King as he wanted to be seen. It was pure propaganda. There was an alternative. The magnificent title page depicted what would happen to those who advocated treason and opposed the Royal

Decree. The '*The Byble in Englyshe*' could then go out to Parishes locally. Yatton churchwardens accounts for 1539 show the Great Bible ordered to be set up for free and accessible public reading. The significant sum of nine shillings and eight pence was laid out 'for a bybyll'. What effect this had as the Great Bible came into church, courtesy of Royal authority can only be conjectured.

The Yatton records for 1542 record the usual balance of funds brought forward into the care this year of John Irysch and one Thomas Partrych (the funds are unusual in that they mention a small coin not in legal currency by the name of 'dandepratt' as well as 'Irys grots'; both to the value of 14 shillings). But then comes an ominous reference. Dandepratts and grots will nicely pay for a new levy.

1542 – "Payd for the Kyngs subsyde (subsidy)   13shillings 4d."
1543 – "Payd to the Kyngs collectors   8 shillings"
1543 – "Payd for 2 bokes for owr professyon   8d."

This is most likely "A necessary Doctrine and Erudition for any Christian Man", the Bishop's Book published that year and known as "The King's Book, "Henry's project to start educating people and priests so they would not look to Rome or the old superstitions.

1544 – "Resevyd by the wardens for the Kyngs bere
    this present yere   33 shillings 4d"

It is not clear what this refers to. But the intrusion of royal authority continues.

1544 – "Payd to Syr John Danyell for the subside making   8d"
    "Payd to ye same for making a byll of the subside   7d"
    "Payd to Syr Jo. Danell for hys wages   25 shillings"
    "Payd for rydng to Charleton at ye vysstation   7d"
1546 – "Payd in expenses for goyng to ye Kyngs vysytors   3d"
    "Payd to Syr Christover of Kynston at ye visitation
    for making a byll   2d"

Royal authority is endeavouring to ensure that everyone is being briefed about what is now expected of them. Levies must be paid for. Festivities are held in 1545. The merrymaking brings in £3, 8 shillings and 8 pence. This is a sizeable amount though eclipsed by the tavern ale at Whitsunday the following year when £4 14 shillings came in or in 1547 when over £5 income came in at 'Wysontyde' and the same again at Hockday- though less at 'Mydsomer'.

Handed in for Burning

In that year of 1547, the church wardens have to pay '*for setting further sowdears*' (soldiers). This cost them 30 shillings on one occasion and 12 on another. In 1548, a muster at Banwell requires a charge of 15 shillings and 4 pence on the parish. There is clearly public unrest. The Tudor State is taking no chances.

The Chantry Act of Edward VI, December 1547, confiscated the possessions and endowments of chantries and free chapels. The following year, Chantry Commissioners went round the country listing and assessing the value of the endowments. The lands were subsequently sold off. One of these was Claverham Free Chapel. The Commissioner responsible for North Somerset was Sir Miles Partridge. He had been a royal servant at the end of the reign of Henry VIII. But events took a tragic turn. He was one of the chief supporters of Edward Seymour, the Duke of Somerset. When the Duke was brought down by John Dudley, Earl of Warwick and later Duke of Northumberland, Sir Miles was hung, drawn and quartered. Edward VI's Chantry Commissioners report that the inhabitants of Yatton had bought the old chantry Chapel of Claverham. Endowments were annexed to the State Treasury. This had no doubt been closed for some time. The nominal incumbent was a scholar of 18 who had been unable to perform his duty.

In 1548, the Yatton churchwardens have to pay out for a '*bybull of the largyst volume.*' It will cost 11 shillings. This is highly significant. Yatton Parish church now has a full Bible to be read out in services. This is the Great Bible of Henry VIII. Yet there is something wrong here. It is the date.

By then Henry was dead and the child born when he had agreed to the Great Bible, was now on the throne as Edward V1. Was the Great Bible lost, stolen or removed by reluctant, conservative elements amongst those who opposed the move? The indication is that Royal decrees were not taken up with enthusiasm in the Moor.

It is in 1548 that the real changes come. A new Vicar is appointed, Dr William Lyson. Given the speed with which he adapts to Elizabethan settlement, he is likely to be an appointee in sympathy with the Reformation. At any rate, William Lyson will have to deal with a very different scenario. Gone are outlays on wax, lamps or poor relief. The image of *'owre Lady in ye chaunsell'* is now removed. *"Thys yere the sylver crosse of owr church was sold by Master Kenne'* to pay for sluice gates at Wemberham in the parish. Though no doubt for the purpose of sea defence, that this happened in the same year may point to theological reasons for selling off the goods of the church. More was to come. A bull for the King's Commissioners at Bedminster has to be paid for. A pulpit is to be erected. A book called 'paraphrasus and Erasmus' will cost the wardens 21 shillings and 4 pence. This is a series of homilies that the priest can read out. His job is not now just one of taking the mass but of preaching, of teaching the people. The mass must now be understood by the people.

"Payd to Syr Nicholas Poore for wrytyng ye masse in Englych   8d"

November 1550 saw another huge change for the villagers. The Bishop of Bath and Wells, along with his colleagues, was ordered to ensure that stone altars and communion rails were removed from every church. Along with receiving communion in both consecrated bread and consecrated wine, all believers were henceforth invited to take part in the full benefits of Christ's death and resurrection. The Rood Screen was taken down. This must have caused a great shock. It had been nine years in the making and been the pride and joy in village faith for a hundred years. If publicly burnt outside, the impression must have been dramatic. A cry went up.

In 1551, the Wardens have to pay out for *'a boke for the Communion'* at a cost of 4 shillings and 4 pence. This presumably is the Book of Common Prayer, Cranmer's great achievement. The old Mass books have to be handed in for burning. One can imagine the scene. The villagers have been told for generations that their faith was a way to ensure safe passage from a life of toil and offer a way to heaven. Now the very Mass that kept them in eternal life was up for grabs.

The first Act of Uniformity had been put on the statute book in 1549. By Whitsunday, every minister is required to use the new Prayer Book and none other. The alternative is fine, deprivation of living or imprisonment. There was henceforth a standard, imposed by Government, which all ministers must follow, the Prayer Book which will now be a manual for worship and doctrine. The old Canonical hours were gone. In their place were Matins and Evensong. Cranmer's Litany was included but there were some aspects that the priests on the Moor had been used to that were pointedly excluded. No longer would they prepare for the Mass in the same way or elevate the Host. Invocation of the saints or belief in purgatory no longer featured in the expression of faith. Transubstantiation was out. So was use of Latin in favour of the quest for simplicity that enshrined use of the English language. The reading of the whole Bible was substituted for a variety of readings including those from the Fathers of the Church of early centuries.

The Book of Common Prayer was a far-reaching change that was to affect greatly the kind of faith practiced on the Moor. It became a manual of private devotion as well as a book of public worship. The religious life of these communities was to rest in the future on Bible and Prayer-Book. Saints had to take a back seat; processions were retired. This was to alter the spirituality of the people of the Moor.

It was not of course the end of the line. No sooner was the ink dry than Cranmer began making notes about developing the theology and practice of the Prayer Book even further in a Protestant direction. The result was that Wardens and Priests on the Moor had to absorb further legislation. The Second Act of Uniformity of 1552 was a re-construction of the Prayer Book to be enforced amongst clergy and amongst laity. The villagers were obliged to absorb the fact they are compelled to attend the revised services. For the recusants – those who refused to attend services that the law prescribed – there were to be penalties. The people could see for themselves what the changes involved. The word 'Mass' was omitted. Their priests were no longer allowed to use vestments; the Protestant surplice was now the order of the day. All mention of the saints and the holy angels was removed.

When the priests were obliged to act differently, come out from behind the Rood Screen and speak to the people, thence to conduct Holy Communion in the vernacular, the effect must have been dramatic. To some it must have seemed that what they had been used in the conduct of their faith had been profoundly affected. To others, there was welcome surprise in being able to follow the liturgy for the first time. There is a *'tabull in ye chansell'*, possibly a substitute for the *'awter'* (altar).

Compared with towns that accepted reform somewhat faster, the people of the Moor faced change with bewilderment. There is no protest such as the Pilgrimage of Grace in 1536, ruthlessly suppressed. In Exeter a group of women prevented workmen from pulling down a rood screen in the priory of St Nicholas.[263] Yet in Yatton, wholesale clearance of items during Henry VIII's and Edward's reigns was met by a lack of response.[264] There was no Prayer Book rebellion as in Morebath.[265] The villagers protested in other ways. It is highly significant that there is marked fall in income. From a balance of about £20 a year, after that year of change 1548, the balance fell to £8. Income from the Ales and sources of voluntary revenue had dried up. Enthusiasm waned. The Reformation was greeted by only grudging acceptance.

Much came down to the persuasive powers of the government at local level. We have noted the intrusion of royal authority in the churchwarden Accounts. Every year now, the King's Officers conduct visitations to which parish representatives are obliged to come. For Yatton in 1549, this is held at Axbridge, nine miles over the hills. An inventory of church goods must be brought for scrutiny. That year, the old Manor of Yatton was surrendered to the Crown by the Bishop of Bath and Wells.

The changes are not only ecclestiastical. There is a new social concern. In 1549, for the first time, there is poor relief, paid to 14 men of the parish. Here were seeds of what became the Elizabethan Poor Law. Yet the impact of the Reformation profoundly affected the visual look of churches. Yatton Parish Church now looked very different. Rood screens, vestments and some church plate had been sold off or destroyed. The walls had been whitewashed. Even the altars had been demolished and replaced by wooden tables in the naves. Objects that had previously played an important part in the local religious practices: altars, images, statues and candles that were a focus for devotion and burial were put somewhere in store. The final injunction of Edward's reign concerning church goods occurred in January 1553, giving instructions to seize all surviving items except linen, chalices and bells. All other goods had to be sold, and the money sent to London. Sacred items had enormous symbolic value and for Yatton churchwardens to sell them off must have been alarming. To be custodian of church plate was part of the job.

In November 1554, the anti-papal legislation of Henry VIII was repealed, heresy laws re-enacted and the nation solemnly absolved of its sin. At a stroke, the Cardinal Legate, Reginald Pole, admitted the entire country back into communion with the Church of Rome. The villagers are aware of these changes at national level. In 1556, the Wardens record a charge for reading a Papal Bull to be read in these domains.

The following year, expenses are charged in connection with a visitation at Bedminster of the Archbishop of Canterbury, now Cardinal Pole. But it was the Diocese that held regional jurisdiction. The Wardens charged to the parish the cost of a trip they made to Banwell *"unto my Lorde bysshoppe to axe his counsel for thei tabernacull"*. No doubt this was related to the way their world had been turned upside down in the last twenty years of Reform. How should they now respond? Over a ten year period, the accepted ways of devotion and familiar landmarks of faith had been removed. Parishioners were perhaps adjusting. There were no Protestant martyrs here such as there were in the south east. Yet it is clear the veneer of practical Protestantism the villagers had imbibed was rather thin.

When Mary became Queen, everything connected with the old Catholic faith was restored. The altar, missal, manual, sacred bell, candles, censer and frankincense were back. The rood loft was replaced, destined as a make-shift construction, nothing on the scale of the previous one. The 1557 accounts speak of 'Rode makyng' and paying John Brodmore to wash the images. Restoring the old religion costs 45s 9d for four service books,12s 4d for a new stone altar and 26s 8d for plate. But in November 1557, Queen Mary died. The Warden accounts speak of 3d paid out for a visitation 'for the continuance of Mary', presumably prayers for her soul. There are many signs that Mary's restoration was welcomed by the people. Catholic Church ritual was restored locally with little compulsion.[266] In the Diocese, 36 out of 266 churches had no proper altar in1554. By 1557, 86% had complied, including Yatton. Once, the inside of St Mary's would have been a sight to behold with colourful statuses, images, wall-paintings and stained glass windows. The villagers must have hoped that their church would recover its former glory. It was not to be.

The Final Transformation

The generation that live out their lives on the Moor from 1558 to 1603 live in the shadow of a great Queen. In short order, Parliament passes the Act of Supremacy, recognising the Sovereign as Head of the English Church and the Act of Uniformity which stipulated that the Prayer Book is the only valid service book to be used in Parish Churches. Apart from Mary's

Bishops and a few hundred clergy who refuse the settlement, there is little outward protest though perhaps reluctant acquiescence.

1559 Accounts refer to the final revolution. *"For taking downe the Roode.... expenses at the plucking down of the Images"*. '*A bocke of the injunctions*' has to be purchased and '*drawyng the koppye of the bryfes of the stattutes*' has to be paid for. 1560 sees Church Wardens Thomas More and John Warre paying '*for taking downe the alter*'.

Dr William Lyson is still Vicar. Despite ten years of upheaval, he accepts this final transformation of the Parish Church. The fact that after 1558 there were no more Church Ales is significant. He may be a Protestant minister in what is an essentially Catholic village. Elsewhere, the accession of Elizabeth did not have the same immediate impact on merry - making as did the fast-track Reform under Edward.[267] At any rate, William Lyson will be Vicar of Yatton until 1588, the year of maximum crisis for Elizabeth, the year of the Spanish Armada. Spanish invasion was partly prompted by the death of Mary Queen of Scots in 1587 which sent shock waves throughout Europe. Wardens must pay for ringing the bells on her death.[268]

Local militias, the Home Guard of their day, were available for the national defence. A Muster Roll for 'the tithing of Yatton" in 1569 shows 25 'ablemen' ready to defend their district. 'Trayned bandes' included 12 archers, four pikemen, some horsemen and six billmen (a pole arm with a wide cutting blade, sometime with hooks added for extra effect!).[269] By then, the replacement of the feudal system with the imperial concept of kingship meant that Tudor monarch were no longer dependent on the landowning aristocracy for support. Christopher Kenn, lord of the Manor at Kenn supplies the armour. Their weapons included bows with arrows. These tried and tested weapons, were replaced a little later, in 1595, with the threat of Spanish invasion still ever present. More power was needed from the new guns that were coming in as Tudor technology advanced, such as the arquebus, referred to in the Muster Roll, a match-lock shoulder gun that led directly to the musket.

In that year 1595, it was clear the church spire was a hazard. Three masons came to examine it. One was called Jenings, one was called Bristoe but the third went by the unusual name of *"out of ye forest"*. They were paid 2 shillings each though *"out of ye forest"* was rated at an extra 4 shillings. A labourer was employed *"for ii days work about ye steeple"* at one shilling a day. The Bishop gave his warrant and, soon after Easter 1596, the work began. Ropes costing 13 shillings and 8d were brought along with poles.

The spire was taken down and laid on the lead roof. Three men were employed to remove them and another to clean the lead. There was a problem in paying for the work. The Vicar of the day, Mr Clapham, had to contribute personally and the churchwarden accounts show they took a year to pay it all off.[270] It seems an epitaph on final transformation of the Parish Church: a focus of faith, a whole way of life and eternal life. Painted piety and vibrant colours of faith were forever gone.

Chapter Eleven

A Sea of Troubles

Some eighty years are about to pass. In the period between the end of Elizabeth's long reign and events of 1688, the 51st and 52nd generations will play out their lives on the Moor before the years close over them.

Devotion is strong. The Moor seems untroubled by the actions of the Puritans, who loudly asserted that the Reform was incomplete. With the single exception of the new Quakerism, Christianity on the Moor took the form of a moderate Anglicanism with religious instruction based on prayer-book and a new version of the English Bible. Samuel Ward was one of the translators of the King James Version- a member of the Second Cambridge Company, responsible for the Apocrypha. He held the absentee office of the Prebendary of Yatton as well as the Archdeaconry of Taunton. His diaries show him to be a conflicted man, struggling with his conscience over his indulgence for food- especially plumbs! Yet the project he helped oversee was to be foundational in the spread of English-speaking peoples across the globe and hold undisputed sway both in public worship and personal faith for 300 years.

By 1611, the new Bible was ready. Devotion was now to be strongly linked with the source book of the Christian faith. Since 1543, the parish priests of Yatton were required to read one chapter of scripture every Sunday. Four years later, the epistle and the gospel had to be read in English. Cranmer's Prayer Book helped mediate the vernacular Bible to the villagers. The Vicar of Yatton was required by Archbishop Whitgift to have his own personal copy of the English Bible. But which one? There were numbers of translations emerging from the religious ferment. It was King James who gave an impetus to the first English Bible produced by leaders of the English Church in order to have an official version that was sanctioned by Church and State.

It is not clear if the Vicar, Thomas Clapham, or his Wardens, bought the new Bible immediately. The preamble states that it is 'appointed to be read in churches' yet there does not seem to be a force of ordinance to oblige parish churches to equip their lecterns with the 1611 version. Yet the connection with Samuel Ward made it at least politic that Yatton invests in a translation that patently has the King's blessing. The lyrical quality of this Authorised Version will evoke acoustics of the spirit that shape the faith of generations. They grow up reciting the 23rd Psalm (most of it Coverdale's) or the pattern prayer well-known in earlier times as the 'Our Father'.

Wills attest the level of popular devotion that was rooted in the Bible. The will of John Wornell, Gentleman of Yatton, proved in 1637, left to his son James *'my ring with my Arms engraven on it and my Bible; son Joseph to have the lease of the Parsonage House at Yatton.'* A Bible is a different emblem of spirituality, a different world than an earlier will of say 1534 when an Isabella Horte left 10 shillings to Yatton Parish church, an equal amount to the mysterious Chapel of St James and to a priest *'to sing for my soul and all Christian souls by the space of one whole year £6.12.4.'*[271]

Biblical rationalism co-existed with a great deal of superstition. Scofula, tuberculosis of the bones and lymphatic glands was popularly known as the "king's evil." From the time of the saintly Edward the Confessor had come the belief that the sovereign's touch could affect a cure. The custom reached its peak during the Restoration: Charles II is said to have touched more than 90,000 victims between 1660 and 1682. A case before the Quarter Sessions for the County of Somerset concerned a John Harris of Yatton who directed his nephew to cover up that he suffered from the King's Evil. Harris' nephew was discharged from his apprenticeship because of it.[272]

A Marriage of Two Families

Shortly after his death in January 1593, a monument was erected in Kenn Parish Church to Christopher Kenn, the last of the Kenn family to occupy the Manor. His third wife Florence, daughter of a John Stalling, had originally been housekeeper.

Lady Florence left her mark in Yatton. In 1620, her will was generous to the poor. *"First I commend my Soule unto the hands of Almightie God my merciful and loving father, in Jhesus Christie his sonne my merciful and loving Saviour and Redeemer by the merittes of whose precious deathe and passion I do assuredly hope and believe that I shall have eternal life...... I give and devise to the poore of the parishe of Kenn the somme of five pounds of lawful money to be distributed at the time of my funeral. Also, I give and devise to Ten poore women of the same parishe of Kenn to every one of them a gown...I give and devise the Church House of Yatton for the better relief and maintenance of the poor".*[273]

The old Almshouse still bears the name of Lady Florence Stalling. When she died in 1621, her legacy dated the 18th year 'of our Lord James' had to be confirmed by 13 good men and true that she held the Manor of Yatton from the King 'incapite through military service.'[274] Her husband was a soldier, Nicholas Stalling, who died from war wounds in 1605, the year of gun-powder plot. The curiousity is that Nicholas was brother to her father, John Stalling. It seems Florence had married her uncle.

The monument at Kenn depicts Christopher Kenn along with his two daughters. One of the two daughters is Elizabeth. When she was a rich heiress, Elizabeth Kenn wrote a long letter to King James 1 explaining why she didn't want to marry an old man, the Earl of Orkney. He was a hanger-on, coming down from Scotland with James, looking for a rich plumb! Instead, she went on to marry John Poulett of Hinton St George in 1614 and became the ancestor of the influential Poulett family.

The Pouletts went on to become major landowners in the Somerset aristocracy, whose stately home was Hinton St George. Elizabeth took her father's estates into the marriage, including the Manors of Kenn and Court de Wyck.

Here were two important families coming together.

"One of the best and most ancient families of Somerset"[275], the Kenn family derived their wealth and status from their land holdings. Their core holding was the Manor of Kenn and one third of the adjoining Manor of Kingston Seymour. They added to their lands as a result of marriage. Sifting through late medieval documents is complicated by there being six John Kenns in a row, father and son. One John Kenn died in the year 1438. There is a reference in the wills to guardians appointed on his death to hold estates in trust until his son and heir, Robert, then only ten, was of age.[276]

"Commitment to John Inyn, Knight, by mainprise of John More, gentilman, and William Gascoigne, gentilman, both of the county of Somerset, of the keeping of all the lands late of John Kenne of the said county, gentilman...... to hold the same from the death of the said John Kenn until the full age of Robert Kenne his kinsman"[277]

Robert Kenn lived until the year 1453. Most of his estates were granted in May 1454 to James, Earl of Wiltshire, beheaded in March 1461 following his capture at the battle of Towton during the Wars of the Roses. The core holding of land is then held by Isabel, the widow of Robert Kenn until another son John, comes of full age.[278] John Kenn (1450-1504) who married Elizabeth Newton, daughter of Sir John, whom we met in Chapter 8, is an important man in the county, escheator in the County of Somerset in 1483.[279] His grandson, Christopher Kenn, who supplies armour for the National Guard, was Sheriff of Somerset in 1575 and JP for the County of Somerset in 1591. His heir through his housekeeper Florence Stalling is Elizabeth Kenn.

By the early 17th century, the Pouletts also went back a long way. A hundred years before, Sir Amias Paulet began to develop a country home befitting his new position in society as Sheriff of Somerset. One of his tasks was to sentence the Curate of the nearby village of Limington to be placed in the stocks for disorderly conduct in the revelry at the local fair. The name of the young Curate was Thomas Wolsey, future Cardinal of England. Wolsey never forgot it. Probably on a trumped up charge, a copy of the Bible translated by William Tyndale was found in the possession of Amias Paulet during his time at the bar in London. Wolsey forbade him to leave London for several years.

By the time Sir Amias died in April 1538, his son and heir, Sir Hugh had already served as Sheriff of Somerset and Devon. Two years later, Sir Hugh was one of the Knights appointed to bring over Anne of Cleeves for the disastrous marriage to Henry VIII in 1540. Throughout his life, his eldest son, another Amias was a strongly principled Puritan. He went on to serve for three years as Ambassador in Paris, a position he was never comfortable with. He wrote, *"I am Jack-out-of office and I thank God for it"*.[280] But his most famous appointment was as keeper of Mary Queen of Scots. She protested to Queen Elizabeth that Sir Amias was biased against her as a result of his time in France. Elizabeth was unrelenting. It was Sir Amias who came to Mary at her final prison at Fotheringay to inform Mary that she was to stand trial and against Sir Amias it was that Elizabeth directed her anger for carrying out her wishes.

The 2nd son of Sir Amias, Sir Anthony succeeded him in 1590 as heir. He was not in good health, dying ten years later at 38. His eldest son John, born in 1586 in Jersey, returned to Somerset to take up a position in society and won a Parliamentary seat in the year 1610. This was the family that Elizabeth Kenn was to marry into.

Problems were to follow the marriage. James 1 had never trusted the Puritans and suspicion fell on this staunchly Puritan family early in 1615 when the Rector of Hinton, Edmund Peacham, was charged with treason. Regaining favour after a few years, John Poulett and Elizabeth went on to receive the new King, Charles 1 on his accession in 1625 en route to review the fleet at Plymouth. Elizabeth played hostess later that year to the Duke de Montmorency, a French Huguenot leader. John Poulett was created 1st Baron Poulett in 1627. As Lord Poulett, he remained loyal to the King and attended the Council of Peers at York which Charles called in September 1640.

The curious aspect to this story is how the Poulett family, staunch supporters of the Reformation, ended up as staunch supporters of the Crown rather than Parliament. At any rate, land on the Moor was to remain with the Pouletts until 1815 when there was a massive land sale. One of the daughters of the first Lord Poulett marries Thomas Smythe and when he passes away, she catches the eye of Thomas Piggott, who had purchased nearby Brockley Hall. It was the start of a marital association between Pouletts, Smythes and Piggots. Clearly, both short and long-term fortunes of the Pouletts were extended by when John Poulett married Elizabeth Kenn.[281]

Elizabeth Kenn, who married John Poulett in 1614

Tsunami

In January 1606, the fourth year of the new reign, the coast around Kingston Seymour witnessed a tsunami. The devastation is recorded in the parish church:

"An inundation of the sea water by overflowing and breaking down the Sea banks; happened in this Parish of Kingstone-Seamore, and many others adjoining; by reason whereof many Persons were drown'd and much Cattle

and Goods, were lost: the water in the Church was five feet high and the greatest part lay on the ground about ten days. WILLIAM BOWER"

William Bower was probably the Curate. The devastating flood disaster he recorded killed 2,000 people along the Bristol Channel coastline.[282] Whether the disaster was caused by a combination of freak high tides and hurricane-force winds or a rare tsunami similar to the one that devastated Asia in December 2004 is a matter of debate. *"An Atlantic tsunami created our greatest environmental disaster, and it could happen again,"* claimed a Professor of Astronomy at Cambridge University.[283]

Local records describe the event and its aftermath. An area was affected from Barnstaple in north Devon, up the Bristol Channel and the Severn Estuary to Gloucester, then along the South Wales coast around to Cardigan; some 570 km of coastline. A ten metre high wave moved up the Bristol Channel at speeds of up to 100mph, giving no warning to people caught in its path. According to historical accounts, sea water rushed inland and inundated some 200 square miles of land across Somerset and South Wales. The sea water at Burnham went inland as far as Glastonbury, making it the largest and most destructive flood in British history.

But was a storm was really to blame? On December 13, 1981 the biggest storm in the West Country in living memory occurred. Low pressure in the Atlantic forced sea water up the Bristol Channel, and combined with high tides and snow melt to bring crashing waves over the sea wall at Burnham and Weston. It was a heavy storm, but does not match up to the force of the 1606 flood which clearly is no ordinary storm.

The idea that the flood was due to a tsunami was first put forward by Haslett and Bryant in a paper published in 2002 in the journal *Archaeology in the Severn Estuary*. Haslett and Bryant argued that the flood was caused by a tsunami because:

1. Some historical accounts indicate that the weather was fine e.g. *"for about nine of the morning, the same being most fayrely and brightly spred, many of the inhabitants of these countreys prepared themselves to their affayres."*

2. The sea appears to have been "driven back" i.e. retreated out to sea, before the wave struck.

3. The wave seemed as *"mighty hilles of water tombling over one another in such sort as if the greatest mountains in the world had*

overwhelmed the lowe villages or marshy grounds. Sometimes it dazzled many of the spectators that they imagined it had bin some fogge or mist coming with great swiftness towards them and with such a smoke as if mountains were all on fire, and to the view of some it seemed as if myriads of thousands of arrows had been shot forth all at one time." This is very similar to descriptions of more recent tsunami, such as the tsunami after the eruption of Krakatau in 1883, where accounts refer to the sea as being 'hilly'. 'Dazzling, fiery mountains, and myriads of arrows', is reminiscent of tsunami on the Burin Peninsula (Newfoundland) in 1929, where the wave crest was said to shine like car headlights or Papua New Guinea in 1998 where a wave was frothing and sparkling.

4. The speed of the wave appears to have been faster than a storm flood as the wave is *'affirmed to have runne …. with a swiftness so incredible, as that no gray-hounde could have escaped by running before them'*.

In the summer of 2004, Haslett and Bryant embarked on field work in the area to record any physical impacts of the proposed tsunami that might still be left in the landscape. They estimated that, when it struck, the wave increased in height to 5.5m (18ft) along the Somerset coast, at about 14.5 m/sec (32mph). On the flat coastal areas the tsunami was able to penetrate a considerable distance inland. The maximum inland penetration possible was estimated at just under 4 km (2.5 miles). A possible cause of the proposed tsunami is not yet known, but the possibilities include a landslide off the continental shelf between Ireland and Cornwall, or an earthquake along an active fault system in the sea south of Ireland. This fault system has experienced an earthquake greater than magnitude four on the Richter scale within the last 20 years so the chance of a bigger tsunami earthquake is a possibility.

At any rate, the surge overwhelmed the stone and lime sea defences at Kingston Seymour. It moved remorselessly across the low-lying land, much of which lay at sea level or under. How many *"Persons were drown'd"* Bower does not tell us. The impact on a village of some three hundred people must have been devastating. Some 4,000 acres in Kingston and Kenn Moor district were flooded.

Algerian Pirates

Tsunami was not the only external events to arise from the sea and menace the inhabitants of Kingston Seymour.

"The most cruel trespassers to these shores were the infidels, an Algerian pirate crew, who landed here in 1636 to carry off some parishioners of Kingston Seymour into slavery"[284]

One can imagine the astonishment, terror, and despair of these country folk, whose world was bounded by the parish in which they lived, finding themselves confronted and seized by outlandish strangers. No record tells us whether the men were taken to row in the galley, or the women to serve in the harem. An England without newspapers hardly learnt of an incident which happened within twelve miles of its second largest city.

This story was corroborated independently by a very elderly local resident who had it passed down in his family. North African pirate raids were not new. There are reports of similar incidents in Devon in the 1520s, associated with the expansion of Turkish power. They are not far-fetched. Bristol merchants had begun to trade with North Africa from the 2nd half of the 15th century. A regular English traffic along the Barbary Coast of Morocco was emerging by 1151. By the mid 1620's, the value of Bristol's trade had grown significantly during the past 50 years. Markets in North Africa had continued to grown considerably. Sugar, molasses, fruit, gum arabic, saltpetre, ostrich feathers could be found along the Barbary coast. Even gold could be obtained there. In return, this was a natural market for English cloth, lead and tin, timber and items re-exported from the continent.[285]

But worse trouble lay ahead than pirates Civil War was barely five years away.

A House Divided

Generally, Somerset was loyal to the crown during the Civil War. Though North Somerset escaped most of the fighting, it could not escape the consequences. Heir to the local estates of Kenn and Court de Wyck, Lord Poulett raised men and money for the King's cause. In the swing of war, Royalist armies captured nearby Bristol in July 1643. A weekly contribution of £1,500 was imposed upon Somerset after its fall.

By 1645, the miseries of the war seemed endless. *"For month after weary month the armies fought and foraged, pillaged and plundered, reducing a fruitful countryside to ruin and desolation."*[286] Organised neutralism in the form of 'clubmen' began to spread, a peace-keeping association intended to keep the foraging armies away to *'preserve ourselves from plunder and all other unlawful violence'*. In the face of marauding soldiers of either side, church bells sounded the warning. Men armed with pikes set themselves between cavalry and roundhead, encouraging them to drink together rather than fighting. As one banner of the clubmen proclaimed *"if you offer to plunder or take our cattle, be assured we will bid you battle."*[287]

The flame spread throughout Somerset. Villagers of the entire area around nearby Brent Knoll set upon Royalist soldiers who ransacked the district on Good Friday 4th April 1645. Sympathies in North Somerset gradually leaned towards Parliament. The yeomen farmers realised which way the tide was turning and had more to gain from a Parliamentary victory. However, most of the clubmen were genuinely neutral though ready to take action against plunderers of either side.

By July 1645, Prince Rupert, bottled up at Bristol, was desperate for new troops coming from Wales. Parliamentary ships operating from nearby Steepholm and Flatholm blockaded the Bristol Channel. Ships carrying Welsh and Irish troops slipped through and attempted to land at nearby Portishead. The clubmen were there to stop them. Prince Rupert had a hostile population on his hands. Villagers from the local area, including no doubt the Moor rose up against soldiers under the royalist Sir Thomas Aston when they came to plunder. Prince Rupert attempted to march through nearby Wraxall but the clubmen blocked his path. A Royalist Squire tried to whip up the crowd in a nearby village by trumpeting roundhead contempt of the Prayer Book. A man from that village dismissed it out of hand. The Squire had lied like a knave, he said.[288] Yatton did not seem to see the tramp of armies. Its inhabitants would have fought in the different armies, contributed to the raising of regiments and almost certainly to the protest of Clubmen against soldiers.

In the wake of Cromwell's victory over the King at Naseby, Speaker Lenthall of the victorious Parliament authorised a Circular in September 1645 calling on county committees to take action. There was now a new reality. Presbyteries of ministers and lay elders must be formed. Royalist clergy were disbanded. Those who used the Book of Common Prayer were proscribed. A fifth of Somerset clergy had to go.[289]

The Vicar of Yatton, Stephen Berrier, survived the war, the 1650's commonwealth in Cromwell's time and the first years of the Restoration monarchy despite being temporarily ejected. That implies he was a strong Royalist sympathiser. Berrier managed to support himself. The Commonwealth Parliament dissolved Deanery Chapters, Canons and Prebends, associated with Cathedrals. A Glebe Terrier in 1650 listed the holding of land for the Vicar of Yatton for his support following these measures. Ten acres was available for hime to farm or farm out.[290]

The old views of the Commonwealth under Cromwell as a time of bigoted repression cannot now be sustained. *"Not all Puritan were graceless adherents of a negative, ant-life morality, rejoicing in the destruction of cathedrals and works of art."*[291]

It was often men of property such as the yeomen farmers, who were opposed to popular amusements, to fairs and ales. When in 1649, Somerset Justices of the Peace prohibited revels and wakes because of mutinies and contentions, there was nothing new under the sun. There were no books published advocating Sunday sports or in defence of rural revelry.[292] Maypoles and Morris dancing were out in Yatton; so was Christmas. Some Puritans did smash stained glass and deface statues and ornaments but they were a small island in a sea of apathy. What seems clear, however, is that this is when there was damage to the Parish Church in Yatton. To go there today is to realise that violence has taken place. Statues of the Newtons were vandalised. Richard and Emmota's chest tomb has been moved from its original location. Some of the heads on one side have not been vandalised, whereas heads on the other three sides suffered damage in the era of the Puritans. The 1650's were a violent time for many churches. We can imagine the disturbance- the entrance perhaps of soldiers or iconoclastic local inhabitants spurred on by the new regime. Radicals of the Civil War...who were they? The mood did not last long.

The Cromwell regime in the 1650's was a stage that the nation passed through on the way to the restoration of Charles 11nd. It was a conservative reaction. Justices of the Peace had already made a come-back as local authorities. Yeomen farmers and lower classes began to feel the impact of high taxation to pay for the wars and a large standing army. The upper echelons of society began to unite. Old enmities were forgotten. Suspicions lingered. Lord Poulett, who had played a key role in the Royalist armies, was temporarily imprisoned at Taunton in April 1658, then released.

Then came the Restoration of the monarchy and of Christmas. The iconoclasts of Yatton had had their day. Two years after the events of 1660 came a further ejection. The Vicar of Yatton, Stephen Berrier, was clearly no Puritan or he would have gone in 1662 when so many clergy who could not support the restored Church and State were removed and subsequently persecuted. He has managed to chart a course along the middle of the road to stay out of trouble. He will oversee the use of the 1662 Prayer Book that represented Anglicanism in its final form for a long time.

A Tax on Chimneys

There are descendants of the Kingcott family alive and well in Somerset today and in many parts of the English-speaking world. The Kingcott family lived at Chestnut Farm in Yatton continually for three hundred years, from the year 1640 to 1940.

The Kingcotts owned the land they farmed. In social status, they were on a par with business merchants, country squires and many clergy. The Kingcotts kept out of the civil war. Many yeoman farmers obtained furnishings from Royalist homes that were ruined during the conflict. Rugs, desks, mirrors, silver and chairs were there for the taking. Yeoman farmers such as the Kingcotts were literate and built small libraries.

There were other branches of the family. Before income tax, the Government came up with ingenious means of raising revenue. In the Georgian age came a tax on windows. Before that, between 1662 and 1690, the Restoration monarchy taxed hearths, or stoves from the occupier, not the landlord. It was collected in two instalments, Lady Day and Michaelmas. From 1664, all those who had two chimneys were required to pay two shillings per chimney. If stopped up chimneys were discovered, the tax was doubled. In the Somerset Hearth tax returns of 1664-5[293], a sonorous note records that John Plenty had to pay extra because *"he hath stopt up two"*. Hearth tax returns indicate the size of houses. In all, 103 people paid hearth tax that year in Yatton. Some were then exempted *"by reason of his povertie."*

The tax was a source of nearly £30 revenue. "The Hearth tax for Somerset 1664-65" mentions a John Kencott. He was poor and did not have to pay tax. A Mr Crabb of Bristol was the owner of the property in which John Kencott lived. The same record of Hearth tax mentions a Joanne Kennycott, presumably a distant relation. Joanne was slightly better off. She was obliged to pay two units of Hearth tax to the tune of two shillings and also four shillings.

Life went on in the village communities. As well as Hearth Tax, the Poor Rate was a regular feature of the outgoings of parish and people such as the Kingscotts. In 1685, when Charles IInd died and James IInd became King, it was levied at 1s 6d in the pound. A John Galton was churchwarden then. Along with 40 sheep, John Galton left other disbursements for the poor.[294] Sometimes the parishes were in conflict with each other over the Poor Rate. A law suit took place between the assessors of Yatton and the parish of Kingston Seymour because the assessors had taxed certain lands. Its occupiers refused to pay. The incident was important enough to be referred to in the back of Kingston Seymour Parish Church to this day.[295]

In the local courts in 1655, the larceny of sheep in Wemberham area of Yatton came to attention. That this was held in the Quarter Sessions of the Ecclesiastical Court shows how much the church was still involved in every aspect of local life.[296] The economy of the people of the Moor is highlighted by Ecclesiastical Court Records in the 1680's. Cows, sheep, apples and eggs were vital. John Davis owned eight cows and 40 sheep. The cows gave him a thousand quarts of milk (at 1d a quart) and the sheep provided some 40 lambs (each worth three shillings and six pence) as well as about 100 Ilbs of wool (at about ten pence per pound). Eight calves yearly brought were worth ten shillings each. Along with his apples (two shillings each for the 100 bushels) and 500 eggs (at four pence per score), John Davis' personal economy amounted to about £26 of income. He did complain that his cattle were both unprofitable and barren.[297]

In 1635, only half parishioners signing the Church inventory, the Terrier, were able to write. By end of the century, all could. At least some education was taking place..

The tone of the age was moral seriousness. In a time when Prayer Book re-iterated and reminded people of the perils of sin, sin as a crime against God and the community was a real force in human life as strong as any of the physical forces that were being charted by Isaac Newton. In 1672, local Magistrates brought an action against John Syms of Yatton, 'charged to be the father of a bastard child begotten on the body of Ann Goodenoth.'[298] An order was made for his arrest by Edward Gorges, one of the Justices of the Peace. Thomas Terry, the local constable apprehended John Syms, who spent the night in the village lock-up. Someone helped Syms to escape rather than face Magistrates, probably the village constable himself, who was, after all, only a volunteer. There was no dedicated police force in those days.

In the religious convulsion of the period, new ideas and movements arose, all in the name of the coming millennium. The monopoly of the State Church was eroding.

The Quakers of Claverham

In the year 1673, land was given in the village of Claverham for the "people called Quakers". The donor was Robert Dawson in Yatton. His will stipulated that a small *"plot or parcel of ground"* was to be given *"as a burial place for the said people called Quakers in those parts and for others, who, being separated from the world's worship shall desire here to be buried."* The will recognised that those who are *"reproachfully called Quakers....refused those idolised publique burying places commonly called (though falsely) consecrated or holy ground."*[299]

It was not just a burial ground. Robert Dawson's will went on to stipulate that *"on the said ground may be built a house for the said people called Quakers to meet together to the Lord their God."* The parcel of land was to be theirs for 2000 years.[300]

The Friends named in the Deed provide a social commentary on early Quakerism in Somerset. Of the ten Friends mentioned as Trustees, three are said to be yeoman farmers. Yeoman farmers feature amongst the early members of the Meeting House as does a John Galton of Yatton, a clothier.

How did there come to be Quakers in Claverham? The movement began with the remarkable mystic and leader George Fox in the 1650's. There is no record that George Fox ever came to Claverham or to visit its new Meeting House. The spark came from those who heard travelling preachers at fairs or large outdoor gatherings.

As one of the largest cities of England, Bristol was a local base for the Quakers as it was to be for the Methodists 90 years later. In 1654, only 2 years after George Fox began the movement, John Audland and John Camm were two of George Fox's Valiant Sixty who came to Somerset after taking meetings in Bristol. A couple, John and Mary Whiting, opened their home to them. That led to their holding meetings for Friends to gather and wait on the inward light. The reputation of Quakers in Bristol suffered when James Naylor, another of the Valiant Sixty, allowed himself to be manipulated into thinking he was Messianic. At his death in 1660, he uttered words that sum up a better spirit, a spirit that was to inspire those early Friends.

"*There is a Spirit which I feel, that delights to do no Evil, nor to revenge any Wrong but delights to endure all things, in hope to enjoy its own in the End. Its hope is to outlive all Wrath and Contention, and to weary out all Exaltation and Cruelty....As it bears no Evil in itself, so it conceives none in Thoughts to another. If it is betrayed it bears it; for its ground and spring is the mercies and forgiveness of God.*"[301]

The Quakers of Claverham would need to drink deeply of such a spirit in all they were about to face. In the 1660's, local Friends began to think of having a Meeting House. Their vision was for a place to meet with an adjoining burial ground and some accommodation for a poor widow or a couple to act as caretakers.

Under the impact of the Clarendon Code that sought to curtail unofficial meetings, persecution was intense. Initially, the Quarterly Meetings that were a feature on the Quaker landscape had to be held at Illchester in south Somerset. This enabled Friends who were in prison to attend. Among them was a Quaker from Yatton by the name of George Harris. Imprisoned at Illchester prison in 1662, his name occurs on the prison list as giving 10 shillings "*towards the supply of such of our fellow prisoners who have not sufficiency of those outward things to afford necessities.*"[302] Conditions were harsh. Prisoners had to arrange their own upkeep. No food brought and you starved! It was a generous act by this Yatton Quaker, himself a prisoner.

The memoirs of John Whiting, son of John and Mary of Nailsea who had first opened their home to the travelling preachers, reveal constant harassment by the authorities. These were dissenters who objected to paying tithes for '*mayntaning of steeple houses*". A Charles Marshall was praying in Claverham meeting house when the authorities disturbed the meeting. Pulled between the gallery rails, he was seriously injured as a result. In 1681, John Whiting records a raid by three Justices of the Peace - Sir John Smith, John Piggot and Edward George. The first two names were to become inextricably linked in the later history of North Somerset. They commanded the Friends meeting there in silence to depart. The Quakers refused. The Constable was ordered to throw them out and keep them out. But the Quakers were ordered to pay fines - "warrants for distress" as they were called. They were forced to sell valuable cows which represented their livelihood. Two cows worth 6 pounds ten shillings were sold to Justice Piggot for 5 pounds. According to the 19th historian John Rutter, writing in 1829, this Quaker meeting place was one of many in the district visited regularly by William Penn, the coloniser of Pennsylvania.[303]

The Society of Friends greatly influenced Claverham. It became known as a 'dry village', a village without a pub. It was a different story in Yatton where there was an Inn, the Prince of Orange. Earl Poulett owned the inn until selling it on in 1813. The so called 'Ale House Recognisance' stipulates that the lessee may not allow card games, draughts, dice or bagatelle. Bull, bear, badger baiting is out along with cock fighting. No drinking or tipling is allowed during the hours of divine service on Sunday.[304] Built in the mid-17th century, it would have been strange for the Inn to be named after a Prince of Orange who arrived on the scene some 50 years later. There was an earlier Prince of Orange, a William who married the daughter of Charles 1 in 1641 who fits the bill. Nevertheless, there was a Prince of Orange who was to come towards the end of the century and further change England.

Finally, the years of persecution were over for the Quakers. The 1689 Toleration Act allowed dissenters to meet for worship provided they had a certificate for their meeting place. The Quarter Sessions at Michaelmas that year saw 51 licences being issued in Somerset. Claverham was amongst them.[305]

By then, the events of 1685-8 had taken place. Was it really a Glorious Revolution, the civilised, non-violent new start that laid the foundations of our national liberties? This was the view taken by Lord Macaulay in his 19th century 'History of Britain." But according to Steve Pincus, Professor of History at Yale,[306] revolutions do not occur when rulers prove themselves to be numbling and inffective at responding to changed circumstances. They occur when modernising programmes begin that trigger instability and upheaval. Far from being a misguided reactionary, James IInd set out to create a modern, rational Catholic State. It was a short-lived experiment. James quadrupled the size of the army. Inns such as the Prince of Orange in Yatton were required to quarter troops or lose their trading licence. He attempted to use the new Post Office as a tool of political surveillance and packed Parliament with his supporters. It did not succeed. Trying to suppress Protestantism, not just the radicals such as the Quakers of Claverham, but the Anglican opposition who constituted the overwhelming majority in England, was not practical politics.

England was not Catholic. In 1686, the Yatton Vestry paid out 6 shillings to church bellringers for ringing the 5th November. Memory of the Gunpowder plot had by that time become hugely iconic as an anti-Catholic symbol.

The events of 1685-8 produced a reaction that amounted to revolution, a competing view of how the State should be organised. So it was that another Dutch Prince, led a revolution that was just as radical as what happened in France or Russia later on. It changed Anglicanism from a persecuting force to a tolerant polity that recognised there were different roads to faith. The Quakers of Claverham were free at last.

There was another result of the transformation of 1688-9, reaction though it was. It helped move England in the 18th century from a largely agrarian society to a manufacturing one. The village communities of the Moor will no longer represent the pattern of life for the majority of English people. A new reality was on the way.

Chapter Twelve

THE BITE OF A MAD DOG

During the next hundred and twenty years or so, at a life span of forty years or so, three generations will rise up, play their part and then fade from remembrance. Many of the acts of the 53rd to the 56th generations of the people of the Moor since the Romans came are recorded in the parish records. It would be helpful if we had access to their thoughts and emotions. All we have though, even in the detailed parish records of Kingston Seymour, are references to some of those who lived and died. These would not have left their names to posterity were it not for an Oversight task fulfilled, a job paid for, a sickness or smallpox attended to or a punishment when the parish required correction for a miscreant.

The year 1703 saw a great storm throughout England. Today people remember the near hurricane of 1987. But the 1703 storm seems to have been on a greater scale. There are reports of whole trees being uprooted and flying through the air in Scotland, devastation throughout the country and seventeen Royal Navy ships wrecked. The Western tower of Llandaff collapsed and a chimney stack fell on the Bishop of Bath and Wells in their palace. Bishop Kidder and his wife were both killed. The storm was recorded in the Kingston Seymour parish records.

"November ye 27th [1703] ensuing ye inhabitants sustained great loss of Cattle Sheep and Corn with many mows both of corn and Hay; the violent tempest breaking down, the Sea-Banks let in the Salt-Water."[307]

1714 witnessed the changeover of dynasties. The event did not go unnoticed in the village community of Kingston Seymour. The churchwardens paid to mark the occasion. *"Spent ye Kings Coronacon day- £10"*. This was a great deal of money in those days. As Head of State, the new King had to be honoured.

1719 – "Pd and spent on King George's birthday   5 shillings".

Twice as much was spent on Mayday that year, another major celebration complete with maypole and fair. The new King was King George 1 who did not prove popular in the country, despite the celebrations on the Moor. People did not know what to make of this Prince of Hanover who did not speak English. There is no record of his ever visiting the area. Nevertheless, this was an occasion to be marked. We can imagine bunting, dancing on the village green and liquor for a street party or two.

Amidst the Deism of the times and general weariness about wars of religion, it was less likely now that you would be hauled up for witchcraft or heresy. Nevertheless, many aspects of church life constituted examples of moral offences, beliefs, conduct, private relationships or non-payment of tithes that came before the law.

In 1731, one Richard Read is accused of 'laying violent hands' on a Margaret Yeels, who was visiting church that day. As the Vicar was in the pulpit, he pulled Margaret out of the pew, injuring her. Twelve years later in 1743, one Thomas Norris was being hauled up before the Church Prebendal court in Wells to face charges related *"to his soul's health and the Reformation of his manners and more especially concerning his irreverent and indecent behaviour to the Rev Robert Creyghton, Vicar of Yatton."* Norris had been interrupting the Vicar whilst performing his ministerial functions, for *'contemptously treating the sd Robert Creyghton and his ministerial ffunction and for quarrelling or brawling in the Church".*[308] All be warned!

Then in 1749, an order of Penance is being recorded in the Bath and Wells Diocesan Records, for Ann Paydon of Yatton. She has been *"living incontinently with Roger Heale of Yatton and having been by him begotten with child and by her voluntarily confessed."* What she had to do to put matters right publicly was to stand in a white covering in front of the pulpit for the whole service. The Vicar, still Robert Creyghton, was to preach a sermon against fornication and adultery. At the end of the service, she had to say, *"I am right heartily sorry for the same and faithfully promise never from henceforth to offend in the like again".*[309]

Moral seriousness was not a Victorian invention.

Life in an 18th Century Community

The glimpse that the village communities on the Moor reveal of the 18th century is both rich and partial; partial because there are few windows on what is going on nationally, rich because the internal life of the communities is clearly brought out. These are not large communities. The Bishops Register for 1699 shows that in Yatton there were 12 Baptisms, three marriages and 23 burials. Throughout the first half of the 18th century, baptisms run at about 25-30 per year.

The churchwarden accounts for Yatton hold a distant mirror up to the late medieval period and the tumultuous changes of the 16th century when all the old certainties collapsed. Those for the parish of Kingston Seymour hold an equally fascinating mirror up to life in the 18th century. High quality information comes to us from 1705.

The documents reveal a community generally at ease with itself, with little crime or outside pressure to disturb it. Civil War is the repository of the memory of a few grandfathers. No armies are rampaging nearby. Villagers are free to get on with their own lives. The enemies are different now. Poverty and disease get the attention of the community. Following the great flood, villagers have to maintain a part of the sea wall assigned for upkeep.

In Kingston Seymour, the demands of the State carried financial implications that must have seemed a continuous burden.

1716 – "Pd for expenses of assessing the King's tax   2 shillings and 6 pence"

A source of State income in the 18th century was land tax. In 1755 it was four shillings in the pound. John Pigott Esq, local landowner, had to pay £5-18 for Ham Farm in Kingston Seymour. In 1782, there are new occupiers. The tax is still £5-18. Clearly inflation has not had much effect in those intervening 27 years. Then there was window tax. This was publicised in a curious way in Kingston Seymour in 1726.

"Pd for singing ye window's tax rate   1 shilling."

In addition to forms of taxation imposed by the national Government – that did not yet include income tax - there were local rates to pay for the poor, for the roads and parish expenses. Then there was the local militia, the home guard of its day.

1715 – "settling the list for the militia   6 shillings and 6 pence.

There were expenses towards the upkeep of the Parish Church at the heart of the village. In 1722, three sacks of lime were required to whiten the church. Presumably, it had not been done since the 1650's when the puritan influence tried to promote simplicity rather than the riot of colour that had characterised churches for centuries. But it needs maintaining. John Noble is paid £1 that year for carrying out the work.

The Book of Common Prayer was the staple diet of the churches.

1734 –"Pd for a Common prayer book   14 shillings.

Bells were rung on 5th November; less about fireworks than an anti-Catholic protest. Anglican devotion is real and meaningful and far from plain. In 1754, the parish pays out the enormous sum of £30 for *"beautifying ye church."*

Illness was another enemy.

1710 – Pd William Godwin for curing someone's leg   7-5"
1710 – "Pd Doctor Bonyman for several cures on the poor people"

There is very little by way of medical expertise available in the village. The services of a surgeon are referred to in the parish record. There was also a midwife. In severe cases, the poor were sometimes helped in a hospital, possibly at Bristol.

1724 – "Pd for 2 yrs for ye hospital   16 shillings"
1767 – "Pd for phisick and medicine for Sarah Roper   1 shillings 9 pence."

'The itch,' or scabies, was a problem that comes up a few times in both Kingston Seymour warden books and those of Yatton parish. In 1770, Hannah Walker had three girdles paid for out of parish rates to help cope with it.

But it was the spectre of smallpox that haunted the villagers.

1756 – "Wm Nobles' family in ye smallpox- 10 shillings.
1759 – "Tending James Hakins in the smallpox and many
*   other necessities   18 shillings – 9pence ha'penny"*
1779 – "Pd for curing Tho and Mary Wiles in the smallpox   6 shillings."

The village communities boast a Court House. In Kingston Seymour, the house was the official residence of the Steward of the Manor. The Steward- a man of considerable status - was expected to have a residence in a prime location. In 1725, Court House had 71 acres attached to it. In 1777, a Samuel Filer from Backwell bought the property at the same time as the sum of £106 was raised 'on the sale of Right of Advowsan in every third turn.' Clearly, the presentation of the Rector every three occasions was important financially! This is an enormous amount.

The economy was much less dependent on the old Manor as a unit of production. Nevetheless, Manor courts still took place two or three times a year. Every ranking member of the village was supposed to attend. You could get a fine if you didn't - rather like a parking ticket in contemporary society. The Court Roll for 1682 cites *"Roger Jennings Esq, a freeholder of this Manor, for not appearing here this day to do his duty for which we avorne (fine) him eight shillings".*[310]

This was not much of a deterrent; the same names often appear as non-attenders in the court records of Kingston Seymour. The powers of the Manorial Court were limited. One main concern was the need to maintain local bridges. In 1784, the Court orders a Mr Cox to replace a bridge. In 1785, he is again ordered to replace the bridge. Mr Cox clearly realises that its powers of enforcement were limited.

But something is changing. In 1788, the local Court requires that land forming part of the Common pound should be repaired by the lord of the Manor of Kingston Seymour. If he does not, he faces a twenty shilling fine. The lord of the Manor is no longer dispensing justice in the name of the King. He is now himself subject to the law. This item reveals something else. In the year 1810, the Parish pound again needs to be repaired on pain of a £5 penalty. Maybe this is the effect of inflation during the Napoleonic war or it reflects growing irritation with the lord of the Manor.

Education was never systematic in those days. But some attempt is being made to educate the children of the rural poor.

1754 – "for schooling of ye poor children   £2 – 13 shillings- 6 pence"

In 1764, a Mr Andrews is paid for teaching the poor children. Later Warden accounts refer to a Sunday school in the village.

Being nearby the sea, Kingston Seymour had to deal sometimes with drowning. Reports in 1779 reveal a local tragedy. 6 shillings had to be paid *"for taking up the child at sea".* The mother is paid 1 shilling for drink to bury her child. A coffin cost 5 shillings but a man was also re-imbursed in food and drink for burying the boy."

Justice was severe.

1751 – "Pd for stocks and whipping post   1 shilling"
1786 "for 3 days journey going to Taunton   15 shillings"

To go outside the village, people had to allow a long time just to get to a destination. Including the business to be done there (no doubt connected with Crown Court Sessions), a round trip to Taunton of just under 40 miles takes three days. Transport could also be dangerous. Folk memory is that of Highwaymen lying in wait in Brockley Combe, on the Bristol Road.[311]

In 1760, George 111rd comes to the throne. His coronation day is marked locally. It will cost £1- 2 shillings, nothing like the scale of the outlay for George 1st forty six years before. In 1763, prayer was made for *"ye young Prince,"* the future George IV. The Hanoverians are well established.

Awareness of wider events varied. When in 1749 the War of the Austrian succession was over, on April 25th that year the parish spent £1-8 shillings and 4 pence" on *"ye thanksgiving for ye Peace".* For the most part, war, even the Seven Years War, receives little attention in the parish records. A generation later, you would hardly know that the French revolutionary wars were taking place except for references from 1793 to military service. The parish is required to raise men for the Royal Navy and for the local militia for home defence. In 1798, the ringers are paid 10 shillings and 6 pence for bells to mark *"when Admiral Nelson gain'd victory over the French."* News of the battle of the Nile was evidently received with huge joy in Kingston Seymour. Horatio Nelson is now a celebrity Admiral.

But the most intriguing reference in the churchwarden's records concerns a remedy for the bite of a mad dog. One wonders how many rabid animals were encountered.

"To cure ye bite of a mad dog.
Take of rue pluk't from aye stalk   - 6oz
Of garlic a little bruised   - a ¼ lb
Of Venice or common treacle   - a ¼ lb
Boil all these in two quarts of ale, till its shrunk.
To a man or woman give a spoonful evening and morning for seven mornings.
To a boy or girl, six. To an infant, three. To other eventures, three spoonfuls a morning."

A similar cure in 1735 in the Bath Journal spoke of a cure that a sailor, George Cobb, had seen in the East Indies result in a cure even though signs of madness had already appeared. Instructions were clear enough-*"repeat ye the same 20 days!"*

The Spirit of Philanthropy

What to do about the poor had been a problem for generations. It really did seem as if the poor were always with us. The Elizabethan Poor Law had been an attempt to solve the problem in 1603. But in the absence of any cushion to support those not in regular work, the issue would keep returning.

In 1705, a parish worker, James Plumer, can expect to be paid one pound and five shillings. By century's end, the schoolmaster receives that for one quarter's work and the equivalent amount for a labourer is £2-10 shillings. How much is this worth today? Estimates of inflation over such a period are at best approximate but to give an idea it is necessary to add three noughts to multiply by 100.[312] The labourer's wages are about £250 for a quarter, £1000 per year- all that to bring up a family on!

In Kingston Seymour in 1705, the Parish pays *"Abraham Williams for his necessity"* three shillings and three pence. That year, John Tippett the overseer of the poor rate has to travel to Gloucester to prove that a marriage is genuine. It costs him two shillings and six pence. The parish has a Poor House. In 1705, it will cost 12 shillings to maintain. But relief is given for heating and footwear.

1711 – Pd for a loade of coale for the poore   *16 shillings.*
1724 – "for a pair of shoes for Wm Hurde   *2 shillings and 6 pence"*
1751 – "shoes and mending for ye Poor   *£1 - 3 shillings"*

Some families needed regular help. In 1726, a John Taylor is allowed a quart of ale each day. He does work for the parish sometimes. Thirteen years later, men need to be paid to restrain his son *"who went crazy one night."* The next year, he is being granted some cheese. In 1751, there are expenses for *"shaving Taylor (being crazy)"*. Things didn't improve. In 1769 the parish has to pay men for looking after John Taylor *"in his craziness"*. The children of the poor often needed financial support to begin apprenticeships.[313]

In the 18th century, people could not have got by without the generosity of those who were better off. Philanthropy was a notable feature of community life. People relied on it. Later, in 1819, a Commission under the chairmanship of Lord Brougham investigated the state of charitable provision in England and Wales. The relevant report for Yatton describes various charities that were set up in the 18th century expressly to help the poor. Two pieces of land were dedicated by Robert Davis, a yeoman farmer of Yatton, *'who gave to the poor inhabitants thereof receiving no relief'* the rents due. By Lord Brougham's day, these rents totalled 35 pounds.

There was a stern reminder in Brougham's Report of the moral seriousness with which poverty was regarded in the 19th century compared with an earlier period. Davis' provision was criticised as being distributed among the poor of the parish *"without a sufficient regard to character"*. This stemmed, Brougham's Commissioners said, *"from a mistaken belief that the poor had an equal right to the relief, whatever might be the cause of their poverty"*. The churchwardens of the day were told in no uncertain terms to adopt a more careful choice of the objects of relief, *"having regard to their manner of living and bringing up of their families"*. Only those who could safely be described as "the deserving poor" should be helped. In short, 18th century Poor relief was too generous![314] The poor were clearly responsible for their poverty.

The Yatton Vestry Minutes, in effect the Parish Council, date from May 9th 1787. Their first meeting records the parishioners adjourning to the Prince of Orange to form a committee for the relief of the poor of Yatton. The very first charitable act was to disburse twenty sacks of potatoes.

But still private charity was essential. A Notice in Kingston Church reads, *"Mr Edward Sess of this parish gave 20 shillings yearly on Twelfth-day to be paid out of his land lying in the parish for ever. Ten shillings for preaching a sermon and ye other ten shillings to be given to the 2nd poor having no relief- in bread."* An eye-witness remembers this still happening well into the 1940's, except the custom had settled on Evensong on Christmas Day. After the 3rd Collect, bread would be distributed. One old woman put the two loaves offered to her in a sack but did not stay for sermon![315]

This was not the only bequest to the poor. John Lane's charity in Kingston Seymour allowed for payment to a schoolmaster for teaching eight children. In Yatton church are plaques recording disbursements by Christopher Battiscombe, a gentleman, and also Sarah Plenty. The Plenty families and the Battiscombes loom large in accounts of 18th century life in Yatton; their names are enshrined around the walls. Both gave 40 pounds; the interest was to be given to the poor.

Those bequests were just part of acts of generosity by benefactors in the 18th century. Some help for the poor was to be given in the form of bread or bread vouchers, some for the education of children. Small grants are given to young people for books and other items for an education. The

Society of Friends placed great emphasis on education. In 1729, a local Quaker, Richard Durban, gives £5 is given for Claverham Meeting House. His legacy contains another gift.

"*I give and bequeath all the rest and residue of my Personal Estate, Goods and Chattels unto my friends....in trust and for the use hereinafter mentioned. My will is that my Friends in Trust before- mentioned do lay out my substance in free land forever, or to put it out to interest...to be bestowed on the Teaching of a school for poor children for ever, at the discretion of my Trustees, and after my Trustees decease to whom they should appoint in trust for the said school".*

The school was immediately established. Mary Maskell and Sarah Corse were appointed to teach *"a parcel of poor children"*. The first schoolmaster was Jonah Thompson. His salary is £20 per annum- £20,000 in today's money. This was long before the activity of Hannah and her sisters.

Hannah and Her Sisters

In the winter of 1773-4, Hannah More, a beautiful and cultured woman of 28 years of age first visited London in company with her two sisters. In the home of Sir Joshua Reynolds, the acclaimed portrait painter, she fulfilled a life-long ambition to meet Dr Samuel Johnson. The great Doctor was impressed. He told Sir Joshua's sister that Hannah was one of the rare people who, *'thought it a less evil to dissent from the opinion of a fellow-creature than to tell a falsity".*[316] When in April 1776, Dr Johnson visited what he called 'The Sisterhood' in Bristol, Hannah urged him to 'take a little wine'. His reply is, characteristically, a classic. *"I can't drink a little, child; therefore I never touch it. Abstinence is to me as easy as temperance would be difficult."*[317]

Johnson used to tease Hannah More about her strict religious views, which may have formed the basis of the dislike that his biographer, Boswell, had for her. Not a single mention was made of Hannah in his biography, despite the great man's visits and encouragement of her literary talents. For Hannah was at one and the same time, a poet, a playwright and an evangelical. She moved in literary circles that included not only Samuel Johnson but David Garrick, the greatest actor of his day. Hannah went on to become an activist in the cause that began to engage evangelicals and many other Christian groups at this time, the abolition of the slave trade. She corresponded with John Newton, boycotted West Indian sugar in her tea, was friendly with William Wilberforce and agitated against the many merchants from '*my savage city*'[318] of Bristol who made their fortunes from the triangular trade. This was the infamous route by which ships from Bristol sailed to West Africa, exchanged goods and trinkets for slaves and then loaded up with sugar and molasses for import. By now, Hannah was associating with members of the Clapham Sect, the group of prominent evangelicals who campaigned against social evils. Following a visit by Wilberforce in 1789 to the cottage she had built for herself at Cowslip Green in Somerset, she became concerned about the education of children in nearby Cheddar. The result was yet another cause this remarkable woman took up.

And that is how she enters the story of these communities. Hannah More began a series of schools in the Mendip area of North Somerset. Not only Cheddar but Shipham and Nailsea were the focus of schools to educate the rural poor. Then there were the so-called 'lesser schools,' Sunday schools and places for evening reading classes. By now the number of schools and pupils had increased and Hannah and her sister Patty found it challenging to bring effective supervision.

The school in Yatton had a good beginning. Church bells rang. Local gentry and clergy alike gave full support and local people volunteered to collect money to clothe the 130 children who were on the initial roll. Hannah More was pleased with the unusually civil manner in which she was received. "*The whole village seemed all gaiety and pleasure*". She even held Yatton up as an example when 40 guineas were given by local gentry and farmers so the poor could be clothed. One farmer brought seven sons to the Sunday school so they could learn to read the Bible. Not long after, he lost his wife in childbirth. Down the nave of Yatton parish church he went, leading his long family procession and carrying the infant in his arms. Hannah and her sisters evidently found it a strong encouragement that he had been spiritually sustained in this supreme trial. Despite this event, the school tailed off as teachers and numbers began to diminish. 'Aversion to religion materially increased,' wrote Hannah More. "Before it was hatred in disguise; now it was decidedly open." In 1800, Hannah was forced to close the Yatton school and transfer to Chew Magna, a 'populous, ignorant and wicked' village, which would benefit from Hannah's efforts. "*After struggling and toiling at Yatton for many years, we reluctantly quitted it.*"[319]

By our standards, the curriculum in Yatton school was limited. As Hannah More herself explained, "*the grand subject of instruction with me is* the Bible itself".³²⁰ She said that "*in teaching in our Sunday schools, the only books we use two little tracts called 'Questions for the Mendip Schools'....the Church catechism..... Spelling books, Psalters, Common Prayer - Book and Bible.*"³²¹ Yet the school needed to be closed.

What had gone wrong? The challenge of effective supervision no doubt played a part, but then no more than anywhere else presumably as the sisters were forced to spread themselves to meet the need. There was another reason, connected with Hannah's own statement about instruction based on the Bible. Hannah More was an evangelical with strong leanings towards Methodism. Methodism had, however, just gone its separate way from the Church of England. It has arrived in Yatton.

The Mendip Annals of Hannah and Martha More record an unusual sight at nearby Congresbury in 1798. A Mr Biddulph was preaching. Clearly he is no established Anglican clergy.³²² Farmer Baber and Mrs Avery of Yatton took all the children from Hannah More's school to hear him. She writes that this took place in the church at Congresbury. "*It was a great feast to hear such a preacher as Mr Biddulph*" records Hannah More. Trouble was brewing and it proved to be "*another scene for Satan.*"

"*The clergy, however, took great offence at it and summoned the farmer and Mrs Avery before them, to receive their public reprimand for daring to hear a Methodist. But the overpowering and apt texts of Scripture quoted upon them by the farmer and the calm and sensible replies of the mistress threw them into the greatest confusion and they were glad to put an end to the scandalous debate, threatening the mistress, however, with their vengeance.*"³²³

Hannah has brought in a Methodist minister, no doubt stimulated by her own evangelical sympathies to want to convert the children. Here is the likely source of source of friction with the Parish.

A Fork in the Road?

The 18th century was an age when steam power began to work machinery. But there were other, older sources of energy. The Domesday survey does not record any mills locally³²⁴ but by the 13th century, there were two mills powered by wind. Then came coal production, smelted as coke. Nationally, production of coal by 1780 was three times what it was in 1700. Seams at nearby Nailsea and small shafts around the Moor contributed to this though the main production was in the massive coalfields elsewhere in Britain.

The narrative of industrial revolution is not just the old farming v new manufacturing. As well as harnessing coal and steam to drive machines, there was a revolution in agriculture going on at the same time. New methods, new approaches to rotating crops and above all, fencing in common land has meant that yields are increasing far beyond the imagination of the peasant farmers with the strips of land they farmed. It was now no longer feasible for everyone to take their animals on to the Common. By Act of Parliament, Claverham Common is enclosed early on in 1750. 193 acres were divided up and allocated according to land rights anyone could demonstrate. New owners were required to plant hedges or dig ditches to mark the boundaries. A larger enclosure takes place around Kenn village in the year 1810. Much distress is caused though in the long-term, the enclosures result in far greater productivity. Folk memory is that of a land-grab; poor people driven from small holdings and deprived of their rights of common ground for their geese and their pigs.[325] Yet the arable land here and new pastures were mainly realised because of waste land being put to use.

These were not separate developments. The availability of both food and work fuelled population growth. Agricultural productivity began to rise, faster than in France which witnessed national convulsion in 1789 due, in part, to hungry crowds and failing harvests. It was as well that the land yielded more food; there were many more English mouths to feed. To that extent, rural economies such as on the Moor were very much part of the industrial age. The transport system was also improving in the last decade or two of the 18th century. Greater yields in the newly enclosed fields could be taken to hungry markets. These developments went hand in hand. They led to fast export-led growth based on manufacturing, the engine of wealth-creation as the railway age dawned.

It is in the latter half of the 18th century that the transformation of the English landscape begins. The ups and downs of a primarily rural economy represent a fork in the road. From about the 1780's, the Moor will diverge in its growth from other communities that up till now have been about the same size. The national scenery changes from a predominately agricultural economy to one based on manufacturing. Waltow Rostow, the American economist and adviser to President Johnson referred to a 'take off into sustained growth' in the UK around 1780.[326] The plane had been taxiing and revving up for a while. Now it will accelerate into the industrial age.

Chapter Thirteen

SOCIAL TRANSFORMATION ON WHEELS

THE MOOR IN 1841.

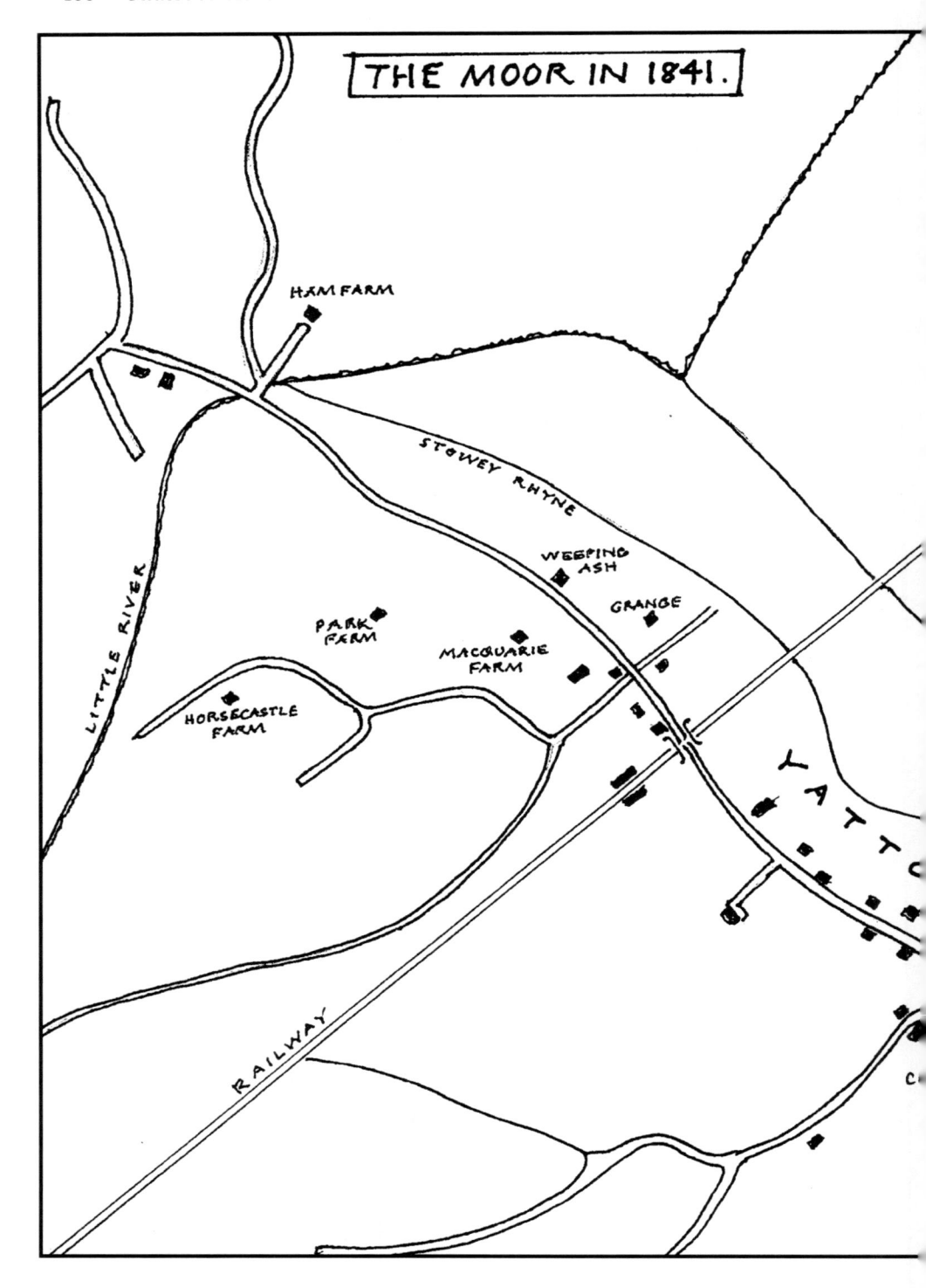

Let the Stones Talk 167

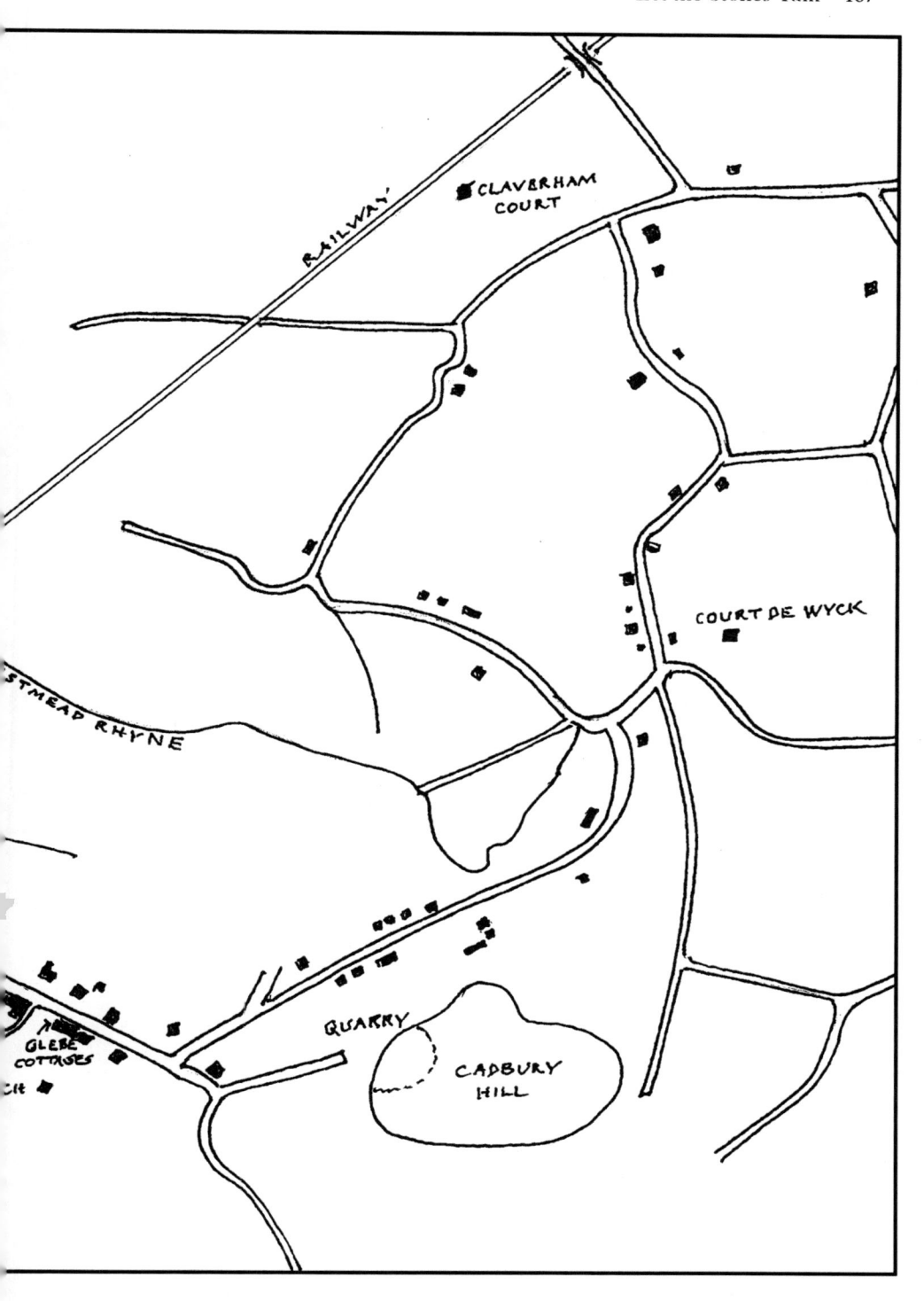

The spotlight falls on one particular generation, those living in 1840 to 1880. The 57th generation, the mid - Victorian, will see dramatic changes to its way of life, more so perhaps than any generation that had lived on the Moor before.

Queen Victoria has been on the throne for three years. In 1840, she marries Prince Albert of Saxe-Coburg. It was the year of the Penny Post; the year too when children could no longer be dispatched up dirty, claustrophobic shafts to sweep chimneys.

Nationally, the last two generations have witnessed a transformation in the conditions of life. Between 1751 and 1781, the population of England grew from 5 ½ million to 7 million. By 1841, it had more than doubled to 15 million. With the exception of London, the cities of manufacturing and trade overtake the old centres of population. In 1790, country labourers were twice as numerous as town labourers. By 1841, the reverse was true. Expansion of population and manufacturing from about 1780 onwards brought about social metamorphosis. It was economic change on a scale that the world never been seen. Across the country, new machines could be heard clanking night and day, heralding powered manufacturing that transformed the world far more than any class - war revolutionaries with fire in their minds.

For Britain as a whole, industrial production and services are becoming more important. Britain in the mid-19th century is going through enormous changes in the transition from land to town and city and from agriculture to manufacturing that we call the industrial revolution. Factory life has come to stay. Increasingly people realise that the tide of transformation could not be rolled back. As the Prime Minister Sir Robert Peel put it in 1842, *"we cannot recede"*.[327] The seventy years between 1821 and 1891 saw the contribution of farming to national income drop from a quarter to a twelfth (even though the amount rose in real terms). The trend away from agriculture was set to continue.[328] It would be a long time before machinery did the work of weary men and women - or farm animals. A Yatton Man, James David, wins the Bristol Agricultural Society prize in 1843 for the best yoke of working oxen.[329]

Horse-drawn power had been seen on the Moor for centuries. In the Middle Ages, that had been supplemented by water-power. It sparked off what some claim to be the first industrial revolution.[330] Various watermills are recorded in documents around the rhynes and tributaries feeding the River Yeo, which was tidal as far as Congresbury until the early 19th century.

What drove industrialisation was a marriage of coal and iron to produce power on an entirely new scale. In any discussion of why Britain was the first country to go industrial, two forms of capital are usually included. One was the wealth that had accrued, often from the slave trade, resulting in large amounts that lay waiting to be invested by wealthy landowners such as dominated North Somerset and also businessmen, eager to plough the new wealth into further profits. The other factor was entrepreneurial capital; a climate conducive to coffee-shop discussion of new ideas, open to harnessing scientific ideas to new technology.

Coal had become the universal power source. It was well-known in the domestic hearths of the Moor. In December 30th 1834 the Vestry Minutes record a sack of coal being granted to Florence and Hannah Lukins as they were on poor relief. Coal had been mined on a small scale for centuries, contributing as much as wind-power does today. Until the 18th century, wood was still THE fuel on the Moor. Woodlands had been carefully managed so growth could keep up with demand. Now, landowners are on the look out for valuable minerals as well as valuable land for agriculture. In 1847, coal is discovered locally. A vein between three and four feet thick was found on the estate of John Hugh Smyth-Piggott, the local landowner. Its proximity to the railway line meant that the black gold could be loaded at the small pits and taken anywhere. Local iron had been mined for a while in the district; the ore being sent to South Wales. Now the writer expressed the opinion that Yatton could see its own mini-industrial bonanza.[331] Further reports showed how it was the strong belief that coal existed on his estates that led J. H. Smyth –Piggott to go boring in the first place.[332]

The countryside saw its own transformation. Yields doubled and then quadrupled. There was an agricultural revolution through selective breeding and the enclosure of the people's common land that has vastly increased yields. Yatton is not destined to become a major centre of manufacturing. It will, however become an industrialised village with small enterprises - a tannery and later, a furniture factory The Industrial revolution was not in any case built on large factories. Returns from around the country in 1851 indicated that over two-thirds of firms employed less than ten people.[333]. What the Moor did experience was a revolution in transport that will change life dramatically for the villagers. In 1841, the railways arrive.

At the same time, the villagers are obliged to wrestle afresh with some age-old problems that will define them; not with the worst effects of overcrowding, slums and factory labour such as their counterparts were compelled to elsewhere but with rural poverty, agricultural depression, the impact of the railways and the need to do something to educate the children of working people. How the mid-Victorian generation addressed these issues will occupy us in the next part of our story.

1841 saw a Census that still yields high quality information about the people who lived on the Moor. It was complemented that year by a tithe map that draws a picture of a different kind, that of dwellings, fields and common ground –in short the pattern of settlement. To ensure proper recording of tithes to support the church, in 1841, a tithe map was drawn up for Yatton. There had been estate maps before, especially of the estates belonging to the landowner, Earl Poulett. This was more extensive.

In the 1841 tithe map, built against the walls of the church is a stable with a first floor schoolroom and the village lock-up. This three room jail will later be demolished to make room for a new stable and bier-house for coffins. Only the bier-house will survive long-term. Next to it and at the heart of the old medieval village, is a bucket and chain over a well that has been used by poor people since the Middle Ages. That will be replaced soon by the village pump. Then there is the Glebe land. Called Poundsfield in the 1851 Census, this provides an income to pay the Vicar. At the edge of the Glebe, facing the main road through Yatton is a row of ten small cottages. In the 1850's, the aunt of the new vicar, Henry Barnard, sketches the cottages from the Vicarage over the main road. Her drawings remain, though the cottages were pulled down. The cottages have one room downstairs and one room upstairs, reached by a ladder. Eight of the cottages were thatched. These are seen on the front cover of this book. Cramped conditions are a far-cry from the grand house at the other end of the Glebe. This is still called the Rectory in the 1841 tithe map but it is in fact the Prebendal House, for the absent Prebendary based in Wells, the oldest house in the village. The 1841 tithe map clearly shows the village community clustering round Church and glebe land. Farms adjoined the main street and there was little housing. By 1881, the picture has changed. Housing runs up and down the street. Shops abound. What changed was the arrival of the railways.

Social Transformation on Wheels

Dramatic advances on transport had arrived. There were no turnpike roads or canals to the Moor, only large numbers of drainage ditches, or rhynes. It never had a canal. A map of 1842 shows the route that had been proposed thirty years ago of the nearest canal to Yatton, the Bristol and Taunton. Canals had been a feature of the English countryside since James Brindley was employed by the Duke of Bridgwater to construct a channel from the Duke's colliery to Manchester, eleven miles away. That was back in 1759. Innumerable Acts of Parliament followed, asking that canals be cut. Canals were needed because industry needed cheap transport to move heavy coal and iron. The golden age was 1790-1794 when 81 Acts were passed. The Bristol and Taunton Canal was proposed in 1810[334] and authorised the next year. It was never cut north of Bridgwater. The 1842 map shows the channel was expected to run down the Gordano valley, through the hills via a 600 yard tunnel and thence down south to Banwell. The Canal would run across Kenn Moor and Yatton, near the present station. If it had been dug, the area would have developed differently. Kenn Pier would have seen a branch line to the Nailsea colliery. A wharf in Yatton would have stimulated industrial development.

It was not to be. The previous year, the railways came. Modern Yatton was built on 50% railway, 15% furniture production (the nearest that Yatton came to industrialisation at the beginning of the 20th century) and the rest agriculture.

The first main line in the district was between Bath and Bristol. This was the famous Great Western railway and Isambard Kingdom Brunel was its engineer. The London end of the 118 miles of track was ready by 1838 and the final section (from Chippenham to Bath) was in place by May 1841. The line terminated at Bristol. Then a new company was formed.[335] The purpose of the Bristol and Exeter Railway was to extend the line to the West Country. Once again, Brunel was its chief engineer and once again, the railway used the broad gauge of 7ft 0¼ inches between the rails. Brunel favoured this over against the 4ft 8½ inch breadth between rails that eventually became standard. Because the goods wagons could hold more, it was reckoned to be more economical. That was how the railway came to the Moor.

The world was changing. Newspapers reported that the Bristol to Exeter line was being laid down quickly. *"Works on this railway are proceeding at a fast rate"*. Taunton, it was boasted, will soon be within 6 hours of the metropolis.[336]

In 1841, the Bristol Mercury reports the preview outing for shareholders to see the results of their investment. Their locomotive was called 'Fireball.'

It ran out from Bristol, re-doubling its speed as it came near to Yatton. There to meet the shareholders was a band, striking up 'See the Conquering Hero Comes' while the shouts of the assembled crowd rent the air. *"All along the line, the villagers welcomed their strange visitor with every demonstration of applause."*[337]

On 14th June 1841 came the big day. The Bristol and Exeter Railway line was opened as far as Bridgwater. The project is mentioned in the Vestry Minutes for September 5th 1842. On 6th March, if as it appears the railway company has not paid the Highway rates, they are to be asked to pay. The line was in immediate use. Within a few months, the papers were reporting a Bazaar at Wrington Rectory, made feasible by the railway to Yatton and a coach from there.[338]

Accidents, or near accidents were a hazard from the outset. In April 1842, there was a hue and cry because an engine at Yatton station had set off by itself. Clearly the brakes were not working or had not been applied. Reports speak of the consternation of the villagers as they saw the locomotive rushing past. It was not until Bridgwater, much further down the line, that the train ran out of steam.[339]

Railway incidents began to be reported on. In 1850, a railway steamed into Yatton station bearing guests from Bristol for the annual Clevedon ball, now accessible by train. Chaging at Yatton, the guests were taken the few miles up the branch line but the brakes failed. The train went through the station, plunged off the track and ended up on the road outside. Fortunately, no one was hurt.[340] Three years later, there was a similar incident, this time in reverse. The mid-day train left Clevedon to transfer to the main line but the man responsible for changing the points (who bore the title of 'policeman') failed to do so. The train continued its journey and plunged into engine sheds at Yatton. The roof collapsed on top of the train, which continued its journey, ending up in nearby fields. As well as the driver, many passengers were injured.[341]

A new criminal offence began to be noted, the ticket offence. One defendant claimed he had not alighted from Yatton station but had been round the back of the line all along. This was contrary to what a policeman saw and a porter corroborated it. The miscreant was made an example of; fare dodging was happening all too often.[342]

Yet the railway was highly successful. A Tudor style station was built to show that Yatton was junction of some importance. By 1844, there was a hotel. In time, the junction will be intersected by various light railways. A branch line was opened, from Yatton a few miles up to Clevedon. A report to shareholders of the Bristol and Exeter Railway Company could highlight this as an example of what a Branch line can achieve. 3,000 passengers booked tickets in the months before the line opened. In the event, 8,000 people travelled. It was highly encouraging to shareholders.[343]

Yatton Railway Station c1920

In February 1869, the first sod of earth was cut for the Yatton and Cheddar Railway. Tickets for the Grand Ball that night cost 2-6d. The next day, the navvies moved in. Progress was swift. By August, the line reached Cheddar. Then by Easter 1870, the line reached Wells. The railway was a lifeline for these rural communities. For many, trips to Clevedon on this line, including Sunday school outings, were a highlight of the year. This 'strawberry Line' took fresh strawberries from Cheddar to London. The line will be supplemented by a light railway from Portishead and Clevedon through to Weston- Super-Mare. It will service the farming community. Kingston Seymour will have four halts where milk churns can be loaded. The railway will transform the potential for marketing milk and help convert many farms away from corn in the years of agricultural depression, to diary farming. It was access to wider markets for agricultural produce that was the gift of the railway age to the Moor.

The old agricultural society began to change. There was more freedom, greater mobility. Generally, steam engines were few and not large, averaging

20 HP in 1880. They took a long time to replace horse and cart. But the locomotives were the largest and most powerful engines of that generation. Across the world by 1880, almost two billion people a year travelled on them. Between 1841 and 1846, £87 million was raised in the UK, six times the level of public investment in rail travel a decade before.[344] Profits from industry and manufacturing were feeding railway investment, *"the most massive effort of public building as yet undertaken."*[345]

Counting the People

The real suprise in the Census data is in the proportion of those born locally. In 1841, 99% of the population of Yatton were born in the village. By 1881, the proportion has dropped dramatically and only 26% were really local. 60% were born within a ten mile radius. This is testimony to the social transformation wrought by the railways. Trains began to run earlier. In 1865, the first train to Bristol was at 9.03am. By 1877, you could catch a train at 7.06am. The age of commuting had arrived.

Yatton itself had been larger than either Weston super mare or Clevedon until now. In 1801, Yatton had 1,147 people living there compared with 334 for Clevedon and only 138 for Weston-super-mare. But that is before the railways meant that Victorian people could discover the delights of a seaside resort.

In 1821, Yatton has had 225 inhabited houses, 271 families and 1516 inhabitants. By 1831, even without the railways, that figure has risen to 353 inhabited houses, 370 families and 1865 inhabitants. Yet as more housing has gone up, there is less overcrowding- just over five people per house compared with nearly seven only ten years before. The Yatton Vestry Meeting of December 1830- in effect the Parish Council- is considering the best way of employing labourers. Not long after, they are taking note of the increase in the population that the new Census showed up.[346]

The acquisition of land and estates in North Somerset by the new landowner, John Hugh Smyth-Pigott, brought fresh investment to Yatton. A survey of 1841 shows that, compared with a comparable survey of 1821, new buildings had begun to go up. A comparison of the average amount spent each year on aggregate to extend and repair the roads shows a steady increase. Half as much again year on year was spent in the 1830s compared with the 1820s.[347]

By 1841, Yatton has 1649 inhabitants. Of 605 people with occupations, 188 are agricultural labourers along with 54 male servants who have more permanent farm work. There are in addition 36 farmers. In all, 46% of its employed people work directly in the land compared with about 60% in 1831. This figure of 1649 inhabitants in 1841 is set to rise again. In 1851, 2,063 people will be living there- the highest figure until the village grows again in the 20th century.

Yatton men continue to win agricultural prizes and were successful cattle-dealers. At a Christmas farm show in 1856, prizes for best bred oxen, pigs and Southdown sheep go to local farmers.[348] Two extraordinary size pigs of a celebrated Berkshire breed belong to a Kingston farmer, John Bryant.[349] The area remains dependent on agriculture. Its five communities have a life of their own, separated by fields, rhynes and history. One farmer, William Hayman Naish, sends off to Dorset to acquire the next batch of sheep. The shepherd/sheep driver sleeps where he can and trudges that long journey by day. Local family memory is that it took a week to get back to North Somerset via drove lanes. The last sheep batch from Dorset will be in 1896.

Driving sheep to market c1910

Our look at the Mid-Victorian generation begins with the Hungry Forties. The worst sufferings of the working classes were in the years 1838 to 1842[350] when unemployment was combined viciously with low wages.

Agricultural wages, after rising a little in the middle of the previous decade, had fallen again and fell sharply.

The Manor is still the basis of the local, agrarian economy. Records of the 'Court Baron of Yatton Rectory' are a document of village life until the Ecclesiastical Commissioners took over the prebendal estates in the 1870's.[351] The Manor Court would have been held at the old Rectory next to the church; later meetings were held at the Prince of Orange hostelry in the village. The Manor system is in place until abolished under the Right of Property Act of 1875.

The writing had been on the wall for the immensely strong agricultural interests for thirty years. The repeal of the Corn Laws in 1846 by Sir Robert Peel was a political defeat for landowners as the dominant special interest group. Farmers moved from corn to horn, from wheat to livestock. Chilled meat began to come in. At the same time, improved methods and mechanisation meant that yields were expanding. The annual productivity growth of 0.4% between 1860 and 1910 continued the trend of the previous 150 years- though comparing poorly with the USA and Canada.

By 1880, European society ran the world. It was set to dominate the globe in a new age of Empire. And it was based on industrial capitalism, born of the coal and iron that had started a revolution a hundred years before. The railways that had come early to the Moor and excited its inhabitants now left tracks across an entire planet.

But by 1880 too, the great agricultural depression was affecting the British countryside. A combination of cold springs and wet summers took their toll. 1879 saw the worst harvests in the 19th century. It co-incided with cheap corn flooding the home-market. Great Britain was no longer the workshop of the world. It had been overtaken in industrial production by Germany and the USA. But Britain faced stiff competition from America in another way – wheat. Cheap and plentiful corn from America was gathered by combine harvesters that were practically unknown in Britain. It was brought east by the new railways, shipped by steamship to Britain and sold more cheaply than British wheat. There were now no Corn Laws to protect the British farmer. The price of wheat had fetched 44 shillings a quarter, then 50 shillings in 1877. Now it dropped- dramatically. By 1885, wheat fetched 32 shillings a quarter.

Many farmers were faced with ruin. As the price of wheat plunged, social distress amongst labourers rose. Young men left the countryside in search of work. As the 1880's dawned, trade was depressed in the towns as well. Farmers on the Moor turned much of their land into pasture for rearing cattle. That at least could compete, even with imports of frozen meat. An increasing population demanded more milk, butter and eggs. Market gardening and fruit growing became prosperous, though much less than could be gained in a good year from corn growing. Agriculture was to struggle on, flatlining until the First World War had to be endured by the next generation of the people of the Moor.

Chapter Fourteen

On a Street Corner in Yatton

On a street corner in the village of Yatton in 1840, four people pass each other. In a rural community such as this, they will be aware of each other's existence and acknowledge perhaps with a passing nod or a longer chat.

William Derham is 56. He is a skilled tailor, local businessman, and a leading light in Methodism. As Overseer of the Poor he has been a pillar of the community.

He is perhaps talking with James Kingcott, described in the Census the following year as a yeoman farmer- or is he a shoemaker? James' wife Jane is 64, the same age as him. Their son William was baptised on an April day back in 1812 as Napoleon was about to invade Russia. By now, William is 28, also a farmer. Eight years before there was a family tragedy. William's cousins in Kenn, John and James Rowley, have been implicated in the burning of hayricks that led to the last public hanging in England at the scene of the crime. John has swung for it. James has been transported to Australia. Meeting the next passer-by evokes wistfulness from James Kingcott. He had a daughter called Eliza who died when she was that age.

Eliza Gregory is seven, daughter of a Quaker family who have lived in the area for over a century. She is with her father, Bishop Gregory, who is also a respected member of the community. Bishop Gregory currently farms in Claverham but already he is thinking of moving back to Yatton where he grew up. Eliza's mother Sarah will die on the same day as William Derham.

But passing them is a strange character. Eliza knows him because this old tinker comes to the door to grind scissiors and sell his wares. Isaac Joules was born in 1770 - or was it 1780? Following the loss of his wife Merrily, he has been inconsolable, trudging the dusty roads of the Moor. These are his last months in the village. Next year he will be admitted to the workhouse and die of the dropsy.

We will follow briefly the fortunes of these passers-by as they live out the various meanings that life held for them.

Faith and Adversity – The William Derham Story[352]

In 1840, Yatton has its own forge, wheelwright, chandler, beer shop, baker, butcher and tailor. The tailor is William Derham, a prominent family in Yatton.

It is likely that Yatton Methodism started in the same way that it spread elsewhere. People who were touched directly in the evangelisation passed on the fire to others who became upwardly mobile. Wesley's dictum '*work as hard as you can, save all you can, give all you can*' resulted in habits of life in which Methodists did well for themselves. 'How can I stop these people getting rich?' had been Wesley's lament. As with the Early Church, craft communities were often the key to spreading the gospel. William Derham, the driving force in 19th century Methodism in Yatton was a tailor who then becomes a pillar of the community, taking on a position of Overseer.

The year William Derham was born, John Wesley's movement was legally constituted as a religious body separate from the Church of England. How the Derhams come to the personal salvation that was the hallmark of Wesley's preaching is not known. The appeal of Methodism was different to that of the Parish Church. The most important difference was a strongly personal note. It was possible to know God for yourself. Forgiveness was not just mediated through sacrament, it was an experience to be received, an inward witness. "*The arms of love that encompass me would all mankind embrace!*" the Derhams sang. "*He breaks the power of cancelled sin, he sets the prisoner free. His blood can make the foulest clean, His blood avails for me!*"

William Derham's father, Joseph, was a tailor from Backwell who in the year 1773 married Mary Cox, a lady from the nearby village of Dundry. They soon settled in Yatton. Children follow in quick succession. William, their sixth child is born in 1784 and baptised that August. Earl Poulett was the local landowner in those days. Rent books show Joseph making payments for a property for his growing family. Business evidently prospered. Mary dies in 1794. William has to endure the loss of his mother when he is ten years old. Within a year, he has a step-mother. Joseph will marry a Murford Rogers from Nailsea. By 1799, according to the Copyhold documents for the Manor of Yatton Rectory, owned by Earl Poulett, the Derhams obtain a desirable residence that will befit prosperity. An outhouse and fields are included in the deal. William, one of his son's, is sixteen. Five years later, Joseph is dead.

William Derham now continues the family business. In 1805, he married Penelope Shephard from Locking. Penelope is six years older than William. She joins him in the house that is also a draper's shop. A year later, they celebrate the arrival of their first child, a daughter named after her mother. Joseph, named after William Derham's father, is born in 1808. He will be William's eldest son.

In the year 1822, William is granted a Dissenter's certificate. He is allowed to use his home as a meeting place for Methodists. What he and local people of the same convictions had done for public worship is not known. It may be that a pattern of Sunday worship at the Parish Church and weekday class meetings elsewhere was followed.

By this time, Penelope has given birth to eight children. Three boys are born to them who do not survive. The parish church register records the death of their son William on November 12th 1819. He was only one day old. Significantly, the funeral service is taken by a Minister John Hamden. He is not Church of England. Such is William Derham's standing in the village that a Methodist minister is allowed to take the funeral at the Parish Church. The three boys are interred in the graveyard of the present Methodist Church. But three daughters have survived, Elizabeth, Peninnah and Mary. In all, Penelope has had eight children.

In January 1825, William Derham purchases another property, a long leasehold on 'Seven Acres' in the High Street, the site of the present Methodist Church. He pays £656 and 5 shillings for this. A cottage and a new meeting house are quickly built to accommodate the Moor's growing Methodist movement. A Dissenter's certificate is quickly granted and by October 15th, 'Seven Acres' is registered as a meeting place. William and Mary continue to live in the Lower House Yatton that has been their home and draper's shop for many years.[353]

Adversity is a constant companion. In 1827, the shop is broken into and a quantity of printed cotton is stolen. (see Chapter 18) That August, his stepmother, Murford Derham dies. She is 79. William has growing standing in the community. In March of that year, he is appointed an Overseer of parish rates. His Methodism has not been a bar to this. He is firmly a member of the Middle Class that in Victorian Britain represented a fifth of the population.[354] Shopkeepers, clerks, businessmen and professional types such as doctors and officers in the armed forces were a strong and emerging force in society.

Joseph Derham, William's eldest son follows his father into the family business. William has sent him to London to learn to become a master tailor. Romance and learning went hand in hand. Joseph returns with a London girl, Elizabeth, two years older than him. By 1829, still only 21, Joseph takes on an apprentice of his own. His protégé is Aquila Keene. Aquila joins the family business in December that year. Apprentices were expected to live-in and adapt to the family ways. Shortly, Joseph will marry Elizabeth.

Aquila has a brother, David. By 1833, he too is in Yatton, learning to be a tailor. He is just 13. Both brothers are being affected by the religious fervour of the Derham family. That August, William Derham's youngest daughter Mary attends a prayer meeting. Her uncle, who lives in nearby Wrington, later records with enormous joy that his niece is now 'saved'. He is a Wesleyan Methodist local preacher. She is 12 years old. Something is happening with David Keene also. A fellow Methodist, a Mr Collings from Nemphnett, writes to congratulate him on an "early religious experience". He encloses a book to guide him. David now holds a probationary membership ticket of the Yatton Methodist Society. A year later, he holds full membership. Sharing the same household and religious fervour, the two young people are attracted to each other. David is 14, Mary is 13. Yet Mary is not well. Her uncle writes that a severe illness has left his niece *"with almost constant pains in the head, which serves to depress her natural good spirits."* Nevertheless, a youthful romance blossoms. Mary Derham loves flowers. She sends David tiny pressed campions and daisies. His subsequent keepsakes include a poem from Mary entitled "A Field Flower", extolling the virtues of the humble daisy by comparison with more exotic flowers. Mary uses an unusual pseudonom, 'Montgomery'.

David's artistic interests are flourishing, in addition to his religious experience and knowledge of tailoring. Mary's cousin John sends him "a few easy airs" to practice so he can learn music. His romance with Mary is also blossoming. David asks Mary Derham for a letter for him to keep. A letter seems unnecessary when they are seeing each other every day in the same household but in November 1835, she complies. It is full of religious exhortation reflecting the fervour of the Derham household. It is as well she did.

By now, David's brother Aquila Keene is courting William Derham's second daughter Elizabeth. William does not discourage these relationships between daughters and apprentices. In 1836, Aquila has completed a seven year apprenticeship. He and Elizabeth Derham are now in a position to marry. David and Mary would undoubtedly have attended, celebrating their brother's (and sister's) love, thinking about their own future.

It was not to be. That December, Mary catches influenza. It weakens her further. The summer of 1837 sees Mary recovering sufficient strength to visit her uncle's chapel at Wrington and the new chapel at Worle. But this is to be her last summer. Bronchial consumption takes hold. Anticipating the end, Mary comforts her grieving family. In January 1838, she dies, just two months short of 17. Her grief stricken uncle preaches at her funeral. A copy of his sermon survives as does her uncle's "Memoir of Mary Derham", printed in the Wesleyan Methodist Magazine that August.

As for David Keene, two locks of hair are a memorial of Mary. She had given one to him with words he will treasure always.

"This is to lock
Within your heart
All that would tend
To mar my peace."

The other lock of hair was cut off by David, heart-broken. It was kept within intricately folded paper. David writes on it, "cut off after death, my first love aged 17." He will not forget his first love. He emigrates to build a new life. Twenty years later in January 1860 he is a naturalised American citizen and respected Minister of his own church in Milwaukee, David visits England alone, leaving his American wife and baby son at home. David goes to Yatton to make *"a pilgrimage to her grave."* Evidently, he has with him the only letter she penned to him. *"She was a sweet girl"*, he writes, *"and with a heart of deep religious feeling. Few love letters can be found to equal this in its religious sentiments....I have not forgotten the sweet memory of Mary Derham."*

Despite these personal sorrows, William Derham would have been encouraged by the growth of their brand of Christian experience. In September 1837, Yatton Methodism was officially registered. In 1838, six months after Mary died, a Sunday School was established. Years later, Aquila has become a Wesleyan Methodist minister. He has left tailoring. His training was expensive in terms of books. But he recalls the "almost nightly meetings" that will have done so much to train him. So does tragedy. Susan, the first child born to Aquila and Elizabeth dies just two months after Mary has passed away. Elizabeth's sister Peninnah attempts to comfort the sorrowing parents.

Then Aquila has a posting. He is to go to Worcester to begin his first Methodist ministry. His influence over David is strong. David Keene becomes a lay preacher. From seventy miles away, brother Aquila asks for copies of his sermons and sends some of his own so he can help guide him.

Still mourning Mary, David is restless. Aquila writes, though not as often as he would like. Maintaining contact is expensive. "*When the National Blessing of a Penny Postage shall be conferred upon us, you may expect to hear from me more often*".

By then, Elizabeth has given William Derham another grandchild with the promise of another on the way. Now 56, William Derham is hugely influential in Yatton Methodism but things are not always going as he would like. When in January 1840, David Keene is examined before a Mr Ward, the Yatton Methodist Minister, Aquila is critical that standards have dropped. He suggests to David that Yatton is not contributing as much to the life of the circuit as it should. If all had been in the hands of David's "worthy master" William Derham, things would be different. How will the area manage for lay preachers now David is to be a full minister and move on?

There is friction within the church and very likely, quarrels within the Derham family. Both Peninnah and Elizabeth, Aquila's wife put the friction down to Joseph's London wife. If only everyone will "forgive and pity!" Evidently, their sister-in-law was responsible for a dramatic scene when she burnt her Association tickets "*declared herself no longer a member of society and wishes Mr Ward [the local Minister] to erase her name from the Class paper*" [the list of members]. Tranquillity and happiness were in short supply, she laments. Aquila was asked to intervene but he, a newly qualified young preacher, refuses to second-guess a decision of the Board regarding the examination of a lay preacher who seems to have been turned down.

It is possible that this was related to the setting up of another type of Methodism. Until that time, Wesleyan Methodism was the only form of Methodism that people would have known. There is no record of the Primitive Methodists coming to Yatton.

But then comes the remarkable legacy of William Bryan. By birth Anglican, by influence Quaker, by choice and temperament Methodist, William Bryan had a conversion experience similar to John Wesley. A farmer's son, Bryan felt called to preach in places where there were no preachers or preaching places. In 1814, he became a wandering evangelist, subject to no ecclesiastical superior and taking the Bible only as his rule of life. William Bryan became a popular preacher and tireless evangelist. As their numbers multiplied, those who gathered to hear him in homes or farmhouses built chapels. Around 1840, Horsecastle Chapel was built in a poor hamlet on the edge of Yatton. The Methodist rules of 1742 were accepted by these Bible Christians, as they became known. They even encouraged women preachers! But their installation amongst people in the hamlet of Horsecastle is instructive. Here were those who were poor, the agricultural equivalent of the industrial urban poor crowding into the cities of the time. The Bible Christians appealed to these people who were probably only partially evangelised by the Parish Church.

At the time of the encounter on a street corner in Yatton in 1840, William Derham is about to witness further tragedy. Peninnah Derham, who had rejected David Keene's interest in proposing marriage, writes to her would-be-suitor in June 1841 that her sister Elizabeth, Aquila's wife, is in poor health. So are their two children, Susan and Mary. It was unfortunate that they are all being nursed at the family home at Lower House Yatton because William Derham is undertaking extensive renovations. The roof had been taken off both the kitchen and half the shop. The upheavals do not help. A month later, little Susan lay dead, followed a few days later by her sister Mary. Then, in September, having witnessed this double-shock, Elizabeth passed away. Aquila had seen his entire family wiped out and William Derham had lost another daughter as well as two grandchildren.

It was not the end of his troubles. James Brown, a prominent London preacher well-known in the circles that the Derham family moved in, was visiting Yatton and evidently quite taken with William's eldest daughter Penelope. By now, she is 35. Here is an opportunity for marriage, to escape dependence on parents that haunted Victorian women and, with good fortune, find domestic bliss and children. There was a moral panic about old maids and 'the surplus woman question'. The 1851 Census will show that nationally, there were 1.4 million spinsters between 20 and 40 and over 300,000 'old maids' over 40.[355] Penelope has no wish to enter these statistics.

But William is reluctant. He has lost enough daughters. Nevertheless, in February 1842, Penelope Derham goes off to marry her preacher. She has left Yatton for London but her father keeps a tight hold over her money. He stipulates that it will revert to the Derham family if she dies. He must have felt the family were breaking up. Bereaved and heart-broken, Aquila Keene goes to labour in Glasgow Methodism, where he is to be appalled by the poor, walking barefoot in winter. He will marry again and continues to look to old William Derham as a father-figure as he moves from circuit to circuit. His brother David decides to emigrate to America and apply for the ministry of the Episcopal Church. He will find love but will never forget Mary Derham, his childhood sweetheart.

The Vestry Minutes for March1842 record William Derham appointed as Surveyor for the poor rates. He will keep accounts of those on Yatton east side of those who pay poor rates and those who require assistance. That is the last local office William seems to have held. By 1848, William Derham will not be on the list of parish officers. Since 1827, he has served the community as well as founded a local movement. In Yatton was on the circuit for meetings such as held by the Bristol branch of the British and Foreign Bible Society.[356]

In 1844, William will give the shop to his son Joseph, a tailor, though perhaps lacking the skill of his father and grandfather before him. Aquila reckons that his tutoring has dropped in standards so all is not well. Joseph is married and has a growing brood. Joseph's sister Peninnah has been Governess to his children. Though unmarried, she has a strong love for Mr Hurd, the family doctor. Marriage is out of the question. It was said that her partial blindness that came on in January 1846 was a result of her affection and grief over Mr Hurd. By August she is dead. Old Penelope Derham wrote a harrowing letter to David Keene, describing the suffering her daughter had been compelled to endure. The medical practice of the day has not helped. Peninnah is 30. Her mother has seen six out of her eight children die prematurely. Penelope wishes David would write more often. Aquila, by now at Durham assures her that he and his brother could never repay the Derhams for their kindness.

Joseph Derham, William's son, is living next door to the shop. In 1851, he moves back to Lower House and takes over the shop. William Derham, now 67, and Penelope retire to Joseph's house *"which they had fitted up very comfortably"*. William Derham remains active in village life and exhibits the earnest attitude of moral improvement. He is host in October that year to a meting of the Temperance Society. There was no restraint with roast beef and plum pudding which the guests heartly tucked into before some of them signed the pledge.[357]

In January 1844, newspapers record a public meeting of the Total Abstinence Society at the Wesleyan Chapel. Several people came forward and signed the pledge. Tea was served.[358] The abstinence instinct was strong. The Wesleyan Methodist Conference had, only three years before required the use of 'bona fide' wine for communion. A Temperance Declaration would not attract many signatories. All that gradually changed. There was a growing sentiment amongst Methodists at this time in favour of total abstinence and that the Church should lead the way in temperance reform for the good of the individual and for the welfare of society.[359] 1858 saw Abraham Strong, a beer retailer convicted of keeping his premises open on a Sunday morning. He was fined 40 shillings.[360]

As part of building a lasting church work, Sunday schools were a vital part of building the next generation of church as well as educating children. The Ecclesiastical Census for 1851 records 78 children in the Sunday school. The papers report that the Wesleyan Methodist, William Smart, is in the chair of the district Sabbath school association for 1851. The children had been given Bibles and hymn books.[361] Then later that year, the annual sermon is preached for the Wesleyan Sabbath School Association. The Bristol Mercury spoke of children assembling in a nearby orchard, eating plenty of tea and cake, reciting various items to the guests. Parents will be gratified, it was said, that their children are able to receive religious instruction.[362]

Two years later William Derham is dead.

The founder of Yatton Methodism has seen his faith carry him through adversity after adversity. He leaves the shop and Lower House to his son Joseph but the cottage, house and garden around the Meeting House to Joseph's boy Theophilus Sheppard Derham who was then only eight years old. Penelope lives to see her beloved eldest daughter return to Yatton in 1860 after the death of the London preacher James Brown. She lives to see her grandson Theophilus marry a local farmer's daughter before she dies in September 1871 aged 93.

What she does not live to see is further tragedy. The Minutes for 3rd October 1874 of what is now in effect the new ratepayers meeting record that Mr Theophilus Derham, successful as Postmaster as well as draper, has been appointed to the office of Vestry Clerk. Before the end of the year, he is dead. He is only 30. His mother, the London born Elizabeth who had caught the eye of Joseph Derham all those years before, dies the same year. Three years later, Aquila Keene re-visits the scenes of his youthful ministry and is saddened to see Joseph having to endure paralysis. By 1881, he is dead.

In 1840, it is three years since the Wesleyan Methodist Chapel (or meeting house) had been officially registered for religious services. The 1841 Tithe Map shows that the chapel is under the ownership of William Derham. His family ensure that the old chapel had enjoyed a rent-free period of over 60 years. In 1887, the foundation will be laid of a new Chapel, the present building. In 1887, land is purchased for £50 next to the old Meeting House founded by his father. At a cost of £850, a new chapel is built, the present Methodist Church. By now, there was no separate branch of Methodism in Yatton. Labels will change. In 1857, two groups of Methodists unite to form the United Methodist Free Churches. That name will remain until 1907 when they unite with the Methodist New Connexion and Bible Christians to form the United Methodist Church, then the Methodist Union in 1932.

There is an interesting postscript to this story. In August 1858, the Bishop of Bath and Wells was to have preached at a church event to mark the opening of a new parish school in Kingston Seymour. His Chaplain arrives on his own. The Bishop has met with an accident. Consternation sets in. The Chaplain has not come with a sermon and no visiting clergy wish to preach at a moment's notice. However, in steps a visiting American preacher who just happens to have a sermon in his pocket. The preacher is David Keene, armed with Holy Orders in the Episcopal church and qualified for the occasion![363]

A Tale of Farmers, Families and Revenge- The Kingcotts[364]

In 1840 on our hypothetical street corner, James Kingcott is well known in the village of Yatton. His family are amongst the oldest families in the parish records. We have met members of this family as they played out their lives in the 17th century. Richard Kingcott and Sarah Pool were married in 1769. Many of their children are baptised in Yatton Parish Church. Sarah will be buried in May 1822 aged 72.

Their oldest child, Martha, baptised the same year as their marriage, will marry Thomas Rowley. The sons of Martha and Thomas, John and James, will become infamous.

Of three of their other children, Sarah, Richard and Betty, little is known. Sarah Kingcott is buried in September 1816, aged 40. Like her sister Patience, she will never marry. Another son, Job, is baptised in May 1782. He is 29 when he marries Sarah Vowles. The marriage lasts only two years. By September 1813, he is dead.

Of their other son James Kingcott, much more is known. He was born in the year 1776. Marrying a Jane Vowles in 1805, the year of Trafalgar, they will give birth to seven children. Parish records show that their daughter

Eliza was buried on May 7th 1815. She is 7 when she dies. James is a yeoman farmer though with varying occupations alongside that. In the last two baptism records of his children, he is down as a shoemaker. That will be entered on his death certificate. In 1841, James is described in the Census as a yeoman farmer. Jane is also 65. They farm at Horsecastle, in those days a hamlet distinct from Yatton. Their daughter Ann and her three children are living with them. Ann is a widow. A 13 year old servant boy called Charles Neade is with them. As the 19th century unfolds, it will be rarer for children to be formally employed below the age of 14.

Their son William was baptised in 1812. By now, William is 29, a farmer. Three years later, in 1844, he will marry. With his wife Sarah, he will farm at Well Cottage, Claverham. Before the Enclosure Act re-shaped Claverham, this was a fairly sizeable house; two rooms and two storeys together with a four fields and a garden. By 1841, the land had been whittled away. Now all that remains is the field out the back and the garden. They have made two cottages for labourers out of the one property. This is where William and Sarah live and work for five years. Then she will die, aged 39. After a 2 year interval, William will re-marry to an Elizabeth Rimmes who is the same age.

Two years after that, in October 1853, William's mother Jane passes away, aged 79. She had a rupture of a blood vessel in her stomach. Within two days, she was dead. The informant is illiterate. He signs with a cross. Despite having chronic bronchitis, her husband James last until March 1854. Their widowed daughter Ann is witness to his death. In his will, James remembers his children and growing cluster of grandchildren.

Chief mourners at their father's funeral will be William Kingcott, his son in Claverham, Ann and William's brothers Sylvester and George. Sylvester will live until 1898 at the age of 82. The records describe him as a butcher. He and his wife Elizabeth feature in the 1891 Census for Yatton. They have eight children. Their grandsons will fight in the Great War. Brother George married Love Ford in March 1837 and have 10 children- the oldest born that December. They will move around the district though the 1881 Census finds them farming 100 acres in Yatton. George lives to 1885, aged 71. His wife will live for a further nine years before she passes away aged 80. His brother William survives him by two years. Both William and his two wives are buried in Yatton Churchyard. The inscription on the tombstones of Elizabeth and Sarah, his spouses, bears a solemn message:

"Watch therefore for ye know neither the day nor the hour when the Son of Man cometh." Below William's name is another verse from scripture- "thy will be done."

But why were the children of James' Aunt Martha so notorious?

One night at the end of October 1829, a Kenn farmer, Benjamin Poole was awakened by a neighbour to tell him that three wheat stacks he had in a nearby field were on fire. *"I found all the stacks on fire"* he told the Court, *"and a noble fire it was."* A neighbour was urgently called to help but it took all of three hours to extinguish the fire. The damage was assessed at some £50 (worth £12,000 to £15,000 by today's standards). A week later, he told the Court, he saw John Rowley, James KIngcott's nephew and two others wheeling a cask of cider. It was around three in the afternoon. They stopped, sang a profane song, flung up their hats and gave a cheer. There was evidence to convict.[365]

The authorites were vigilant and decided to make an example of the suspects. John Rowley along with a small farmer of 15 acres called William Wall and a labourer, Richard Clarke were arraigned for public trial. John Rowley is single and about 30. He already has a criminal record for assault. Richard Clarke, nephew of the man who alerted Farmer Poole to the blaze, is 19 and under suspicion also of stealing two sacks of potatoes and some sheep. William Wall is 35 and under a cloud of suspicion for stealing two lambs and receiving four sacks of potatoes. Also implicated in the case were John's younger brother James Rowley, who is 19, John Old, who is 19 and also down as a labourer, and William Wall's wife Mary. She is accused of making the means to fire the wheat stacks- rags, flint and tinder.

The case makes for dramatic reading. It turns out that William Wall had been prosecuted for selling cider without a licence and that the man who told on him was Farmer Poole. Isaac Old turns King's Informant and says he heard William Wall say that tonight would be a good night to burn the hay stacks in revenge. His actions save his brother, who is sentenced to transportation for life. James Rowley is also reckoned to be an accomplice and he too is to be transported. So is Mary Wall, William's wife. She has seven children, the oldest of whom is 13.

But for her husband, John Rowley and Richard Clarke, there is no manumission. They were convicted at the Somerset Assize of arson. The authorites are concerned about the breakdown of law and order. A spate of incidents has taken place recently. Nationally, social distress is resulting in hayrick burning becoming copycat crime. Some areas had a local tradition of incendiarism. It doesn't stop in the 1830's. In East Anglia, eight fires took place in November 1870 alone.[366] But the fact is that in 1830, sheep stealing, potatoe theft and setting fire to wheat stacks were hanging offences. No mercy is to be shown.

In Ilchester jail, the prisoners await their execution. A cart comes to the jail. It will carry them and their coffins to their place of execution. The High Sheriff is insistent. This is not to be outside the jail but at the scene of the crime. The prisoners sit under guard for the six hour journey back to the village where they have lived and played. Now they will die here. Local family history recalls the cart on its solemn passage through Yatton, the prisoners contemplating their coffins and their final end.[367]

With them at the last are their families. The prisoners are refused permission to speak to them. Also present are the High Sheriff and three magistrates – among them John Hugh Smyth-Pigott, the local landowner.[368] A squadron of mounted javelin men are in attendance, armed with halberds, a cross between a spear and an axe. The authorites are taking no chances; the Bath Yeomanry have been called out for this is a lawless place and a rescue might be mounted. Watching the proceedings that September day is a crowd estimated at between 10-20,000. Before the noose was tied, the prisoners were given leave to say a few words. *"Cider has been my ruin"* said Richard Clarke, *"the ruin of us all." "I should not have been here if I had not opened a cider shop"*, declared William Wall. *"If I had listened to my wife, I should not have come to this. Lord, forgive me all my sins"* John Rowley could only add, *"I have nothing more to say. I hope they will take warning by us."*[369]

They said that John Rowley and William Wall died quickly as the wagon hurried away from under them. Richard Clarke suffered rather longer, the grisly sight of slow strangulation watched by a hushed crowd. When it was all over, the Chaplain for the occasion addressed the crowd. John Hugh Smyth-Pigott thanked him for the solemn message that would have done much good in re-inforcing public order.

There are sad postscripts to this story. William Wall's widow Mary is transported. Her seven children will never see their mother again. With her newborn son, David, born in Ilchester jail three months after William's execution, she will be sent to Tasmania. David will be with her throughout that long voyage but will live in that land for 2 years. John Old will also go to Tasmania. James Rowley will not make it. After languishing in the prisonhulks of Plymouth, the Surgeon's Case Book for the SS Strathfieldshay records his going on the sick list during the long voyage to Australia and then passing away in August 1831 from an epileptic fit.

No doubt to stay near him, his mother Martha Rowley later moves into a house on the field where her son was executed. Farmer Poole, who may well have been innocent of informing on the unlicenced cider sale, ceases to sign as a member of the Kenn Vestry in 1834. Local feeling may well be against him. He is dead by 1839.

William Wall's children are taken in by local people. In April 1830, before his father was dead, there is an account of bread distributed to some poor local people because of a fine on Isaac Old to the value of ten shillings and sixpence. Among the beneficiaries is one of the Wall children, George, who is one year old.

The Kenn hangings are a tragic story. This will not be the last public hanging. That will have to wait until the year 1868. But it is the last public hanging at the scene of the crime. The High Sheriff has insisted on this to put a stop to the lawlessness of Kenn people and as a deterrent to the burning of hayricks.

Security and Stability: The Recollections of Eliza Gregory[370]

If the William Derham story represents the newer forms of Christianity that were influencing the Moor in the nineteenth century, the Clarks of Claverham represent an older non-conformity that was still powerful. So strong was this non-conformist conscience that Claverham, home to Quakerism in the area, was not allowed by Council rulings to sell alcohol. It was a dry village.

Life as a Quaker in nineteenth century the Moor is well illustrated by the diaries and memories of Eliza Clark, nee Gregory, hitherto unpublished. Eliza was a cousin of the Eddingtons born in March 1833 and lived to the year 1919. She was a member of the Gregorys, a family of Quakers that had lived in Pucklechurch, outside Bristol. Edward Gregory was registered in the Parish records there in February 1668. One of his daughters, *"Joanna Gregory of this Parish was buried in woollen on April 9th 1678."* To encourage the wool trade, a law had been passed that wool only should be used in burials, a law not repealed until 1814.[371] A descendant of theirs, Edward Gregory, came to the Moor in 1742, to Park Farm, rented by his father-in-law, Thomas Hipsley, from Earl Poulett, the local landowner. Thomas Hipsley was one of the Friends who drew up the inventory of the Trust bequeathed by Richard Durban in 1729. A Quaker tradition was unfolding. The move from Pucklechurch to Yatton is referred to as 'the migration' in subsequent family narratives.[372]

Thomas Hipsley's own father, Samuel from Cleeve, was imprisoned for non-payment of tithes. In turn, Edward Gregory's son bought the farm house when Earl Poulett wanted to sell estates in North Somerset to pay for a larger property. Gregory's lived there until 1876. One member of the family, Edward Gregory's granddaughter Debbie, showed how Quakers were far from an austere religious group. A Captain Vallis had proposed but on return from a voyage had found her

"Father went to Claverham this morning in order to attend Peter Morris and Debby Gregory's marriage, he being one of the overseers."[373]

A few years after, Peter Morris died. Debby continued to operate the shop they had set up. One day, a carriage drew up. It was Captain Vallis, now a rich man from trading in Newfoundland. He had heard of the death of Peter Morris and wanted to see Debby again. In 1798, they were married.

How a marriage was enacted in Quaker circles is well illustrated. A family diary records an Edward Gregory "entering into the solemn covenant of marriage" in 1785 with a large company of Friends. About 80 or 90 dined and celebrated the occasion. The writer, Betty Gregory, experiences a huge shock five years later when her own husband went suddenly *"to everlasting rest. I was in Yatton when the change came. I cannot describe my feeling when I first heard the melancholy news of having so near a friend so suddenly removed, he having been a kind husband to me and a tender father to the children which makes his loss truly great to us, but being well satisfied that our loss is his gain.... I hope and desire the Almighty to be a husband to me and a father to the dear children"* (23rd and 24th July 1790).[374]

The social life in the family diaries is full of references to taking tea with sisters and brothers in the movement or going by pony and trap to the Monthly Meeting for waiting on the inner light. One member of the family, Elizabeth Gregory, was very active in schools in Yatton village in the 1790's.

Eliza Clark's grandfather, Thomas Gregory, rented many acres of land from a farmer of land between Wemberham, Yatton, and Kingston Seymour across the fields, some of the richest lands in 'the marsh' as it was known. Back in Claverham, a Meeting is held in 1824 about levelling the old burial ground and keeping graves in rows. The second name in the burial register is that of Mary Eddington, a widow aged 64. Again, the name is significant.

Thomas Eddington from Kingston Seymour had a son, William, who became a Friend. He married at Claverham Meeting House and died in 1806. At Rock House in Yatton where he lived was where Richard Durban's school was based.[375] His wife, Mary Eddington died peacefully in April 1825, surrounded by eight of her children and some of the grandchildren. Seeing her peaceful, placid countenance, they could not but believe *"that her purified spirit, dismissed so gently from its tenement of clay had entered into the rest prepared for the righteous."*[376] When the mortal remains of Mary Eddington were interred at Claverham, *"a solemn and impressive meeting was held."* Her daughter, also Mary, was said to be a *'handsome girl' with long black hair reaching down to her knees'*. A descendant of William Eddington of Rock Road, Arthur Eddington, is to become a famous Quaker scientist and interpreter of Einstein. He stayed in Yatton sometimes as a boy.

Sarah Eddington was married in 1811 to Bishop Gregory- who always got teased about his Christian name! He is described as *"possessed of sound judgement exercised with Christian concern and a regard for the feelings of others"*[377] Later, Bishop Gregory became an elder and overseer of the Society of Friends in Claverham. The family moved to Claverham Court, a well proportioned Elizabethan property with ample space for the ten children that followed. This is where Eliza was born on 12th March 1833, the last of twelve children.

Eliza's first memories include hearing an anti- slavery poem, *'The Little Blackamoor'*. When Eliza was nearly four, her parents went to London for the Yearly Meeting of Quakers. Eliza was taken ill. The doctor prescribed leeching. *"I know the exact place where I was nursed by the fire and the dreadful creature put on my chest."*[378]

'Home' was incredibly important for 19th century lives. Mugs and later silver-framed photos breathed an air of domesticity. 'Home-sweet-home' was hung from many parlours. Families were large; to have less than seven children would have been considered a small family.[379] Eliza's situation was fairly common. Sometimes fathers lost track of how many children they had sired and whose they were. 'Onward Christian Soldiers' was a hymn that was to be well-known on the Moor. Its author, Revd Sabine Baring-Gould was also author of 16 children. He once asked a little girl at a party whose child she was. 'I am your's Daddy!' she cried, bursting into tears.[380]

This was the time when the Railway came to the Moor. With the coming of the railways built by Quaker engineers the station made Yatton more the trading centre. Eliza remembered 1840-1 when the railway was laid out across the farm fields. *"When it was completed, this was a wonderful place to us and here we played when the trains were running...the sheepdog chasing the train to see if he could get beyond it. But the glorious thing was to dare the engine driver by standing on the rails till he would sound the whistle to frighten them off."*[381]

Books for a teenage Quaker girl included 'Paradise Lost,' and the life of the 17th century French quietist, Madame Guyon. Eliza remembers more sober monthly meetings and also Temperance meetings being held at her home; the latter being especially rowdy. As well as Methodists, Quakers were solidly behind the growing movement to refuse alcohol as a social evil. It was *"kept going by meetings, teas and picnics and other amusements in which all took part; a gay, happy social time and very informal."*[382] This was part of the non-conformist conscience about social evil.

Eliza enjoyed a happy childhood for the most part, ranging over the fields and living a free and independent life with few restrictions. *"Implicit obedience, however, was required of us"*. The meetings at "dear old historic Claverham House where we had to sit for 1 ½ hours at least she describes as *"bi-weekly martyrdom."*[383]

Childhood games were played in the country lanes and on nearby Cadbury Hill. Yatton churchyard was another area to wander around. In 1842, the family left Claverham and went to live in Yatton so the churchyard was close by. Eliza's father was a respected member of the community. He owned Somerset House in Yatton. Kingston Seymour Parish Vestry Minutes contain the following entry:

"Jan 26th 1843- James Griffin in the chair. James Jenkins to be bound as a parish apprentice to the lands belonging to Bishop Gregory of Claverham. Bishop Gregory is deemed a proper person to have the care of James Jenkins."[384]

One of Eliza's cousins, Henry Gregory, had eleven children. He lost membership of the Friends through "marrying out." Henry was a stout, well-made man, the wearer of top boots. Fond of drink, he returned from Backwell Fair and fell into a narrow stream and drowned. This was in 1834. 'Marrying in' was much more the rule. Eliza records a family wedding at Claverham Meeting House in 1845 where her first cousin, Catherine Naish (the only child of John and Lydia Naish) was married. A prayer was written down.

"*Thou knowest O Lord, those who have come hither with prayerful hearts before Thee, beseeching Thee that Thou wouldest be pleased to bless the dear young people who have just entered into solemn covenant before Thee...Grant O Lord that all may experience that glorious liberty wherewith Christ sets His people free from sin, so that when all here shall terminate they may be made to meet to join in singing Alleluias to Thee the Lord God and to the Lamb.*"[385]

This could have been the prayer of the most fervent Methodist meeting in Yatton at that time. Eliza records a key difference in worship style, however; the 'purgatory' of the long quiet meetings. A cousin records a dream she had about heaven.

"*I was given to feel that the object of life is to gain heaven; that it can only be entered by passing through this world; that to the true believer Heaven has already begun and death only refers to the body and liberates the soul to enter into the fullness of life; that Salvation is entirely through our Saviour; that there is perfect safety in Him and that we shall never be weary of loving and praising Him.*"[386]

Eliza's memories are an insight into social history of a 19th century family on the Moor. An elderly Aunt considered that to loll around was disrespectable. Bed was the place to lie down; sofas were an unwelcome concession to the frailty of the flesh. Yet Friends were neither isolated nor austere. One of the Gregory cousins, Edward Churchus, travelled in an overnight coach in 1810 to witness the funeral procession of the old King George IIIrd. His elderly mother Mary wore a lavender-colour silk dress with a pair of scissors attached to her side from a silver chain.

1858 saw Eliza recording a Comet, "*a never to be forgotten and most glorious sight; the whole sky a blaze of colour.*"[387] She attended Sidcot School, the Quaker establishment as a weekly boarder, travelling there in a two-wheeled carriage called a 'gig', securely tucked in between mother and father. Eliza went on to marry John Aubrey Clark, part of the Clark shoe factory family of Street, her childhood memories well and truly over. By then, her parents had died. Her mother, Sarah, died on the same day as William Derham.[388]

It would be a mistake to think that the best years were behind Quakers and that their movement gradually lost impetus in the eighteenth and nineteenth centuries. The railway that Eliza Clark saw being built became an engine of change in the communities of the Moor. Yatton itself with its own station is more important than Claverham as a trading centre. The Claverham Meeting closes in 1866 and will from now be used as for occasional Meetings. Three years earlier, land has been bought in the centre of Yatton by Trustees for the Society of Friends. A substantial meeting house is built in 1866 to become another feature on the ecclesiastical landscape. Amongst the Trustees are two prosperous grocers from Yatton, Francis and James, both of the Gregory family. A cottage belonging to Samuel Avery is included in the transaction. The name is significant. Thomas Avery and William Avery were amongst the early members of the Society of Friends in Claverham back in the 1670's..[389]

On the 2nd March 1867, a public meeting was held to open the new centre. This was at the same era as the substantial Masonic lodge is built up the road, taking over Larchmount School. The records show it the opening Meeting witnessed a packed house. By 1868, one year on, *"the Committee thankfully believe that the benefits anticipated from its opening have been more than realised... A Meeting for scripture reading is regularly held on the First Day (Sunday) evening. These have been attended by many of the inhabitants of the village, and have often been times of spiritual refreshment."*

The Notice went on, "The advantage of a Meeting House close to the population of the vicinity is shown by the large attendance at several Public Meetings held since the opening of the Meeting House."[390]

How many attended regularly? At the end of 1887, there were ten males and twenty six females.[391] By then, the Society of Friends has begun to question the need to keep open the old Claverham Meeting House, now nearly a hundred and sixty years old. Permission is refused because of the burial ground there. As a postscript, it is the Claverham Meeting House that will survive longest, still in use today. In 1912, when Eliza is nearly 80, the Yatton Meeting House has declined. It will be sold to become part of the Infant School in the village. Burial ground stones will be sold in 1965 to go to Claverham to join the final resting place of Friends from previous eras.

When she was a girl, Eliza recalled Isaac Joules the gipsy coming to the house with sand, which was always used on the stone floor of the kitchen. "I think he also used to to grind knives and scissors", she writes. *"He would search for snails which made a useful and nourishing diet for his family."*[392] Who was this enigmatic gypsy?

A Tale of Love and Loss - A 19th Century Gypsy Family[393]

Isaac Joules the gypsy

Isaac Joules is the last of our passers-by. He is a tinker, 60, or is that 70 years of age? This is his last year wandering around the Moor.

In the churchyard at Yatton, there is a burial plot known locally as 'the gypsy graves'.

The visits of travelling gypsies were welcome. Gypsies bring supplies and items that were not easy to buy locally. They also bring news. Before the Enclosures, Mendip gyspies could roam where they wished and pitch their camps without let or hindrance. Once land was enclosed, it was a different story. They had to resort to semi-permanent sites such as a quarry or a field. The Joules were given the right by the Smith –Pigotts, the local landowner, to use Brockley Combe.

It was from sites like this that old Isaac Joules used to venture. He was well-known in the area as a wandering knife grinder. Many stories were told about old Isaac. It was rumoured that he was held in awe as king of the local gypsies. Isaac had the power of the 'evil eye' and could bring bad luck to those he took a dislike to. When he went round from village to village, local boys would tease him. If something went wrong subsequently at home, it must be because '*somebody have a bin worritating wold Isaac*'. Isaac played up to the rumours that surrounded his ability to cure sick pigs and sheep. He muttered cabalistic phrases when he administered the potions.

There were other stories told about him. It was said that Isaac was no gyspy but the son of a wealthy farmer who had given everything up for love. Abraham Joules, a descendant, was convinced that the family were Smyth- Piggotts, the local landowners. Arguably, Isaac's features were not those of a genuine Romany. None of this can be proved, despite the wish to evoke romantic stories from the materials to hand. The factual basis is that Old Isaac Joules did marry a gypsy girl called Merrily. Whether or not he gave up everything for her, he and Merrily did get married.

Born in 1782, her maiden name was common to many people plying a trade- Cooper. Merrily was probably twelve years younger than Isaac. By all accounts, she was dark in complexion and possessed of an uncommon beauty. When she was 29, Merrily gave birth to Richard. Three daughters followed, Caroline, Fancy and probably Matilda. Two years after the birth of Matilda, in March 1827, Merrily was dead. Her death entry in the Parish records reads 'Mersella.'

Isaac was distraught. He never got over it. Inconsolable, whenever his travels brought him back to Yatton, the old knife-grinder would spend the night by her grave. The epitaph he had inscribed is very touching. "*Here lies Merrily Joules, a beauty bright. That left Isaac Joules – Her Heart's Delight*"[394] It was a tale of love and loss.

For fourteen years Isaac trudged the country lanes of North Somerset, sometimes exercising his passing acquaintance with the healing arts (as he put it) but often posing for a sketch at a guinea a time or a portrait. He died in April 1841. Isaac had been admitted to the new workhouse at the Axbridge Union of local Poor Law authorities. Sometimes, workhouses functioned as hospitals. Isaac died there of the dropsy. His death was certified by the Master of the workhouse- Onesiphorus Millard. Isaac's occupation was entered as 'tinker' and his age given as 61, which points to a brith in 1780. Finally, his remains were lowered beside Merrily's, his lost love, and they were re-united in death.

"*The funeral took place in Yatton of Old Isaac, King of the gypsies where there was a very large assembly of the black-eyed bruettes,*" reported the press. Evidently it rained; the reporter of the day described the heavy wet and cold that descended. Tempers frayed and the 'funeral baked meats' got knocked about in a huge row.[395]

One of Isaac and Merrily's offspring went on to dazzle local people and break a few hearts. Caroline must have been a sensation. She became known as the Queen of the Coombe at Brockley. Sometimes, Caroline even held court at the Brockley Hall itself. A local farmer of substantial means tried to woo her by showering her with gifts. Caroline was adamant. Offers of marriage were rejected. She refuses to exchange the open sky for tiled roofs and solid walls; the 'wind on the heath' means more to her. There was other interest. A Somerset landowner, probably Smyth-Piggotts, made a provision for her. This is interesting and possibly significant though it does not establish whether there was a family link with her father. Queen Caroline had no known children.[396]

Fancy Joules, another daughter of Isaac and Merrily sometimes took the name 'Fancy Cooper'. She got into trouble in 1856; summoned on a charge of telling fortunes with the aid of playing cards. Apparently, Fancy had gone to a house in Weston and persuaded a servant girl to relieve herself of £4-10s. Clearly, this was rather more than crossing her palm with silver.

It is likely, though not certain, that Matilda Joules was her sister. The fact that Matilda was born in 1825 points in this direction. 7th January 1854 found her on board ship to seek a new life in Dayton, Ohio. Matilda was 29, the same age as her mother had been when giving birth to her eldest son. Six years later, Matilda went on to marry a Levi Stanley from a gypsy family in Devon. The networks of contact that brought them together in the gyspy community can only be conjectured. But somehow the epithet 'King and Queen' attaches itself to them as it did to Matilda's sister and mother before her. Matilda dies in Vicksburg, Mississipi which General Grant assaults in the Civil War. Maybe they were present at the siege? At her death, Matilda was 53. Branches of the Joules family in America come from Matilda and Levi Stanley. When Queen Matilda was buried, reports said that a vast crowd came to pay their respects, that a thousand carriages had to be turned away and that the service was taken by a minister from the United Brethren Church.

As for Richard, Isaac and Merrily's firstborn, he was born in 1811 and lived until he was 56. Through the gyspy community, he married a Jane Wells, a girl from a gypsy family at Wells, and had seven children with her. They made their home at Bleadon, near Weston. The cause of death was disease of the throat- cancer or diphtheria. On the death certificate, his occupation was entered as horsedealer. "In memory of Richard Joules", runs the inscription, again at Yatton near his parents rather than at Kewstoke where he lived and died. His widow went on to live to the remarkable age of 92. Dying in December 1898, the entry on the certificate for the cause of death reads, 'senectus'. Jane was buried near her husband Richard.

"*A mother from our household gone, a voice we loved is stilled. A chair is vacant in our home that can never be filled,*" runs the epitaph. Newspapers reported that a large crowd from the village assembled in the churchyard when she died.[397]

It has been very difficult to verify if there is anything to the stories that Isaac Joules was a Smyth-Piggott who was disowned- or was he a Wiltshire farmer's son? These are community stories and with all such narratives, what is most important is what it tells us about the community in which they were repeated. What is clear is that the Smyth-Piggotts gave the Joules certain rights to camp at Uphill and Brockley Woods and were kindly disposed to them. It is also the beautiful Caroline, the Queen of Brockley Combe to whom a rich landowner took a shine. A puzzle remains over who bought such a prime spot in the churchyard and paid for railings and headstone. Admirers? Or was this a family tradition of 'going to town' for the last caravanserai?

Isaac and Merrily's eldest son Richard goes on to have seven children. One of them, William, is only 33 when he died, probably at Ilminster. A strange tale was told in later years. An old inhabitant of Ashill Somerset, still in that village in 1938, told of how one day, some sixty years before, a gypsy named Joules approached the local vicar to say his wife had passed away. The grave had been dug when one morning an order came through from the Vicar of Yatton to say that the corpse should be buried there. Mr Joules paid the sexton for digging and then re-filling the grave and hurried off, with his wife's coffin to Yatton. To that day, the old inhabitant remembered Mr Joules giving him a fowl before he went.[398]

Amongst Richard and Jane's offspring is Henry Joules, born in 1833 when Richard is 22. Like his mother, Henry will live to a great age, dying in 1929 at the age of 96. Along with Richard's children and his grandparents Isaac and Merrily, Henry is also buried in Yatton churchyard, the family burial ground. One of his sisters, Genty, born in 1855, will live to the year 1941. She will tour the area, selling clothes – pegs and brushes. Her elder sister Drusilla will live to 98. Local people remembered this old woman sucking a clay pipe by the side of the road. The life they will live continues for a long time to come. At Bleadon, there is a problem when the Great

Western Railway Company want to purchase the area where they made camp. The Joules protest loudly that they have lived there for many years, in effect claiming squatter's rights. The image of bed-ridden Mary Joules, Henry's widow, being forced to move means that many local people are up in arms. This is too much. They can stay.

As ever, life was not easy being in a minority. Gypsy kids had rough times in school. A descendant, Abraham Joules was the first in the line to settle down, buying a small holding with some land. A brilliant gardener, Abraham will be well remembered by his living descendants and local people who still speak of his ability to splice and graft trees, even being able to graft a rose onto a bramble! Other family members will live out their lives; many will be buried in Yatton churchyard. But the folk and family memory of Isaac Joules and Merrily, his heart's delight, will live on.

Chapter Fifteen

THE DAY BEFORE YESTERDAY

It is now the year 1920. As people are living longer, many of the 58th generation that lived on the Moor since the Romans came, born around 1880, are still alive. But they have had to endure terrible times. One in eight of men of fighting age in the villagers have not come back from the Great War. Their names are recorded on War Memorials in the villages. The 40% or so of the 44th generation who perished through Black Death left no trace of their lives and names. This was different. The years after the First World War saw the greatest act of collective remembrance in our history. On the Moor, it had been mooted three years before.

12th April 1917 – the Vicar thanks the congregation for the Easter offering who thought that something should be done as a war memorial. The restoration of the churchyard cross was seen to be an appropriate response.

April 24th 1919- the Vicar spoke of those who had fallen in the War and the also of the War Memorial to be erected in the village with the high object of honouring the fallen. A vote of sympathy is extended to all the relatives of those who had died.

Year after year until this day, the villagers will gather to remember the young men who never returned. The closed curtains and barely suppressed grief following the arrival of the dreaded telegram meant that 36 families were traumatised for life. Silent pain accompanied a member of the church ladies' choir. She never saw Dad.

In the Second World War that the next generation had to fight, all the men of Kenn came back. In the Great War it was a different story. Three boys from the village never returned from the war. One of them was an orphan boy, Anthony Marchant. His mother, Aggie Bailey had never married. She had gone to an orphan home to ask if there were any boys she could raise as her own. Bringing a three year old into her home that day, she could never have thought she would live to see him die.[399]

Then there were the wounded. One of Dorothy Tutcher's uncles was wounded in the First World War and became shell-shocked. *"I remember seeing a piece of shrapnel hanging out of his cheek,"* she recalled.[400] Another uncle died in the flu epidemic of 1918-19, immediately after the end of the Great War. A lot of people died that winter from flu. The hospital had to wait for someone to die so they could get a bed.

Heather King's Aunt Elizabeth had a sad life. Her husband Oliver Simms was one of the Yatton boys who did not return. He died at the first battle of Ypres at the end of October 1914. The men had to make their wills before they went into battle. Elizabeth had been left £127 and had to go out to work. She became a midwife. Her mother Laura came to Yatton to help bring up the two daughters that, along with £127 were the legacy of Oliver Simms. Three bloody years later, brother-in-law Ted Cook fought on the same battlefield. He managed to survive the third battle of Ypres, became a Bristol policeman but fought and lost another battle, this time with pneumonia.[401] When he died, in January 1927, the streets were lined with people and every blind in the village was drawn. 70 policemen were in attendance. Rev Hughes from Kenn officiated. It was, according to a Bristol newspaper, one of the largest funerals seen in Yatton for many years.

The 59th generation of villagers will now experience a revolution in power. Elsewhere in the country, modern England was built on coal. It had been combined with iron to forge the industrial revolution. Apart from the steam locomotives they saw every day, there was little machinery in evidence on the Moor. Cast-iron products were available in the home. And coal filled the skuttles of better-off homes, enough to require coal merchants such as Ron Clements in the village of Yatton. There were three or four coal merchants in the area in those days to feed the demand.[402]

Yet farming technology had not changed for centuries. Across the Moor, power still came from using animals. Horse drawn implement pull up potatoes. Mary Langson's father carried on as a village blacksmith, shoeing horses on Wednesdays and Fridays in the 1930's amidst other jobs of wrought iron-work, bonding for wheels, farm machinery repair and even making wooden coffins which his wife used to line.[403] He charged 12 shillings and 6d for a set of four shoes. By the 1950's, as mechanisation had taken hold, only Friday shoeing remained.

It was not until the Second World War that milking machines installed to mechanise farms. Until then, cows had been milked by hand. Tractors now rumble across the fields – a new sight just as steam locomotives were a hundred years before. Two forms of power now revolutionise the lives of the villagers, electricity and the petrol engine.

There was gas lighting in the streets in the 1920's, Mr Slocombe used to come up on his bike with a stick, 2 wires hanging down either side. He would pull one up to put the light down and when it was time to turn it on at dusk- pull the other one to turn it off at dawn.[404]

In the 1920's, electricity was now being generated by huge coal-fired power stations. This provided power at the point of a cable. And it was available in the home. House by house, cottage by cottage, electrification came to the village communities. A local man, Bert French, recalled the day that the power was switched on. It was like the Illuminations.[405] Each house had 3 lights and a power-point for free. In turn, electricity fuelled the creation of labour saving devices.

For most of the 1930's there was no electricity in Kingston Seymour. In their village shop, the Summerells had nine lamps to attend to every day. The lamps were either hung or were put on the walls for safety. To get their water meant a bucket on a rope dropped down a well. In time, they were able to invest in a pump. Then the great day came when electricity was available. Annie Summerell's husband Jim wired the house and was all ready to connect. An iron, a radio and then appliances like a toaster and a grill heater became regular features of life, courtesy of power at the end of a cable.[406]

Eileen Viney's parents had a brand new house in 1928 in Claverham when they got married. The great day came when they had a gas oven because coal gas came to Cleeve, piped from the gasworks in Yatton. It fed a boiler downstairs from which her father heated water to bring buckets upstairs for a bath. Local cottages had to make do with a tin-bath in the kitchen and, if they were lucky, an outside toilet that flushed. Coal gas also supplied lighting. Her mother came round lighting gas lights around the house. All that was to change in a remarkably short time. Electricity meant light and heat; an electric fire and electric iron. The electricity people came round in 1933 and did a demo of the appliances possible. They brought with them a plate showing what had been cooked.[407] Gone were the days of arriving home amidst gas lighting and candles to go to bed with mother's anxious words, "don't spill the wax!"

The second form of power that revolutionised the lives of the generation born around 1920 was the petrol engine. It was a social revolution powered by the oil that began to dominate the global economy. Small, cheap family cars became popular. The villagers became wedded to oil, to the car. Cars got off to a slow at first in the villages. Then they took off. Agricultural machinery became commonplace; tractors based on oil and other forms of mechanisation achieved yields far beyond the ambition of the farmers of former generations in the village.

Roger Manning's father was a carpenter/wheelright by trade making the wheels and the carts, all of which were horse-driven. Yatton was still a small, industrialised village. *"Mother used to know everybody who lived in Yatton- it was much smaller then."* Uncle Henry worked in the Tannery.

100 people worked there in the 1920's. As cars took hold of life, demand for wheelrights inevitably fell.

High Street Yatton

approaching the station in pony and trap c1920

For most of the 1920's, there were almost no cars in the villages. Horse and cart took people and milk churns all over the county. Buses in Bristol were horse-driven. Behind the Vicarage in Yatton were some old paddocks where the Vicar kept his horse and a pony and trap. The Headmaster and doctor and a few traders and farmers had a car but that was as far as it went. The owner of the ladder factory, Mr Starr had one of the first Jaguar cars in the country.[408] Gradually, the democratisation of the car came within reach of more and more people. In the 1930's Eileen Viney's family owned a car – an Austin 7 with a soft roof.[409]

Mr Travis with his portable hardware store

A bus service made Bristol accessible in the 1920's. Increasing traffic meant the Bristol to Weston road had to be widened. Few owned a car in Cleeve before the war. Only moneyed people and landed gentry had a car. Ordinary folk did not until after the war.There was very little on the main road; mainly bikes, some motor bikes and the postman coming round with the mail on his horse. The letters were in his pouch, not that there was much mail in a country district except for the big houses.

Returning from Canada where his father had emigrated, Len Burdge grew up in Yatton in the 1920's and 30's. *"Your world was round here then. You cycled everywhere. Then in the 1930's we had a car- a little 2 cylinder Jowett. With petrol at 10 1/2d a gallon, you could travel out the village"*.[410] For those without the new means of transport, even with the railway, it was a static life. Most never left the village until after the Great War. A trip to nearby Clevedon marked the first outing.

Others used a punt in the form of a round tub to row on the rhynes. You could go for miles on them in the 1920's; you could row a boat to Clevedon. Every winter, the Moors were flooded near Kenn. People came skating from Bristol with lanterns.

The pride and joy of the Summerells was a two seater Rover they had painted blue with yellow wheels. Petrol was a shilling a gallon though there were different grades in those days. A short run out over the Mendips was all that the family were able to manage most weeks. Sometimes there was a show on in Bristol on a Saturday night they liked the look of. For a shilling, an attendant would take the car, park it and give it a rub down before handing it back. Occasionally, a much longer trip was possible. The south coast of England and the bays between Lyme Regis and Bournemouth was popular. Such a trip meant long hours of work to make up for the time lost.[411]

The development of a mass national consciousness did not occur in Europe until the 19th century. It involved the shift from an agrarian society to an urban and industrial one and from a folk to a national culture through schooling, mass literacy and communication and an increase in the mobility of the population. Apart from the first, these trends shaped the village communities in the twentieth century. Despite excellent transport links, the Moor never became an urban or industrial centre.

There was, however, one important exception. In 1904, Sidney Wake had come down to Yatton in order to set up a factory to make furniture for schools. Originally, Sidney Wake was from Brighton where he made school slates. Together with an associate, Wake and Dean's factory became Yatton's industrial revolution. Business boomed. Soon, the factory was employing up to six hundred people, mostly men. They came from the district as well as the immediate locality. There were three mills in those days. Upstairs they worked on school furniture. Downstairs they made furniture for churches and Government offices.[412]

The impact on the Moor was huge. It offered considerable employment. Sidney Wake owned a well-to-do house in Yatton, near the Station. As a large local employer, Wake and Dean will hold the factory until 1955 when it changes hands. 30 were employed at a ladder factory and at its height, a 120 at the Tannery in Claverham. Maybe half the people in the village worked for the light industry now scattered around Yatton than being labourers, paid only 30 shillings a week.

Born in 1916, Mollie Lukins was a child of the Bell Inn at the south end of the Village. Her father was also the village undertaker as well as a builder. In the war, he was forced to go to Wake and Dean's factory, which was converted to the incessant production of munitions in the First World War. At the National School, where children went from aged 5 to 14, Mollie met her future husband, Ron Clements. He was Chief Prefect, taking the names of people who talked if teacher went out of the room. Ron Clements had come to Yatton as a little boy in 1915. His mother was the first district nurse. At that time, newborn children of some of the poorest families were wrapped up in brown paper.[413]

Rural poverty persisted. Lots of children didn't have enough to eat in those days.[414] Both the Stones and May families in Yatton had nine children. Sam May used to sleep under the table; there was only one room only upstairs. Old Mr Stone would come back drunk on Sunday lunchtime. Sometimes, Mrs Stone threw Sunday lunch at him in the yard. Such families just got by. Porridge and dripping toast were commonplace. To get by people used to catch small animals such as rabbits. On Kenn Moor, there were experts at living off the land. Old Joe Cox would stroll out with his ferret and an hour later return with a rabbit in his hand. Living near the coast, some became proficient eel- catchers or knowing where to find duck eggs.[415] Everyone had a garden. Evryone had an outside toilet that emptied into the ditches. Those houses that located were on the bank of the River Kenn drew their drinking water from it.

In Cleeve, there was no electricity until the 1920's. Most of the villagers did not have water in their homes until then either. Names like Bishop's Well Farm recall the quest for a safe water supply. Rita Quarrington's grandfather had a job that relied on a way of ensuring water supply that is a far cry from the 20th century. In the 1890's, he was a water diviner. It was a full time job; he got paid for it. No one would build a house in 1800's unless you had water. *"My daughter can do it- it's a gift,"* he would say. The other side of Cleeve Parish Church there was a Farm. The Doctor lived there. Here was a well where villagers could go for water. Rita's father had half a field for his horse, half to grow his vegetables which would be taken to Bristol on his horse and cart every day. He was still going up to Bristol in the 1920's when his horse dropped dead. Rita's house, built in 1939 included the new electricity, boasting two round pins. Around them, candles were still being used in some houses.

Some housing was built at Cleeve in the 1930's; until then it was mostly fields around the village. The men worked on farms, as gardeners for big houses, farm labourers, in the Tannery at Claverham or in the Quarry at Plunder Street where they would sit, chipping away at the open rocks.[416]

There were poor families on the Moor and large families also. At one of the village blacksmiths, Mary Langson's family had nine children. A loaf of bread was given to poor families once a year, who typically, would have two bedroom houses in which to bring up six children.[417] Sleeping top to tail in a large bed was how things were for the Knott family with seven children to accommodate.

Many did not have their own home. When they married, it was common to lodge with people until housing could be available. Ray Wathen' parents took in lodgers. Otherwise they couldn't have afforded to send him to grammar school. There was a great need for social housing.[418]

In time, the new version of the old Parish Vestry, the County Council, started to provide social housing at Henley in Yatton. In 1938, a family had the chance of the first house to become available in the village of Kenn.[419] Compared with the rural slums they had lived in before, this was heavenly revolution. One family of nine had lived in a one room cottage with a bedroom area under the sloping roof. Few dwellings for agricultural labourers boasted what came to be regarded as proper facilities. Drinking water required a trip to the well at the bottom of the field and there was only a bucket for a toilet.The poor in a village like this were really poor, not like other rural areas where perhaps the farms were larger. There were no services of any sort in the village. There was no gas, no electricity, no piped waters, no sewers. The first person up in the morning had to find enough dry sticks to start a fire.[420]

Rural poverty was endemic on the Moor. Agricultural labourers might earn only 28 shillings for a 56 hour week. In the Horsecastle district, the 'Trafalgar Square' cesspit was always overflowing. Three or four cottages around the pit were little better than hovels. The workhouses were closed in the 1920's but there was always the Almshouse. Here was the village pump with its supply of water and a handcart for a village fire with buckets on the side, to be pushed in an emergency. Three men used to live upstairs. The rooms had a bed, a geranium or two and an open fire where the residents cooked.[421] Len Burdge's family visited old ladies in the Almshouse where a few lived in one room.[422] They did washing for local people at 2/6d a time in exchange for dinner. On Monday lunchtime, Win Hook used to pick up the rent of the of the washerwoman at the Almshouse, Mrs Brown, who paid 6d a week for her room. She would take the finished washing to Mr Ebden, Reader at the Parish Church and schoolmaster at the National School.[423] Life was demoralising for the insiders. Once, an old gentlemen from the Almshouse went and drowned himself; another cut his wrist.

In Yatton, farm labourers did not earn very much though they could get free eggs and free milk. There was more of a social divide in Kingston Seymour. Until gentrification after the 1960's, Kingston Seymour was a community marked by great poverty.

Coal lorries would be cleaned out with fresh straw and used to transport children of Band of Hope for the annual outings.[424] Although a low crime area by the classifications of the day- the village bobby would give recalcitrant youths a clip round the ear – behind closed doors, family violence went on. In the 1920's, Aggie Bailey in Kenn village was somehow surviving on 50 pence a week war pension. No doubt because she had lost her orphan son in the war, Aggie often had rows with her neighbours because of the way they treated their children.[425]

In the 1920's, industrial unrest meant coal miners on strike in South Wales or Radstock. They came to places like the Moor looking for work. There was little. Most of the men of Kingston worked on the land but there was not enough work for the villagers in Kenn. Some went every morning to the tile factory in neaby Clevedon; others found work at Wake and Dean's furniture factory in Yatton where there was a job for life if you kept your head down.[426] Five working farms in Horsecastle area at the north end of the village meant there was generally work in Yatton itself. Women would take in washing or work scrubbing steps. Children could work in some of the larger houses around, earning 9d a week with Farmer Price.[427]

For this 59th generation, the days of parish relief, pauper's graves and workhouse are gone mercifully. The Liberal Government of 1906 onwards has brought in National Insurance and Unemployment Benefit. But medical attention such as pregnancy meant trips to the doctor across the Moor to Nailsea. That was before there was any National Health Service. Doctor's bills had to be paid. Bills amounting to £20 through a pregnancy were not uncommon. For a shilling a week, you could pay into a hospital scheme. That would be enough for a family. If you reached 60, you were lucky. Local people recall how their families would only fetch the doctor if they had to.

"Why didn't you come to me before?" the doctor would ask. *"I couldn't afford it". "I would rather treat you now for cheap than see you in your coffin"*, came the doctor's reply.[428]

Even with its darker side, it would be inaccurate to misconstrue Yatton as a hard place in which to live. The village is recalled with great nostalgic affection, a long high street flanked by nearly sixty shops. This was a self-contained community. There was a shoe shop, a drapers (staffed by a Mr Tutt with had an ear trumpet he put to his ear), a men's tailor, a jewellers, a number of sweet shops, a chemist where you could buy vinegar and Beecham's pills at 2d a week. Children found it intriguing to see the cobbler take nails out of his mouth to do the shoes. This was a complete village.[429] There were 14 farms in Yatton between the wars. At least three firms supplied milk from local farms to people in their horse and cart. Villagers go out with their jugs to take a pint or a quart from the churns. And then there was the bread man who brought buns, seven for six pence. The top one was the one with the icing!

There were bigger congregations at church in those days. Not that everyone went. An interesting comparison can be made of rural church attendance in the early 1920's compared with a generation later. According to the service registers, barely 20 people on average would attend the 8am service at Yatton Parish Church but the 11am service did not do appreciable better with only 17 or 18 people turning out for Matins and a sermon. Clearly numbers swelled appreciably at Easter and Christmas (which had a service at 7am also!) but this is hardly sign of personal and active faith.

Perhaps we are witnessing in these statistics the fate of official Christianity in an age of doubt. What are things like at the end of our period? In 1960, service registers noted that average attendance at the 8am was 38. By then, the pattern of service included Holy Communion at 11am. Attendance here ran at 41 on average. We are not seeing modern surges of zeal here either.[430] It has to be said that much depended on the Vicar and what was on offer. Crucially, the role of the parish church went far beyond attendance on a Sunday. The attitude seems to be that church was there if needed, principally to give meaning to life's milestones.

The old contrast between chapel and church was not hard and fast and did not easily sit with class divides. The well-to-do Dyers of Kenn Court were Chapel people; only becoming church when the Vicar asked Mr Dyer if he would become church warden.

At the Parish Church in the 1930's, Church was at the heart of the village. The Village Hall, Girls Friendly Society, the Band of Hope, Church fetes. Magic lantern slides in the village halld charging 3d for children- most activities were connected with church.[431] Church would attract people from the Almshouse and also, many local children. Horsecastle Chapel saw 100 children in the Sunday school, mainly from the labouring classes. It was easier to send the children to church so parents could have a lie in rather than go yourself.[432]

In Cleeve, some farmers went to the Methodist Chapel which was well-attended – there was little sense of a social divide. In Yatton itself, the picture varied. Children from north end (Horsecastle) were Chapel people. They went for the most part to the undenominational school. Children didn't really mix and went to activities organised by the Chapel. Some children went to the undemoninational, others to the National (Anglican) School.[433] The Methodist church was in the middle of the social spectrum.

Basket weaving at Church of England National School c1935

With their emphasis on abstinence and temperance, the Methodists used to lecture on the evils of drink. There was quite a bit of drinking. At 10d a pint, Cider was cheap. Some women went through difficult times with husbands coming back and beating them. Wives would wait by the gate to get money immediately after a man got paid before he went drinking.[434] Some poor families in Yatton were, it seemed, mainly because the father used to drink.

As an important junction, Yatton station was busier than ever. Bert French's father was a signalman, working at Yatton station, which had become the 3rd biggest junction on the Great Western Railway.[435] 80 people were employed there. The signalbox had 130 levers. The engine pulled the coaches to Clevedon and then to avoid using valuable time decoupling and placing it at the front of the train, the engine pushed the train back to Yatton. Strictly speaking, this was against regulations. On a typical day in 1925, four coal and mineral wagons and something like seven goods wagons would be received. 53 cattle trucks went over the line that year along with 2000 milk churns. The last train of empty wagons came through in June 1963.[436] The Moor was criss-crossed with railways. What the locals called the Light Railway went from Portishead to Weston Super-Mare in those days. Kingston Seymour had its own halts, one mini-station even having its own waiting room. On the railways, a refreshment boy was employed to sell chocolate and cigarettes in the 1920's. He was paid the princely sum of 15 shillings a week plus 6pence for every pound of items he sold. A new stall was opened in 1932 by Wymans. It was busy. A manager was employed plus an assistant manager, two boys carrying chocolate and cigarettes, and six boys full time on paper rounds.

One of the paper boys was Bert French. He would report at 7am to meet the paper train from Bristol, sort the bundles and then catch the 8.10 to Cheddar. At Axbridge, he collected his bicycle with its front carrier then delivered papers in Axbridge, Cross and Weare. There were many magazines as well - perioidcals such as The Tatler, Doctor's Journal, Farmer and Stockbreeder, Titbits, Woman's Weekly, Comic Cuts and the Rainbow. Once a werk, Bert French collected the money plus one penny for delivery. His wage was 10 shillings per week.

New forms of entertainment were made possible by the growing mobility and technology. A trip to London by train was just about possible on a half day. With mass circulation newspapers, a family was able to keep in touch with the wider world. In 1917 or 18, Jim Summerell was one of the first people in the area to get anything on the wireless he loved to tinker with. Building a set with coils and wires and with instructions from books, they waited for ages for something to come through. When it did, the sound was that of music with very little speaking.

The era of mass society had well and truly arrived. Cheap newspapers and the wireless were freely available. Rural areas such as the Moor only began to feel this after the First World War. Until after the next war, the majority of villagers would remain in the locality in which they had grown up. In the village of Kenn in 1934, there was only one telephone.[437]

In Eileen Viney's home as a child of the 1930's, there were newspapers every evening- The Bristol Evening World. And there was wireless. At first they came with batteries and you had to go up the road to get them charged. Then the day came when the family had an electric wireless.[438]

By 1912, the first films were shown at the Curzon cinema in Clevedon, at the other end of a short train ride. Now one of the oldest cinemas in the country with a continuous service, the original Picture House seated 200 people, boasted mirror front doors, hanging baskets and an organ to accompany silent movies. The first showing, on April 20th, was a special charity screening of a newsreel film about the sinking of the Titanic. Proceeds of £2 2 shillings went to the Lord Mayor of London's Fund for the survivors and relatives.[439] Hereafter, cinema became part of the experience of the villagers on the Moor. You could go to the picture house in Clevedon and get the last train home. As a young girl, Win Hook would go to Clevedon for 3d on the train to see Charlie Chaplin and other silent movies until the talkies came in. Other leisure pursuits remained beyond the reach of most ordinary people who never travelled far afield or had a real holiday. The men went to the pub and the women to the Women's Institute or the Mother's Union. In the old First World War hut, socials, dances and skittles used to take place in Cleeve.

Social attitudes struggled to keep up with changing times. Unmarried women from better off families were chaperoned on trips out if they went with a young man. There were many richer people around. Even at the Horsecastle Chapel in the poorer part of the village, well to do people would drive there sometimes in the early 1900's on a pony and trap. The ladies would wear their new outfit and Easter bonnet.

The Parish magazine recorded the gender imperatives of contemporary society. *"Housework is not a drudgery but an adventure with wind in its sails. House-work equips a girl with business acumen, self-reliance and self-forgetfulness and crowns her with the dignity of a queen, her rightful kingdom, the kingdom of love"*[440]

In Yatton, the Village Hall used to have its annual Flower Show as well as billiards and snooker. It was a place to go for local kids. Such memories pay fond tribute to a slower place of life. Yet that did not mean a rural idyll.

Bert French's father went on strike in 1926. He was a socialist, strongly imposed to what was still a class-ridden society. Bert was not persuaded that communities such as on those on the Moor meant rural heaven. He grew up acutely aware of the social divide and the conventions of the day. *"If you didn't touch your cap to a lady, you were in dead trouble"*.[441] Bert French wanted to work on the railway but had a lazy eye so that was out. Instead, he went to work for a butcher who had his own slaughter-house. Bert asked the Butcher for a raise of half a crown but that was refused, despite him being one of the richest people in Yatton.

Dot Tutcher's father learnt to doff his cap to the local landowners. When Mrs Smyth-Piggot went on a Sunday afternoon drive once, she spoke to him sharply. "You call me Madam!" It was a lesson he never forgot.[442]

Another local lad recalled the days when 'respectable' denoted the families who were poor, did not mix and went neither to church or chapel. *"I remember during our last days at school, Oliver talking wistfully to me knowing I was going to start a career on the railway. 'Of course', he said, 'your family is respectable; mine isn't..'"*[443]

Class-based social injustice was endemic. One Yatton woman, Mary Wride, lived past her 90th birthday. But to her dying day, she remembered what had happened to her daughter Cissie. Cissie had gone into domestic service in Torquay in the 1920's. The Coroner recorded an open verdict on why she had fallen off the cliff but her family and employers knew the truth. Cissie had left the house where she worked in tears. Her employer had accused her of stealing. A pound note had gone missing from her purse. The accusation of being a thief and the threat of losing her job was more than the lonely young woman could bear. Her employer later found out she had wrongly accused Cissie. When he came back from work, her husband came back and told his wife he had borrowed a pound note. Dreams of a new life for Cissie, away from the poverty of the small South Wales mining village where she grew up, had all gone tragically wrong. All for the sake of a pound note. Mary Wride later lost her son on D-Day, then her husband in a mining accident.[444]

In Cleeve, there was a strong sense of a class- based society. The Sinclairs were landed gentry, giving the George V playing field to the village. There was a THEM-business people and other landed gentry, 50 in all at the most and US- the manual workers. That was to change after the war as Cleeve became commuter land.[445]

It took time to break down insular, prejudicial attitudes. Sometimes these were expressed in autograph books. *"God made the little niggers, He made them in the night. He made them in a hurry and forgot to make them white"* – autograph book of Marjorie Court of Claverham.

A Parish magazine at the end of the twenties waxed lyrical about the future. *"1929 finds us looking out upon a world with its doors flung wide open to us."*

It was not to be. This was the year that the Wall Street Crash helped to trigger the Great Depression which did so much to bring the Nazis to power in Germany.

War!

Like their parents, the 59th generation have to endure another terrible war. The Second World War brought planes criss-crossing the skies above the inhabitants. Many young men are called up to fight. Young women were determined to do their bit- women like Win Hook who drove lorries in France and jeeps for Generals.[446]

How did war touch the life of a country parish?

In 1940, Yatton Station was host to King George VI and Queen Elizabeth. The Royal train stayed at the station for two nights. Cows were removed from nearby fields so they would not disturb the King and Queen. Those two nights saw no shunting and no goods train to Wells or Clevedon. Sawdust was laid to deaden the footfall of the Royal bodyguards.[447]

Bert French is a full-time fireman in the War, reporting for duty in Plymouth to face incendiary bombs coming down in thousands on the city. By day, Len Burdge is in a reserved occupation, producing food to keep the country alive. By night, he is on ARP duty locally. Heather King's mother is making gas mask cases. *"I can see her now doing on an old trendle sewing machine making these for someone to collect...... those were the happy years. We all mucked in."*[448]

Daylight raids brought bomb damage such as water mains bursting. The inhabitants cheer as British fighters chasing the enemy bomber, who, to gain height, releases its bombs. They mourn a big mine meant for the sea missed the water and went down in Kingston Seymour, not far from the sea wall. Five locals die that day. The people live off bread and dripping, a little meat such as rabbits and vegetables. You didn't waste the earth above an air raid shelter. It was good to grow cabbages on it.

Bristol was the 5th most bombed city in Britain. When a bomb was dropped on Kenn village Ray Naish sat up to find he was covered in plaster and glass, lucky to be alive. Kenn Church suffered slight damage.

School children watched a low-flying enemy aircraft on its way to the Horsecastle end of the village where it dropped eight bombs.Italian prisoners of war, and later Germans, were held in tin huts at Congresbury. Prisonerswere escorted through Yatton on work detail. *"The Italians used to make coffee for us and do any jobs that needed doing. Some never went back."*[449]

"In the war, Italian prisoners of war were in the village. One came and worked on the farm. He had to go back at night. I remember him as a tall young man. The Italians went and German prisoners of war replaced them. One of these was Josef Rices, He stayed until 1947. There were also Polish soldiers who had fought for Germany."[450]

On Claverham Moor there was a decoy. Flairs were lit to look like a town on fire. Often it worked. Bombers would bomb the flairs. Barrage balloons were thought by local people to be effective; the nearest ballon was at nearby Hewish. Other areas of the Moor are also set up as decoys, to confuse the Luftwaffe into bombing the countryside instead of Bristol. Bread baskets are set on fire in Kings Woods on Roddy Hill to give the effect of burning buildings.

Women over a certain age are wanted for the Land Army.

Evacuees came in their hundreds. Cleeve House was full of evacuees from London., Children from Bow bells and Bermondsey suddenly had to get used to life in a North Somerset village. Evacuees in the village worked at Wake and Dean. One family took in Jewish children- Jan and Felicity from Czechslovakia. Jan's father was a well-known musician in Czech. She never heard from her parents again. The local children had lessons in the morning, the evacuees in the afternoon. Some mothers came to stay. As their husbands were in the forces, that didn't matter.

The evacuees were brought to Cadbury House. Now it is a smart country club but during the war, a school was on the site. St David's School was small. Only about 60 pupils attended. It offered boarding for boys along with a few day pupils. Many pupils were Jewish refugees from Austria and Germany who would join in, eating stew for lunch, bread and margarine for breakfast and tea with cake on Sundays. The uniform was a black blazer with white on the pocket together with a black cap with a white ring. This gave rise to the nickname of 'liquorice allsorts" by villagers as they saw the boys in the village as they visited the old sweet shop on Frost Hill where they could spend their sweet coupons.[451]

The war did not pass Yatton people by. They were constantly reminded of it. There was a Wings for Victory week in June 1943 that aimed to raise £20,000 for 4 Spitfires. The actual result was £43,229. It was a huge achievement for a small village and one that demonstrated the profitability of its farmers. In the wake of the ceasless demand for food, raising food production was the need of the hour. Now there was work for everyone and it was profitable. Yatton cattle market functioned as a centre where once a fortnight, you could bring your steers to feed a hungry nation- and get a good price for it! Over 250 cows were brought in on one day. You had to book a slot.[452]

The Home Guard in the district was the 7th Somerset (Long Ashton) Battalion consisting of about 2,500 men and also women auxiliaries. One of its Companies was based in Yatton.[453]

Another way the war touched the life of a country parish was the incessant demand for food. An eyewitness records Yatton market functioning as a cattle collecting centre. Once a fortnight, people would bring steers to the centre to be bought to feed a hungry population. One day set a record. Over 250 head of cattle were bought in. You had to book the slot several weeks before.[454] Farmers were experimenting with a greater use of machinery. Until the war, they had been using horses. That began to change. Massey Ferguson tractors became a vital part of the agricultural landscape across the Moor. Rabbits and eggs provided food for the local population.

In 1943, the area is allocated to the Americans, as part of the build-up for D-Day. Nearby Brockley Coombe was a transit facility for moving troops from one part of the UK to another or for the invasion, using ports in the Bristol area such as Portishead. The US 4th Division 1st Army was based here as was the 298th Field Hospital in training. The inhabitants get used to seeing a great many GIs in jeeps. About one in eight of these were black Americans. This is where the villagers encounter racial prejudice.

Local women would go out with the GI's. Sometimes, these would be black. "*They came into our village hall*" recalled Rene Cook.[455] "*The coloured soldiers were great dancers, swinging you here and there, real jitter-bugs. Father used to cycle to the village hall.' Don't you dare leave this hall until I collect you', he'd say. Coloured soldiers and whites didn't mix though. The coloureds went to the Lord Nelson pub; the whites to the Starr Inn. The black*

GI's were gentlemen though. They knew the position they were in. Were we going to treat them the same as other Americans?"

The camp was segregated. There was an all-black camp or black end of Brockley camp. And there were black and white clubs in Bristol. Sometimes, there were fights between white and black soldiers in a Nailsea pub- using knives and forks. One Clevedon girl married a black GI that caused a great comment. General Benjamin Davies- the only black General and in command of supply troops at Brockley, expressed subservient gratitude to another general of supply, General Less. *"He even let me use his shower!"*

Prejudice was not just confined to white Americans. At nearby Weston, the wife of the Vicar of Worle caused a sensation. It was all reported in a Sunday pictorial magazine and even discussed in Cabinet. The Vicar's wife had made it clear in wriiten advice what any respectable women should do in the presence of black men; leave a cinema immediately, leave a shop immediately.[456]

Then came the end.
Tuesday May 8th 1945 – V.E day!

The Post-War Years

When Britain emerges from the Second World War, she still rules ¼ of the people on the planet. But the country was exhausted. Rationing cut even more deeply into what ordinary people were allowed to have in any week. It was a make and mend culture that affects the people of the Moor. Building New Jerusalem will also transform England's green and pleasant land here in another way. The Beveridge Report, published at the height of the war, had signposted the prospect of no more squalor, no more children stunted because of the kind of rural poverty seen in these communities. A new National Health Service meant that health care will now be free at the point of need.

Wartime petrol rationing ended in May 1950. With it, appetite for consumer goods grows. Demand for economical, British-made family cars grew. Cars such as the Standard Vanguard and the Morris Minor were found everywhere on the Moor. The Ford Popular lived up to its name.

For many local people, things did not change in the village until the 1950's and 60's. With the growth of financial services in Bristol, commuting became a way of life. It was the legacy of social transformation brought by the arrival of the railway back in 1841. Population remained at about the two to three thousand mark up to the 1950's. This was not much more than a hundred years before. Then it will mushroom. Road by road, housing was extended. The numerous local shops, so fondly remembered by local people as the mark of self-contained community, began to go until a supermarket in the 1960's symbolised that the people of the Moor are in a new time.

An old way of life had gone forever. The 60's heralded high-speed social change, one effect of which was that people oriented themselves around their own needs and happiness. It would no longer be instinctive to think communally. Yet a remarkably strong sense of community prevailed, offering the hand of friendship to strangers. Churches were to remain at the heart of their communities as they had for centuries. For the 60th generation to have lived on the Moor since the Second Legion came to occupy in Roman times, the future had arrived. It no longer lay over the horizon.

Epilogue

THE GREAT YATTON FEAST

On Friday 8th January 1886, an enormous public feast took place. The ox roast is still within folk and family memory: how it turned into a riot with hundreds of yobs from Bristol coming down on the train as ox was pulled off the spit.[457] Communal feasting was a feature of Parish life in Merry England. Extracts from contemporary newapapers described the memorable event.

The fatted ox had been roasting all Thursday night for public distribution. The ox was put down to the fire between 11 and 12 o'clock on Thursday night, and those attending it throughout the night had no pleasant task, as the gale that blew from the north-east till 3 o'clock was followed by driving sleet and rain for a couple of hours, during which the kitchen, which was built in the open field, was partially roofed in with an iron shield or bonnet.

The dining tent was in Mr Wyndham's field. There was an ornamental arch erected at the entrance to the field, and over the engine was displayed the motto, 'welcome to all'. On the reverse side, 'long life to all donors.' The band of the first Gloucestershire Engineer Volunteers gave their services. The Clevedon amateur Fire Brigade marched in wearing their uniforms.

They came literally in thousands. The Committee, with an ox weighing 8 cwt, 2 well-grown sheep, 300 quarterns of bread and sundry hogsheads of 5X ale and cider, had provided for a thousand. But nothing short of a miracle would have fed and satisfied 5,000 hungry persons who thronged Yatton village that day.

An old lady of 84, journeyed from Kingston Seymour and she remembered feasting on the last ox roasted whole in the neighbourhood, 76 years before, when the first sea-wall of Kingston Seymour was completed.

Hundreds of Bristolians journeyed in by rail. So crowded was the midday train that when the miscellenaeous throne de-trained in Yatton, the platform was crammed from end to end, and hundreds leapt the fences without giving up their tickets.

The Committee had arranged to seat and dine, 580 at a time but after the arrival of the 1.15 train, the crowd, finding the knife and fork business already commenced, burst into the tent, carried away the side canvas, raided the tables and so upset all the arrangements. All was confusion and turmoil and the huge tent was packed with a huge mass of struggling people, each one of whom seized anything within his reach. Two or three had a dispute over the head of the beast, another clutching 2 lbs of solid meat, very underdone, was triumphantly holding it aloft in his clenched fist. A still more hungry visitor, dexterously dashed it from his hold, and there was a scramble for it as it fell.

The whole affair started with the best intentions and the most generous motives, proved such a Saturnalia that, although it made Yatton more lively than it had been for a century, probably another century will pass before Yatton people consent to roast a second ox!

Part Two

THE MID-VICTORIAN GENERATION
(AN IN-DEPTH LOOK)

Chapter Sixteen

THE UNDESERVING POOR

At Claverham House in 1851, Daniel House, an agricultural labourer has taken a lone child, Joseph Meachy, who is two years old. He is not the only orphan in the village. William Webber is 5 months old, taken in by another farm labourer. There is no national provision for retirement and pension. In the village of Claverham in 1851, three people regard themselves as retired. All are in their 70's. At the bottom of the pile were six paupers. The age of the paupers varies. Ann Thomas is 90, Eliza Avery is 40 and John Burge is 76. James Burge is listed as a farm labourer as well as pauper. He is 32. One pauper is 77, another 62.

In 2010, amidst Government action to find savings from a national overdraft, the idea of restraining the welfare budget by ensuring that benefits only went to the deserving was back on the agenda. Announcing drastic cuts to public expenditure, the Chancellor George Osborne referred twice to the deserving v undeserving poor.[458]

There is nothing new about the kind of analysis that periodically returns in social and political discourse about the problem of the poor. Karl Marx spoke of the '*lumpen proletariat....in all towns quite distinct from the industrial proletariat. It is a recruiting ground for thieves and garbage of society*".[459] In the 1880's, commentators spoke of 'a social residuum'. Later on, by the 1950's, the residue of society had mutated into 'problem families.' In the 1960's, analysts used the term, 'disreputable poor'. Then in the 1970's, there was talk of 'a cycle of deprivation,' or 'cycles of disadvantage'.[460]

What to do about the poor was an enormous problem for mid - Victorian Britain. Rural communities as well as urban towns and cities wrestled with the issue. They had done this for centuries but this time, there is a new moral seriousness that signified a return to Elizabethan attitudes. If people were poor, it was their fault.

Poverty was a headache for the people of the Moor too. Parish records recorded what these days would be regarded as secular business. Back then, there was no distinction. In February 1825, the Vestry minutes for St Mary's Yatton record that the Commissioners appointed by the King were keen to ensure that only grants for poor inhabitants of the village be accepted, not poor parishioners per se. Some of these might after all live outside Yatton. Churchwardens were required to ensure that regard be made for the "*objects of relief, that is the moral conduct and behaviour of those who are to receive the bounty; whether their general habits of life and mode of bringing up children be such as to render them worthy objects; since undoubtedly, it was not the intention of those who left money for charitable purposes to have it disposed of to those who were notoriously profligate, idle and disorderly and therefore undeserving objects".*[461]

The poor rate was fixed on that occasion at one shilling in the pound. To help local poverty, rate-payers had to find one twentieth of a given sum in proportion to the value of their property. But 'undeserving objects'..... who were these characters?

By contrast, the Yatton Vestry Meeting for January 1st 1838 said that those who have worked or are widows of labourers are to be regarded as "deserving characters". No one would be regarded as deserving poor if they were addicted to drink or if they neglected public worship. The deserving poor are in three categories - over 60, over 40 and over 30. 'Deserving poor' are set against those who seem to be milking the system, clearly undeserving. The Vestry minutes record how this might be judged.

'September 2nd 1828- Martha Gregory to be committed under vagrancy act is she continues to apply for poor relief'. By the time of the 1841 Census, Martha is 55.

The Vestry meeting on November 5th 1833 had resolved that such paupers as Vestry thinks fit shall have the mark of YPP in some conspicuous place on their clothes to distinguish them as belonging to the parish of Yatton. They were to wear this social label for as long as they were designated a pauper. It was a badge of stigma.

Other cases are clearly more deserving. Or are they? In the 1841 Census, there is reference to a Robert Rogers. He is a young man of 15. He is mentioned in the Vestry Minutes of August 14th 1832 providing for the children of the late Nehemiah Rogers. A jacket, trousers and shoes will be given to Robert, a frock and skirt for his sister Louisa and jacket trousers and shoes for his younger brother Thomas. By 1841, Robert has gone into the shoemaking trade himself. Loiusa is 13, a female servant, and Thomas is 14, an agricultural labourer. They appear to have lost their mother by this time though there is a grandmother on the scene, Martha, aged 69.

Another name or two from the 1841 Census might be mentioned. Ann Jenkins is now 31. The Vestry Minutes for September 11th 1832 had allowed two shillings for Ann Jenkins during an illness. A few weeks later she is granted a further 2/6d in her illness. A Deborah Lovell is to be paid for lodgings for Ann Jenkins. Deborah is described in the 1841 census as being in independent means. She is 51.

In 1834, a new Act of Parliament had been passed. *"In pursuance of an Act of Parliament passed in the 4th and 5th year of the Reign of His Present*

Majesty King William the Fourth entitled 'An Act for the Amendment and better Administration of the Laws relating to the Poor in England and Wales', the Poor Law Commissioners do order and declare that the Parishes and places together with all hamlets, tythings....shall on the eleventh day of April next be united for the Administration of the Laws for the relief of the Poor, by the name of Bedminster Union."[462]

That was how the communities of Kenn, Kingston Seymour, Cleeve and Yatton came to be included in a scheme that was to represent the terror of the working classes. They had to contribute to a common fund for purchasing and building the Bedminster Union workhouse at Long Ashton. A Board of Guardians was to be constituted and elected annually. Any ratepayer could be chosen or put himself forward- men only at that stage!

Quickly, the Poor Law Commissioners is referred to in parish records. Then comes the first reference to the dreaded workhouse. On January 27th 1835, John Cook's poor relief is to be stopped until his son quits the workhouse where he was provided for. February 24th 1835- Joseph Hopkins is paid 6d a week for the next fortnight for pillow cases until one of the Assistant Overseers for the poor in Yatton can make arrangements for his reception into the workhouse.

The workhouse needs provisioning. Saturday March 1841, *"All persons desirous of contracting for the supply of bread in the undermentioned districts are requested to send in tenders with samples".* Yatton, Kingston Seymour and the village of Kenn are included in number 3 District. Weekly consumption is estimated to be 130 loaves.[463]

At first, Yatton clergy might take funeral services for their own people or at least their deaths were recorded in the parish registers. On September 10th 1843, for instance, a John Cook was buried in the Long Ashton (Bedminster) workhouse.[464]

The new Poor Law was not as generous as the old system of poor relief. As Parish records also make clear, the problem of the poor remained. Desertion, old age, sickness, widowhood, unemployment and injury meant that many people were forced to apply to the relieving officer. Recourse to Poor Relief was a necessity for up to a third of households in the 19th century; possibly a half had applied for assistance at some point in their lives. The proportion amongst rural labourers was even higher.[465]

There was a rate levied for the relief of the Poor. In Kingston, the annual amount of poor-relief previous to the New Poor Law had been £126. In

1859, 3d in the pound has been allowed for the relief of roads; 6d in the pound for the relief of the poor. The Poor Rate and the cost of maintaining the Poor House in Yatton fell to owners of property. The rate had gone up - from 3d in the pound in the early part of the 18th century to a shilling in the early part of the 19th. It seemed as if work has always to be carried out on the upkeep of the Poor House. In Kingston in 1841, the Parish has exacted 6d in the pound for the relief of the poor. The amount fluctuated, decreasing as the workhouse came into effect and as people complained about the burden..[466]

The new workhouse was the last resort. 'Abandon all hope who entered therein'! Inmates would be segregated, stigmatised and find it enormously difficult to break free from the shackles. This was systematic social devaluation. The workhouse is not the only possibility. The alternative was the local Almshouse. This was not without difficulty. In October 1840, churchwardens, acting with the Overseer of the Poor serve the occupants of the Poor House *"notice to quit the apartment provided by the Parish of Yatton."* They have one month to depart.[467] A new accommodation list is drawn up. The Vestry Minutes for January 6th 1841 *"pay Thomas Bishop 6d a week until such times as the parish house is ready to be occupied"*.

On 10th April 1843, the Vestry Meeting examines the pauper list. The Board of Guardians is to be consulted on stopping upkeep paid to Martha Osmonds for a woman in lodgings in her house, commonly known as the old witch. Also, John Beacham's boy was to be designated an apprentice bound by the parish. That year, there are five Assistant Overseers for the west side of Yatton; five for the east side.

In 1851, the Almshouse contains around 30 people. In 1895, it will come under the administration of the Parish Council. Nearly 100 years later a Trust will be set up with the aim of renovating the building by using social housing grant to bring it back into use as accommodation for local people in housing need. The Trust will not be able to secure sufficient funding. They will sell to a housing association. When they die, poor villages will be buried in pauper graves, probably near the present Chapter House of the Parish Church. Pauper graves constitute one strategy of social de-humanisation; representing silent objects - people whose voices were not heard.

What to do about the lunatic paupers remained a problem. The Parish wrote to the Poor Law Commissioners about it. The reply in February 1841 was that a new bill being placed before Parliament ought to address the problem. It took four years.

In 1845, legislation created the Lunacy Commissioners. Lord Shaftesbury is the Chairman, though he can only give Monday afternoons to this work. The powers of the Lunacy Commission only extended to the insane in workhouses. Sometimes they championed wrongful committal. But classification was controversial. The problem was getting an adequate definition of who was insane and who was not. Were the old, the feeble, the harmless and the helpless to be regarded as lunatics? Assessment criteria were part of the problem in that they created labels. The Victorians feared moral contagion. In effect, the problem of the lunatic pauper became an aspect of Poor Law administration.

The Election of Guardians for the Poor Law was reported in the press. The Bristol Mercury could announce that Henry Beakes and Robert Williams would represent Yatton in 1860-1 along with James Dyer from Kenn and Jacon Harding from Kingston Seymour.[468] There had been complaints about the fairness of administration. Why should it be that the interests of Bedminster, sending six Guardians to represent 19,241 inhabitants, should be swamped by 28 Guardians representing country parishes totalling 18,420?[469]

The problem of the poor remained. So did the culture of moral seriousness. In December 1862, an Emma Field along with 'her bastard child' was ordered to be removed from Yatton Parish to Weston Zoyland. Sorting the problem out involved travelling to Weston Zoyland, applying for deposition and removing the paupers. In all, the case of Emma Field and her child cost £2-10 shillings to resolve..[470]

Illegitimacy is a grave social stigma. The Register of births in the Long Ashton workhouse from the parish of Yatton shows many children who are illegitimate.

> January 1870 – Mary Ellen, daughter of Clementina Rowley of Yatton is born. She is illegitimate.
> January 1872 – Henry, son of Anne Denmead is born. He too is illegitimate.
> February 1875 – Lucy Cooksley from Yatton has given birth to twin girls. Celia Cullen from Yatton gives birth to a son the following week. All are illegitimate.

There was no way legally to force someone into the workhouse. Increasingly, the workhouse held those who were unable to function outside it - the sick, the old, the feeble, the infirm as well as the insane.[471] Always, dogging the issue there was the problem of definition of the insane. Victorian doctors and administrators never could agree on a working definition.

Life in the Workhouse in 1881

In 1881, the bookend at our look at the mid-Victorian generation, the Long Ashton workhouse for the Bedminster Union is limited to 420 inmates plus 150 pupils for the schools. The paupers are engaged on stone breaking, oakum picking, gardening, carpentry, tailoring, shoemaking and farm work. Three outdoor labour officers supervise the work. The Labour Master, Albert Bobbett, is paid 23 shillings per week. On 11 January that year, it was agreed to help Henry Weldly, a poor person residing in the workhouse who wanted to emigrate to St Louis, Mobile, USA.; *"the necessary steps to be taken and £6 to be given for the purpose"*.[472] In one week in March, Kingston contributes £105 to the workhouse, Kenn £46 and Yatton £282.

In 1881 George Gage from Yatton is both a vaccination officer (for which he is paid £20) and a collector for the Guardians, taking 5% of money collected. He is not the only Yattonian. The surgeon John Hurd is also there as a public vaccinator. He is paid as per contract on number of cases. The Matron is a Mary Stone, paid £45. She has been there since Sept 1873. An assistant matron who is from the workhouse, Emma Tilley, has been doing that since September 1872. Her salary is £20, not as much as the Head Nurse, Martha Halley, also from the workhouse, paid £30. A schoolmistress, Henrietta Clarke is paid £32. The local Guardian for the Workhouse is William Naish, farmer. John Griffin, landowner, is Guardian for Kenn and John Wallis Guardian for Kingston. John Griffin is still doing this job ten years later.

The Register of Deaths at the workhouse commence in 1866. Between then and 1881, 14 people from Yatton will experience that great dread of our ancestors, to die in the workhouse. The average age at death is 61. James Beacham will live to the age of 80, passing away on Christmas Day 1887. Members of his family have lived in the Poor House in Yatton or have been detained at Her Majesty's pleasure.[473]

Emigration

One solution the parish adopted to relieve the financial burden was to help the poor to emigrate. On April 13th 1832, it was agreed by a large majority to allow George Hookey and family of Claverham to go to America. £5 is to be given to enable this. Parishes helped many poor people to new lives in the British colonies. Between 1837 and 1847, Poor Law Unions assist 9,500 emigrants; 4,800 going to Canada and 4,000 to Australia.[474] It was cheaper than paying out long-term Poor Relief.

Rowntree's survey of rural poverty showed that many agricultural labourers coped with rural poverty either by moving to the towns or moving overseas.[475] But it was not just the poor who emigrated. Between 1841 and1881, many families from Kingston Seymour will emigrate. One family, the Bakers, will end up in Chicago. Yet it is Australia and New Zealand that will take most families emigrating from Kingston Seymour. In 1840, by the Traty of Waitangi, New Zealand became a British colony. *"Bristol Mercury, June 20th 1840 – Mr Jennings, late Chief Clerk to the New Zealand Company will be happy to communicate with anyone relative to emigration to this new colony....free passage is procured for agricultural labourers and similar trades."*

Emigration to Australasia seemed to both a new world and a promised land. Letters home reported that even the dogs get more to eat out there than labourers. You don't have to sit under a hedge gnawing a piece of bread and an onion. Working people get to eat the best joints, washed down with whiskey! Letters home read like biblical descriptions of well endowed trees bowed down with fruit.[476]

One name comes up regularly in the Vestry Minutes in the 1830's is that of the Jenkins'. Richard Jenkins is a Butcher and a Wesleyan Methodist. He had been baptised in Yatton Parish Church in July 1804. The parish has been involved. *May 23rd 1833- Mr Manning to be asked if he will take Richard Jenkins' son Daniel. June 18th – Ann Jenkins paid 1 shilling per week while she is in the infirmary. August 27th 1833- Ann Jenkins 2 shillings during an illness and lodgings to be paid Oct 23rd 1833 - Richard Jenkins pay to be reduced 1 shilling and 6 d a week as his son was now in work. Daniel Jenkins to have a pair of shoes.*

In 1844, Richard Jenkins is living in a local tenement rated at three pence ha'penny. The Vestry Minutes record that Richard Jenkins earns himself two shillings and six pence for repairing 'the gout from the [village] pump' in late April that year. In March 1848, the parish agrees to advance up to £20 from poor rate to assist Richard Jenkins, his wife and their seven children to emigrate to Australia. They sail from Plymouth in July 1848. The voyage on the SS Andromeda takes nearly four months. Once in Australia, Richard Jenkins will set himself up as a butcher.[477]

It was not the only ship from Britain to carry a Yatton family that year. In June, the SS Berkshire has taken George Hunt, a labourer. George has been educated. He is employed on board as a ship schoolmaster and given £5 for it. On arrival in Australia, he is employed as a teacher by a Doctor and then in a Church of England school. His brother John is employed as a Hospital Assistant at sea. In Yatton he was a gardener. In Geelong, New South Wales, he will continue in that role. Elias Hayes, his wife Matilda and their 18 month old daughter are granted £20 to emigrate in 1849 on the SS Nelson. The voyage is full of sadness. Their daughter dies of diahorrhea on the voyage. Matilda gives birth to a premature baby who dies shortly afterwards. In 1851, the SS Statesman takes a Yatton housemaid called Maria Nash to Geelong. Maria will find work with a Minister of Scotland for £14 a year.

June 1852 sees another Yatton man emigrate to Australia. Henry James Lyon is a carpenter who embarks on a voyage on the SS Sir Edward Perry, arriving in Geelong in October. There is someone else from Yatton on board. Sarah Young is a domestic servant. When they arrive that October, the immigrants are conscious they have had a safe voyage. The ship's Master, William McLeod, is thanked with a certificate to record his kindness and gentlemanly manner.

On a fine warm day in August 1854, George Cook from Kingston Seymour sails with his family from Plymouth on the SS Panama. In addition to carrying people, the SS Panama has stopped five days for a cargo of hoop iron, paper, tobacco and goods for local merchants. Despite being rather crowded 'tweendecks', emigrants enjoy tropical conditions. Only three deaths are recorded, from *scarletina and exhaustion*.' In all, 275 immigrants arrive safely. Most single men and women were Irish but the families were from south –west England. Three months later, the Bristol Mercury announces the death of George Cook in Portraig, South Australia.

It is when agriculture was in difficulties at the time of the depression in farm prices that many sail from Kingston to try their luck overseas. John Hugh Price is born in Kingston Seymour in October 1858. With his family he sails from Plymouth in April 1880 on "The Windsor Castle". It arrives in Rockhampton, Queensland, Australia. Out there, John Hugh Price marries an Elizabeth Cook, another Kingston emigree who had sailed on the SS Lobelin from Plymouth in 1865.

Free passage is granted to encourage domestic servants, 'greatly in demand'. The cost of the voyage is 16 to 40 guineas. Everyone who paid for their own passage gets 40 acres of land. Otherwise, they will pay between 5 and 15 shillings per acre.

Though villagers from the Moor will not have realised this at the time, all this was part of a movement of English speaking peoples across the world. It became fashionable later to recall emigration through the filter of imperialism and exploitation of native lands and peoples. But colonisation was much more nuanced. It involved what has been described as 'a settler revolution.' English settlers constructed clones of their societies that then bought in goods, capital and above all, people, from the old land they had left. Far more than the 'imperial' label suggests, settler nations were co-owners of the great enterprise of building an Anglo-world.[478] Without knowing it, families from the Moor had become stakeholders in a global enterprise.

Chapter Seventeen

SOCIETY IN LAYERS

The People of the Moor

Overall, the numbers of those who live on the Moor stay the same as the 19th century unfolds. This is where paths diverge for the new industrial towns that grow exponentially. We have no way of knowing how many people of the Moor are amongst those thronging the new population centres. These were years of displacement of rural populations.

Rural occupations are diverse- and becoming more so. In 1841 in Yatton there are 102 female servants, 11 Carpenters, six charwomen, 20 dress makers and bonnet makers, strawbonnetmakers and milliners. Then there is Jesse Gillard, the Saddler, James Escott the horse keeper, John Day the Blacksmith, Francis Day the writer, Mary Belsey the Governess, Charles Coles the butter dealer, John Lukins the Beer House keeper, George Willins the lime-burner and George Neades the Constable.[479]

Kenn is a village of just over 1000 acres. In 1841, there are 324 inhabitants. Of the 109 people listed as being in employment, 38 are agricultural labourers working on a casual basis and 17 are farmers. There are also 18 male servants who have longer contracts. Officially, 73 people work on the land; two out of three. There are also 16 female servants (14% of those employed); as well as assorted occupations such as a miller, (Elijah Hookway), carpenters such as William Lukin (aged 40), a tallow chandler (Thomas Sprod) and two publicans (Thomas Parsley and Joseph Pooles). Life will continue much as always. Between 1841 (no 1 in the new Marriage register) and 1881, 39 marriages were solemnised. At about one marriage per year, there will be many who remained unmarried. Around Kenn in 1810, the Moor has been enclosed. This provoked resentment as a land - grab by rich, powerful interests.

Kingston Seymour is a slightly larger parish- 2600 acres. In 1841, 81 out of 147 (or 55% of listed occupations) are agricultural labourers or farmers. The picture has not changed significantly by the 1881 Census - out of 160 listed occupations, 60% (95) are either agricultural labourers or farmers. In many cases, holdings of land were too small to make a living from. In 19th century Kingston Seymour, there were some dairies but farms mostly grew corn with many orchards dotting the landscape. Wheat was milled locally; there was a windmill at Kenn and a tidal mill at the sea wall. The coming of the railways changed that. Wider marketing of milk became possible.

Counting the people of the Moor- population in 1840/1880

	1841 census	1881 Census
Cleeve	298	333
Claverham	330	276
Kingston Seymour	376	293
Kenn	324	289
Yatton	1649	1805
Total	2977	2996

The contrast between the 1841 Census Data and that for 1881 is in Appendix 1.

Claverham in 1881

The Census for Claverham in 1881 provides a snapshot of rural lives at the other bookend. Besides 22 farmers, 26 agricultural labourers and seven farm servants, there are eight domestic servants (10% of the women in employment). One of these, Mary Vowles, aged 45, describes herself as farmer's housekeeper. Four children between 10 and 14 are employed. But there are plenty of other occupations. There is employment as a housepainter, an engine cleaner at the tannery (which uses eight labourers), a grocer/draper, a blacksmith, a haulier, a hay dealer, a baker or a milliner. For the women, you could choose between being a marketwomen, a needlewoman, a charwomen, a launderesses, a dressmaker or a domestic servant.

One village blacksmith is a woman, Mary Sampson. She is 59. Her younger brother Charles is 54 but he is down as a 'blacksmith's domestic'. Mary has been widowed. There is a village nurse, Caroline Clake, now 42. Like her mother, Charlotte, with whom she lives, Caroline is a widow. Another woman, Mary Light, registered as a monthly nurse. She is 46 and listed as unmarried despite having a grown-up son and two daughters and three other children. Emma Peterson is 38. She is an agricultural labourer widow of no occupation. She lives on the farm run by Richard Binning.

Richard Binning is a retired farmer in an age when people rarely retired. He is 80 and lives with his son George, on their farm. William Hunt is 77, described as a general labourer in 1881. One man is entered as a retired agricultural labourer. He is James Taylor, aged 86. George Brown is 55. He is a railway labourer. His son William, has become Blacksmith's labourer. Another son, William, is 14 - an agricultural labourer.

The village pauper is female. Then there is Joseph Duckett, 15 of age, a letter carrier. Wallice Gregory is the village carpenter. He is 45 and employs 6 men.

Behind the Census data stands a record of social transformation. Death rates begin to fall. Fewer children are being born. Children under the age of 14 account for just over a third of the population in 1841; by 1881, this has dropped to just under a quarter - from 34% to 24%. In both years, 30% of the people are in work.

Nationally, the main occupation is farming. Agriculture is by far the largest industry in 1851, employing nearly two million people. By 1871, this has declined to 1.5 million. For the Moor as a whole, in 1841 60% of those in work are employed on the land. Forty years later, only half as many work on the land. Claverham in 1841 had 21 farmers and 44 agricultural labourers. By 1881, that had declined to 12 farmers and 26 agricultural labourers.

The proportion of those working on the land clearly declined as the 19th century wore on. This is clear from the Parish registers as well as the Census. Of those bringing children for baptism in 1815, 26 were agricultural labourers and 15 were farmers (who might also have been labourers with small holdings). In all 85% work on the land. The proportion of agricultural parents declines significantly.

| 1815 – 85% | 1835 – 75% | 1855 – 43% | 1875 – 43% |
| 1825 – 63% | 1845 – 49% | 1865 – 53% | 1885 – 35% |

It is testimony to the prominence of agriculture on the Moor that its farmers were rated very highly. On December 12th 1840, a prize for the best set of six ewes was won by a Yatton farmer. The previous week, William May received a prize for the 2nd best milch cow at the Clevedon Agricultural Show. William May is an auctioneer as well as farmer. In February 15th 1841, he is acting as agent for the sale of house contents from a fine home in Clevedon; the furniture being of first rate quality.

The Life of Landowners

By the beginning of the 19th century, landowners were instrumental along with their tenant farmers in enclosing the land. It marked the end of the field strip system. Yet the old pattern of a few landowners still dominating the skyline was beginning to break up. As we saw in Chapter 11, estates in North Somerset including Kenn, Kingston Seymour and Yatton had come into the possession of the aristocratic Poulett family after marriage to Elizabeth Kenn in 1614.[480] The Poulett family came to own most of the land in and around the Moor down to Weston, Later, the land in Yatton belonging to Earl Poulett was sold off between 1812-15. He had to pay his dues on land tax and help fund his estate at Hinton St George. In all, the sale of substantial lands in North Somerset raised the immense sum of £67,295 and 10 shillings. The Big Sale transformed the High Street of Yatton as well as transferring ownership of surrounding lands. Tenant farmers remained, letting their small holdings from new owners living outside the area. But new owners for the High Street and the road connecting Yatton with Claverham meant some investment.

Amidst these transfers of property amongst the landowning class, one family became especially prominent. The Rev Wadham Pigott had already owned the Manor land of Ham and Wemberham. When in 1815, his niece, Ann Provis married the son of Sir Hugh Smyth of Ashton Court, Wadham Piggott stipulated that the name and arms of the Pigotts should be added to the new family. Wadham Pigott died in 1823 but by then, John Hugh Smyth-Pigott was well established in North Somerset. John Hugh was the illegitimate son of Sir Hugh Smyth of Ashton Court. 1824 sees John Hugh busy buying up estates in Yatton.[481] He now became very much the local landowner. Owner of nearby Brockley Hall, many lands on the Moor had been added to his estate. But by 1848, the money ran out. Lavish expenditure on paintings, statues, a library of 6,000 books and developing the lands around Brockley Hall on a grand design had incurred debts of £30,000 - a huge amount. There was only one thing to do. The next year saw a massive sale of the Smyth-Piggott estates. Some were sold in his lifetime to pay for his debts.[482] By the time he died in 1853, much had gone. After his death, much of his estates in Yatton were valued and sold off in 1857.[483] The archives also show that he had a son, described as having lunacy, who needed legal redress to ensure provision in his father's will. This is how the case of 'Pigott v Pigott' came before the courts.[484]

In 1821, Earl Poulett had sold Cleeve Court, a grand home for a gentleman, to the Rev Thomas Shrapnel Biddulph of Worcester College Oxford who also snapped up the Manor in Yatton.[485] It carried responsibilities. As lord of the Manor, he was now owner of the Poor House. He also owned the substantial property of Cleeve Court, on the hill outside Cleeve, together with its cottages.

Land continued to be broken up. In 1848, the whole ancient territory of Yatton Manor was up for sale. The vendor proposed to include Cleeve Court plus a number of small farms and woods to total 1860 acres. A good profit is likely with an investment- probably £3,300 per annum could be realised and this did not take into account the advantages to be gained from coal, iron and other minerals being discovered. If a buyer for the whole estate is not available, it can be divided into smaller lots starting with the sale of the Manor of Yatton.[486] Sometimes, land sale went too far. An action was brought in 1856 to recover 9 ½ acres of land on Kenn Moor that had been under the copyhold of Lord Hinton (the Pouletts by another name). The land had been part of a marriage settlement by the tenant farmer. Now the owner wanted it back![487]

The big houses in each village- the Hall or the Manor where the Squire and Rector reside, are a link with fashionable trends in the outside world. John Hugh Smyth-Pigott owned Kingston Seymour Manor house. This old mansion dates from Edward IV, whose favourite badge, the rose-en-soleil, appeared on the west gable. The Gentleman's Magazine for 1835 regard the mansion as the *"one of the most perfect and interesting specimens of ancient domestic architecture in the county of Somerset"*.[488] That was before the fire.

Kingston Seymour Manor House c1840

Traditionally, landowners ran the show. But with the rise of the Victorian middle class, landowners such as the Smyth-Piggotts and Pouletts were no longer able to shout the loudest in the political agenda. A survey known colloquially as 'The New Domesday Book' showed that land was concentrated in far fewer hands than the landed gentry sought to demonstrate. Still more than 40% of the land nationally belonged to fewer than 1,700 people.[489] Until 1880, landowners constituted the great majority of those leaving £500,000 or more at death.[490] Inequality was entrenched. When the 2nd Earl of Yarborough died in 1875, the stock of cigars he possessed was sold for £850. That represented more than 18 years income for the agricultural landowners who lived and worked on his Lincolnshire estates.[491]

Even compared with European aristocracy generally at this time, never was so much owned by so few relative to so many.

The Middle Classes

Then there were the Middle Classes. Next rung down from landowners were farmers of substance, farmers holding 100 acres or more. One such yeoman farmer in Claverham in 1842, Mr J.G. Cox, was a notable member of the Royal Agricultural Society.[492] He is the Secretary of the Tithe Authority in the district. Another farmer of some substance in Claverham is Joseph Manning. He has 125 acres. In 1881 he is 63, married to Harriet, a lady from Kingston Seymour. He describes himself as a *"farmer of 125 acres employing 3 agricultural labourers."*

White collar workers were in a different mental universe from manual workers. They felt that they were different. Even in a strongly agricultural village like Kingston Seymour, there were middle class families like the Stuckeys, one of the mainstays of village life. In 1841, William Stuckey is a described as a 'chairman'- he hired out wheelchairs. William keeps a lodging house. There are two more members of the wider family in the same line of business. Another family member is a 'fly proprietor,' the owner of a light carriage of two wheels that functions as a fast, horse-drawn taxi. These are lower middle class occupations. George Stuckey is a haulier, James farms and retails milk, Thomas is the post-master, George also keeps lodgers. Little has changed by 1881. Thomas is now a carriage proprietor. Alfred Stuckey (listed as a dairyman from Kingston Seymour in the 1881 Census for Claverham) gave land for the Chapel in the 1860's. His nephew,

Walter Stuckey was born in the village but left as a boy and ended up as a butcher in Clevedon, having married a lady from Kenn whose father kept a lodging house in Weston Super Mare.

In today's terms, the family generally were upwardly mobile. Victorian respectability meant different things to different people. To the artisan worker, it meant independence. To the better-off, respectability meant deference to their social superiors higher up the ladder but respect from those below your station in life.[493]

On the Moor, the wealth of the new rich, the industrialists, the nouveau riche is absent. But there are doctors, shopkeepers, teachers, an accountant, a lawyer and clergy. These are professional people. The clergy were upper middle class, - though the best of them were no less faithful for all that and possessed an uncanny ability to reach across social divides. Sons and daughters of the more educated clergy that the Moor succeeding in attracting tended to marry within the rank society assigned them. As advised in the Bristol Mercury, Yatton people would have read of the marriage of Mr James Hurd to Julia Wickham, daughter of the Rector.[494]

The Bell Inn Yatton c1880

There was a large gap between skilled workers and unskilled labourers. An observer in 1849 contrasting the West End of London to the East End commented that the change was so great, *"it seems as if we were in a new land and another race"*.[495] That would no doubt have been the case between social groups on the Moor. It may have felt to the rising middle class that the labourers were from a world they had left.

The Campaigns for the Reform Bill and against the Corn Laws gave the middle classes generally a political identity that they had not enjoyed before. In 1831, Lord Brougham can equate the middle classes with *"the wealth and intelligence of the country, the glory of the British name."*[496] The middle classes were well represented amongst the people of the Moor, though not on the scale of the new urban society where they comprised about a fifth of the population. The proportion of the 2.1 million adult males in England and Wales who paid income tax was about 20%. You had to earn more than £100 a year to cross the tax threshold.[497]

In Yatton, in 1841 about one in eight occupations were middle class. Depending in how one defines the term, that proportion has not changed much by 1881. What has changed is that there are more skilled artisans. Each village on the Moor had its own middle class. In Claverham, the record of those who were resident on the night of 30th March 1851 lists seven members of what might be called middle class. These include:

- Four Farmers of significant size (not small holdings)
- One clergy (Rev Richard Symes)
- One shopkeeper (Isaac Gregory- by the 1881 Census, he is 53, described as a grocer and draper. He has done well for himself and managed to retire.)
- One Proprietor of Land

Out of 155 occupations in total, that means barely 5% are Middle Class.

For the agricultural tithing of Cleeve in 1881, there are slightly more in what might be termed the Middle Class socio-economic group. Perhaps 8% of occupations fall into this rather arbitrary category. Who would fit in and qualify is a matter of debate. William Baber, a 'farmer of 132 acres employing two boys and three men presumably does as will Ann Beakes, described as a widow in the 1861 Census with a 100 acre farm and two men. But where does William Eacott, Master Blacksmith, come on the social ladder?

There was a general feeling that the income of the rising middle classes was not keeping up with expenditure. They were getting poorer, or felt they were! In a well –publicised essay published in 1875, the author complained that it is a *"substantial truth ...which cannot be denied that the life of the vast proportion of the middle classes was becoming more difficult and more costly by the year."*[498]

Clerks on the Moor, like James Grainger, Solicitors General Clerk in Cleeve in 1861, were poorly paid. In London, clerks could find work in banking, insurance or the Civil Service; in the provinces, there was widespread pessimism about their prospects.[499]

Throughout society there was a strong ethos of conformity, of deference. Deference ran deep. On the Moor, it was Mr Derham, Mr Gage etc. Dress code was strong. The middle class both expected the deference due to them as well as the aristocracy and exuded respectability. This made for uniformity, for social control. How far that kept crime at bay is a matter of conjecture.

The Life of a Labourer[500]

The main social group in the countryside were agricultural labourers. The Ridleys of Cleeve represent the lives of this particularly important segment in rural worlds. In the 1700's, Ridleys are mentioned in Yatton parish church records as peasants.

For England as a whole, the census information for 1851 shows nearly one and half million agricultural labourers, labourers and farm servants. The labour force in the countryside was at its height. But as a proportion, fewer people now worked on the land. Twice as many were working in the factories and mills of the new Britain. By 1891, half a million fewer people were employed in farming. Because the population was growing sharply, by 60% in this period, this represented a decline from 20% to 10% of the labour force. In 1851, farming was still the most important industry in Britain. Twenty years later, more people were finding work as domestic servants than as workers of the land.

Agricultural labourers had done well during the Napoleonic wars. Their wages increased over the 19th century by 40%. But the average increase for British workers generally was over 70%. The impact of trade unionism in the countryside meant that farm wages increased in the 1870s but returned to previous level by the 1880's.[501]

The agricultural workforce comprised men with particular skills and the casual labour, taken on for a week or day at a time. Their labour is always subject to the vargraries of weather and whim, of available work and available pay. An official Return to the Poor Law Commissioners in 1834 revealed that some labourers lost between 8 to 12 weeks through lack of health, wet or winter.[502] Almost all the fathers of agricultural labourers were agricultural labourers themselves. Hours were long. The best estimate is that, nationally, working hours averaged about 65 per week in 1856 and fell to 56 in 1873, remaining at that level for the next forty years.[503] This was a substantial drop but still the life of labourers was a life of labour.

The ratio of farmers to agricultural labourers fell at this time. In 1831, there were five and a half labourers for every farmer. By 1871, it was four to one; in 1891, there were about three and a half agricultural labourers for every farmer. This was a significant loss of hired hands. A labour shortage arose. Wages rose. Agricultural labourers were earning more proportionately compared to landlords or farmers. Yet real incomes never rose above half of what a labourer could earn in industry.[504] The entire increase in cash available to a farm worker between the 1820's and the end of the century amounted to no more than the princely sum of 5 shillings a week and that only if you were fully employed.

There were demarcations between agricultural labourers (who were the casual labour, paid daily or weekly) and the farm servants on a more permanent contract. Many workers were farm servants; men like Daniel Bendle at Kenn in 1841. These were labourers who were employed for a given period, able to change farms and occupations. They did not expect to stay in farm service for the rest of their lives.[505] For England and Wales, there was a big contrast between the pattern of farm service in the industrial north, where it was much higher, and the more agricultural south of the country, where it was lower.[506] According to the Census data, there were 21 male servants in Claverham in 1841. By 1881, these distinctions are breaking down and most land workers are entering their occupations as 'farm labourers'.

In the 1841 Census, there is mention of one such agricultural labourer, Thomas Ridley. He was born in the year 1815 at nearby Wrington. By the 1841 Census, he is 25, married to Mary. Born in 1808, she is seven years older than him.

Now they have a son. George Ridley is mentioned in the 1841 Census as 2 years old. The years pass. George meets a young lady from nearby Nailsea, Eliza Sprod. The 1861 Census shows she is the same age as George. They have a little son, John. His birthplace is recorded as Nailsea, like his mother. Maybe their eldest son was born out of wedlock.

The stereotypical image of rural worlds is that of thatched cottages of agricultural labourers around the village green with the inhabitants contentedly drinking cider. The reality was very different. This was no Thomas Hardy novel. The beauty of the English landscape nestled a contrasting reality- the poverty and rude lives of its inhabitants. Year after sweaty year, its farmers and labourers wrestled and struggled with a small area of soil, hoping for the right balance of sun and rain in order for the miracle of renewable growth should again be repeated.

In the 1870's, the family will vacate the one bedroom cottage they have been living in with their six sons and one daughter, Elizabeth. Eight people to one cottage was not unusual in those days. But a house had become available down the road at the bowling green. Not everyone had or could afford a horse and cart. George and Eliza and their sturdy sons pick up their furniture and all their possessions and walk with it over the fields. It was a startling sight, watching a family trudge across the fields with their belongings. The Ridleys will not have been worried at what anyone thought. Their new house provides larger accommodation for the family. There are four large bedrooms. It is an ample, healthy environment. Very likely, George got the house rent free. He is a gamekeeper for the local landowners, the Smyth-Pigotts, who now own most of the land between there and Weston Super Mare.

Life for agricultural labourers was hard, very hard. It was only in the 1880s that change really began to set in and the old patterns of infectious diseases, poor diet and poor health began to shift. Calcium deficiency was rife.[507] The quality of food was hampered by the cost of fuel, the lack of safe water and the means of cooking. Gas ranges only became common towards the end of the 19th century. There was more tea; consumption rose in this period from 1.6 lb per head in 1841 to 4.9 lb per head in 1881.[508] Often, the best of what food was available went to the adult male breadwinner; the women and children had to go without.

All this meant that bread was still the basic food item in the family diet. A labourer might only see fresh meat once a week. He had to go his daily round on a bread and butter pudding at best.[509] Limited diet meant height differences between the classes. Children of farm labourers, were, according to the British Association for the Advancement of Science, three inches shorter on average than children of professional people.[510] It is well known that recruits for the First World War from the poorer classes were shorter than others.

Labourers were usually allowed to keep a pig if they rented a farm cottage. A great deal of the pig would be salted. This supplied bacon several times a week and often represented the thin margin between famine and feasting.[511] The scarcity of bread and food generally meant that poaching was rife in rural areas. Pheasants were fair game. So were rabbits and pigeons. Gardens and allotments were a help but probably contributed no more than a tenth of family food.[512] When times were hard on the Moor, the working man took the best of diet and clothing; his wife would go without. Any meat going went to the father, then the sons. It was enforced vegetarianism.

Eliza Ridley will live to the year 1888. She dies at 48, worn out with having produced ten children. She is still producing her last child in 1880 when her daughter in law is pregnant with a baby that will be born in 1881. The next generation has arrived. But Eliza is in trouble. She has breast cancer. It has to be done. They chloroform her and cut her breast off on the kitchen table. Mercifully Eliza survives. But she will only live eight years after the birth of her last child. George Ridley lives on for fifteen years as a widower, dying in 1903. Their sons lived out their days with a range of occupations and experiences. They are by no means following their father on the land.

Their son John finds work at the Tannery in Claverham. He is listed in the 1881 Census as a Tanner's labourer. In 1877, at the age of seventeen, he had married Mary Taylor. Like his mother, Mary is also from Nailsea. Both women are pregnant at the same time. She will give birth to Norman. John will go on to make a bit of money and own a property. Exactly how is unclear. But it is enough to put a roof over their head in Clevedon to house John and Mary and their family. In 1891, John Ridley is described as Head of Household, now 31. He and Mary have three sons and a daughter. John is employed as a Finisher Tanner at Claverham Tannery. Ten years pass. The 1901 census shows he is in Claverham. By now he is a 41 year old Farmer. John and Mary have four children.

Great great grandfather to the current local resident is Joseph Taylor, listed as seven years of age in 1841. In 1851 Joseph is still living at home; he is 16. Like his Dad, he is a farm labourer but down too as a pauper. In 1861, Joseph is now head of house, with three children, the eldest of whom is Mary. In 1871, Joseph is registered as a tanner; Mary is 12, listed as a scholar. In 1881, neither are in Claverham. Joseph is in Cleeve, now listed as Tanner's labourer. By then, Mary has married John Ridley.

One son of George and Eliza Ridley, Samuel is 21 by the time of the 1881 Census. He will go on to join the Royal Navy and take part in military action in China in 1900 to suppress the Boxer Rebellion. He will serve as a rating on HMS Penelope, 'Old Pepper Pot' as she was called; a ship that features later in 1943 in the relief of Malta.

In 1876, another son, George, is born. He is the second son to be called George after his father. The first-born George has not lived beyond his birth in 1865. Another son, Alfred, is born in 1874. His work is that of coachman at Brockley Hall for the Smyth-Piggott family. Alfred claims to have originated the many ghost stories while serving there as a coachman; walking and waving to the occupants clad in white. One day, attracted by the tales of mystery and imagination, Sir Arthur Conan Doyle will come. Alfred acts as butler on duty the night he visited. He served the great writer and the master of the house with whiskey as they wait for the ghost to appear!

Woman's Work

Intersecting class in Victorian society were the imperatives of gender.

Agriculture was undoubtedly one of largest categories of employment for women. Nationally, it was about 25% in the period 1851 to 1881.[513]

The idea of women going out to work can seem to belong to a later period when women had to fight to have jobs and on do those jobs in equal terms. One of the conceits of the twentieth century is that this is when women began to go out to work on a mass scale. But in rural worlds such as the Moor, women have always worked. The Census disguises the extent of this because it failed to recognise those who worked part-time. There was a considerable disparity in Somerset generally between the census information and how much work was undertaken by women.[514] Their labour was hidden under that of the head of household. They are the silent objects of rural life. 30% of occupations in Yatton in 1881 were held by women.

Women were involved at all stages of the agricultural workforce. There was a great deal of overlap in these rural communities between domestic service and farm work. A typical day might start at 6am milking. Then would come preparing breakfast, preparing meals and taking food to the men in the fields. But as well she might have to care for the pigs, pick potatoes and help with the harvest.[515] It was harvest that involved all hands to the pump. Wheat had to be planted using a small hand-held digger to make a hole for the seed.

Many rural families could not have survived otherwise. A contributor to a Parliamentary Report on the Employment of Women and Children in Agriculture said that in the west of England, there were few families where the wife and children were not involved in farm labour.[516] The husband's day work contributed only around half of the income of an average family. The remainder was from the wife, earnings from children when they picked up gleanings and from harvest labour.

In 1841 in Kenn, there are ten farmer's wives who would no doubt be involved in farming. Kingston Seymour shows thirteen farmer's wives helping to keep the farm going in 1841. No doubt farmer's daughters and wives of agricultural labourers would also have been recruited at harvest times. Forty years later in Kingston Seymour in 1881, an additional 37 women list their occupations as farmer's wife or as the wife of an agricultural labourer. That means that the land generates employment in this village community for 82% of its people. Again this figure does not take into account the numbers of children available to help at harvest time. Neither does it take into account the cross-over between female domestic service, employing twenty women at Kingston Seymour in 1841, and farm service. Taking food to the men in the fields, looking after the pigs, grooming the horses and doing the housework was all of a piece in many a farm. There was no demarcation.

The work was hard. A rural doctor in 1843 reported that women dairy workers frequently complained of *"pains in the back and limbs, overpowering sense of fatigue..., want of appetite, feverishness"*.[517] The Census at Kenn two years before identified a number of women who worked in the fields as 'female servants', women like Betsy Smith, aged 20, Sarah Jones, only 15, or Rebecca Hilana, a year younger.

For women to be employed as agricultural labourers and female farm servants was to go against Victorian ideals of what constituted femininity. As Lancashire farm labourers told a Royal Commission on Labour later in the century, *"we keep our women at home, which is their proper sphere."*[518] Agricultural labour is *"most destructive to the female character"* fulminated an earlier report on the employment of women and children in agriculture. *"It tends to tarnish the purity of their minds and feelings and to make them mannishly coarse.*" Field work resulted in a "*loss of evening comfort to their husbands,*" rendering them unfit for domestic duties.⁵¹⁹

The exception was the image of the milkmaid, such as Eliza Goodland at Cleeve in 1881. Eliza is 20. In rural memoirs and Victorian novels, dairy work represented fertile nature in its purity. But there was another reality- the simple struggle to make ends meet. Going into the fields may not always have compensated for the cost of someone to look after their children or of clothing. For some it was worth the attempt.

In 1881, the largest farm, at Claverham Court, is owned by a lady, Mary Winter, who describes herself as a 'farmeress'. In 1871, her husband John was Head of Household and described as both landowner and farmer. But now, Mary is head of household, a farmer of 174 acres employing five men and a boy. She is 64 and has seven daughters all of whom list their occupations as farmers, along with her son William. Her brother's widow Elizabeth. lives with them as does one of the farm servants, Edward Durbin. In 1881, Edward is 56. A decade earlier, he has described himself as an 'indoor farm servant'. His father William worked on the land along with Sarah, his mother who was 8 years older than William. On the Winter farm in 1881, Ellen, a 16 year old girl from Congresbury, is a domestic servant. The night of the Census, there is a visitor. He is Alfred Verry, an accountant's clerk. Unless he is wooing one of the older sisters, Alfred is probably checking the books.

Women were not just active as fieldworkers. They were involved with domestic service and a variety of other occupations. In Kingston in 1841, women were shopkeepers, a schoolmistress, charwomen, a needlewoman, dressmaker and those who labelled themselves as 'assistants'- very likely to the farmers whose household they are listed under.

Marriage was the ideal for young women in the communities of the Moor. Out of every 1000 females in England and Wales in 1851, 859 would be married at least once by the time they reached 50. It was an exit from life-long dependence on parents and conferred a status that later generations would begin to find in the workplace.⁵²⁰ However, there was a downside. Strict social penalties awaited those who married outside their social rank. There was little of the concept of 'society' in these small communities yet a young woman from landed gentry would rarely have married a son of professional people. Opportunities for women shrank with the decline of traditional industries. But there was always domestic service. It was not second best for salary. Cooks and maids were relatively well-paid compared with their industrial cousins.[521] Nationally, probably one in three women experienced domestic service at some point in their lives. Domestic service occupied more women than any other type of work. In a typical year between 1851 and 1881, anywhere between 1.1 million and 1.8 million women earned their living from being cooks and bottlewashers, housekeepers, nurses for a household or the chambermaid.[522] At the end of the century, the Board of Trade could describe domestic service as the biggest industry for either men or women.[523]

They did not necessarily do the washing. That was farmed out to a washerwoman. But when the washing returned, there was the ironing to do. That was only the start of their labours. A typical day might run from 6am to 8pm with a break one afternoon and Sunday evenings if she was lucky. Whenever a domestic took the child in her care out for a stroll in Yatton, she would be dressed in a black dress. She must not talk to anyone, least of all an agricultural labourer. Serving a meal to one of the posher homes was not complete without her white apron and cap. A blue cap meant she was scrubbing. Largely due to domestic service, marriage was often delayed; 10% of the population never married at all.[524] In Claverham in 1881, 26 out of 83 women of employable age were unmarried. It was a lonely and hard working life, relieved sometimes by a walk over the fields before returning to a lonely evening.

Chapter Eighteen

EDUCATING THE RURAL POOR
(AND OTHER STORIES)

Keeping the Parish Going

Contemporary accounts give a vivid account of what life would have been like in the villages of the Moor. How will the villagers handle such matters as enabling them to move around, dealing with crime in their midst, hazards to health and the task of educating the children of the rural poor amongst them?

On a cold winter's day in January 1847, George Banwell does a day's labour breaking stones. For that, he will earn 1 shilling and 6d. He is 35, fit and able.[525] The Accounts for the Surveyor of the Highways in Kingston Seymour show that in all, the parish pay out £6 -17 shillings and 8d for Highways upkeep that year, mainly to keep the drains from clogging up. One consequence of the enclosure of agricultural land is that more roads will be laid down on the Moor. Turnpike Trusts managed major roads but local roads were the responsibility of the Vestry Meeting. The highways needed repairing and extending. A rate was levied to pay for work on the roads as a proportion of how much your property was worth. In 1842, John Heale of Yatton will be asked by the Vestry Meeting if he could let out his quarry on Frost Hill so that its stones could be more economically utilised in road maintenance.

In 1859, John Denmead, John Blew and two others are appointed surveyors in Kingston; in effect, bosses to the workmen. Charles Baker and Richard Stuckey were voted to be village constables; Samuel Wallis and George Gage are Church Wardens.[526] In all such decisions, the Rector has a very large say in the running of the parish. He is chairman of the Vestry mtg, along with local farmers - Charles and Samuel Griffin, William Gage, Charles Gould, Charles Demnead and George Price.

How did these communities work? Before the growth in public administration during the 19th century that brought in the Parish Council, the Parish was run by the Vestry Meeting of the church. This recalled earlier times when Parish and church were one. At first, this met on the first Friday of the month. Later, in 1790, had been changed to meeting after the main service in church. Fridays were thought too conducive to indecent behaviour; too "big with evil tendencies." The Vestry had many duties to perform. The Parish tax of the times was paid to various bodies that had a claim on the inhabitants. Mostly those who were better off paid it, mostly those who owned property. It was not until 1871 that a Local Government Board was to supervise such matters as sewage, paving of the streets, upkeep of the roads and refuse collection. The Board also took over the responsibities of the former Poor Law Commissioners.

Until then, landowners and farmers were responsible to play their part in keeping the sea away and help drain these North Somerset levels. The magnificently entitled 'Yatton Jury of Sewers' had the responsibility for the district. They had to oversee the drainage of the Kenn River, the Little River at Phipps Bridge near Wemberham where it flowed into the Yeo and the sea wall at Kingston Seymour. In addition there were the innumerable drain ditches called the rhynes.

At the end of the year, the people come to pay tithes – one tenth of the yearly farm produce which is the proportion that had always been give to support the clergy. In Yatton Edward Jones is assessed in 1840 @12 cows, 6 calfs, 3 pigs+27 geese.[527]

Readers of the Bristol Mercury in 1861 will read that John Blew is putting his farm up for auction the following week. Village handbills gave further details but with the farm went livestock, hay, grass and straw.[528] This will cause a problem. A case will be heard nine months later when the new owner, George Gage, should pay the tithe bill. He had been presented with a demand for £21, a considerable sum and it had accrued in the time when John Blew had been tenant farmer. John Blew maintained he had paid a full measure of tithes on entering the farm in March 1848 and it was most unfair that he should have to pay on leaving it. The Court decided in favour of the defendant. George Gage had to pay up![529]

Philanthropy is alive and well. The people of the village were engaged in charitable works. This tradition continued into the 19th century. Voluntary service was derived from a generous sense of benevolence. Nevertheless, the social problems faced by the mid-Victorian generation were beyond the scope of philanthropy or indeed individual parishes or towns. They required action by the State.

With the growth of public administration during the 19th century, national Government was looming larger in the lives of the villagers. After 1832, more are able to vote in a General Election. *Saturday September 12th 1840 Bristol Mercury– "we the undersigned Barristers at Law, having been duly nominated and appointed to revise the list of voters in the Eastern Division of the County of Somerset, hereby give notice that we shall make a circuit and hold courts at several places.....Congresbury at the Ship and Castle Inn, Friday 26th Day of September, to revise the list of voters of Yatton and Kingston Seymour".* In 1840 in Kingston Seymour, there are 29 registered electors of whom 15 were free and 14 occupiers. They go across the fields to nearby Congresbury in order to cast their vote.

The social profile shows a contrast between Yatton itself and the rural communities surrounding it. Essentially, the division in the villages was between landowners, well-off yeoman farmers and a smattering of professional people and between the great mass of small farmers and agricultural labourers. In Yatton there was more of a middle class. More people can vote. When in 1867, the middle classes are enfranchised in full, the increase is dramatic. Nationally, the number of registered voters doubles. For Yatton, the all-male electorate rises from 96 to 182.

Crime and Punishment

The Victorians did not invent jails but they certainly placed more emphasis on locking people up than previous generations. Justice was rough in those days. In 1840, a convict in Tasmania obtained a conditional pardon. After that, all trace of him is lost. William Hipsley had arrived in Hobart in August 1828 on board the 'Bengal Merchant', a captivity hulk of 503 tons. He had been sentenced to transportation but was lucky to escape the death penalty. A quantity of printed cotton was stolen from the shop owned by William Derham, the Methodist draper. The theft was the work of Joseph Willmot, a Congresbury shoe-maker, who took it to the house of his brother-in-law, William Hipsley. It made no difference when the Constables arrived. Hipsley, a farm labourer of 45 was in possession of stolen goods. In Yatton, the village pound, the pillory, the stocks and the village jail, the lock-up built near the church the previous year, are all prominent.[530] The door led directly to the Constable's room; behind that were the windowless cells at the rear. That was where they were held before both men were taken to Illchester and sentenced to death. It was a mercy that Hipsley's commutation to life imprisonment stood despite having escaped. He went back to his wife and family in Yatton and was promptly re-arrested. The enforced emigrant now had no hope of ever seeing them again.[531]

Yatton Vestry Minutes October 11th 1840 - pay the Constables bill for handcuffs. To keep law and order, there had been constables around the village for a while. In 1827, the year of Hipsley's so called crime, it had been felt necessary for Yatton Parish to appoint an extra constable."*That it be taken into consideration before the next church meet to select a proper and vigilant person to serve the office of constable.*"[532] It may be that the rough justice in this case stirred resentment. The following year, 1829, a reward of £5 is to be offered '*for the detection of those offenders who wilfully pulled down part of the Lock-Up*'. Crimes and incidents were constantly occurring though on a small scale compared with urban areas. For it was in that year of 1829 that the Home Secretary, Sir Robert Peel, established a police force in London. It was not until 1856 that local counties are compelled to follow suit. The local Poor Law Guardians of the Bedminster Union are, however, solidly against establishing a Constabulary for Somerset. In the Spring of 1840, they present petitions in the Quarter Sessions at Wells trying to prevent this.[533] The Vestry Minutes that year show Parish leaders trying to sell materials from the lock-up.[534]

Few people locked their doors. Trust went hand in hand with community. Exceptions were noted, marked down as deviant from social norms, spoken of in hushed tones.

1840 October 31st - Joseph Rainess aged 14 to be imprisoned for 3 months with hard labour for breaking and entering the home of William Burdge, stealing 20 shillings and some bread and cheese. To be twice severly whipped."

The question begs itself in this era of the 'hungry forties'. Was he just hungry? It was, let it be said, comparatively easy to break in in those days. Yet penalties were harsh. On a day in October 1843 when Somerset men were transported to Australia for ten years for breaking and entering, one James Parsons was sentenced for stealing a shovel in Yatton. He got six weeks. He was lucky. Somebody else stole a pair of scissors at Wrington and got six months.[535]

Once, in 1853, a Mr John Symes was found guilty at the Petty Magistrates sessions of taking live coals from the fire and heaping them on to the marital bed. Patience Symes, his wife, accused him of putting her in godly fear. The bedstead and bed went up in flames though there was no report of the house burning down. This may have been intended to drive her away.[536] Crime did not just involve men. In 1858, the Courts indict Sarah Burge of Yatton for assaulting a local lady, Mary Sampson.[537]

Keeping law and order was a problem even for a smaller community like Kingston Seymour. In February 1854, there were six Constables for the year ahead including George Gage and John Blew. This seems a lot- six constables for some 300 inhabitants- until we remember that some of those names are of prominent local farmers with powers of arrest, rather than acting as the village bobby.

But social responsibility was strong. The boundaries of respectability and expectations were both powerful and patrolled. Liberal sentiments might abound in politics but society was profoundly illiberal. In June 1856, the papers reported the case of 'an unnatural son.' A George Thomas from Yatton was summoned by the Overseers of the poor rate for failing to maintain his elderly father. The situation was compounded by his having promised to maintain his father when the latter had given up his business as a carpenter and wheelright to him. The son had refused to pay and as a result, his old Dad was now chargeable to the parish. The Bench were of the opinion unanimously that this was shameful conduct. The defendant was ordered to pay him 2s-6d a week which he maintained he could not afford and would have to go to prison if forced. That, said the Bench is exactly where he would end up if he did not fulfil his responsibility- considered an obligation, not just a legal duty.[538]

Village life went on. "Last week", so 'The Era' of London reported in December 1844, *"some diabolical wretch mangled a horse belonging to Mr Charles Parsons of Cleeve while the horse was standing outside the Prince of Orange Inn. The wretch cut off a portion of the horse's tongue and mutilated the jaw. A reward of ten guineas is offered for the perpetrator of this infamous act."*[539]

People lived and died, had babies, went bankrupt. In 1847, Silvester Atherton, a village butcher in Yatton attends a first hearing for insolvency to the Bristol Court of Bankruptcy.[540] Many cases affecting the Moor that come before the courts are of local people appling for bankruptcy proceedings. Times are hard. Bankrupts include a Yatton leather worker,[541] a tiler and a plasterer.[542] Times become hard for money scriveners,[543] William May the auctioneer,[544] and Mr Wyatt, a farmer.[545] Civil cases were held at the Bristol Assize; one such claim in 1860 involved a thousand tons of iron ore that had been deposited at Yatton Station and not delivered.[546]

The railways generated new crime. Courts imposed a fine of £1 for travelling without a fare in 1859,[547] six months later came a celebrated case of a mangled body by the railway line which had been cut in two.[548] In those days, the villagers could face 5 shillings for being drunk; £1-10 shillings for obstructing a policeman[549] Nevertheless, the courts could be lenient. An arsonist setting fire to a house in Yatton belonging to William Palmer, did not receive the full sentence he warranted due to a plea of mitigating circumstances. The prisoner's uncle said he had been orphaned and left friendless in the world. Nine months hard labour was imposed instead.[550]

Some incidents investigated by the Coroners of the day were tragic. In 1864, a man called Charles Chaplin was drowned at Kingston near the river. Despite attempts by a boy on the bank opposite who saw it all and tried to help, Charles Chaplin drowned.[551]

The Queen's Highway

Accounts of the Highways Surveyor for Kingston Seymour demonstrate that even in a rural community, there were other types of labourers than just agricultural labourers. The duties of working on roads in and around the village include picking ruts, cleaning drains, spreading stones and keeping the roads open.

April 30th 1842- Stephen Pippet 5 days labour rate at 1shilling and 2d per day.

May 21st to 28th 1842- William Denmead 6 days labour at 1shilling and 2d per day.

Over the next year, there are 120 days when Stephen Pippet will work, scarcely 1/3 of the year. What other work is available to him and how much he is the only breadwinner for the family we cannot tell. His wages have varied a little. For the 1st 41 days of his work, through the spring and summer of 1842, he is paid 1 shilling and 2d per day but in November 1842 through to end of the March 1843, he has been paid 1 shilling a day- 2d less. This will continue and represent a cut in household income from 7 shillings a week to 6. With such slender margins, the strain on household income may be imagined. By contrast, his mate, William Denmead has worked for 219 days over that year. He has been paid at the same rate though for 89 days of his labour, he was paid at 1 shilling per day.

William and Stephen do not have things all stitched up between them. Other workmen are applying for work. George Collins and Joel Bishop are working for the surveyor, often at the same time and doing the same work. But they are being paid 1shilling and 3d per day. The difference is that some is contract work. William and Stephen are on day labour. Day labour in all will cost the parish £24-9shillings and 6d that year; contract labour £10-10shillings and-10d.[552]

This means that Stephen Pippett's wages for that year amounted to barely £6- 7 shillings. William Denmead is luckier. He will earn just over £12 that year.

George Collins will carry on working for the Surveyor, breaking stones and cleaning drains. In the 9 months from April to December 1859, he will be given 58 days of worth of work. Wages have risen. He is now being paid 1 shilling and 6d compared with 1 shilling and 3d 16 years before. Something happens. He does not work between January and March 1860. His place is taken by William Shenton, who gets 48 days of work at the same rate. What has happened to George Collins? There is no contract work available that year.[553]

Health and Medicine

As the 19th century wore on, a multiplicity of local authorities and administration sought to deal with the nation's problems. Centralisation was opposed tooth and claw but gradually Public Health, the Police Force, schools and factory inspection were seen to be the legitimate role of Government. Yet this went hand in hand with bodies such as Poor Law Unions, Turnpike Trusts, local Boards of Health, Highway authorities and Schools Boards.[554] Parish Councils inherited the job of the Church Parish and Vestry Meetings; Borough Councils were responsible for towns or cities.

Along with public administration for a civilised society, the 19th century brought with it a greater conscience. There was heightened awareness of the large numbers of infant deaths and of unsavoury living and working conditions in which people had to live their lives. People were concerned about such issues as sewage and refuse disposal, the housing of animals, the water supply, prevention and control of disease, registration of hospitals, the notification of births and the causes of deaths. The trajectory of concern was that awareness of social evil agitated a conscience that led to studies that raised public awareness and finally to Goverment action. The Poor Law Commissioners have interested themselves in the conditions of poverty in the countryside and the problems of community health. Its report in 1838 argued that *"the expenditures necessary to the adoption and maintenance of measures of prevention would ultimately amount to less than the cost of the disease now constantly engendered."* Sanitary surveys proved that a relationship exists between communicable disease and filth in the environment. From now on, safeguarding public health is the job of the engineer rather than the doctor. In 1842, Edwin Chadwick, Secretary to the Poor Law Commission published his *Report on the Sanitary Conditions of the Labouring Population*. It startled the nation. The number of deaths in one year from Typhus alone was double that of the lives lost by the allies at Waterloo. The evil of overcrowding compounded the lack of sanitation. This is why death rates showed no sign of falling. The available housing could not keep up with population swelling on the scale it did. That led to the development of conditions that were breeding grounds for disease and poor health.

The situation was only a little better for the rural poor on the Moor. By our standards, overcrowding was normal for the large families the villagers often had. References to labourers living on cottages on the church glebe lands in the centre of Yatton are of one up and one down. An ex-cottage for farm labourers in Kingston Seymour would consist of one room for living (where the parents sleep) and one bedroom.[555] The floor is made of compacted earth. There would be an open chimney- 7 foot wide. No means of cooking is available beyond a pot over the fire. Family recollections are of hovels with at best, tiny spiral staircases leading to a carmped first floor where there was a single bedroom. In the double bed, the children would sleep, trying to settle down for the night - three at one end, two at the other. Len Burdge's father and his grandfather before him were small farmers. In 1840, William Burdge's family come into possession of North End farm in Yatton.[556] A few pigs and some cattle meant the farmer could just about make ends meet. But the agricultural labourers who worked on such farms lived in hovels with a rotting roof.

Across the 19th century, middle classes paid out something like 8-10% of their income on housing whereas workers paid up to a quarter. The very poor were compelled to spend over 30% of their meagre income on having a roof over their head.[557] Living standards were slowly rising. Gradually, houses came to boast a particular room for a given purpose and to be further away from their neighbours.

In Kingston Seymour, examination of the Burial Registers demonstrates a clear change in the profile at which people are dying in the 19th century. Between the start of the Register in 1813 and 1841, the burial numbers were as follows:

Children 0-5	Age 5-20	20-40	40-50	50+
38%	6%	10%	6%	40%

By 1881, the situation has changed significantly. Eight out of the nine people who died that year are 50+. What was making a difference was not the conquest of disease; smallpox was the only major mass disease to have a cure found by 19th century science. In our period from 1840 to 1880, if you survived infancy, you ran the gauntlet of typhoid (such as claimed Prince Albert in 1861), tuberculosis, diphtheria, scarlet fever and dysentery. The poor additionally were prone to typhus, courtesy of body lice. The difference came from better public health and more effective sanitation which began to get cholera under control by the 1860's. In the wake of the cholera epidemics of 1832 and 1848 in London and the provinces, Boards of Health were set up by Parliament to establish loal boards of health and to address such issues as water supply and drainage. A typical village had no drainage system or artificial water-supply. It was not until 1875 that a Public Health Act laid down rules for sanitation that every owner of every house had to obey.

In this way, many aspects of the villager's lives gradually improved. Entries about smallpox had been common in the parish records of the 18th century. The discovery of a vaccination by Edward Jenner in 1796 changed all that. The first mention of smallpox in the Cleeve school records is in 1872 when Mrs Harding, teacher and wife of the Headmaster, catches the terrifying disease. Happily she recovers.

In mid 19th century England, there was a sharp contrast between rural parishes inland compard with coastal or marsh areas. A child born in watery areas around 1861 could expect to live to no more than 31 on average, compared to 44 in drier areas of the countryside. The murder mystery is partly explained by a surprising suspect; the presence of malaria.[558] Often described at the time as marsh fever or ague, it was malaria nonetheless. Folk memory is that this affected the marsh areas.

The annual mortality rate for England and Wales was around 22 per thousand in 1863-7 and 19 only 20 years later. By the First World War, it was down to 14. Infant mortality was a different story. The number of deaths of children under the age of one per thousand live births was still some 156 in 1871 and 144 in the five year period to 1880. It did not fall significantly until the next century.[559] The Moor bucks this trend. By 1861, half way through our period, life expectancy was as high as the average person nationally would not experience for another 60 years.

At first, child mortality is rife. Examining the Kenn burial register shows a frightening number of times the Vicar of Yatton is called to come to bury a child three miles away. One can imagine the knock at the door, the bearer of sad news, a request brought, an arrangement made and the departure of Thomas Wickham, David Clerk or Henry Barnard by horse to console sorrowing parents and commit a baby to the grave. Of those buried in the village in the decade from 1813, when the 19th century record begins, exactly half are infants under the age of 1. Then the proportion falls.

1820's	1830's	1840's	1850's	1860's	1870's	1880's	1890's	1900-1914
36%	25%	22%	12%	17%	7%	7%	8%	5%

If a child survived its first year, it was vulnerable to infections from diarrhoea or to respiratory ailments, especially in the winter and spring. Or it might fall prey to whooping cough, measles, scarlet fever or diphtheria. The last three culprits killed older children between 5 and 14. There were unintended consequences. Then as now, classrooms were a breeding ground for disease. Compulsory education after 1870 brought children into greater proximity for longer periods. When members of the family fell ill, parents resorted to the traditional 19th century remedy- opium. Intended to pacify children, it would be some time before the debilitating effects of opium would be realised. In the winter, respiratory ailments were joined by typhus fever, spread by lice on the body. This was worse in crowded living conditions in the towns but could be a problem in larger villages. In the summer, typhoid reared its ugly head, aided and abetted by contaminated water and the deadly fly.[560]

If you were seriously ill on the Moor, there was no hospital to be rushed to. The nearest hospital was in nearby Clevedon and later, Weston Super-mare. For those who could make the trip, there was Bristol Royal Infirmary. Locally, Kelly's Directory for 1875 lists Thomas Hardwick as *'Relieving Officer and public vaccinations officer'*. There was in addition a surgery practice in Yatton at that time under the name of Hurd and Sayer. By the 1883 Kelly's, the practice is firmly under the name of John Hurd, "*surgeon and medical officer, Yatton District for the Bedminster Union*" (linked to the workhouse). He has done his training at Edinburgh. Dr Hurd is also a founder member in 1867 of a local Masonic Lodge. He is joined by comfortably off local people, able to afford the considerable sum of 5 guineas for the initiation fee. The social profile included solicitors and JPs, engineers, various merchants, teachers and Henry Shiner, the father of the auctioneer in Yatton. In time, all Yatton doctors and some clergymen will join. Agricultural Lodge no 1199 moved to assembly rooms in Yatton and eventually, to Larchmont Hall, still prominent in the present village.[561]

Victorian medical men such as James Hurd were not highly regarded unless they were consultants. Country surgeons were looked down on. Miss Marrable in Trollope's 'The Vicar of Bullhampton' had the clear notion that the son of a gentleman *"should earn his income as a clergyman, or as a barrister, or as a soldier or as a sailor. Those were the professions intended for gentlemen. She would not absolutely say that a physician was not a gentleman, or even a surgeon; but she would never allow to a physic the same absolute privileges which, in her eyes, belonged to law and the church."*[562]

Since health care was privatised, medical practice in Yatton was often fraught. In the Vestry Minutes of April 21st 1835, Mr Callahan a previous surgeon presents a bill to the parish for attending to Ann Jones. Having had no prior order from the parish, this was refused. The parish did pay up on July 28:h when he attended Ann Jones at Weston and on September 22nd, paid for the confinement of the wife of a Mr Jones.

Medical practice continued to exercise the minds of local people. The press reported that Rev Richard Symes, Vicar of Cleeve, had given £2-2shillings for the Bristol Royal Infirmary.[563] Local interest was greatly aroused in 1848 by the press report that Harriet Wilson of Yatton had partaken of a vegetable compound of some sort and begun to complain of pain in the stomach. To everyone's surprise, she then passed a tape worm that was no less than 8 yards long! The public were informed that if they wished to see this specimen for themselves, they had only to apply to Harriet Wilson for the privelige.[564]

Educating the Rural Poor

As the 19th century unfolds, schools will develop considerably both in number and scope. The first Government assistance towards the education of the masses is given in 1833. The Liberal Government of Earl Grey votes £20,000 towards building 'school houses,' designed to help voluntary organisations such as the Church National Society. Educating children in rural poor was a priority. Further village schools are being opened. Kenn village school was opened in 1832. By 1897, demand had grown and an extension was added. Kenn School lasted until 1953.

1834 saw developments in education as well as trying to deal with poverty. The Church of England National School in Yatton is built that year. The Government granted only £72 towards its cost. John Hugh Smyth-Pigott, the landowner, gives £30. The villagers have to find the rest. Deeds show that £103 and 3 shillings was raised through a bazaar. A collection from one of the vicar's sermon yielded £13 and 3 shillings. Charles Coleman in the village was paid £110 for grounds and his cottages to build the school, the contract going to a Joseph Thomas for £294 17 sh -6d. Articles of Agreement between Joseph Thomas and the Vicar, David Clerk were "*to erect a school house on a parcel of ground pointed out by the aforementioned David Clerk.... the whole of the above works to be done in the best manner with materials of the best description*[565]." A receipt dated July 26th 1834 records the first of three payments. In all the school was built for £612, 17 and 3. Receipts matched this.[566] The vicar is to oversee the school. It will come under the inspection regime of the day that the Diocese arranged for schools within its province.[567]

Then in January 1844, the Vicar, Rev D.N. Clerk, wrote to the Secretary, Committee of Council of Education at Downing Street (which was how education was handled administratively at the time), to inform him that a new school masters residence had been constructed.[568] Desks and forms will cost £9- 5 shillings in 1854.[569]

Another village on the Moor has had a school since 1810. It is going strong in 1841, courtesy of a naval commander, Captain Jenkinson, who rents Cleeve Court from Smyth-Pigott, the local landowner. Captain Jenkinson let the school house to a redoubtable character, William Harding. Alongside his wife, William Harding was village schoolmaster for no less than 45 years. It was a life-time of service and vocation. He educated several generations of village children. In 1841, the vicar of the new parish church at Cleeve, Richard Symes will perform seven baptisms. Amongst occupations of fathers that year will be labourers, a farmer, mason and blacksmith and schoolmaster. William Harding has brought his own son William for baptism.[570] William junior was educated at the village school under his parent's watchful eye.

In 1861, when he had already chalked up 25 years service, William Harding saw the opening of a new school in Cleeve. £560 was needed for its construction, of which the National Society gave £250 and the Government £207. The school was to be transferred to the parish and was built by money raised by the vicar, Richard Symes. The Vicar acted to ensure that the land together with school was not sold off. It remained small- in 1885 60 children attended. Truancy was rife; no doubt so children could help in the fields. The records show the schoolmasters having to explain to the Inspectors reasons for non-attendance. On one occasion, a James Edwards was reprimanded for throwing mud against the school walls. On being given three strokes on the hand by a wooden cane, his father entered the school and made a scene. The Vicar instructed the parent to come to the school and apologise or his children would be dismissed. That was in 1881. That year, the Hardings retire, the Vicar testifying to the universal esteem in which they were held.

The site of Kingston School is given by the lord of the Manor, John Hugh Smyth-Pigott. The Rector and Churchwarden have the responsibility. It will cost £740. Two-thirds of that cost has come from local people, the rest from the National Society for the Church of England. A first plan is ready by August 1857. A year later, the school will be opened. At first, volunteers ran the school, pending the arrival of a village schoolmaster, James Flack. The 1861 Census shows that he came from Richmond, Surrey. He will stay for 11 years. Then Mr Turner will be the village schoolmaster. His appointment co-incides with new National Regulations requiring a properly kept log-book. For this is now the period of the extension of mass education after 1870.

A meeting of the Chew district Schoolmaster's Union in 1856 could affirm that 1 in 14 of the population now attended Church of England schools. New schools had now been opened locally. The cost of each scholar was reckoned to be about £1 each year. Gender imperatives of 19th century British society stand out. First prize for darning stockings went to a girl in Yatton, a Miss Earle. But it was also said that all children should know something about physiology and anatomy.[571] Girls were trained in their future role as the weaker sex. Femininity meant obedience, self-restraint and obedience. Girls did not have a mind. That at least was the stereoptype of an entrenched ideology of subordination.[572] The reality was more nuanced. There are many examples of boys being untypical and told of the joys of learning obedience or having a richer education. Girls had a less one-dimensional education than this stereotype suggests; their love of learning being encouraged.

Education was not only improving the minds of young ladies, it offered opportunities for employment. "Wanted"- ran an advertisement in 1858, "*a young lady to teach in a school. Must be thoroughly competent to teach music and singing.*"[573] Some would make money from private tuition. In March 1883 comes the obituary of a veteran schoolmistress Sarah Carpenter. She was 88. After starting a prep school for young gentlemen in Long Ashton in the year 1830, she went to reside at Yatton, educating the sons of an officer who had made his mark in *"the late Egyptian campaign"*[574]

In theory, Forster's Education Act of 1870 provides education for all. 15 shillings was now available per pupil per year, including attendance and results in the 3 R's. Disraeli's Government of 1874 then broadens the curriculum by reducing payments by results in reading, writing and arithmetic but encouraging subjects like history, geography and even singing![575] With national education, the numbers of teacher rose significantly. Yet salaries rose only modestly; most found it hard to make ends meet and maintain the respectability they felt they deserved. The average salary for male teachers in 1875 was £109 and £65 for females but only if you had a certificate to teach (and most did not). They were not rated highly by their own system. A Government minister compared the idea of consulting teachers about what should be taught with *"asking chickens with which sauce they would be served."*[576]

By the standards of a later era, schools then involved strict discipline and rote learning. Boys were beaten and no answering back would be contemplated. Teenagers had not been invented- in any case, children left school at 14 to enter the world of work which society had already marked out for them. In his novel "Hard Times", Dickens describes how education on a production-line breathed in and out the spirit of industrialism.[577] Thomas Gradgrind was a parody. Nevertheless, for many, school offered a rich potential to get on and begin to explore a different world, wider horizons and a community beyond this one. Education can be deeply subversive; it undermines the idea that this is all there is and that the status quo should be accepted uncritically. Gradually, as the influence of schools proceeded apace across the Moor, villages were enabled to imagine alternative worlds.

The Unleisured Classes

It must be remembered that leisure in rural areas like the Moor in the nineteenth century is limited. The Church had little competition and could still do business as the social hub. Bristol could offer music halls, horse and dog racing and football. 19th century Memoirs contain references to travelling players, entertainers and exhibitors of curiousites (such as the incredible bearded lady). One farm labourer was so stunned by his encounter of theatre he compared it with his first kiss.[578]

Leisure in the rural areas was more limited. In Kingston Seymour, a Saturday night drink would see an old gentleman sip cider and sing the Psalms through- all of them! 8 or 10 men would often gather on a cider farm on a Sunday morning, get round a barrel, have a slurp and pass it round.[579] Children were resourceful to find opportunity for toys but as in every age, play could be hazardous. In September 1840, children were playing in a yard at Yatton when one boy removed the pin from a cart so he could swing it around. The cart collapsed with such force on one of the boys that his body was crushed; he lost his life in a few minutes.[580] For women, life in the community would provide opportunities to chat as well as work. Indeed, within living memory of anecdotes from parents, there were 19th century people who had never ventured beyond Congresbury in their entire lifetime. For others, there was much greater awareness.Even before the days of mass circulation set aside lengthy reports of speeches in favour of headlines and opinionated sensation, newspapers were growing in both size and reach. There was from 1870 a more local paper.

A Yatton man reading the Clevedon Mercury and Courier for Saturday February 5th 1870 would read about a range of world news, including an American feminist who was connected with Mrs Stanton, the suffragette leader. He would read that Frederic Summers of Clevedon begged to inform gentlemen that he had been appointed agent for the celebrated Garston prize ale. He would read of Lea and Perrins Worcester sauce, Horniman's tea, Beecham's Patent Powder and Byrant and May's new safety matches (the public was warned of 'dangerous imitations'). If he was reading the newspaper a few months later, on April 16th, our literate friend would read of the state of education in the country. "It is clear from the statistics laid before Parliament on this subject that the state of education in this country amongst the lower and especially the pauper classes is sadly deficient. Let our millionaires pay". Then in September, he would read of the Franco-Prussian war that would have such terrible consequences for France, unite Germany and help prepare the stage for the Great War of 1914 he might live to see.

News of happenings far away was scarce and travelled slowly. Newspapers helped promote awareness of national events. In 1872, Cleeve school records a holiday in thanksgiving for recovery of HR Prince of Wales from dangerous illness. When he was buried in May 1910 as Edward 7th, this was also noted. All this could be read late into the evening if desired.

Lamps were lit using oil, whale oil at first. Then as whales were hunted and exploited, the paraffin lamp became the means of reading.

Realisation of a world beyond meant a changing context in which the church operated. In 1854, the Christmas fare on offer was reported by the press with nostalgic affection. The old traditions of the wassail, of St George and the Dragon, the Yule log crackling in the hearth, the old English mead, are, it was lamented, dying out. Yet attachment to good meat remains strong. All is well![581]

Chapter Nineteen

LIKE LOSING A FATHER

In 1857, the death was recorded of an old man who had passed away on the train between Yatton and Clevedon. It was a cold January morning but the verdict was stark- "death by the visitation of God"![582]

This strikes us as being more than an insurance classification. The religious awareness was still prominent, though less pressing than in earlier centuries. Church influence remained strong. In 1846, a Christian group, the Society of Bristol Union Youths, meets at Yatton to engage in a round of change ringing. Afterwards they partake of an excellent dinner and propose some loyal toasts.[583] Two years later they repeated the demonstration. It says much for the role that church played in the community that upwards of 300 people cheered them on in much the same way that their forbears would cheer a spectator sport.[584]

The secular hypothesis that religious ideas and practice are inexorably pushed to the margins and influence people's thinking less, was in those days as much about the dislocation of community as being about loss of faith. As rootless labourers flocked to new centres of expanding population, towns grew and industrial cities swelled. Social metamorphosis elsewhere resulted in the connection between faith and community starting to break down. Yet the communities on the Moor retained their existence and character as areas where the church is the centre of the village.

There is now a new parish church on the landscape. It is in the former hamlet of Cleeve and is a marker to a new community in the making. Collinson, the Somerset historian, had described Cleeve as "a tithing and hamlet."[585] For most of this narrative, Cleeve has been a cluster of farms. In Greenwood's map of Somerset of 1822,[586] separate communities are named as Cleeve Court and Cleeve House.

On June 20th 1840, the press reports that Thomas Simmons from Yatton wins 3rd prize in a sheep shearing contest. But the big local news that day was to read of the consecration of Holy Trinity, Cleeve. That had been a few years coming. Cleeve had been part of the Parish of Yatton, along with Kenn. When Kenn became a separate parish, the Rev Richard Symes, who had been Curate in Yatton since 1829, concentrates on the hamlet of Cleeve. With the agreement of the Vicar, he begins to hold services in the school room. Fast forward the tape ten years and building work is in progress. Cleeve is to have its own church.

Buckler's drawing of Holy Trinity Church, Cleeve c1841

The Bishop of Bath and Wells, in company with his son and the Archdeacon of Bath, came to Cleeve to open the church. No longer was Cleeve to have a Chapel of ease as an adjunct to Yatton. The ceremony was a grand occasion. The ex Rector of Yatton, Canon Barnard, Rev Clerk, current Vicar of Yatton and Rev Richard Symes who would be the new minister, all attended. Proceeding from Cleeve Court where the party had been received by 'the gallant Captain Jenkinson R.N.", the church was duly consecrated and the sermon preached. It was significant that the sermon described the weakening of the historical church as being due to its following vain Roman pretensions and that claim of the Pope to supremacy was a modern invention. For this was the era when Newman, Keble and Manning were giants in the earth and the Oxford Movement was calling many to a rediscovery of the Church's Catholic roots. The Victorians were trying to re-capture the faith of the Middle Ages.

But for now, the Church of England was described by Archdeacon Byrmer as 'the poor man's church'. The increase in dissent, he explained, was due to lack of space and place in the national church. The hamlet of Cleeve could now boast its own church, 'a neat and substantial edifice in the neat Norman style' as the paper said. After the Bishop and party had gone back to the gallant Captain Jenkinson's for 'a cold collation' and local notables had been fed with with sermon and ceremony, the children of the hamlet were regaled with cakes. A new church was soundly launched.

Three years after the village of Cleeve celebrates its own church, it becomes a civic entity in its own right. Now it will become a distinct community and form one of the five distinct villages whose biography we are describing. It is one amongst hundreds of new churches to be consecrated in the mid - Victorian spate of church-building, religion will help to provide local identity and social glue for a new generation.

The prophet of the free market, Adam Smith, remarked that the Established Church would not go out so hard and fight to win souls because it felt it was in a monopoly position. As Archdeacon Byrmer was well aware, Anglicanism is not the only game in town. Individual psychology of religion plays a far large role in shaping people's views in spiritual matters than they realise. Most people will be unaware that they have come to a view of what is the right approach by what is right for them. How individuals like their faith mediated to them is ultimately attributable to previous experiences and preferences. General William Booth, founder of the Salvation Army in 1865 expressed it very well. "I like my religion as I like my tea – hot!"[587]

By 1851, there were different types of church springing up in the 19th century to join the Quakers that had been meeting for 150 years. As an alternative to the Parish Church, a spiritually-minded soul could attend the Wesleyan Methodist church in Yatton and a chapel in Horsecastle, then owned by the Bible Christians. After 1851, this would be added to with a Congregational Chapel at Kenn, a Methodist chapel on the hill at Cleeve, another Methodist chapel, this time in Claverham and a Plymouth Brethren chapel in Kingston Seymour.

How many people were in Church? In 1851, Victorian England received a considerable shock. Despite priding themselves on being a church-going society, the number actually in church was shown to be little more than 40%. This was based on a census that had been conducted that year, not just of the population but of the population actually in church at the end of March. The figures for the Moor are illuminating. Those who came that day to Morning worship, afternoon (usually early Evensong) or children in Sunday School were recorded.

Church-going on the Moor in 1851

Church	Morning worship	Afternoon/ evening	Sunday School
Holy Trinity Cleeve	70	140	40 (both services)
St Mary's Yatton	100	150	47 (both services)
Quakers (Meeting House)	46		
Bible Christians	40	50	61 (both services)
Wesleyan Methodists	40		78
Kingston Seymour	75	150	30
Kenn	20	40	30
Total	391	530	286

How does this compare with the total population? We know that the population of Yatton with Claverham that year was a high point it did not attain again until a hundred years later. Taking the highest figure to avoid double counting (not necessarily a proper procedure), assuming about 30% children and including Cleeve (since many Claverham labourers attended church there), the figures point to about 25% of adults being in church together with about 1 in 3 of the children in the various Sunday Schools. At Kingston, nearly half the village are in the Parish Church that day though less than a quarter of the village are worshipping in Kenn Parish Church.

As a post-script, the question in the 1851 Census about religious affiliation will not be asked again for 150 years though it is safe to say that 'Jedi Knight' had not been thought of back then! The question will be asked once more in the last Census for 2010 where it will be possible to record data on-line, again inconceivable in 1851

The Methodists have been in Yatton since the end of the 18th century. Its founder, John Wesley left a record of over fifty years of evangelism and open air preaching, from first hesitant steps in 1739 in Bristol to his death in 1791. "*He combined passion for rescuing people with an equal passion for educating them in righteousness.*"[588] Bristol was a major base for Wesley; part of his triangle for the re-evangelisation of Great Britain. He also followed the coal mining communities down North East Somerset in order to preach to them. Yatton was not on his circuit, though his Journal does record him climbing Brent Knoll and praying for the surrounding area.

Gradually, an evangelical revival permeated many Anglican churches and ministers. The reaction of local clergy to Hannah More and the visiting Methodist preacher we noted at the end of the 18th century suggests that Yatton parish church was not influenced in this way. The pattern of class meetings, local societies, circuits and conference grew into each society becoming a local church with its own ordained ministry. Though having a distinct identity in its own right, each local meeting felt it was a church yet part of the wider catholic and apostolic church.

The Methodist Chapels attest to the vigour of evangelisation in 19th century England. Wesleyan Methodists are strong; the village was on the Banwell circuit recorded in the Methodist Conference annals as recording a steady increase in these years.

The Primitive Methodist movement, which appealed mostly to the labouring classes, had established a District in Bristol in 1848. As a Methodist historian was to write, the evangelisation was not achieved by *"study and application of evangelistic strategy and tactics...when we read the intimate journals of the men who did the work, or of those who came under its influence, we feel we are moving in the region of spiritual forces. The missionaries themselves.....were men of one idea which possessed them, and made them indifferent equally to the good and to the evil things of the world, to its toils, privations and often to its ill-treatment. We cannot but feel that strong faith, prayer, zeal, allied with common-sense, cheerfulness and tact, had more to do with the revivals than had deeply considered methods of prosleytism."*[589]

Nineteenth century religious movements have complex roots. The chapel in Kingston Seymour was founded in 1863 as an offshoot of a Clevedon Chapel. It was planted to enable non-conformist farmers to get to a service more locally. Commitment to milking and the incessant round of farming jobs made that a practical necessity. One of the new Trustees of the Chapel is John Victor, the pastor of Copse Road Chapel in Clevedon. Though associated with George Muller of Bristol, a leading light amongst Brethren, John Victor is a Wesleyan Methodist minister, the same branch of the faith as William Derham. There is a good deal of cross-over and interaction between movements that influenced the Moor.

The Bible Christian Methodists last until 1865 but then sell Horsecastle Chapel to a new movement that had been emerging, the 'Plymouth' Brethren. Much is made of the religious-cum social divide of Church and Chapel. How did that play locally? In the mid-Victorian generation, Len

Burdge's Grandfather was Chapel, a regular at the Horsecastle Chapel built for the Bible Christian Methodists, then used by the Brethren movement. There is social divide; he didn't have much time for church.[590]

Yet there is a surprising degree of inter-changeablity between chapel and church in Kingston that belies the idea that the social divide between church and chapel is rigid. It also belies the notion of religious divide that stemmed from the very founding of Brethrenism itself as a reaction to the spiritual state of the national church. Whatever the doctrinal necessity for forming separatist movements, maintaining the purity of their witness did not preclude them from participation at a local level in the Christian life of the Parish. Of the children of Phoebe Hardwick and Francis Stuckey, one son married a Church of England wife and neither son maintained chapel attendance. Their daughter Frances remained staunchly Chapel though three of her sons in turn married girls from Church and ceased to have Chapel as intrinsic to identity. Socially, chapel and church would mix though folk memory is that chapel goers would drink less alcohol, some being abstainers, though most would allow themselves cider. Most of the farms had presses. Home brewed wine was made by most farming families. Phoebe Hardwick endeavoured to make her children pledge not to play cards though not all their children went along with this.[591]

For many, it was the introduction of Catholic rites and practices into Anglicanism that could not be tolerated. This movement towards Rome was the trigger to become non-denominational. Bible teachers began to hold meetings locally; the Moor was firmly entrenched in non-conformity and on the preaching circuit. Polly Yeates held large Bible classes at Horsecastle Chapel. Sunday schools at the various chapels are thriving. One family memory is that the Congregational Chapel next door at Kenn was always full of children.[592]

In 1880, two further churches are being planned. One is a new build for the Wesleyan Methodist Church in Yatton. They have outgrown their existing place of worship that has served this generation since its construction in 1837. The second church building is in the village of Claverham. Along with Yatton Church, two miles away, from its dedication in 1840, the church at Cleeve has been the parish church for labourers and farmers who dot the fields of Claverham. But the labourers are using it less and less. They do not want to mix at such close quarters with the better off farmers and landed gentry who worship at Cleeve. There is concern for the spiritual welfare of these Claverham labourers, who are, it seems, in danger of living godless lives characterised by drunkenness. The moral seriousness of the times is exercised about unofficial ale houses and cider barns. There is no official pub – for because of the Quaker influence this is a dry village (though in the 1861 Census, Hannah Rogers is entered as a publican). To reform manners and ensure that Christianity comes to the labourers of Claverham, the solution of the Diocese is to erect a Chapel where agricultural workers need not feel it is 'them and us'.

Rural Rides

It would be a mistake to let the non-conformists have all the best tunes, so to speak. The ties that bound the clergy to the people were fully as strong in the Church of England as anywhere. When it was feared, wrongly as it turned out, that what was now the parish of Yatton and Kenn would lose the Rev David Clerk, relieved parishioners sprung a suprise on him and his lady. One evening, a crowd of 200 were waiting for their vicar in the school room that he had set up. In his short time, David Clerk had set up a school in Kenn, overseen the establishment of Cleeve as a separate parish and won the hearts of all by *'his pious spiritual welfare and friendly pastoral care.'* Not surprisingly, the vicar was visibly moved. He would pass on the silver plate given to him to his children in due course so they would understand their father's labours in Yatton were highly valued. He spoke of receiving the gift in recognition firstly of being an ambassador of the King of Kings, knowing that *"you are not insensible of the favours of God towards you or unconscious of what a Saviour has done for your souls."* The cheers were loud and long, rounded off with the national anthem. A special verse had been added to commemorate the birth of a Prince, the future Edward 7th.[593]

Attitudes towards the Church of England may have improved by what had happened nationally. In 1836, a bill was introduced by the Liberal Government to try to sort out the vexed issue of tithes. The annual amount was often greatly resented by local people, especially if they were non-conformist and attended a Chapel. The Journal of John Skinner, Rector of Camerton, shows how much the Vicar's demand for his tithe would cause antagonism amongst local farmers.[594] He wrote, however, just as a Report was looking into the problem. The result was a bill requiring that all tithes should be paid now in money. Gone was the annual bargaining between incumbents and farmers about the barter value of agricultural produce. The basis of valuation was the average market price of wheat, barley and oats over a seven year period.[595]

Church life in Yatton is well illustrated by a Bristol journalist in 1845. Joseph Leech wrote regular reports on his visits to churches in the area. His title affectionately recalls the celebrated Rural Rides of William Cobbett earlier in the century. *"Churchgoer Rural Rides- Calls at Country Churches"*.[596] David Clerk was Vicar.

When Joseph Leech visited Yatton, he found a congregation almost wholly composed of farmers and labourers. He asked an old rustic hanging about what kind of a preacher the minister was. *"I like a loud preacher – one to make the old church ring agin, like Parson B., a fine speaker that knocks the dust out of our hearts and the ould velvet cushion. Mr Clarke is a good preacher for some; but I am old and getting hard o'hearing; he goes so fast I can't always understand him, as it were."*[597]

The Vicar spoke at such a rate that the congregation lost their places and laid down their prayer books in resigned frustration. The sermon was rattled off as fast as the service. Yet Churchgoer had to admit that *"morning, evening and midday', the vicar performed acts of charity and visited the sick. What a man does in the pulpit is, Churchgoer admitted, nothing by comparison with what he is in the parish. Morning, noon and night, the Vicar is seen heading off on an errand of mercy. It is by such labours, that the clergy will make the parish a moral place, replete with wholesome and healthy habits. The simple habit of talking to the ploughman and reaper in the field or the labourer in his homestead counts for far more than eloquence."*

Church Hall & Institute, mid-19th century Yatton

The Church at Kenn had its own curate, under the auspices of the Vicar of Yatton. The 'Jackson's Oxford Journal' reported in May 1844 that Rev John Acres BA had been appointed to the assistant curacy of Kenn.[598]

The Church at Kingston also had its curate that year. In August, the church press reported that Rev Henry Wilkins Norman had been appointed to Kingston Seymour from New College Oxford.[599] This was a first Curacy. Within two years, it was being reported that the Rev William Cartwright had been appointed to the perpetual Curacy of Kenn. He was also an Oxford man.[600] By then, Kingston had a second Curate- a Rev Wadham Pigott Williams who, as his name suggests, was related to the landowners. It was from such family connections and another Oxford background that the clergy was often maintained. Nationally, curates were from less prominent backgrounds and reliant on preferment from a patron. It was who you know.[601]

Kingston shares a Rector with nearby Bleadon, Rev. David Williams. He rides on horseback to Kingston Seymour once a Sunday to take a service. He was instituted in 1820 and died in 1850. As well as a being a sportsman and learned theologian, William is described as a valued member of various antiquarian and geological bodies. Such were the wide ranging interests and pursuits of the country clergy.[602]

His successor was another colourful character. In 1854, the year of the Crimean War, the press announces the death after only four years of the Vicar of Kingston Seymour, Rev John Hawtrey. He had served in his younger days in the Dragoons and had gone on to preach and lecture at Holy Trinity church at Windsor, where, it was said, he had won the esteem and affection of the Royal household cavalry.[603]

John Hawtrey's successor was a name to be conjured with locally.[604] The Rev. George Octavius Smyth-Pigott, previously Curate in a Devonshire parish, was now Rector in a Somerset parish where his relatives were lord of the Manor and therefore patrons. They had asked the Bishop for the man of their choice! G.O. will be Rector for 38 years until January 1892. The lytch gate is erected in his memory. He and his wife do much good in the parish. That is more than will be said for his son, G.H.

Though he is by now serving elsewhere, local churches have enjoyed the ministry of Revd John Acres, the first perpetual curate of Kenn, who rides a horse over to take services. It takes him an hour. 1860 sees a major restoration of the Parish church in Kenn. John Acres pays up the last bills of the restoration. It bankrupted him. But the parish want him back as their minister. The Diocese builds a vicarage; a stone-built house that still exists. It has cost £1000 to re-build the church. Considering that farm worker's wages are then around seven shillings per week, where does the money come from? A few wealthy people contributed and John Acres clears the debt. But mostly the restoration seems to have been financed by a local rate from the parish.

Yatton Church was not added to in the Victorian church building spree but between 1870 and 1875, a major restoration takes place. Box pews were removed and the organ relocated. 15th century floor slabs were replaced with tiles on a timber floor. Still in private ownership, the north transept (de Wyck chapel) and the Newton chapel were not restored until 1905/6. Floors were then laid with mosaic tiles.

Between 1830 and 1880, about 600 ordinands entered the Church of England each year. Their numbers did not keep up with the rising population. In the 1860's few curates were granted more than £100 a year. The Times observed in 1867 that *"the Church will always remain more or less like the Army. The value of a living is like the value of a commission.... Officers do not expect to live upon their pay, and incumbents do not expect to live upon their tithes and stipends."*[605]

Money remained tight. Even Clergy needed private means. Outside our period, in 1897, the Vicar, Wardens and Sidesmen wrote a joint letter to the Ecclesiastical Commissioners for England to ask for consideration to be given about the stipend.

"You are doubtless aware that the depression which has passed through so many country parishes has also largely affected this one, to the extent that at the present time, after usual fees are paid, the Vicar does not get so much per annum as an ordinary mechanic; the result of all this being that since the last ten or twelve years since the retirement of the late Preb Barnard who did such yeoman service in the Parish towards restoration etc) we have had no less than five vicars and one curate in charge.

So poor is the living that no man who has not had private means, can keep on. This sadly militates against the spiritual welfare of the parish.

Your honourable board will also doubtless be aware that Yatton has become practically a suburb of Bristol, having all the disadvantages of the suburb of a big City without the corresponding advantages of a large population to get support from. Our present population is about 1800. We have no wealthy people among us though everyone does his share and have been sadly taxed to keep the Fabric and the School in anything like decent going order. ...In addition to the Parish Church, a Mission church about 2 miles distant has to be maintained, and all this work has to be done by one man, for the Vicar cannot afford to keep a curate".[606]

At the time of Rural Rides, David Clerk had one year to go. He would be succeeded by Henry J. Barnard who was to serve the mid-Victorian generation throughout our period and to leave an enormous mark upon the community. Henry Barnard was a Cambridge man. Having been to Yatton many times in the days when his father was Rector, he felt a strong bond with the villages, enough to make his service his life-work.[607] In 1858, the press report his marriage. Henry Barnard chooses as his bride Helen Sotway, daughter of a Manor house owner in Stanmore, Middlesex. How they meet is unknown. But it is clear that they come from the same social background.[608] The Census returns show that Henry is ten years older than Helen.

Both Vicars were fondly remembered for reaching across the social range to people like Polly Green. "Everyone in the village knew Polly Green" On her death, the newspaper mourned a character, who wasn't quite sure how old she was except that she was fond of birthdays. *"How she escaped being killed by the furious drivers to the station who make Yatton Street a region of danger is wonderful. She was once knocked down by a vehicle but got the better of the shock".* A regular attender at church, she frequently had to be assisted out, much to the excitement of the Sunday school children.

For most of the mid-Victorian generation, Henry Barnard MA was Vicar of Yatton from 1846 to 1884. He was evidently much loved; a household name in Yatton for many years after his death. He oversaw the schools, restoration of the church in 1872, and social change, instituted a daily service, a weekly communion. When he died, there was much ignorance and roughness amongst the inhabitants, according to accounts of the time, but the Vicar was glad to see the improvements and progress during his time in Yatton. His tall and upright figure was often seen bending to enter the cottages of the poor. He had been completing his studies at Cambridge when Queen Victoria visited. Gallantly, he spread his college gown in front of the Queen as she descended from her coach in the manner of Sir Walter Raleigh. In an earlier century, a courtly career might have followed from such conspicuous gallantry. But Henry Barnard felt the call to a country curacy. He served his title parish at Compton Martin but was then appointed to *"the large and important parish of Yatton-cum-Ken."* At that time, services had alternated between Yatton and Kenn, in the morning and afternoon. In unostentatious labours, he served for 38 years, baptising a whole generation of villagers. When he left, some villagers had said, "*we shall miss him not for one month or for two or three but for always*". Another villager said, "*it was like losing a father.*" His only reason for leaving the parish was so that young people would benefit from more active ministry. He had, he said, never received an unkind word in all his time there.[609]

When he died in 1891, a newspaper eulogy was fulsome. "*No Church has ever been served by so valuable a class of men as the English clergy. They are separated by a wide chasm from the peasant clergy of Russia or other lands. It is their distinctive character to be not only the priest and the scholar but also the gentleman. It is not their learning or their scholarship which is valuable but their powers of sympathy with all classes. In manners and education they are more than equal to the squire while they are ready to visit the poor man's cottage, or sit by the bedside of the ignorant or the needy without pride or condescension. The good parson is the friend of his parishioners. To this style of man, the subject of our remarks belong.*"[610]

Religion continued to flourish in the countryside. At the end of our period in 1881 in Kingston Seymour, Charles Griffin has been making £1 contributions each year at Easter for 6 years. Henry Stuckey has been giving ten shillings. Charles Griffin has to reign back his giving to 10 shillings, which is what he was giving throughout the early 1870s. Henry Stuckey has not been able to give at all that year. It does not matter since the number of personal subscribers is growing. There were 15 in 1871 and 21 in 1881. George Banwell, who helped dig the roads in the 1840's, is paid a year's salary at £5 for caretaking and an additional five shillings for washing the church. He will be paid five shillings also for ringing the bell for the 8 am service. He has a brother, William, described in that census as a blind agricultural labourer. Expenditure will go on at this level for a while. Four years ago in 1877, the committee have had to pay out £1 10 for the repair of the church roof.

The pattern was familiar; there was a DNA about it based on the Book of Common Prayer – Matins, Evensong, Communion and litany. It was, along with Cleeve, Claverham, Kenn and Yatton, a pattern of Church-going that was characterise life in an English country community.

Yet new traditions were being formed. The Harvest festival was now a notable item in the diary. An item in the Clevedon Mercury for September 1864 records a harvest service. Portions of scripture were read by the Rector of Kingston Seymour and Revd John Acres, incumbent of Kenn. The sermon was preached by a visiting preacher who took a text from Psalm 147. The altar was decorated with evergreens and flowers. Over the chancel were words from another Psalm- "Thou crownest the year with Thy goodness and love". A field nearby provided the means for a major village social event. The strains of the Clevedon Promenade Band emanated from a large tent. A large 'welcome' sign overhang the entrance. Inside the tent was decorated with banners and mottoes including some that simply read. "Long live our vicar and his lady" and 'Prosperity to Kingston farmers'. Games and feasting followed until time was declared at 8pm.[611] Harvest festival was clearly here to stay!

Part Three
ON REFLECTION

Chapter Twenty

THE SIGNIFICANCE OF SIGNIFICANCE

History, any history, is a field of interaction. Like particles encountering each other in frenzied action and reaction, many factors jostle together to create fresh patterns. In every field of historical study, environment, natural forces, religion, ideas, inventions, creative minds, political communities and social forces collide with personal stories.

One way of viewing the past is to see it as a collection of random events, moving with each other in endless interaction like a force-field. The comparison with physical forces is attractive. A quantum field involves random activity that, in accordance with Heisenberg's Uncertainty Principle, cannot be precisely located. Yet somehow, the weirdness and randomness generates order. History breaks down arguably into a group of fields, a system of interacting factors such as individual life events, discoveries, social changes and the exercise of power. The challenge for the historian is to decide and de-limit how large the field should be.

I have chosen a district of North Somerset as a field of study, an area that is rich in history. The district is surprisingly self-contained, a field that has few external influences and events to shape it. From post- Roman times, the Moor has not known the tramp of armies, the intrigue of politicians or the impact of famously creative souls. No cities were built here; no significant towns were constructed. Yatton was spared the march of generals and soldiers. No Parliaments were assembled here; explorers or entrepreneurs did not beat a path to the district.

History rolled on. Yet most of the people of Yatton Moor were unconcerned. Their lives revolved around the cycle of ploughing, planting, watering and harvesting. They were concerned only with the next harvest. Then, all hands were required to work in the field. For many inhabitants for most of the year, it was a struggle just to get enough food to eat, mindful of an intimate relationship with death that pervaded life. The daily round of menial tasks will result in wresting from the earth its fruit, accompanied with hope and prayer that the annual miracle of growth will be repeated once again.

The Moor has been strangely apart as if the stream of time and change has been diverted around it on its progress to the sea. A life lived in the thirteenth century will be little different from a life lived five hundred years later. Still for the peasant, though neither for the priest nor powerful came the relentless need to plant, to plough, to reap and to sow before it all begins again.

The narrative history of the Moor is primarily that of a rural community, indeed a set of five communities. One of these villages, Yatton itself, becomes an industrialised village only in the 20th century. Yet the coming of the railways wrought its own social transformation in the generation after 1841. Within a single generation, the community becomes radically less autistic, far more open to new people coming in who had not been born there. The internally generated social experience of villages where 99% of the people then alive had been born gave way by 1881 to a situation where barely a quarter was. It might therefore paradoxical to investigate this district as an unfolding slow-motion drama of English history, a microcosm of our national narrative.

Yatton was itself the subject of a 19th century Victorian melodrama. The *Hull Packet* literary newspaper for March 12th 1841 contains an intriguing reference in referring to Blackwood's magazine where, it is reported, the adventures of Mr Titlebat Titmouse have reached the point of being duly elected MP for Yatton. All this is in exciting soap opera called "Ten Thousand a Year". The fiend, readers are informed, has married Lady Celia. The author is spinning the plot out far too much. Later on, as befits every Victorian melodrama, the miscreants have their just desserts.[612]Titlebat Titmouse is confined to a lunatic asylum and the hero, Mr Aubrey, recovers Yatton. There is a nearly tragic footnote to this story. During a production on the stage at the Adelphi theatre that November of 1841, just as the false claims of Tittlebat Timouse to the estate in Yatton were being exposed, someone in the audience raised the cry of 'fire!' There was nearly a rush to the doors except that the manager came on to assure the panicking audience that it was just a stove burning too fiercely.[613]

But in real Yatton, it could be said that not much is happening. It is stage scenery for village lives where people live, love and lose, as they did everywhere else. Our story is not trying to lay claim to exceptionalism about these small communities. Yet if we attempt to tune in to the themes that are playing in the background of this narrative, there are a number that can be detected that reflect wider social and political forces. At least five such influences should be mentioned by way of example.

First the shifting sands of political communities of which the Moor is part. The Dobunni tribal entity yields after AD43 to a Roman presence. Henceforth, it is an area of Britannia with its own Villas and settlements. In apparently post-Roman times, a new hill-fort society that is essentially Old English and Celtic is part of the Byzantine orbit. Towards the end of the

6th century, the Germanic Saxon system is the dominant society. Over five hundred years, 'misty with obscurity', regional tribal groupings under such leaders as King Ine and Alfred of Wessex gradually meld into something called England, working through the vicissitudes of Viking insurgency. The arrival of Norman lords meant that the district was now under the control of medieval landowners such as barons, local lords of the Manor and powerful Bishops. From then on, the story of the Moor is the on-going biography of any part of England except that swirling loyalties in the Wars of the Roses and loyalty to the Crown in the Civil War did not result in the district being a battleground.

Secondly, the story of the Moor is inextricably bound up with the search for the sacred. From the time when Romans took over the hill-fort site on Cadbury-Congresbury, religion has been intrinsic to its landscape. Adoption of the hill-fort by Christian people may have become the basis of a community that morphed into a church centre in Saxon times. As sacred geography covered every square inch of England, the Moor found itself as a separate parish that was a jig-saw piece of an international ecclesiastical system. The parish was part of a Diocese that in turn looked to Rome. All this was to change dramatically in the English Reformation. Yet religion continued to be essential to the fabric of life. The identity of these village communities was defined by faith. How the villagers saw themselves and the lives they played out was rooted in a religious worldview. Church and community were not separate spheres, any more than there were such distinct entities as Church and State in the two hundred years or so after the Norman lords dominated the area. Like space-time, Church-State was a combined field of belief, belonging and behaviour. The church that looked to Rome was something that almost everyone in the social and ecclesiastical commonwealth of European nations shared in common, despite the claims of its Bishop. Congruence between religion and state authority offered a model for the Papal claims that became hotly contested in early modern times.[614]

As an expression of their faith, the villagers want to build a three-dimensional building that will stand for the next eight hundred years. Two hundred years later, at the conclusion of a terrible century when they had faced Armageddon, the villagers set about expanding their church, reaching out beyond themselves in search of transcendence. The people of the village looked to the sacred building in their midst as a gateway to God, both similcrum and sacrament of divine presence. This is who they were and what sort of community that was witnessing the march of generations; people of faith, people who were on their way to the next realm heavily represented in their midst. This is why the Reform was such a shock. Familiar boundaries of faith and practice that defined their lives had moved. The character of their religion was to alter profoundly over the next few centuries of a journey into modernity. From church and community being one organic whole, church now lay at the heart of the villages.

It was to remain that way. When the founding fathers of sociology were writing, they took for granted that religion was gradually losing its place in social and political life. Secularisation was an encroaching tide that could not be stopped, *"the process by which religious thinking, practice and institutions lose social significance"*[615] Berger distinguishes three facets of secularisation- socio-structural in which functions traditionally operated by religious institutions (such as education and law-making) are now performed by secular agencies. There is the cultural aspect in which the role of religion in art, music, philosophy and social sciences has declined. Then there is the secularisation of individual consciousness in which fewer people use religious categories to make sense of the world.[616] Bruce argues that the secularisation of individual consciousness means that each generation is steadily more secularised than its predecessor.[617] All this is challenged by the persistence of belief without belonging as Grace Davie suggests.[618] It is also challenged by the growth of fundamentalism and with that, the persistence of social divisions based on religion.

Though secularity now meant that people saw the world differently and that alternative approaches to life were on offer, there was not on the Moor that dislocation of faith and life that marked rural flight to the cities elsewhere. Rural ways of life prevailed; religion helped shape identity for rural lives.

A **third** way of reading the narrative of life on the Moor is to see it as a study in the formation and sustaining of collective identity. Inevitably, a historical construction of the past is a process of negotiating the forms of belonging and difference which construct social life and which constitute identity. Narrating the past and the psychology of remembering (or repressing) the past is an ineradicable part of the human condition. It involves the construction of collective identity – the sense of who we are - the experience of confronting other ways of life and the general experience of change and contingency.[619]

During the last two hundred years, modernity has been engaged in a project. The project is the compression of the world. Awareness of an expanding world has, paradoxically, gone hand in hand with its shrinking. This is the essence of modernity; that "society becomes seized with and pervaded by this idea of ceaseless development, progress and dynamic change, by the restless forward movement of time and history."[620] Some commentators have called this, the compression of time and space[621]. Distance has been annihilated. The villagers can now go anywhere, anytime. The stock of experiences has expanded along with horizons. From living to little more than fifty years if fortunate, villagers are now surprised if someone does not live to at least the biblical allotment of three score years and ten. Eighty years is considered commonplace. Central to the project of modernity is the idea of progress, that change is irreversible – you can't turn the clock back. It is also cumulative. One generation stands on the shoulders of another. For most of its history, time on the Moor would have been cyclical; the rhythm of life was the regularity of seasons.

The 44th generation had a particular form of collective identity to negotiate- reorientation after the catastrophe of Black Death. Transgenerational forms of remembering become especially loaded in connection with trauma as memories are spoken of with a shudder. The church became a place where community lament and social distress resonated profoundly.

The sense of themselves inhabited by the inhabitants of Yatton Moor was a religious sphere all the more potent because it was assumed; an unconscious worldview permeating conscious practice. How the villagers negotiated their identity was a confluence of both political and religious factors. Distinct communities were formed, each with their own characters and sub-cultures. The churches of Yatton Moor were barometers of their societies, assembly points where the realities of life and death could be acted out and shared, where the community could be sustained. Family influence was enormously potent, especially in small places where if someone sneezed at one end of a village, it was widely reported at the other end. 'Who we are' was closely related to 'how we do things around here.' Culture and identity provided a line villagers drew around themselves to define themselves. Communal identity was vital; it was not an individualistic culture that played on the Moor for most of its history. If you asked someone on the Moor how they were, up to the recent past, they may have responded by saying how 'we' are faring. Daily awareness of the villagers was that of those around them. In time, many influences were at work forming new identities, not just religion and community. Faith became less powerful in promoting a sense of community. Believing without belonging would be the order of things and then, as secularism took hold, belonging without the believing.

A **fourth** theme in reading the narrative history of these village communities is more mundane but in its own way, more revolutionary and rapid than any other change to have affected the character of the Moor. Social change here, as everywhere, was shaped by power, not the subtlety of power-relationships but rude, crude natural forces unleashing their own form of dynamism. At first the fuel was wood and water, supplemented by animal power, especially horse and oxen. In the late 18th century and 19th century, transforming coal into coke heralded use of a power source that far-outstripped its predecessors. Coal meant a thousand domestic hearths could help the inhabitants to cook, to heat their houses and provide iron-working enough to keep the blacksmith in gainful labour. In time, coal gas meant gas lighting too, courtesy of local gasworks. In 1841, coal came to mean something else; steam power that could drive engines, especially those of the new locomotives. The result was social transformation and an influx of new influences on the Moors. Even that was to be exceeded by the impact of new forms of power that arrived in the villages in the 1920's. Petrol engines based on oil allowed cars to come on to the landscape in ever increasing numbers. Electricity provided power at the end of a cable to transform homes, to bring light heat and the promise of release from drudgery.

Lastly, a **fifth** trend could be mentioned, that of the growth of institutions. There was a marked spirit of philanthropy in charities that helped the 18th century poor. An attitude of helping others and voluntarism was energised by religious impulses. The 1830's to 1880's which witnessed an astonishing development, the growth of public institutions. What to do about the poor was not a matter of localism but centrally ordered action. Government dictated what should be done about the poor, the growth of education and public health. Even trading standards affecting what went on in the shops on the Moor was now a proper role of Government.

The Themes of Personal Narrative

But if there are wider forces shaping the social landscape, there are many personal narratives as well permeating the overall narrative. This is where we might invoke an interpretive approach to history. There are many themes that play in people's lives. What is interesting and significant is how they work out these meanings, how they play these themes. What is meaningful to one generation may not repeat itself in the next but it seems undeniable that how people handle the meanings they attach to their circumstances and lived experience tells us a good deal about lives- both past and present. The question is, how we might attempt to interpret people's story?

In a contemporary counselling context, the interpretive task is to attempt to tune in to what is important to the client and to endeavour to find out why. Variants of existential or interpretive therapy suggest that we are meaning-seeking creatures and what is really interesting about us is not some unconscious arena that we can only access in a glass darkly but the meanings we attach to things. The same idea can be seen in qualitative research, rooted in an interpretive view of the world. The urge to count, to quantify, does not capture social reality; we need to develop insights to do with motivations and the understanding people have of their situation. In the historical field, fresh readings of history are constantly being made available, readings that are indistinguishable from the perspective of both Reader and reader.

The stage scenery on which sixty generations have played out their lives on the Moor is a messy blend of fertile drained fields, some higher ground for the villages, surrounding farmland and adjacent hills.

Yet there is an emotional landscape as well as physical. It is the landscape of meaning we wrap around the contours of our world. *"It is never really a matter of the facts per se but the weight, position, combination and significance they carry that is at issue."*[622] What unites personal and social history alike are the meanings that people carry about their lives – for the most part unarticulated in this narrative. For we are not simply talking about a collection of fields and rhynes backing on to Cadbury Hill and wooded areas beyond. Superimposed upon the environment of the Moor were contours of love and laughter, of drudgery and of dreams, of pleasure and of pain, of trauma or tranquillity that moulded the lives of the villagers. As their modern forebears play out their lives on this landscape, it is salutary to imagine what those who went before us thought and felt as they looked at the hills, fields and towers that were deeply associated with their personal stories. Once, such stories popped out as generation after generation unfolds. Then they were carefully placed back in the drawer, to be lost forever.

How would such an approach apply to the texture of the past as described in this history? There are themes that have emerged from the personal stories of those who have touched the life of the Moor. Care must be taken about what might be regarded as defining issues. It is more obvious to spectators from the future perhaps what were the overriding themes of lives.

1. Geoffrey de Mowbray (Chapter 4) – the career of the Bishop of Coutances, the Norman lord who becomes baron over much of the Moor in the 11th century, appears to be about *power and identity*. He was a player in the rude, crude power politics of his day, exhibiting the contest for dominance in a world where there can be only winners or losers. To have come up against him would be to encounter a powerful man whose persona reflected his ambition.

2. Robert Gyene (Chapter 6) – the career of the Mayor of Bristol and successful merchant Robert Gyene was clearly marred by false accusation and *betrayal*. After experiencing the collective trauma of the Black Death, he married Egelina de Wyck, becoming all too briefly lord of the Manor on the Moor. The pinnacle of a hard-won position was then fatally undermined by his enemies. Gyene is exonerated but it is too late for him to enjoy. The fruits of betrayal and false accusation are deadly for him; Gyene dies shortly after.

3. Sir John Newton (Chapter 8) – this late medieval knight, son of a senior Judge, set about establishing himself as a man of substance and position. He becomes MP, marries Isabel de Cheddar who brings with her the Wyck Manor and sets about demonstrating that here is a significant man. The South Porch of St Mary's Yatton is clothing upon him. The *quest for significance* seems to be paramount; he wants to make his mark and be remembered.

4. William Derham (Chapter 14) – here was a man who is motivated by *faith* and hope. The virtual founder of Methodism in Yatton is plying a craft; he will be taking pride in what he does. The skilled artisan becomes Middle Class. *Respectability* is important to him as he takes trusted positions in the village. Derham has obtained a position of social honour.

5. <u>The Kenn branch of the Kingcott family</u> (Chapter 14) – James Kingcott is a respected Yeoman farmer in Yatton but his nephews in Kenn experience a descent into darkness. Informed against at a time of social distress, the dominant theme for a brief period becomes one of *revenge*. It may be that this was impulsive. Nevertheless, revenge becomes the leitmotif of life with terrifying consequences for the family, destructive to those around the men.

6. <u>Isaac Joules</u> (Chapter 14) – the gypsy, if he can be called that, demonstrates a life that from our perspective seems to be replete with wandering romance. Whether or not unproven family fancies have any validity, it is nevertheless clear that *love and loss* defined him. Isaac seems never to have got over the death of Merrily Joules. He was obviously heartbroken. Love and its cost shaped and moulded him; loss is central to his representation and memory.

7. <u>Eliza Gregory/Clark</u> (Chapter 14) - what are we to make though of defining themes playing in the life of the Quaker girl whose diary we deployed? Again there is the inter-play of identity against the factors that might threaten it. Eliza's early experience is shaped by *security*. A safe, affirming home life is foundational to the way she sees her place in the world. Hers is an experience of play, of freedom to explore, of a way of drawing boundaries around the self and her sub-culture that is inspired by faith. While her outlook on life would no doubt have reflected attitudes towards the early Victorian family, love and marriage, it is to the sub-culture of faith that we must look for background influences on a life experience that was available to young Eliza- that and the secure world she inhabits. Family and faith are means by which security is made safe. She would have found it incomprehensible that marriage could be anything other than for life.[623] When she was 25, the Divorce Reform Act took the business of dissolving marriage away from the Church. Then the Married Women's Property Acts after 1870 gave a woman access to her own property.

In taking seriously the themes playing in the background of personal history, we must be cautious about the search for a defining issue. What may look obvious as a candidate to modern people might have astonished contemporaries. Most life is lived in the everyday. From the texture of lives such as these, impulses and motivations may be garnered which help them articulate what was important to them. These seven disparate characters exhibit themes such as:

- Competitive power
- Betrayal
- The quest for significance
- Faith and respectability
- Revenge and passion
- Love and loss
- Security

All such themes are important constituents of human action. The quest for significance is especially crucial here; the diverse ways people look for it and amidst their social context. The significance of significance is crucial to the meanings people articulate as they live out their lives. What people do to search for significance tells us a great deal about what is important to them. These life stances were almost certainly not the defining issue of most past lives in this narrative; for the most part, presumably they got on with the next task in front of them. Yet there is something recognisable about themes such as these. They are familiar. They provide material for inter-subjective recognition.

It is all too easy in studying the past to take up the stance of a tourist, coming to those behind us, taking a photograph as it were and supposing we have captured reality. The medieval period can seem a place that such tourists frequent. We are visitors from another world marvelling at beliefs in ghosts and primitive medicine. Yet those inhabiting the fourteen hundred years of our narrative until we get to early modern times are not alien entities. The comments of the post-colonial African writer Chinwa Achebe surely apply to our attitude to previous dwellers of time and space. *"Africans are not really served by his compassion, whatever it means. They ask for one thing alone – to be seen for what they are, human beings."*[624]

In other words, what was meaningful in past lives is also our story. This is not about alien entities, this is us - back then! With all the caveats about how we can provide an account of inter-subjective recognition of similar experiences, former people of the Moor ask that we can see them as people, living out a human life.

Chapter Twenty One

A Useful Lens?

An Interesting Moment

The study of history is at an interesting moment. Remembering the past has become a growth industry through the History Channel, a constant stream of documentaries and research on family trees. History has been declared dead, outdated and moribund. Yet the very processes that seem to indicate an end of history such as multi-culturalism, globalisation and the success of democracy are probably a western luxury; historical phenomena, belonging to a given moment of historical time.

When at the beginning of our narrative, the Romans conquered the North Somerset levels, they brought with them a concept of cyclical time (what comes round, goes around) that was very different to the way we see the past. History had come to its fulfilment in the Roman Empire. Then came the impact of Christianity in which the sacred life of the seasons and church year was cyclical but also going somewhere like a wheel moving to a destination. That destination was theological and apocalyptic as schemes of history grounded in divine purpose tend to be. God who had intervened decisively in history a few decades or centuries before was moving history towards a conclusion; an end-game marked by judgement and re-creation.

Secular western civilisation has seen history as a narrative of development and progress. It doesn't imply that change is always for the better. The inhabitants of the Moor live far longer and have much healthier lives than their forefathers. They have things to make life easier; their lives are replete with material comforts. Diseases that took lives prematurely are under control; the endemic and tragic child mortality that brought the Vicar of Yatton regularly to take a funeral for a child under the age of one is now in the past. Childbirth is no longer dangerous. Yet the impact of mass society and the life of the troubled 20th century brought its own concerns.

Crafting history as a straight line from past to present means that each historical period has its own style and personality. History has been concerned with institutions, collective agency, causes, trying to be as objective as possible and particular forms of telling the story of the past, of historical narratives that recount something specific. As we noted in the introduction, there is a view of space and time played out in this particular narrative; the way the horizons of the world have shrunk. If the world seems smaller and more accessible to the villagers in these five communities, at the same time it is also faster. The compression of space has been matched by the compression of time, away from the slow-motion of the agricultural year towards speed and rapidity of pace and fast-flying experiences.

As history was de-constructed, the old study of theories of history evolved into the critical study of building historical memory. And yet the constructed narratives of historical memory cannot be divorced from historical theory, the perennial challenge of how to make sense of history. Different cultures have had various concepts of time. In the West, past and present are woven into a representation we call history. Speaking personally, my own awareness of the past was profoundly shaped by imagination but also the perennial desire to make sense of the past. Toynbee's "Study of History" was a strong influence, not so much in its specifics but in its ambition and scope. Unless you dissolve history into a collection of individual narratives, you cannot get away from theories of history that endeavour to see the big picture. Overviews are necessary. It is surely possible to track the influence of events over time; events that affect people and groups simultaneously and collectively. The Moor is strangely devoid of some of these influences, such as urbanisation and industrialisation. Yet the coming of the Reformation and railways, exactly three hundred years apart, brought transformation to these village communities as much as any social revolution.

Here is a proposal for one such big picture. It complements the emphasis on individual narratives we have just been exploring and in fact draws on one aspect, that of the quest for significance as being highly illuminating for the meanings with which people past and present wrap around their lives.

The proposal draws in fact from research into the factors that generate perceptions of being valued or disvalued; the latter being especially revealing. In short, the suggestion is that much social and personal experience is shaped by the value society places on people. Society is busy assigning high or low value to individuals and to groups. Cultures of human devaluation constantly operate with differing effects, based essentially on power relationships. The point is that the devaluing of groups and people collides with our personal worth. The effect on people of being devalued, I propose, is a set of three-fold possibilities:

- Either humans will be demoralised and depressed because their sense of a valuable self withers under these experiences;

- Or people will adopt a stance of resignation, getting on with life and often colluding with a script they have been handed because there is no alternative
- Or people will react with a response of 'I'm worth more than that!' There will be a Protest against the devaluing conditions which stems from the 'value-in-oneself' that has been latent within them. This is what provides the energy.

Arguably, such a thesis could illuminate a good deal of human action within in contemporary life and in personal experiences. There is a major question, though, about the proposition that a reflex of valuing self in the face of human devaluation is an important insight into the way societies function. It is that the kind of response of Protest in the teeth of being disvalued might just be a western luxury. It could be that the thesis is historically specific to our times, perhaps indeed the generation that has seen a good deal of social Protest and the rise of gender equality and civil rights etc.

A way of investigating if this thesis has any merit as a universal insight rather than just being for a highly specific moment in history is to look at a historical canvas and see whether that illuminates the suggestion that devaluation and a value-based Protest can help to explain social processes.

For that reason, what follows constitutes 'academic play'. If the devaluation/value dynamic has any valence and potency, can we see this in the narrative of a community biography outlined in these pages?

Systemic Devaluation

Take the medieval period on which we placed the spotlight in Part Two. The feudal system was a heavily stratified society. On the eight Manors of the Moor, everyone knew their place.

In feudal society, it was access to land that was the basis of rank and status. Though there was a sense that different parts of the pyramid depended on each other, the serf believed that his inferiority was laid down as an immutable rank. Land had been endowed by God. It was to be many hundreds of years before justification of material inequality on the grounds that humans are divinely unequal at birth was replaced by the daring idea that, by virtue of our humanity, humans are born equal, not unequal.

Landowners were not a compassionate group in society. They were contemptuous of the lower classes, proud of their own position and did not see why they should not exploit to the maximum every possible advantage with scant regard for justice.[625] Indeed, the Speaker of the House of Commons after the Peasant's Revolt, Sir Richard Waldegrave, spoke of the *"grievous and outrageous oppressions done..... by various servants of the king and other lords of the realm."* Justice and law are hardly administered to anybody, he lamented. Unless remedied, there was worse trouble ahead.[626]

A mirror image perhaps of the way peasants saw their lot in life was the way they were depicted in tales and ballads. They held a deep grievance about the note of sneering contempt with which they were seen. Like later colonial peoples were depicted, the peasants were aggressive, greedy, sullen, ugly, stupid, discontented and brutish. Above all, as George Orwell was to remark with irony many centuries later, the lower classes smell! Satire spoke of even the villein's soul having no place in hell because the demons refused to carry it owing to the foul smell. According to Knights, the contemptuous peasants have no concept of honour in warfare or in life. The laws of chivalry were extended to fellow members of a Knightly class, not to treatment of peasants!

A serf could not leave the lord's property without permission while a freeman was free to depart, even if he held land that was deemed servile tenement. Nobody but the lord of the Manor had the right to fix rents or the labour required. The lord had undisputed control. Even royal courts were reluctant to interfere. Mixed marriages between those of servile and free status were a legal minefield. Legal remedies available to the peasants were few and far between. There was a legal action called a writ of Naifty which was regularly used by lords to establish someone's status. A writ of Naifty could be used by peasants to demonstrate that they were freeborn- but only as long as they produced a writ in the royal courts. In 1351, in the wake of agrarian discontent after the Black Death, lords attempted to re-establish their seigneurial control of their peasants by legislation. The writ of Naifty fell in to disuse.

Peasants recruited to undertake harvesting for their lord were unlikely to have been very enthusiastic in their task. The productivity of tenants doing their service in one 14th century haymaking was a third less than hired labourers performing for wages.[627] The serfs may have been even less motivated. The problem was that they mixed in the same communities with men and women who were free. This intensified the sense of servile discontent. Servile tenants must have hated their condition. They were at a disadvantage compared with free tenants in the struggle for subsistence.

Farmers leasing the estates of ecclesiastical or lay landlords could undertake some heavy-handed and oppressive actions, such as evicting their tenants without compensation or confiscating the goods of dead serfs. Enclosures- in effect land-grabs- were common. In the Parson's Tale, Chaucer condemns the practice of taking away freehold land that the villeins had acquired that had never been granted by the lord in the first place. It was certainly not his to take back. Greed and covetousness are identified with 'harde lordshipes'.[628] The south – west was notable for being an area where lords could arbitrarily seize goods belonging to the villeins.

In theory, feudal law treated villeins as slaves of their masters in the sense that slaves were a feature of the ancient world. *"It was by reference to the status of the slave, as defined in [Justinian's] Institutes that the status of villeinage was defined."*[629] In practice life things were more flexible.[630] The serfs had to endure a complete lack of rights. The lord had complete ownership of the land. But the lords needed the rents and labour of the peasants, if possible without strife. An eleventh century treatise, 'The Reeve,' advised an estate official to know the best seasons for sowing and reaping, to take an interest in agriculture and treat the labourers fairly.[631]

Amidst the apparent stability, there was also mutual distrust. The peasant revolt shows the extent of "accumulated hatred against manorial lords"[632] Even by the end of the 13th century, the regular week's work provided by the serfs amounted to no more than a third of the man hours the lords needed. It was the lord's full time servants, the famuli, that were the most important part of his labour force. There were many landless men who depended on selling their labour for low wages. It was the beginning of the end of the feudal system, a process fast-tracked by the Plague.

It was not just a vertical class structure which systemically assigned lesser worth to the peasantry of England. There were also gender imperatives. The kind of psycho-social analysis that is proposed here must take into account the commanding position exercised by a husband over his wife. Demographic studies point to a typical age gap between husband and wife of a decade.[633] This would inevitably have helped to cement the devaluing dominance of the former at the expense of the latter. At harvest time, peasant women were paid half that of men

The better off had time at their disposal and an education to help reinforce their position in society. The peasants on the Moor worked long hours in the fields to ensure that the delicate balance between survival and starvation was not upset and that there was enough of a surplus to keep happy the various lords of the Manor who had rights over them. In peasant communities, possession of one or more teams of work animals – mainly oxen – were decisive for the stratified society they inhabited.[634] It meant they were better placed to keep the landowner happy and, into the bargain, give them a grade or two above other peasants.

Late medieval life saw the social order in terms of 'degrees'. A noble at the court of the last Duke of Burgundy wrote that *"of all the good towns, merchants and working men, no long description is necessary, for among other things, this estate is not capable of great attributes because it is of servile degree."*[635] Habits of thought took centuries to shift. Writing in that period, Shakespeare has Ulysees observe that the natural order is enshrined in what was commonly labelled 'degrees'.

"O when degree is shaked, which is the ladder to all high designs, the enterprise is sick! How could communities, degrees in schools and brotherhood in cities, peaceful commerce from dividable shores, the primogenitive of age, crowns, sceptres, laurels, but by degree, stand in that authentic place? Take but degree away, untune that string, and hark, what discord follows!"[636]

The death of the Middle Ages saw new towns and merchant guilds begin to disrupt the agrarian economy. In time, industrialisation brought far-reaching changes to the pattern of life as the new realities of manufacturing and transport took hold of life. These processes birthed the Middle Class and then, in the period from 1780-1830, the working class was born. On the Moor, it was land that continued to confer great advantages but, as we noted in Chapter 16, respectability became owing to professional people and farmers of substance. They held positions of power. It is these power relationships that reflect the systemic devaluation of those at the bottom of the social ladder, the labourers. Their lives and their wives were simply worth less.

In 19th century England, in our look at the mid-Victorian generation, we find a heavily stratified society in which everyone knew their place or were constantly reminded of it. The situation of rural labourers emerges in the literature of the period. Writing in 1854, the novelist Elizabeth Gaskell wrote of rural labourers who laboured *"on from day to day, in the great solitude of steaming fields,- never speaking or lifting up their poor bent, downcast heads. The hardwork robs their brain of life; the sameness of their toil deadens their imagination; they don't care to talk over their thoughts of speculations, even of the weakest, wildest kind after their work is done; they go home brutishly tired, poor creatures! Caring for nothing but food and rest".*[637]

So often in Victorian literature, rural workers are caricatures. George Eliot's novel Adam Bede takes the lives of a village carpenter seriously. Yet when she describes agricultural labourers and those below her own level, she engages in stereotyping. Farm workers 'slouch', their gaze is 'bovine'.[638] As Barry Reay observes in his study of 19th century rural lives, there is a serious problem of invisibility and unwitting collusion between reader at the time and the novelist. It is as if they wink at each other. The description of the doomed Hetty Sorel sounds as if we are being introduced to a farm pet rather than a hard-working servant.[639]

Arguably, Thomas Hardy, feted for his vivid nostalgia, uses the agricultural labourer for comic relief. Tess' parents, in Tess of the d'Urbevilles are trivialised as clodhopping, ignorant simple fools.[640] Henry James observed perceptively, though acidly, that *"Mr Hardy puts his figures through a variety of comical movements; he fills their mouths with quaint turns of speech; he baptises them with odd names."* In the end, *"the only things we believe in are the sheep and the dogs."*[641]

Such devaluation in representation of rural lives reflects the power-relationships of the period. Cultures of human disvaluing were closely bound up with the prevailing social order and mirrored the heavily weighted realities of 19th century class society.

The Protest

As we will now reflect on, the problem of an interpretive approach to history, especially looking for the themes playing in the background of pre-literate people is how we attempt to recover what common people thought and felt from emotions that are buried as deeply as their bones.

The proposal that social experience is shaped by questions of value means that situations and forces such as class, gender and ethnicity are essentially about devaluing those on the receiving end who hold fewer cards. But there are at least three reflex responses to this that tells us a lot about the human situation and how people seem to need inner worth in order to flourish.

One is <u>demoralisation</u>. Most serfs longed to gain their freedom. An elderly bondman of the Abbot of Malmesbury in the 1430's writes movingly of how, if he could be a freeman before he died and his heirs and his blood after him, "*if he might bring that abute, it wold be more joiiful to him than any worlelie goode*". He borrowed £10 from another peasant so that his life-long dream might finally come true.[642]

A second response I suggest is that of <u>resignation</u>. The accepted dictum for handling the peasants was, "*smite a villain and he will bless you: bless a villain and he will smite you.*"[643] This is a common reaction to the devaluing hierarchies of social life. The reaction of most people most of the time is that they go along with the way things are. It doesn't occur to them to break free. A low sense of self is a response to social structures whereby people accept their place in the social order is determined by others and that their lot in life is to go along with it because they simply have no choice.

Even in this response there can be a wistfulness that betrays a quiet Protest. Perhaps many peasants, lower social orders and women were all too aware of the dynamics of their situation. Reflexivity was not lacking. Yet amidst a life that was nasty, brutish and short, to use Thomas Hobbes' celebrated summary, it was easier to feel that but not voice it.

A third response is that of <u>Protest</u>. I do not refer here necessarily to joining a Protest movement; rather the affirmation that human subjects are worth more than the script they have been given, worth more than the circumstances that disvalue them or what was expected of them. Did the people of the Moor feel that they were valuable human beings? When did that sort of thinking begin to come in so as to provide energy for people to protest about their situation?

The truth is there is very little at the best of times about how they viewed their situation. Like women or colonialised peoples after them, peasants are the silent objects of history. Others speak for them. Occasionally, voices can be heard through the silence. The Peasant's Revolt is one such occasion. It was not just England. In France there was a movement known as the Jacquerie. The term Jacques Bonhomme related to the padded surplice called the 'jacques,' worn by peasants in war. It was all they had for protective armour but it was a derisory term used by the nobles. In contrast to the Knights, the peasants were a base crowd who belonged to the soil and could have no possible conception of honour. Popular ballads depicted the peasants as insolent and greedy, unwashed, stupid and credulous.

Yet there were other ballads and stories, including the legend of Robin Hood which was put on in Yatton in late medieval times. This was a statement that ordinary people matter over and against the rich exploitative upper echelons with power.

For their part, peasants reacted with considerable resentment against the deep contempt with which they were held. All this lay behind the violent protest which boiled over in the Jacquerie revolt in France in 1358 and in England in 1381. Sentiments that ran deep in that convulsion echoed a new demand for equality. It is a misnomer to call it the Peasant's Revolt. Village craftsmen, artisans and lower clergy made common cause with serfs and villeins. One of the clergy, John Ball, made a famous speech to the rebels in June 1381 uttering a new truth, "*in the beginning all men were created equal.*"[644] This was the start of a brave idea, that the life of a peasant had as much potential for meaning as a noble. It was an ideology of social protest that was to continue through the English radicals of the 17th century. "*The poorest he hath a life to live, as the greatest he,*" proclaimed Colonel Thomas Rainborrow in the Putney Debates following the English civil war.[645] Social protest was an assertion of equality of value, reacting against systemic devaluation.

Before such social distress, another response was that on rare occasions, a serf could escape his bondage. Two of the characters who throng the stage of the Moor in medieval times were in fact descendants of serfs. One is Richard Rodney whose family come into the story as owners of the Manor of Claverham.

The annals of June 10th 1318 at Westminister in the reign of Edward IInd show a grant to a "*Richard de Rodeneye and his heirs of a weekly market on Monday at their Manor of Bacwell, and a grant also of free warren in all the demesne lands of the said manor and of Stoke Gifford.*"[646]

Richard de Rodeneye was the founder of the family fortunes. He was born about the year 1270. The early pedigree of the Rodney family set out in the Visitation of Somerset 1623 is a fabrication. Richard de Rodeneye or his immediate descendants were trying to disguise their humble origins.[647]

"*It hath been a constant tradition in our family that wee came into this land with Maud, the Emprisse, from forraigne parts and that for service done by Rodney in her Warres against King Stephen the Usurper; Shee have them lands and Estates within this Kingdome*"[648]

The practice was not unknown. Yet the truth was more prosaic. His ancestors were villeins, tilling the lands of the Dean and Chapter of Wells

Cathedral at Mark in the Somerset levels. Rodney was probably the name given to an islet, some firm ground in the marshes like the names Godney and Totney. His grandfather got manumission from the Bishop and Bath and Wells as a serf.

There is no mention of Rodney in contemporary records before 1296 when Isabell Sor, the 'domina de Claverham', gave Richard Rodeneye and his heirs a piece of ground in nearby Backwell to build a mill on.[649] From then onwards, he is acquiring lands in Stoke Gifford in North Bristol (now Rodney Stoke). In the year 1308, the Dean of Wells made a grant of land to Richard and Lucy his wife at a rent of 5s 11½ d in free socage (this meant that the rent was paid in cash, not service).[650] But the reference is intriguing. Richard is evidently buying land used by his ancestors, where they originated.

From 1307, when Edward IInd came to the throne, until he died in 1322, Richard was constantly employed in the King's Service. He was commander of sea walls and dykes 1314 and 16 at the Somerset coast.[651] He was married twice, to Maud and then Lucy. Richard Rodney was knighted at Keynsham in 1316. He had arrived.

There is another descendant of an enterprising serf moving from one degree to another. Robert Gyene, whom we met in Chapter 6. His family was descended from William Gyan of North Curry who in 1264, received manumission 'from servile condition.'[652] Robert Gyene was in essence, a country lad from a small mid-Somerset village who, in today's terms became upwardly mobile. This enterprising son of the soil went on to become a successful businessman in Bristol.[653] He made his mark on society as MP and Mayor of Bristol; a status that was enhanced after the tribulation of bubonic plague by marriage to Egelina de Wyck. It brought with it a position in Somerset, a Knighthood and estates in Yatton.

The vision of Piers Plowman appeared not long after, in 1377 amidst the social distress. Yet something new was taking place. Langland remarks that, though lords of the Manor were offering many inducements to wandering labourers to come and work for them, the latter took advantage of their kindness. *"They deign not to dine on day-old vegetables"*. Instead, fresh cooked meat and fried fish were demanded. The peasants, Langland complains, are ready to band together and associate. It was a revolt in formation.[654]

Yet the Peasant's Revolt four years later did not affect North Somerset. It may well be that the steam was taken out of peasants' grievance by their having been able previously to negotiate strips of land for them to farm. In other words, there was less to revolt against! They had made their protest by getting on and seizing control of their own destiny. This is not to be under-estimated. For the first time in their lives, the peasants can do something for themselves. They are now in a position to move away from the subsistence farming that has maintained a hand-to-mouth existence.

In the early modern age, immunisation against loneliness involved not searching for God so much as turning inwards with the aim of reinforcing one's power of resistance, by introspection, by understanding one's uniqueness, even though at first that might increase the loneliness[655]. The idea of being different maybe stems from Renaissance artists. Before that, people had closed their eyes to their own originality, feeling their way through life by imitation, guided by the memory of established models of excellence, believing that obedience was the way to win both divine and human favour. In the 16th century, Benvenuto Cellini believed he had found a method for avoiding self-doubt. He advised everyone to write their autobiography, not in order to understand themselves but to assert their individuality!

The Protest was there in Shakespeare as King Lear and Shylock show. Maybe it is from Shakespeare that the conscious self began to inhabit itself more self-consciously. The inner space inhabited by the conscious self was explored in the theatre. Shakespeare tantalises his audience with the motivation of Iago who is trying to bring down Othello. He explores personal subjectivity far more than previous writers.[656]

When we fast forward the tape two hundred and fifty years, much has happened. The English revolution, the American revolution and the French revolution have produced deep fissures in the ancient regime. The old rulers found it increasingly hard to hold on to traditional society.

19th century Britain was framed by the impetus towards industrialisation and its social costs. This is not the place to rehearse such movements as Chartism and Trade Unionism. There is little evidence of social demoralisation within this story of an industrialised village community. We might assume that rural poverty did engender strong negative impact upon its human subjects on the Moor but even five or six hundred years after medieval serfdom, we lack access to the thoughts and feelings of the common people to answer how they saw and reacted to their situation.

Other responses to the realities of the social order occurred day by day. A man reflecting on the few options available to him in his life as an agricultural labourer in 19th century Kent pointed out, *"people say why did you put up with it? Because you bloody well had to, that's why!"*[657] The experience of millions surely is that they are greet their lot in life with resignation. They cannot see any way out of their situation and it rarely occurs to them to try to change the conditions of life.

And then there was the response of Protest. Trade Unionism had been extended from the skilled trades of London and other towns until by the 1830's, farm workers were endeavouring to combine their labour. The Government's response, even under a Liberal administration, was harsh. In 1834, worried about rural unrest which seemed to be the result of trade unionism among agricultural labourers, Lord Melbourne, the Home Secretary chose to make an example of six Dorset agricultural labourers. Convicted of assembling for seditious purposes, the Tolpuddle martyrs were sentenced to transportation to Australia. Such was the outcry- even the Times said the crimes did not justify the sentence[658]– that the men were returned home.

A few years later, Chartism struck at the roots of deference. As Harrison suggests, this is why the movement received support from such non-deferential groups as town-based middle class radicals.[659] The success of Methodism in many rural districts is explained by the social divide between well-heeled people who attended the church and working people who worshipped in the humble village chapel. That may help to explain the growth of the chapel owned by the Bible Christians in a poor district of Yatton. It has to be said that the social divide between church and chapel played less than in other areas; it does not seem so formative. Nevertheless, the influence of faith communities both in communicating social division and also its remedy should not be under-estimated.

Joseph Arch, a Warwickshire Primitive Methodist preacher, was founder of the National Agricultural Labourer's Union in 1872. He described how, through the key-hole in the door to the parish church, he saw his father collude in deference to the Squire as they all went up to receive communion. The agricultural labourers had to come last. *"It was as if they were unclean and at that sight, iron entered my poor little heart....I ran home and told my mother what I had seen and demanded to know why my father was not as good in the eyes of God as the Squire."*[660]

There is little sign of radicalism amongst the people of the Moor in response to their situation. If there was a surge to join Joseph Arch' trade union, there is no evidence. Yet people did make their Protest against circumstances that devalued them and wrote them off as being worth less. They became respectable, like the Derhams. There would be many agricultural labourers like the Ridleys; honest workers, proud of what they did and firmly believing that they were as good as anyone else. As they played out the dignity of their lives, such people were engaging in their own Protest.

Life in the countryside was dominated by subtle hierarchies. Census records workers of threshing machines as distinct from a general agricultural labourer or 1st waggoner and 2nd waggoner. The skilled workers, who formed the backbone of farm labour were such people as thatchers, waggoners, ploughmen, or those who worked with horses or cattle. They gained self-respect from their craft in the same way that the village blacksmith would have done.

I am proposing then that societies are shaped by value, by worth. This is in effect another way of speaking about power. For the social structures and individual situations which devalue people are to do with power relationships. Who has the power against those who have fewer cards to play generate value or disvaluing.

The subjective experience of groups and individuals is partially formed by messages constantly being transmitted by society about who are high value people and who are lower down the pile. This may seem to be a matter of relative worth, where one stands in relation to others, but it profoundly affects how people see themselves and others. Assigning social value taps into a sense of 'value-in-oneself' that seems to be basic to the human situation. This leads to the Protest, the reflex reaction of 'I'm worth more than that'. The problem with that thesis is that it is very difficult to formulate it in terms which would show that this response is valid across time as well as being true in contemporary society. Unlike modern times, we have very few examples of what the common people here thought and experienced. We have no access to whether peasants accepted their lot in life or responded to their situation on the basis of inner worth; an assertion of value that superseded the social value assigned to them. This holds true into the 19th century amongst the common people.

In short, because the Moors are full of invisible people, there is no one to articulate the meanings that life had for them. And maybe in the end this is what it comes down to. Grand theories of social processes may have to take a back seat. We do not see a straight forward reflex response to devaluing. We do not discern a one – for - one kick-back of disvaluing and wholesale reactions on the part of peasants or labourers. What we do see are individual decisions to act, to make the best of their setting and engage in indirect Protest; a strange realisation that they are 'worth more than this'!

There is a theme implicit in this Chapter to do with the age –old tension in sociology between agency and structure. What is the relationship between the peasants of 14th century England or the agricultural labourers 500 years later and the poverty in which they can seem to be trapped? Do they have a choice or is their choice an illusion? Does the capacity for Protest, to rise beyond circumstances, depend on some people pursuing a belief that they are worthwhile though staying trapped by the system? It is an old debate. The sociologist Margaret Archer argued that we should not displace the human subject in emphasising the power of social forces to shape and to mould our lives. We must be realistic about the strength of social influence in the feudal or class ridden system but that should not be achieved "*by the radical device of de-centring, dissolving or demolishing the human subject*"[661]

The conditions under which individuals live out their lives are also social structures which shape and constrain potential for individual transformation. The mediating position taken by Anthony Giddens argued that the structural environment constrains individual behaviour, but also makes it possible. Individuals produce society, but they do so as historically situated participants; not on grounds of their own choosing. Structures act not only as constraints upon human agency, but also as enablers.[662] Giddens proposed that the self-identity which is focus of human agency is not inherited or static but a reflexive project – a task we continuously work and reflect on. "*A person's identity is not to be found in behaviour, nor - important though this is - in the reactions of others, but in the capacity to keep a particular narrative going.*"[663]

It is in the hope that the narrative keeps going to which this project is dedicated.

Appendix 1

The Eight Manors of the Moor

1. <u>The main Yatton Manor (12 ½ Knight's Fees)</u> - owned by the Bishop of Bath and Wells. There was no Manor House. Yatton Manor was owned by Bishops until the time of Edward 6th when an aspiring Bishop, Bishop Barlow, had to give up some of his manors temporarily in order to get his Bishopric. In Queen Mary's time (1553-1558), Bishop Gilbert Bourne confirmed this transaction. Yatton was then taken over by the crown until Elizabeth needed the money in the 33rd year of her reign. In 1591, a group of Knights took over ownership. Seven years later, Sir Nicholas Stalling bought it. He had just married the widow of Christopher Kenn, of Kenn Manor and wanted to settle it on her.

2. <u>The Manor of Yatton Rectory</u> - worth two Knight's Fees. There was no Manor House.

3. <u>The Manor of Kingston </u>- William the Conqueror granted this to his warrior Bishop, Geoffrey Bishop of Rouen, who was known as the Bishop of Coutances. His lands were held for life only. In 1197, the 9th year of Richard the Lionheart, the King gave the Manor ('*by fine tried*') to a powerful baron called Milo de Sancto Mauro. It is from him that the name 'Seymour' stems.[664] Milo de Sancto Mauro was part of the baronial conspiracy that resulted in the signing of Magna Carta in 1215. In 1272, Peter, his son, died leaving only one daughter, Maud. Maud was married to the brother of the powerful Bishop of Winchester, Walter de Wengham. Twenty years later, when Maud died, the estate was split four-ways. Various owners came and went, including the Kenn family whom we met

in Chapter 11. One branch of the family gave their name to Jane Seymour, third wife of Henry VIII. Later, Georgian landowner Earl Poulett sold parcels of the Manor to the Smyth Pigott family in 1820.

4. <u>Claverham Manor</u> - also held by Geoffrey, Bishop of Coutance, then by the Le Sore family of Backwell. From there, it came into the possession of the Rodney family before a knight called Capel bought it. At the end of the 18th century, the Somerset historian Collinson refers to three gentlemen who owned the ancient Manor jointly. Around the Manor House, he said, an old court house, large numbers of old buildings and stones have been dug up.

5. <u>The Manor of Court de Wyck</u> - the tiny manor of Wyck and its residence – Court de Wyck, was created during the 12th century by the Bishop of Bath and Wells. This was to ensure that the five other manors that made up the parish of Yatton met their military quota of knights and supporting troops. In the high Middle Ages, this ancient Manor was owned by the de Wyke family, then the Cheddar family held it, from which it came to the possession of the Newton family, eventually passing to the Poulett family. It had a Manor House and its own chapel of which a wall remains. In the late 18th century, Earl Poulett sold the estate. The Manor house became a ruin due to a fire in 1815 and was demolished four years later.

6. <u>The Manor of Kenn</u> - the Kenn family go back to Norman times. The family came to Kenn around 1150 and dwelt there until the 17th century. They added to their lands as a result of marriages, including one third of the adjoining Manor of Kingston Seymour. There were many members of the family line in late medieval England holding the name of John Kenn. One of them (1450-1504) is an important man in the county, holding the position of Escheator in the County of Somerset in 1483.[665] He marries Elizabeth Newton, daughter of Sir John Newton whose name will feature in the biography of this community. After the death of Christopher Kenn at the end of the 16th century, the main line then failed and the Manor passes to the 1st Lord Paulett.[666] *"One of the*

best and most ancient families of Somerset" is how an 18th century historian describes them.[667]

7. <u>The Manor of Wemberham</u> – towards Kingston and Kenn. Little is known of this. In a later era this becomes the property of John Hugh-Smythe Piggott of Brockley Hall.

8. <u>The Bulbeck Manor</u> – this Manor, on the North Somerset levels between Kenn and Kingston, is shrouded in the mists of time. Very little evidence remains. Its stones went, it is said, towards the rebuilding of Kenn Church in the Middle Ages. A dig in 1962 threw up a small piece of roofing tile dated from the 13th century, courtyard with some clay pipe bowls.[668] Local legend has it that the Bulbeck- like the R.D. Blackmore's Doone family- were cattle-stealers and horse-traders. There was a J Bulbeke who was Church warden in Yatton 1496 alongside Lady Isabel Newton. Heraldic history record the family crest of the Bulbecks of Kingston Seymour.[669] A Robert Bulbeck, who died in 1525, owned 6 houses, 400 acres of arable meadow and pasture land as well as 5 acres of woods. He had nine children including a Francis, who died unmarried in 1585 and was buried in Savoy Chapel, London. The name crops up again in a Visitation of the County of Somerset in the Years 1531and 1575. The papers of William Cecil, Elizabeth 1's Secretary of State refer to a civil servant at Elizabeth's court called Thomas Bulbeck, then servant to the Chancellor of the Duchy of Lancaster.[670] A Dorothy, daughter of Thomas Bulbeck of Kingston Seymour, was born in 1609 so time and place fit.[671] Later, a Somerset historian provides a sketch of *"an old tomb of the Bulbeck family"* in 15th century Kingston Seymour.[672]

Appendix 2

19th Century Yatton Census Data - 1841 Compared With 1881

Employment on the Moor – comparing the Census data

	1841 in Yatton	1881 in Yatton
Population	1136	1196
Children under 14	390 (34%)	286 (24%)
% in work	30%	30%
Working on land	60%	30%
Masons	17	8
Shoemakers	9	4
Surgeon/GP	1	4
Dressmakers	7	19
Charwomen	8	25
Bakers	3	5
Shopkeepers	4	12
Teachers	5	9
Railway	4	29
Domestic	87	60

Bibliograhy

SPECIFICALLY RELATING TO EXCAVATIONS ON CADBURY-CONGREBSURY HILLFORT

Anon. 1959c	Cadbury Hill report. Excavations at Cadbury Camp, Congresbury 1959. *Clevedon and District Archaeological Society News Sheet* 18: 2-3
Anon. 1969b	Congresbury, Cadbury Camp. *Archaeological Review* 4: 51. Council for British Archaeology, London
Burrow, I.C.G. & Bennett, J. 1979	A Romano-British relief from Cadbury Camp, Tickenham (Avon). In *Rescue Archaeology in the Bristol Area 1, 1-5. Bristol City Museum monograph 2*. Bristol City Museum, Bristol
Cadbury Hill Project n.d.	Cadbury Hill: Congresbury-Yatton. Wiles, Bridgwater
Fowler, P.J. 1967c	Congresbury, Cadbury Camp. *Archaeological Review* 2: 19. Council for British Archaeology, London
Fowler, P.J. 1968c	Congresbury, Cadbury Camp. *Archaeological Review* 3: 24. Council for British Archaeology, London
Fowler, P.J. 1968d	CadCong 1968. *Current Archaeology* 11: 291-295

Fowler, P.J. 1970d — Congresbury, Cadbury hill-fort. *Archaeological Review* 5: 31. Council for British Archaeology, London

Fowler, P.J. et al 1970 — Excavations at Cadbury Congresbury, Somerset, 1970. Proceedings of the Somerset Archaeological and Natural History Society 114: 101-102

Fowler, P.J., Gardner, K.S. & Rahtz, P.A. 1970 — Cadbury Congresbury, Somerset, 1968: an introductory report. Department of Extra-Mural Studies, University of Bristol

Fowler, P.J., Gardner, K.S. & Rahtz, P.A. 1971 — Excavations at Cadbury-Congresbury, Somerset, 1971. Proceedings of the Somerset Archaeological and Natural History Society 115: 51-52

Fowler, P.J. 1972c — Cadbury Congresbury 1972. Bristol Archaeological Research Group Bulletin 4 (6): 167

Fowler, P.J., Gardner, K.S. & Rahtz, P.A. 1972 — Congresbury, Cadbury hill-fort. *Archaeological Review* 7: 49. Council for British Archaeology,

Fowler, P.J., Gardner, K.S. & Rahtz, P.A. 1973 — Cadbury Congresbury, Somerset. A summary interim report on excavations, 1968 and 1970-3. *Bristol Archaeological Research Group Bulletin* 4 (9): 244-249

Parry, A.H.H. 1994b — Avon SMR 9736: site specific archaeological evaluation Cadbury House country club, Congresbury, Avon. Avon Archaeological Unit, Bristol

Pritchard, J.E. 1896 — Notes on a find of Roman coins near Cadbury Camp (Clevedon). *Numismatic Chronicle* 3rd series 16: 238-245

Rahtz, P.A., Woodward, A., Burrow, I., Everton, E., Watts, L., Leach, P., Hirst, S., Fowler, P. & Gardner, K. 1992 — Cadbury-Congresbury 1968-73: A late / post-Roman hilltop settlement in Somerset. British Archaeological Reports British Series 223

Scarth, Rev H.M. 1878   On an interment found on Cadbury Hill, near Yatton, and on Roman remains found in the vale of Wrington. *Proceedings of the Somerset Archaeological and Natural History Society* 23: 8-11

Allwood, J. 1998c   Archaeological finds at former Roman temple [Henley Wood]. *Weston Mercury* 05 June 1998

Anon. 1964e   Henley Wood [Yatton]. Clevedon and District Archaeological Society News Sheet 19: 1-2

Anon. 1968b   Yatton, Henley Wood. *Archaeological Review* 3: 21. Council for British Archaeology, London

Anon. 1969a   Yatton, Henley Wood. *Archaeological Review* 4: 47. Council for British Archaeology, London

Greenfield, E. 1970   Yatton, Henley Wood. *Archaeological Review* 5: 28. Council for British Archaeology, London

Pullan, J. 1969   Progress at Henley Wood [Yatton]. Clevedon and District Archaeological Society News Sheet 29: 2-3

Watts, L. & Leach, P. 1998   Henley Wood, Temples and cemetery excavations 1962-9 by the late Ernest Greenfield and others. Council for British Archaeology, York

Rahtz, P. 1985   Post-Roman Avon. In Aston, M. & Iles, R. (eds) The archaeology of Avon: a review from the Neolithic to the middle ages: 73-82

General References

1. Gerald of Wales (1978) *The Journey Through Wales*. Harmondsworth: Penguin. Book 1 Chapter 6 p125
2. Meier, C. (1995) *Julius Caesar*. London: Harper Collins.
3. James, S. (1993) *Exploring the World of the Celts*. London: Thames and Hudson
4. Wheeler, M. (1951) *Maiden Castle*. Ministry of Works pamphlet, HM Stationery Office
5. Haywood, J. (2009) *The Historical Atlas of the Celtic World*. London: Thames and Hudson.
6. Millett, M. (1990) *The Romanisation of Britain*. Cambridge. pp51-2
7. Jones, B. & Mattingly, D. (1990) *An Atlas of Roman Britain*. Oxford.
8. Margery, I.D. (1967) *Roman Roads of Britain*. 2nd ed London.
9. Elkington, H.D.H. (1976) 'The Mendip Lead Industry'. In *The Roman West Country*. Ed K. Branigan & P.J. Fowler. Newton Abbot.
10. Green, J. P. (1975) 'Bath and Other Small Western Towns' in *Small Towns of Roman Britain*. Ed. W. Rodwell & T. Rowley. BAR British Series, 15, Oxford.
11. Rivet, A.L.F. & Smith, C. (1979) *The Place Names of Roman Britain*. London.
12. Greenly, E. The Pleisocene Formations of Claverham and Yatton. *Proceedings of Bristol Natural History Society*. Vol 5.
13. CADREX. (1992) *Cadbury-Congresbury 1968-73- A late/post Roman hilltop settlement in Somerset*. BAR Brit. Ser 233. Oxford.
14. Fowler, P.J. Gardner, K.S. & Rahtz, P.A. (1970) *Cadbury-Congresbury 1968*. Bristol
15. Leach, P. (2001) *Roman Somerset*. Wimborne: Dovecote Press p14
16. Van Arsdell, R.D. (1994) *The Coinage of the Dobunni*. Oxford.
17. Cunliffe, B. (1991) *Iron Age Communities in Britain*. London: Routledge.
18. Leach, P. (2001) *Roman Somerset*. Wimborne: Dovecote Press p20
19. Sahlins, M.D. (1968) *Tribesmen*. Englewood Cliffs. Prentice-Hall
20. Costen, M. (1992) *The Origins of Somerset*. Manchester: Manchester University Press. p31
21. Cunliffe, B. (2003) Locating the Dubonni. In '*The Land of the Dubonni*', Council for British Archaeology, South West. Gloucester Symposium 2001
22. Rivet, A.L.F. & Smith, C. (1979) *The Place-names of Roman Britain*. London: Batsford.

23. Leech, R. & Leach, P. (1982) 'Roman Town and Countryside'. In Aston. M & Burrow, I. (Eds) *The Archaeology of Somerset*: A Review to 1500AD. Taunton: Somerset County Council.Ch 8 p71

24. Fowler, P.J. Gardner, K.S. & Rahtz, P.A. (1970) *Cadbury-Congresbury 1968*. Bristol

25. Leach, P. (2001) *Roman Somerset*. Wimborne: Dovecote Press p103

26. Costen, M. (1992) *The Origins of Somerset*. Manchester: Manchester University Press. p44

27. Ekwall, E. (1960) The Concise Oxford Dictionary of English Place-Names. 4th ed. Oxford.

28. Watts, L. & Leach, P. (1996) *Wood Temples and cemetery-excavations 1962-1969 by the late Ernst Greenfield and others*. CBA Res Rep 99,York

29. North Somerset Museum at Weston-Super-Mare

30. *VCH Somerset* 1 [1906], 307, 370

31. Rahtz, P. (1977) 'Late Roman Cemeteries and beyond', in *Burial in the Roman World* ed R. Reece. CBA Research Report, 22, London.

32. Elkington, H.D.H. (1976) 'The Mendip Lead Industry' in Branigan, K. & Fowler, P.J. (eds) *The Roman West Country: Classical Culture and Western Society*. Newton Abbott.

33. Yatton Oral History Project- Jane Bell

34. Leech, R. & Leach, P. (1982) 'Roman Town and Countryside'. In Aston. M & Burrow, I. (Eds) *The Archaeology of Somerset*: A Review to 1500AD. Taunton: Somerset County Council.Ch 8.

35. Leech. R. H. (1981) 'The excavation of a Romano-British farmstead and cemetery on Bradley Hill, Somerset' cited in Aston. M & Burrow, I. (Eds) *The Archaeology of Somerset*: A Review to 1500AD. Taunton: Somerset County Council.p65

36. Morris, J. (1993) *The Age of Arthur*. London: Weidenfeld and Nicolson p1

37. Gardener, K. (2005) **The Last of the Britons - Kings, Thugs or Saints? Somerset & adjoining counties *400 –700 AD*** Papers from a Symposium held at Taunton 26th November 2005 Council for British Archaeology SW.

38. Gardener, K. (2005) **The Last of the Britons - Kings, Thugs or Saints? Somerset & adjoining counties *400 –700 AD*** Papers from a Symposium held at Taunton 26th November 2005 Council for British Archaeology SW.

39. Esmonde Cleary, A.S. (1989) *The Ending of Roman Britain*. London.

40. Archer, S. (1979) '*Late Roman gold and silver hoards in Britain: a gazetteer*'. In P.J. Casey ed. The End of Roman Britain. BAR British Series. 71 Oxford

41. Wedlake, W.J. (1958) *Excavations at Camerton*. Somerset. Bath

42. Faulkner, N. (2004) The Case for the Dark Ages in R. & Gerrard, J. *Debating Late Antiquity in Britain* AD300-700. British Archaeological Reports British Series 365, Oxford.

43. Fleming, R. (2010) *Britain after Rome*. London: Allen Lane

44. Davies, N. (1999) *The Isles: A History*. London: Macmillan p174

45. Harris, A. (2003) *Byzantium, Britain and the West: the archaeology of cultural identity AD 400-650*. Tempus. Stroud.

46. Gardner. K.S. (1998) *The Wansdyke Diktat*. Bristol and Avon Arch Soc. Vol 15, pp57-65
47. Burrow, I. (1981) *Hillfort and Hilltop Settlement in Somerset in the First Millennium AD*. Oxford, British Archaeological Reports British Series 91
48. Burrow, I. (1982) Hillforts and Hiltops 1000BC-1000AD From Aston. M & Burrow, I. (Eds) *The Archaeology of Somerset*: A Review to 1500AD. Taunton: Somerset County Council.
49. Rahtz , P et al (1992) Cadbury-Congresbury 1968-73: A late / post-Roman hilltop settlement in Somerset. British Archaeological Reports British Series 223
50. The Yatton, Claverham & Cleeve Archaeological Research Team
51. Corney,M. (2004) unpub. Copy in North Somerset HER
52. Excavations directed by Jacqueline Nowakowski of the Cornwall Archaelogical Unit.
53. Wooding,j. (1996) 'Cargoes in trade along the Western Seaboard. Ch IV in K. Dark (ed) *External Contacts and the economy of Late Roman and Post-Roman Britain*. The Boydell Press, Woodridge
54. Harris, A. (2003), *Byzantium, Britain & the West – The Archaeology of cultural identity, AD 400 – 650*, Stroud, Tempus. See also Dark, K R. (2001), *Byzantine Pottery*, Stroud, Tempus.
55. www.staffordshirehoard.org.uk September 2009
56. Cadrex (Rahtz et al.), 1992, *Cadbury-Congresbury 1968-73*, BAR-223
57. Watts,L. & Leach, P. (1996) *Henley Wood Temple & Cemetery Excavations* 1962-9. CBA Research Report 9.
58. Leech, R.H. (1980) 'Religions and burials in south Somerset and north Dorset', in W. Rodwell ed. *Temples, Churches and Religion in Roman Britain*. Oxford.
59. Rahtz, P. et al (2000) *Cannington Cemetery*. Britiannia Mono Series 17, London. See also, Petts, D. 2004, 'Burial in Western Britain AD400-800: Late Antiquity or early Medieval?', in R. Collins and J. Gerrard (eds.) *Debating Late Antiquity in Britain AD300-700*. Oxford, British Archaeological Reports British Series 365, 77-87
60. Rahtz, P. (1977) 'Late Roman Cemeteries and beyond', in *Burial in the Roman World* ed R. Reece. CBA Research Report, 22, London.
61. Fowler, P. (2003) The Next Problem. In *'The Land of the Dubonni'*, Council for British Archaelogy, South West. Gloucester Symposium 2001
62. Dunning, R. (1976) *Christianity in Somerset*. Taunton: Somerset County Council.p3
63. Alcock, L. (1971) *Arthur's Britain*. London.
64. Bailie, (1999) *Exodus to Arthur*. Batsford: London.
65. Gunn ed (2000) *The Year without a Summer*. BAR Internet Ser 872, Oxford
66. Keys, D. (1999) *Catastrophe: An Investigation into the Origins of the Modern World*. London: Century- Random House p115
67. Keys, D. (1999) *Catastrophe: An Investigation into the Origins of the Modern World*. London: Century- Random House p117
68. The Yatton, Claverham & Cleeve Archaeological Research Team
69. Garmonsway, G.N. (1972) *The Anglo-Saxon Chronicle*. Everyman

70. Heighway, C. (2000) Heighway Glevensis 33, 5 quoted in *The Land of the Dubonni'*, Council for British Archaelogy, South West. Gloucester Symposium 2001

71. Gardner, K.S. (1998) *The Wansdyke Diktat*. Bristol and Avon Arch. Soc. Vol 15, 57-65

72. Costen, M. (1992) *The Origins of Somerset*. Manchester: Manchester University Press. p90

73. Edwards, H. (1988) *The Charters of the Early West Saxon Kingdom*. BAR British Series 198 Oxford

74. Ekwall, E. (1960) The Concise Oxford Dictionary of English Place-Names. 4th ed. Oxford.

75. Robinson, S. (1992) *Somerset Place Names*. Wimborne: Dovecote Press

76. Costen, M. (1992) *The Origins of Somerset*. Manchester: Manchester University Press. p157

77. Keynes, S. & Lapidge, M. Eds. (1983) Alfred the Great: Asser's Life of Alfred and Other Contemporary Sources. London

78. Aston, M. (2003) *Early Monasteries in Somerset; Models and Agendas*. In '*The Land of the Dubonni'*, Council for British Archaelogy, South West. Gloucester Symposium 2001

79. Aston, M. (1993) Monasteries. Batsford. London

80. Quoted in Strong, R. (2007) *A Little History of the Parish Church*. London: Jonathan Cape p17

81. Pryor, F. (2006) *Britain in the Middle Ages: An archeological History*. London: Harper Collins

82. Roberts, B.K. & Wrathmell, S. (2000) *An Atlas of Rural Settlement in England*. See also Roberts, B.K. (1977) *Rural Settlement in Britain*. Folkestone.

83. Everyman Library ed p55. Quoted in Derry, T.K. (1979) *A History of Scandinavia*. London: George Allen & Unwin. pp17-18

84. Richards,J. (1991) *Viking Age England*.

85. Clarke, P.A. (1994) *The English Nobility under Edward the Confessor*. Oxford.

86. Collinson ,Revd J. The History and Antiquities of the County of Somerset (Bath, 1791), Vol III p617

87. Fleming, R. (1991) *Kings and Lords in Conquest England*. Cambridge.

88. Dyer, C. (2002) *Making a Living in the Middle Ages: The People of Britain 850-1520*. New Haven: Yale p80

89. Loud, G.A. (1988) 'An Introduction to the Somerset Domesday.' In Anne Williams & R.W.H. Erskine ed *The Somerset Domesday*. London p18.

90. Holt, J.C. (1987) *Domesday Studies*. Woodbridge

91. Darby, H.C. (1977) *Domesday England*: Cambridge

92. Exeter Version of the Domesday Book cited in Morris, J. ed. (1980) *Domesday Book (8)*. Somerset Chichester: Phillimore entry no 14 p89c.

93. Exeter Version of the Domesday Book cited in Morris, J. ed. (1980) *Domesday Book (8)*. Somerset Chichester: Phillimore entry no 14 p89c.

94. Baxter, S. (2010) The Domesday Book. BBC2 Documentary

95. I am indebted to the researches of Nicholas Deas for this section

96. Oderic Vitalis, ii, 193; Freeman, E.A. (1878-79) *The History of the Norman Conquest of England*. Oxford. iv,276-7.
97. Trans Bagas (1879-80) Vol 4. In Ellis, A.S. Domesday Tenants of Gloucester.
98. Chibnall, M. Ed (1969) *The Ecclesiastical History of Orderic Vitalis*. 6 Volumes. Oxford.
99. Exeter Version of the Domesday Book cited in Morris, J. ed. (1980) *Domesday Book (8)*. Somerset Chichester: Phillimore entry 63 89a.
100. Herlily, D. (1985) *Medieval Households*. London. p68-72
101. Le Patourel, J.H. (1944) Geoffrey of Montbray, Bishop of Coutance. *English Historical Review* pp129-161
102. Cochrane, L. (1994) *Adelard of Bath. The first English Scientist* (London, note 1.
103. *Domesday Book: Somerset* (Chichester, 1980), 6.1, 6.9, 6.14.
104. Hearne, T. (ed.). *Liber Niger Scaccarii* (London ,2nded. 1774), 1, 86.
105. Smith, A.H. (1956) 'English Place-Name Elements – Part II', *English Place-Name Society* Cambridge, 26, 257, 261.
106. Cochrane, L. 'Adelard of Bath and the Astrolabe', *SANHS* 128, 141.
107. Slicher van Bach, B.H. (1963) *The Agrarian History of Western Europe AD 500-1850*. New York: St Martins p24
108. Duby, G. (1968) Rural Economy and Country Life in the Medieval West. Columbia: Univ of S Carolina Press p330
109. Bennett, H.S. (1966) *Life on the English Manor*. Cambridge
110. Dyer, C. (2002) *Making a Living in the Middle Ages: The People of Britain 850-1520* New Haven: Yale p133
111. Glassock, R.E. ed (1975) *The Lay Subsidy of 1334*. London: British Academy p xxvii
112. Coss, P.R. (1993) *The Knight in Medieval England 1000-1400*. Stroud
113. Brand, P. (1992) *The Origins of the English Legal Profession*. Oxford
114. Prestwich, M. (1996) *Armies and Warfare in the Middle Ages*. New Haven
115. Freeman, E.A. (1878-79) *The History of the Norman Conquest of England*. 6 vols Oxford.
116. Vi Smith,J.B. , 'The Kingdom of Morgannwg and the Norman Conquest of Glamorgan'. In Glamorgan County History, III, pp 1-43
117. Clark, G.J. (1910) Cartae et Alia Munementa quae ad Dominium de Glamorganica 2nd ed 6 vols Cardiff Vol II
118. Archaeological Journal (1871) Vol 28 pp62-63
119. *The History of Cambrai* by David Powel (1584) pp125-126.
120. Clark, Cartae, I (XXV), p38, Glamorgan C. Hist. 111, p286.
121. Griffiths, R.A. (1994) Conquerors and Conquered in Medieval Wales. Alan Sutton.
122. Contributions Towards a Cartulary. Archaelogia Cambrensis (1868) pp365
123. Victoria County History Oxford Vol V, 199, 141, 142.
124. Somerset Record Society Vol 12 no 365
125. Collinson ,Revd J. *The History and Antiquities of the County of Somerset* (Bath, 1791), Vol III p617

126. Holland, T. (2009) *The Forge of Christendom: The End of Days and the Epic Rise of the West*. London: Doubleday
127. Hatcher, J. (1977) *Plague, Population and the English Economy, 1348-1530*. London
128. Kirby's Quest for Somerset (1889) SRS Vol 3 SA 85/88 1st year of Edward 111rd.
129. Somerset Medieval Wills ed Weaver p359 quoted in Miller, E. Ed (1991) *The Agrarian History of England and Wales vol III 1348-1500* Cambridge: Cambridge University Press p717
130. Merlin Merlot, (1993) Père Castor Flammarion. Quoted in, Tuchman, B. (1978) *A Distant Mirror*. MacMillan p174
131. Harvey, S. (1983) 'The extent and profitability of demesnes agriculture in England in the late eleventh century'. In T.H. Ashton ed. *Social Relations and Ideas: Essays in Honour of R.H.Hilton* Oxford pp58-60
132. Grenville, J. (1997) *Medieval Housing*. Leicester.
133. Ham Farm in Yatton
134. Harrvey,S. (1988) *The Agrarian History of England vol II 1042-1350*, ed H.E.Hallam. Cambridge p68-9
135. Dyer, C. (1980) *The Estates of the Bishop of Worcester, 680-1540*. Cambridge. P108-110
136. Harrison, J.F.C. (1984) *The Common People: A History from the Norman Conquest to the Present*. London: Fontana p45
137. I am indebted to Alan Denny in Yatton for his help with this section and generous comments on the book as a whole. Alan is a living enthusiast for the ecclesiastical history of Yatton
138. Denny, A. (2010) *Church Guide to St Mary's Yatton*.
139. Morris, C. (1991) *The Papal Monarchy: The Western Church from 1050 to 1250*. Oxford: OUP
140. Southern, R.W. (1970) *Western Society and Church in the Middle Ages*. Harmondsworth: Penguin
141. Kalendar of Papal Registers, Vol 2, Kal. July 1311
142. Bishopric of Bath and Wells estates 1331 to 1591
143. Dunning, R. (1976) *Christianity in Somerset*. Taunton: Somerset County Council. P8
144. Calendar of the Register of John de Drockensford, Bishop of Bath And Wells. AD 1309-1329.Somerset Record Society fol 283a p290
145. Dunning, R. (1976) *Christianity in Somerset*. Taunton: Somerset County Council.p6
146. Ramsey, F.M.R. ed (1995) *English Episcopa Acta: Bath and Wells 1061-1205* Published for the British Academy by Oxford University Press pxxiii.
147. Dr A.J. Robinson, Dean of Wells. Yatton Church Guide 1931
148. Calendar of the Register of John de Drockensford, Bishop of Bath And Wells. AD 1309-1329.Somerset Record Society p201
149. Calendar of Papal Letters, II 236

150. Calendar of the Register of John de Drockensford, Bishop of Bath and Wells. AD 1309-1329.Somerset Record Society 227a.
151. Common Pleas 86/111
152. Coram Rye Roll 127/27d
153. Common Pleas 164/233
154. Kalendar of Papal Registers, Vol 2, Kal. July 1311
155. Ramsey, D. Ed, (1995) *English Episcopal Acts, Bath and Wells* Oxford, OUP no 170
156. Calendar of the Register of John de Drockensford, Bishop of Bath And Wells. AD 1309-1329.Somerset Record Society p31 folio 30a
157. Somerset Record Society. Vol 1 (1887) Bishop Drockenford's Register Deputatio Coadjutor.p278
158. Somerset Record Society. Vol 1 (1887) Bishop Drockenford's Register Augmentatio Vic. De Yatton. P270
159. Calendar of the Register of John de Drockensford, Bishop of Bath and Wells. AD 1309-1329.Somerset Record Society p290
160. Wilkins, Concilia, ii, pp 735-6, Quoted in Ziegler, P. (1982) *The Black Death*. Penguin: Harmondsworth p128
161. Ziegler, P. (1982) *The Black Death*. Penguin: Harmondsworth p129
162. Mortimer, I. (2008) The Perfect King: The Life of Edward 3rd, Father of the English Nation. London: Vintage p261
163. S.R.O. Bishop's Registers D/P/Yat
164. Dobson, R.B. ed (1970) *The Peasant's Revolt of 1381*. London p63
165. Fryde, E.B. (1996) *Peasants and Landlords in Later Medieval England*. Stroud: Sutton Publishing p32
166. Dyer, C. (1989) Standards of Living in the Later Middle Ages: Social Change in England c1200-1520 Cambridge
167. Statutes of the Realm Vol 1 pp307-8. See also Putnam, B.H.(1908) *The Enforcement of the Statutes of Labourers During the First Decade After the Black Death*. New York.
168. Rubin, M. (1994) 'The Poor' in *Fifteenth Century Attitudes: Perceptions of Society* in R. Horrox ed Late Medieval England. Cambridge
169. Dyer, C. T. In Hilton, R. and Ashton, T.H *The English Rising of 1381*. eds. p34
170. Hoskins, W.H. (1976) *The Age of Plunder:The England of Henry VIII, 1500-1547.* London.
171. I acknowledge the researches of Nicholas Deas and Alan Denny of the Yatton History Society in material and sources used in the preparation of this chapter.
172. Calendar Patent Rolls ,1216-25, 5, 36; Rotuli Litterarum Clausarum in Turri Londinensi Asservati, 1204-24, 1, 338, 354(b).
173. *Feudal Aids 1284-1431*, 4, 307,351, 367, 382.
174. Denny, A. (2008) *Medieval Yatton*. Unpublished paper. p9
175. Somerset Record Office E199/39/31
176. Manumission by Edward the Dean and the Chapter of Wells of William Gyan of North Curry 1264

177. Historical Manuscripts Commissari. Calendar of the MSS of the Dean and Chapter of Wells Vol 1. 1907 p71
178. VCH (1992) Somerset Vol VI p12
179. PRO B. 4976 List & Index Vol 95 p7
180. Calendar of Patent Rolls 1335 p226
181. Cal. Patent Rolls 1330-1334 p 14
182. Van Zanden, J. (2008) The Medieval Origins of the European Miracle. *Journal of Global History. Vol 3 Part 3 pps 337-359*
183. Smith, A. (1974) *The Wealth of Nations*. Harmondsworth: Penguin p 198
184. Cal. Patent Rolls. 1330-1334 p139
185. Cal. Close Rolls. Edward IIIrd July 20th 1340 p433
186. Calendar of Patent Rolls 1335 p183
187. Historical Manuscripts Commissari. Calendar of the MSS of the Dean and Chapter of Wells Vol 1. 1907 p240. Dated July 5th 1337
188. Historical Manuscripts Commissari. Calendar of the MSS of the Dean and Chapter of Wells Vol 1. 1907 p240. Dated 6 April 1338.
189. Historical Manuscripts Commission. Calendar of the MSS of the Dean and Chapter of Wells Vol II, 1914 p104.
190. Little Red Book (full text) www.archive.org/stream *September 2010*
191. Enquisitions Ad Quod Damnum Part 1, pps 170, 371 and 406 respectively
192. Cal. Eng. Misc (Chancery) p94; Cal Patent Rolls, 1354-8, p530
193. Feudal Aids, 1284-1431 Vol 2.
194. Barrett, William. 1789. *The History and Anquities of the City of Bristol*.
195. Knighton, Chronicon Henrici Knighton, ed J. Lumby, R.S. 92 II
196. Boucher, C.E. (1938) 'The Black Death in Bristol'. *Transactions of the Bristol and Gloucestershire Archaeological Society. Vol IX*
197. Cal. Patent Rolls 1348-50. 1348 April 20th Westminster p46
198. Cal Inquis., X, No 100
199. Register of Ralph of Shrewsbury, Bishop of Bath and Wells 1329-1363. Somerset Record Society Vol 9 (1896) item 2280 p591 & 2505, p617.
200. Collinson ,Revd J. *The History and Antiquities of the County of Somerset* (Bath, 1791), Vol III p617
201. Brown, R.A. , Colvin, H.M., & Taylor, A.J. (1963) *History of the King's Works: The Middle Ages*. Vol 1. p161
202. Cal. Patent Rolls 1350-54 August 29th 1351.
203. Cal. Patent Rolls 1350-54 March 5th 1352 p 232 and 279.
204. Cal. Patent Rolls 1350-54 Oct 30th 1353, p522
205. Calendra Misc. Inquisition of Chancery 1348-77 p94.
206. Phillips, S. (2010) *Edward 11*. London: Yale University Press
207. Mortimer, I. (2008) *The Perfect King: The Life of Edward 3rd, Father of the English Nation*. London: Vintage p50
208. Somerset Archaeological Society LXXii p39
209. VCH Somerset (1974) Vol 3 p113
210. Calendar of Close Rolls Edward IIIrd. October 26th 1352 at Westminster p449

211. Cal. Patent Rolls 1354-1358 February 20th 1355 p186
212. Penn, S. (1986) *A Fourteenth Century Bristol Merchant*. Bristol Archaeological Society Vol 104 pp.183-186
213. Cal Patent Rolls, 1351, p179
214. Calendar of Inquisitions Post Mortem Vol X. Edward IIIrd. P89
215. Calendar Fine Rolls. 1352 July 28th at Westminster p338
216. Calendar of Papal Registers, Papal Letters III 1342-1362. 29 November 1350 & 27th November 1352. P466
217. Cal. Fine Rolls. 1461-1471. July 10th 1465. p173
218. Sacks, D. H. (1991) *The Widening Gate: Bristol and the Atlantic Economy 1450-1700*. Berkeley: University of California Press p25
219. I am indebted for the following section to Mr Nicholas Deas of Yatton. William Newton- illegitimate son of Duke of Beaufort from 18th century was Nicholas Deas' ancestor.
220. Ross, C. D. Ed (1959) Cartulary of St Mark's Hospital, Bristol (Bristol Rec Society Vol 21) p103
221. Ross, C. D. Ed (1959) Cartulary of St Mark's Hospital, Bristol (Bristol Rec Society Vol 21) p104
222. List of Enquisitions- Enquisitions and quod Damnum II 26 Henery VI p754
223. Henry Owen, Old Pembroke Families 1902, p88
224. Griffiths, R.A. (1972) The Principality of Wales in the Later Middle Ages. Cardiff
225. Morgan, P. (1987) *War and Society in Medieval Cheshire* 1277-1403. Chetham Society 3rd Series Vol 34.
226. Calendar of Fine Rolls 1471-1485 1476 Jan 25th.p100 Writs of diem clausit extremum after death.
227. Register of Bishop Beyknton, 1443-1465. 1460 p346. Somerset Record Society Vol 49.
228. Register of Robert Stillington 1466-91 Vol 52 1466 p3
229. Calendar of Patent Rolls 1476-85 August 1st 1483 at Westminster p395
230. Calendar of Fine Rolls 1485-1509 1488 p71 Writ after death of John Newton, Knight.
231. Calendar of Enquisitions PostMortem Henry VII Vol II p251
232. Calendar of Fine Rolls 1485-1509 1500 p301
233. S.R.O. D\P\yat/4/1/1
234. Hobhouse, Right Rev Bishop ed. (1890) *Church Wardens Accounts Somerset Record Society*. Vol 4. Printed for Subscribers by Somerset Record Society. London: Harrison and Sons.
235. Weaver, F. W. & Mayo, C. H. (1891) *Notes and Queries for Somerset and Dorset*. Sherborne: J.C & A.T.Sawtell
236. Calendar of Fine Rolls 1485-1509 1498 p252 Writ after death of Isabel Newton, late wife of John Newton
237. Bristol Rec Office ref AC/D10/2.
238. Denny, A. (2010) *Church Guide to St Mary's Yatton*

239. Basford, K. (1978) *The Green Man*. D.S Brewer
240. Hayman, R. (2010) *The Green Man*. Shire
241. Register of Bishop Knyght 1541-1547 SRO Vol 55 p112
242. Somerset Record Society Vol 11. Note 114
243. J Anderson, (1742). *A Genealogical History of the House of Yvery*. Vol I Book V, Ch XIV p421
244. Gentleman's Magazine. Oct 1835.
245. Emery, A. Greater Medieval Houses of England and Wales. Vol 3
246. Denny, A. (2010) *Church Guide to St Mary's Yatton*
247. Bennet, J.M. (1996) *Ale, Beer and Brewsters in England: Women's Work in a Changing World*. New York
248. Hutton, R. (1994) *The Rise and Fall of Merry England*. Oxford: OUP Ch 6
249. Pevsner, N. (1958) *The Buildings of England: N. Somerset and Bristol*. Harmondsworth:Penguin p351
250. Wiles, D. (1981) *The Early Plays of Robin Hood*. Cambridge
251. Denny, A. (2010) *Church Guide to St Mary's Yatton*
252. Taylor, R. (2003) *How to Read Churches*. London: Rider
253. I am grateful for these points of detail to Dunning, R. (1976) *Christianity in Somerset*. Taunton: Somerset County Council.p 11
254. Bossy, J. (1985) *Christianity in the West, 1400-1700* Oxford: OUP
255. Heath, P. (1969) *The English Parish Clergy on the Eve of the Reformation*. Routledge and Kegan Paul p88
256. Strong, R. (2007) *A Little History of the Parish Church*. London; Jonathan Cape. P48
257. Register of Hadrain de Costello, Bishop of Bath and Wells 1503-1518. Somerset Record Office Volume 54 (1939) for 3rd August and 2nd November 1509. De Castello's position was purely nominal. He lived in Rome and was a Cardinal. He was deprived of the See in 1518.
258. Wilson, D. (1976) *The People of the Book: The Revolutionary Impact of the English Bible 1380-1611*. London: Barrie & Jenkins p99
259. Somerset Chantry Grants quoted in Barraclough, M. (1991) *A History of Yatton*. Yatton Local History Society p24
260. MacCulloch, D. (1996) *Thomas Cranmer*. New Haven & London: Yale University Press. p196
261. Ronald Hutton, 'The local impact of the Tudor Reformation', in *The English Reformation Revised* (C. Haigh ed., Cambridge U.P., Cambridge, 1987), p. 155.
262. Duffy, E. (1992) *The Stripping of the Altars*. New Haven, Conn. P394-8
263. Youings, J. (1971) 'The Dissolution of the Monasteries', *Historical Problems, Studies and Documents*, 14, pp. 164-5.
264. Daniell, C. Reaction to the Sale of Church Goods at the Reformation. www.tyndale.org. July 2010
265. Duffy, E. (2001) *The Voices of Morebath: Reformation & Rebellion in an English Village*. London: Yale
266. Haigh, C. (1993) *English Reformations*. Oxford: Clarendon. P215

267. Hutton, R. (1994) *The Rise and Fall of Merry England*. Oxford: OUP p113
268. S.R.O. \D\P/yat 4/1/4
269. www.thetudors,org.uk-tudor-weapons October 2010
270. Letter John Harrison, Vicar, to Clevedon Mercury and Courier August 9th 1901 D/P/yat 23/19
271. 6 books of Wills, MS Collections of Rev Frederick Brown 1888. SA 85/88
272. Somerset Quarter Sessions Records for the County of Somerset. 1666-1679 Vol 4. p153 note 31
273. Will of Lady Florence Stalling, Somerset Record Office.
274. SRO Sa 308/02a Inquisition Post Mortem Florence Stalllinge, widow of Christopher Kenn of Kenn Court and wife of Sir Nicholas Stallinge.
275. J Anderson, 1742. *A Genealogical History of the House of Yvery*. Vol I Book V, Ch XIV p421
276. Victoria County History Vol. X (1972) p182
277. Cal. Fine Rolls, Vol 17,p39 May 21 1438
278. Calendar Fine Rolls, Vol 19, p89
279. B. Record Society Vol 35.
280. Winn, C. (1976) *The Pouletts of Hinton St George*. London: The Research Publishing Co. P27
281. Dunning, R. (2002) *Somerset Families*. Tiverton: Somerset Books P107
282. BBC2 Documentary (2005) *The Killer Wave of 1607*
283. Michael Disney, Professor of Astronomy, Cardiff University. The Times, January 4th 2005
284. Waters, B. (1955) *The Bristol Channel*. London: J.M. Dent & Sons: p181
285. Sacks, D. H. (1991) *The Widening Gate: Bristol and the Atlantic Economy 1450-1700*. Berkeley: University of California Press p47
286. Underdown, D. (1973) *Somerset in the Civil War and Interregnum*. Newton Abbot: David & Charles p86
287. The Desires and Resolutions of the Club-men of the Counties of Dorset and Wilts. 12 July 1645 Journal of the House of Lords. 7, 484 Sprigge. Anglia Rediviva, 80
288. Wedgwood, C.V. (1958) *The King's War*. P467
289. Victoria County History 2, 48
290. Glebe Terrier SRO DD/CC 114106
291. Underdown, D. (1973) *Somerset in the Civil War and Interregnum*. Newton Abbot: David & Charles p170
292. Hutton, R. (1994) *The Rise and Fall of Merry England*. Oxford: OUP Ch 6
293. Donelly, E. Ed (1916) *Somerset Hearth Tax 1664-65*.
294. Somerset Archaelogy and N.H. Society MS Book of Accounts, related to disbursements for Mr John Galton quoted in *Notes and Queries for Somerset & Dorset*, F.W.Eaver. (ed) Vol VII 1902 p201
295. Collinson, Somerset Vol 11, p124
296. SA 85/88 Q3 1/102 108/17,18. 1665
297. Ecclesiastical Court Records

298. CQ3 1\108 116 and 117 1672 116/10
299. Trust and Trust Properties vested in Bristol and Somerset Quarterly Meeting.
300. Claverham Meeting House Guide and Historical Notes.
301. Vipont, E. (1975) *George Fox and the Valiant Sixty*. London: Hamish Hamilton p90
302. Vol 75. Somerset Record Society "Somersetshire Quarterly Meetings of the Society of Friends"
303. Rutter, J. (1829) *Delineations of the North Western Division of the County of Somerset*. London
304. Ale House Recognisance. Prince of Orange dates 2.9.1822 to Eliazabeth Parsons and Samuel Parsons, Yeoman of Kingston Seymour. Q.RLa 1822-4
305. Vol 75. Somerset Record Society.
306. Pincus, S. (2009) *1688: The First Modern Revolution*. Princeton: Yale University Press
307. The Notice on a Board in Kingston Seymour Parish Church.
308. Ecclesiastical Court Records D/D/Ppb 109 1623-1833
309. Bath and Wells Diocesian Records 5th March 1749.
310. Court Roll for Kingston Seymour 1682
311. Yatton Oral History Project- Len Burdge
312. An index agreed by the House of Commons Library, the Bank of England and the Office of National Statistics in 2003 as quoted in Hague, W. (2004) *William Pitt the Younger*. London: Harper Collins p42.
313. d\P\k.sey/p/9/1/1 SRO
314. Reports of Lord Brougham's Commission to Enquire of Charities of England and Wales. 1819-1835. P.S. King London Vol 12 S 663 p161
315. Yatton Oral History Project- Bob Ford
316. Roberts, W. (1834) *Memoirs of the Life and Correspondence of Mrs Hannah More*. London: R.B. Seeley & W Burnside. Vol 1 p54
317. Roberts, W. (1834) *Memoirs of the Life and Correspondence of Mrs Hannah More*. London: R.B. Seeley & W Burnside. Vol 1 p252
318. Collingwood, J. & M. (1990) *Hannah More*. Oxford: Lion. P69
319. Collingwood, J. & M. (1990) *Hannah More*. Oxford: Lion. P90
320. Roberts, A. Ed. (1859) Mendip Annals: A Narrative of the Charitable Labours of Hannah and Martha More in their neighbourhood. London: James Nisbet and Co. p8
321. Roberts, A. Ed. (1859) *Mendip Annals: A Narrative of the Charitable Labours of Hannah and Martha More in their neighbourhood*. London: James Nisbet and Co. p6
322. Or is he? There is a similarity in name with the subsequent leasehold owner of Cleever Court after 1821, Rev Thomas Shrapnel Biddulph. To have two clergy of similarly unusual names in the same locality is curious. An uncle perhaps?
323. Roberts, A. Ed. (1859) *Mendip Annals: A Narrative of the Charitable Labours of Hannah and Martha More in their neighbourhood*. London: James Nisbet and Co. p8

324. Thoen, C. & F. Ed. (1980) *Domesday Book: Somerset*. Chichester
325. Yatton Oral History Project- Ray Naish
326. Rostow. W.W. (1978) *The World Economy: History And Prospect*. London
327. Parker, C. S. (1891) *Sir Robert Peel from his Private Papers*, To J.W. Croker vol ii, p529. London
328. Deane, P & Cole, W.A. (1967) *British Economic Growth* 2nd ed. Cambridge, p 166
329. *The Bristol Mercury* (Bristol, England), Saturday, December 16, 1843
330. Gimpel, J. (1992) *The Medieval Machine: The Industrial Revolution of the Middle Ages*. London: Pimlico
331. *The Bristol Mercury* (Bristol, England), Saturday, March 20 1847
332. *Caledonian Mercury* (Edinburgh, Scotland), Thursday, March 25, 1847.
333. Checkland, S.G. (1964) *The Rise of Industrial Society in England 1815-1885*. London p134
334. S.R.O Q/RUP/32
335. Maggs, C. (2007) *Somerset Railways*. Wellington: Somerset Books p12
336. Trewman's Exeter Flying Post or Plymouth and Cornish Advertiser (Exeter, England), Thursday, April 29, 1841.
337. *The Bristol Mercury* (Bristol, England), Saturday, June 5, 1841
338. *The Bristol Mercury* (Bristol, England), Saturday, August 21, 1841
339. *The Morning Chronicle* (London) Wednesday, April 20, 1842
340. *The Morning Chronicle* (London, England), Friday, January 18, 1850
341. *The Examiner* (London, England), Saturday, January 1, 1853
342. *The Bristol Mercury* Saturday, February 9, 1856
343. **Trewman's Exeter Flying Post or Plymouth and Cornish Advertiser** (Exeter, England), Thursday, September 9, 1847
344. Cole, G.D.H. & Postgate, R. (1949) *The Common People 1746-1946*. London: Methuen
345. Hobsbawm, E. (1994) *The Age of Empire*. London: Abacus p27
346. S.R.O. D/P/Yat 9/1/2
347. S.R.So D/P/yat 14/5/5
348. *The Bristol Mercury* (Bristol, England), Saturday, December 27, 1856
349. *The Bristol Mercury* (Bristol, England), Saturday, December 10, 1842
350. Cole, G.D.H. (1949) *The Common People* 1746-1946. London: Methuen. p304
351. S.R.O. DD/FS 70; DD/SAS c/82 DD/CC 178891, 184957 & 199782 DD/gj c/329 Plans of 821 and 1841. See also Barraclough, M. (1991) *A History of Yatton*. Yatton Local History Society. Ch 15
352. For material in the following section, I am indebted to a set of papers and documents kept in the loft of William Derham's home in Yatton, Brandon House, some of which has been published in *Search*, the Journal of the Banwell Archeological Society.
353. This is now called Brandon House.
354. Bowley, A.L. (1937) *Wages and Income in the United Kingdom since 1860*. Cambridge p128

355. Jalland, P. (1986) *Women, Marriage and Politics 1860-1914.* Oxford p253-5
356. Bristol Mercury March 7th 1840
357. The Bristol Mercury (Bristol, England), Saturday, October 11, 1851
358. *The Bristol Mercury* (Bristol, England), Saturday, January 6, 1844
359. Townshend, W.J. et al (1909) *New History of Methodism.* London: Hodder & Stoughton Vol 1 p529
360. *The Bristol Mercury* (Bristol, England), Saturday, August 28, 1858;
361. *The Bristol Mercury* (Bristol, England), Saturday, June 14, 1851.
362. *The Bristol Mercury* (Bristol, England), Saturday, September 6, 1851
363. *The Bristol Mercury* (Bristol, England), Saturday, August 14, 1858
364. As well as Yatton Parish records, I am indebted for this section to the family memoirs, collected under the reference, Kingcott, L. (2002) *Kingcott: The Family from Somerset.* Eastwood, N.S.W, Australia: Hippo Books
365. Bristol Mirror, August 28th 1830.
366. Archer, J. E. (1990) *By a Flash and a Scare: Incendiarism, Animal Maiming and Poaching in East Anglia 1815-1870*, p 119-25
367. Yatton Oral History Project- Ray Naish
368. *Bristol Mirror, September 11th 1830.*
369. Lilly, D. (1991) *The Ken Hangings: the Full Story.* The Village Pum: Clevedon Local History Society p14
370. For material in this section, I am indebted to unpublished memories and diaries of Eliza Clark, lent to me by the local Quaker group based at Claverham Meeting House, whose Secretary is Councillor Tom Leimdorfer of Congresbury
371. Mann, J.de L. (1971) *The Cloth Industry in the West of England from 1640-1880.* Oxford: OUP
372. Records and Memories, Eliza Clark p30
373. Records and Memories, Eliza Clark p 16
374. Records and Memories, Eliza Clark p 19
375. Collinson, in his history of Somerset suggests that, in 1782, a quarry of limestone was opened in the south-east end of Yatton, 'near the Quaker schoolhouse'.
376. Records and Memories, Eliza Clark p 49
377. Annual Monitor Claverham Society of Friends.1858.
378. Records and Memories, Eliza Clark p 54
379. Banks, J.A. (1981) *Victorian Values: Secularism and the Size of Families.* London. p98-9
380. Purcell, W. (1957) *Onward Christian Soldier: A Life of Sabine Baring-Gould.* London p2
381. Records and Memories, Eliza Clark p 54
382. Records and Memories, Eliza Clark p 68
383. Records and Memories, Eliza Clark p 69
384. SRO D/P/k.sey/9/1/1
385. Records and Memories, Eliza Clark p 74
386. Records and Memories, Eliza Clark p 105

387. Records and Memories, Eliza Clark p 80
388. *The Bristol Mercury* (Bristol, England), Saturday, April 30, 1853
389. Wilts County Record Office 1699/109
390. Yatton Meeting House- Public Notice 5th March 1868
391. Wilts Record Office 1699/109
392. Records and Memories, Eliza Clark p 70
393. For the material in this section I am indebted to the family archives of the descendants of Isaac and Merrily Joules- reference Yatton Oral History Project June 2009
394. Inscription in Yatton Churchyard
395. **The President Steamer'** *North Wales Chronicle* (Bangor, Wales), Tuesday, April 27, 1841 referencing the Devonshire Chronicle.
396. 'Romance and the Countryside', *Weston Mercury and Somerset Herald* December 24th 1898
397. Weston Mercury. 15th December 1898
398. Somerset County Herald, 9th April 1938.
399. Yatton Oral History Project – Ray Naish
400. Yatton Oral History Project- Dorothy Tutcher
401. Yatton Oral History Project – Heather King
402. Yatton Oral History Project – Ron Clements
403. Yatton Oral History Project – Mary Langson
404. Yatton Oral History Project – Win Hook
405. Yatton Oral History Project 2009 – Bert French
406. Summerell, A. (1990) *First Days of Motoring*. A recollection based on her notes.
407. Yatton Oral History Project – Eileen Viney
408. Yatton Oral History Project – Ray and Linda Wathen
409. Yatton Oral History Project – Eileen Viney
410. Yatton Oral History Project- Len Burdge
411. Summerell, A. (1990) *First Days of Motoring*. A recollection based on her notes.
412. Yatton Oral History Project- Monty Lane
413. Yatton Oral History Project – Ron and Mollie Clements
414. Yatton Oral History Project 2009 – Bert French
415. Yatton Oral History Project – Ray Naish
416. Yatton Oral History Project – Rene Cook
417. Yatton Oral History Project – Mary Langson
418. Yatton Oral History Project – Ray and Linda Wathen
419. Yatton Oral History Project – Ray Naish
420. The people who lived in Kenn in the 1934- Ray Naish.
421. Yatton Oral History Project- Win Hook
422. Yatton Oral History Project- Len Burdge
423. Yatton Oral History Project- Win Hook
424. Yatton Oral History Project- Ray and Linda Wathen.
425. Yatton Oral History Project – Ray Naish
426. Yatton Oral History Project – Ray Naish

427. Yatton Oral History Project- Ray and Linda Wathen.
428. Yatton Oral History Project 2009 – Bert French
429. Yatton Oral History Project – Win Hook
430. MacCulloch, D. (2009) *A History of Christianity.: The First Three Thousand Years*. London: Allen Lane
431. Yatton Oral History Project – Win Hook
432. Yatton Oral History Project- Ray and Linda Wathen.
433. Yatton Oral History Project- Win Hook
434. Yatton Oral History Project- Ray and Linda Wathen.
435. Yatton Oral History Project 2009 – Bert French
436. Maggs, C. (2007) *Somerset Railways*. Wellington: Somerset Books p67
437. The people who lived in Kenn in the year 1934 – Ray Naish.
438. Yatton Oral History Project – Eileen Viney
439. Curzon cinema Clevedon. 10th Anniversary brochure
440. Yatton Parish Church Magazine January 1929
441. Yatton Oral History Project 2009 – Bert French
442. Yatton Oral History Project- Dorothy Tutcher
443. Westcott, A. (1988) *Arthur's Village – The Somerset Childhood of Arthur Westcott 1900-1915*. Congresbury History Group
444. Yatton Oral History Project – Vivian Wathen
445. Yatton Oral History Project – Rene Cook
446. Yatton Oral History Project – Win Hook
447. Maggs, C. (2007*) Somerset Railways*. Wellington: Somerset Books p49
448. Yatton Oral History Project- Heather King
449. Yatton Oral History Project- Dorothy Tutcher
450. Yatton Oral History Project- Dorothy Tutcher
451. More Yatton Yesterdays 1997, no 2 p47.
452. Yatton Oral History Project- Ray Naish
453. Hawkins, M. (1988) *Somerset at War: 1939-45*. Wimborne: Dovecote Press
454. Yatton Oral History Project- Ray Naish
455. Yatton Oral History Project.- Rene Cook
456. Reynolds, D. (1996) *Rich Relations: The American Occupation of Britain 1942-1945.London:* Harper Collins
457. Yatton Oral History Project- Jane Bell
458. www.bbc.co.uk/radio4/PM. 20th October 2010
459. Welshman, J. (2006) *A History of the Excluded, 1880-2000. London:* Continuum p6
460. Rutter, M. & Madge, N. (1976) *Cycles of Disadvantage; A Review of Evidence*. London
461. Vestry Minutes Feb 21st 1825 D/P/Yat 9/1/2
462. S.R.O. D/P/yat 13/9/1
463. *The Bristol Mercury* (Bristol, England), Saturday, March 6, 1841
464. S.R.O. Parish registers
465. Roberts, D. (1960) *Victorian Origins of the British Welfare State*. New Haven

466. SRO D/P/key 14/5/9
467. S.R.O. D/P/yat 13/10/2
468. *The Bristol Mercury* (Bristol, England), Saturday, April 14, 1860
469. *The Bristol Mercury* (Bristol, England), Saturday, July 31, 1858
470. S. R.O- D/P/yat 13/3/5
471. Bartlett, P. (1999) The *Poor Law of Lunacy:the administration of pauper lunatics in 19th century England*. London: Leicester University Press Ch 2 and 3
472. D/G/BD 8a/26 sro 11/1/1881
473. Barraclough, M. Bedminster Union Workhouse. *More Yatton Yesterdays*. No 6.
474. Richards, E. Ed (1991) *Poor Australian Immigrants in the Nineteenth Century*. Canberra p57
475. Rowntree, B.S. & Kendal, M. (1913) *How the Labourer Lives*. London p12
476. British Library of Political and Economic Science, University of London, Emigrants' Letters, 1/45
477. Chuk, F. (1987) *The Somerset Years*. Ballard, Victoria, Aus.
478. Belich, J. (2009) *Replenishing the Earth: The Settler Revolution and the Rise of the Anglo-World*. Oxford: OUP
479. 1841 Census information for Yatton
480. S.R.O DD\X\LLY/39
481. S.R.O. DD\FS/17/1/1-3
482. S.R.O DD\FS/18/4/2-3
483. S.R.O DD\FS/17/2/2-4
484. S.R.O DD\FS/18/4/4-82
485. S.R.O DD\FS/70/5/4
486. *The Morning Chronicle* (London, England), Tuesday, May 9, 1848
487. *The Bristol Mercury* (Bristol, England), Saturday, August 9, 1856
488. Gentleman's Magazine October 1835
489. Thompson, F.M.L. (1963) *English Landed Society in the Nineteenth Century*, London p109-50
490. Rubinstein, W.D. (1981) *Men of Property: The Very Wealthy in Britain since the Industrial Revolution*. London p 60-6
491. Thompson, F.M.L. (1963) *English Landed Society in the Nineteenth Century*, London p247-55
492. *The Bristol Mercury* (Bristol, England), Saturday, April 23, 1842
493. Hoppen, K.T. (1998) *The Mid-Victorian Generation 1846-1886*. Oxford: Clarendon p70
494. Bristol Mercury 22nd February 1840.
495. Hunt, E.H. (1981) *British Labour History 1815-1914*. London p99
496. Briggs, A. 'Middle-Class Consciousness in English Politics, 1780-1846', *Past and Present*, 9 (1956), 65-74
497. Bowley, A.L. (1937) *Wages and Income in the United Kingdom since 1860*. Cambridge p128
498. W. R. Greg, 'Life at High Pressure', quoted in Hoppen, K.T. (1998) *The Mid-Victorian Generation 1846-1886*. Oxford: Clarendon p39-40

499. Wrigly, E.A. (1972) *Nineteenth Century Society.* Cambridge.
500. For this next section I am indebted to the family researches and recollections of David Ridley of Cleeve, *Yatton Moor Oral History Project* May 2009
501. Boyer, G. & Hatton, T. (1994) *Rural Trade Unions and the Labour Market in Late Nineteenth Century England.* Economic History Review, 47 pp310-34
502. *Report into the Administration of the Poor Laws. Answers to Rural Queries.* Parliamentary Papers 1834 xxx pp445,488,515
503. Matthews, R.C. O. Et al. (1982) *British Economic Growth 1856-1973.* Oxford p565-71
504. Minchianton, W.E. (1968) *Essays in Agrarian History.* Newton Abbot vol 2 p271
505. Howkins, A. (1991) *Reshaping Rural England: A Social History 1850-1925.* London
506. Mingay, G.E. (1990) *A Social History of the English Countryside*, London
507. Burnett, J. (1989) *Plenty and Want: A Social History of Diet in England from 1815 to the Present Day.* London. p60
508. Burnett, J. (1969) *A History of the Cost of Living.* Harmondsworth. p274
509. Rowntree, B.S. & Kendal, M. (1913) *How the Labourer Lives.* London
510. Floud, R. Watcher, K. & Gregory, A. (1990) *Height, Health and History: Nutritional Status in the United Kingdom, 1750-1980.*Cambridge p.198
511. Yatton Oral History Project- Bob Ford
512. Rowntree, B.S. & Kendal, M. (1913) *How the Labourer Lives.* London p40
513. Higgs, E. (1987) 'Women, Occupations and Work in the 19th century Censuses' *History Workshop*, 23 p75
514. Speechly, H.V. (1999) 'Female and Child Agricultural Day Labourers in Somerset c1685 to 1870. (University of Exeter Ph.D. thesis)
515. Bragg, M. (1976) *Speak for England.* London p48-50
516. *Reports of Special Assistant Poor Law Commissioners on the Employment of Women and Children in Agriculture.* Parliamentary Papers 1843, xii, p.32
517. *Report of Special Assistant Poor Law Commissioners on the Employment of Women and Children in Agriculture.* Parliamentary Papers, 1843, xii, p.21
518. *Royal Commission on Labour: The Agricultural Labourer: Reports upon Selected Districts*, Parliamentary Papers, 1893-4, xxxv, p.337
519. *Second Report of the Commissioners on the Employment of Children, Young Persons and Women in Agriculture*, Parliamentary Papers, 1868-9, xiii, p16
520. Branca, P. (1975) *Silent Sisterhood: Middle Class Women in the Victorian Home.* London. p3-4
521. Ebery, M. & Preston, B. (1976) *Domestic Service in late Victorian and Edwardian Britain.* Reading University Geographical Papers, 42 p93
522. Roberts, E. (1990) *Women's Work 1840-1940.* London p31
523. Drake, M. (1994) 'Domestic Servants' from J. Golby (ed) *Communities and Families*, Cambridge p38-39
524. Wall, R.J., Robin, J. & Laslett, P. Eds (1983) *Family Forms in Historic Europe.* Cambridge Ch 2
525. D/P/k-sey 14/5/5

526. SRO D/P/ k.sey 9/1/4
527. S.R.O D/P/yat 3/2/1
528. *The Bristol Mercury* (Bristol, England), Saturday, October 26, 1861
529. *The Bristol Mercury* (Bristol, England), Saturday, July 26, 1862
530. S.R.O. D\P\yat 9/1/2
531. Journal of Banwell Society of Archaelogy. Search 17 (1981)
532. Yatton Vestry Meeting 24/7/1827.
533. S.R.O Q/AP/a/1/1
534. S.R.O. D\P\yat\9/1/3
535. *The Bristol Mercury* (Bristol, England), Saturday, October 28, 1843
536. *The Bristol Mercury* (Bristol, England), Saturday, March 5, 1853
537. *The Bristol Mercury* (Bristol, England), Saturday, July 3, 1858;
538. *The Bristol Mercury* Saturday, June 14, 1856
539. The Era, Sunday, December 15, 1844
540. *Lloyd's Weekly London Newspaper* (London, England), Sunday, June 27, 1847.
541. *The Derby Mercury* Wednesday, January 21, 1857
542. *The Bristol Mercury* (Bristol, England), Saturday, July 31, 1858
543. *Hampshire Telegraph and Sussex Chronicle etc* (Portsmouth, England), Saturday, January 5, 1850),
544. *The Era* (London, England), Sunday, March 3, 1850,
545. *Lloyd's Weekly Newspaper* (London, England), Sunday, October 27, 1850
546. *The Bristol Mercury* (Bristol, England), Saturday, August 18, 1860
547. *The Bristol Mercury* (Bristol, England), Saturday, February 19, 1859
548. *The Bristol Mercury* (Bristol, England), Saturday, August 6, 1859
549. *The Bristol Mercury* (Bristol, England), Saturday, March 19, 1859
550. *The Bristol Mercury* (Bristol, England), Saturday, August 13, 1859
551. *The Bristol Mercury* (Bristol, England), Saturday, August 27, 1864
552. SRO D/P/key 14/5/8
553. SRO D/P/key 14/5/9
554. MacDonagh, O. (1977) *Early Victorian Government 1830-1870.* London
555. Yatton Oral History Project- Jane Lumkin
556. Yatton Oral History Project – Len Burdge
557. Rodger, R. (1989) *Housing in Urban Britain 1780-1914.* London p10
558. Dobson, M. J. (1997) *Contours of Life and Death in Early Modern England..* Cambridge pp.2-3
559. Woods, R. (1992) *The Population of Britain in the Nineteenth Century.* London p57
560. Creighton, C. (1965) *A History of Epidemics in Britain.* Vol 2 London.
561. Yatton Yesterdays no 9 1992
562. Trollope, A. (1870) *The Vicar of Bullhampton.* Ch 9
563. Bristol Mercury April 14th 1846.
564. *Trewman's Exeter Flying Post or Plymouth and Cornish Advertiser* (Exeter, England), Thursday, April 20, 1848
565. SRO D/P/yat 18/8/1

566. SRO D/P/yat 18/3/1
567. Barraclough, M. (1991) *A History of Yatton*. Yatton Local History Society. p81
568. SRO D/P/yat 18/3/2
569. SRO D/P yat 18/3/3
570. Cleeve Parish Records 1841
571. **The Bristol Mercury** (Bristol, England), Saturday, July 5, 1856
572. Fletcher, A. (2009) *Growing Up in England: The Experience of Childhood 1600-1914*. Princeton: Yale University Press
573. **Trewman's Exeter Flying Post or Plymouth and Cornish Advertiser** Thursday, April 8, 1858
574. D/P/yat 23/19
575. Woodward, E. L. (1938) *The Age of Reform*. Oxford: Clarendon Press
576. Tropp, A. (1957) *The School Teachers: The Growth of the Teaching Profession in England and Wales*, London p18-40
577. Dickens, C. London: Hazell Watson & Viney ed
578. Kitchen, F. (1984) *Brother to the Ox: The Autobiography of a Farm Labourer*. London. pp.164-7
579. Yatton Oral History Project- Bob Ford
580. Bristol Mercury September 19th 1840
581. **The Bristol Mercury** (Bristol, England), Saturday, December 23, 1854
582. **The Bristol Mercury** (Bristol, England), Saturday, January 3, 1857
583. **The Bristol Mercury** (Bristol, England), Saturday, March 14, 1846.
584. **The Bristol Mercury** (Bristol, England), Saturday, July 14, 1849
585. Collinson, W. (1798) History of Somerset- Yatton
586. SRO T/PH/SRO 94
587. Collier, R. (1965) *The General Next to God*. London: Fontana
588. Brigden, T. E. (1909) John Wesley in *"A New History of Methodism"* W.J. Townshend et al (ed) Vol 1 London: Hodder and Stoughton
589. Townshend, W.J. et al (1909) *New History of Methodism*. London: Hodder & Stoughton Vol 1 p580
590. Yatton Oral History Project – Len Burdge
591. Yatton Oral History Project- Jane Bell
592. Yatton Oral History Project- Ray Naish
593. **The Bristol Mercury** (Bristol, England), Saturday, November 27, 1841
594. Skinner, J. (1971) *Journal of a Somerset Rector 1803-1834*. Oxford: OUP
595. Woodard, E.L. (1949) *The Age of Reform 1815-1870*. Oxford; Clarendon Press p491
596. Joseph Leech- *Churchgoer Rural Rides- Calls at Country Churches*
597. Leech, J. (1847) *The Churchgoer: Rural Rides*. Bristol:John Ridles
598. Oxford Jackson's Journel Saturday, May 11, 1844
599. **Jackson's Oxford Journal** (Oxford, England), Saturday, August 3, 1844
600. **Daily News** (London, England), Monday, April 6, 1846
601. **The Morning Chronicle** (London, England), Monday, July 7, 1845
602. **The Bristol Mercury** (Bristol, England), Saturday, September 14, 1850

603. *Lloyd's Weekly Newspaper* (London, England), Sunday, January 1, 1854
604. *The Morning Chronicle* (London, England), Friday, May 5, 1854
605. Haig, A. (1984) *The Victorian Clergy*. London p 3 & 223 quoting The Times 5 Sept 1867.
606. S.R.O Letter Yatton P.C.C to Ecclesiastical Commission D/P/yat February 1897
607. *Jackson's Oxford Journal* (Oxford, England), Saturday, June 20, 1846
608. *Jackson's Oxford Journal* (Oxford, England), Saturday, April 24, 1858
609. As reported in local papers, S.R.O. D\P\yat 23/19
610. SRO D/P/yat 23/19
611. Clevedon Mercury September 1864
612. *The Belfast News-Letter* (Belfast, Ireland), Friday, August 13, 1841.
613. *The Morning Chronicle* (London, England), Saturday, November 27, 1841
614. Womersley, D. (2010) *Divinity and the State*. Oxford: OUP.
615. Wilson, B.R. (1966) *Religion in Secular Society: A Sociological Comment*. London. Weidenfeld & Nicholson pxiv
616. Berger, P. (1970) *The Sacred Canopy: Elements of a Sociological Theory of Religion*. New York. Doubleday
617. Bruce, D. (2002) *God is Dead: Secularisation in the West*. Oxford, Blackwell
618. Davie, G. (1994) *Religion in Britain since 1945: Believing without Belonging*. Oxford. Blackwell
619. Rusen, J.ed. (2002) *Western Historical Thinking: An Inter-cultural Debate*. New York: Berghahn Books pxi
620. Hall, S. & Gieben, B. (1992) *Formations of Modernity*. Polity Press/Open University p15
621. Giddens, A (1984) *The Constitution of Society*. Cambridge. Polity Press
622. E H Carr, *What is History: The George Macaulay Trevelyan lectures*
623. Waller, M. (2009) *The English Marriage: Tales of love, money and adultery*. London: John Murray
624. Achebe, C. (2010) *The Education of a British- Protected Child*. London: Penguin Allen Lane
625. McFarlane, K.B. (1973) *The Nobility of Late Medieval England*. Oxford. P49
626. Hilton, R. and Ashton, T.H (1984) *The English Rising of 1381*. Eds Cambridge
627. Dyer, C. (2002) *Making a Living in the Middle Ages: The People of Britain 850-1520* New Haven: Yale p134
628. Robinson, F.N. (1957) *The Works of Geoffrey Chaucer*. 2nd ed Oxford p252
629. Bonnassie, P. (1991) *From Slavery to Feudalism in South West Europe*. Trans J. Birrell. Cambridge p326
630. Davenport, E. (1906) *The Economic Development of a Norfolk Manor: 1086-1565*. Cambridge.
631. Dyer, C. (2002) *Making a Living in the Middle Ages: The People of Britain 850-1520*. New Haven: Yale p35
632. Fryde, E.B. (1996) *Peasants and Landlords in Later Medieval England*. Stroud: Sutton Publishing p14

633. Waley, D. (1985) *Later Medieval Europe from St Louis to Luther.* New York: Longmans p241
634. Cherubini, G. (1990) The Peasant and Agriculture from Goff, J. L. (ed) *The Medieval World.* London: Collins and Brown.
635. Tuchman, B. (1978) *A Distant Mirror: the Calamitous 14th Century.* London: Book Club Associates p15
636. Troilus and Cressida. Act 1 Scene 111
637. Gaskell, E. (1981) *North and South.* Harmondsworth p63.
638. Eliot, G. (1996) *Adam Bede* Oxford p19
639. Reay, B. (2004) *Rural Englands* Palgrave Macmillan. *p4*
640. Snell, K.D.M. (1985) *Annals of the Labouring Poor: Social Change and Agrarian England, 1660-1900.* Cambridge. ch 8
641. James, H. (1957) *The House of Fiction*, ed L. Edel. London pp268-73. 1st pub 1874.
642. Hilton, R.H. (1969) The Decline of Serfdom in Medieval England. London pp51-52
643. Tuchman, B. (1978) *A Distant Mirror: the Calamitous 14th Century.* London: Book Club Associates p175
644. Oman, C. (1969) *The Great Revolt of 1381.* Oxford.
645. Baker, P. ed. (2008) *The Putney Debates: The Levellers.* London: Verso
646. Cal. Chart R iii 13—01326 p384
647. The Genealogist N.S. Vol. XXVI (1910) copied in the ANH Library for Somerset.
648. The Genealogy of the Family of Rodney of Rodney Stoke. As complied in the 17th century by Sir Edward Rodney, Knt. In the Genealogist N.S. Vol. XVII (1901)
649. The refererence is also from the Genealogy of the Family of Rodney of Rodney Stoke. As complied in the 17th century by Sir Edward Rodney, Knt. In the Genealogist N.S. Vol. XVII (1901). Isabella Sor may be another spelling of Esmania and the Latin tag refers to her as Lady of the Manor.
650. Slocombe, P. (1999) Mark: A Somerset Moorland Village. p28
651. Burke's Peerage vol ii 1999
652. Manumission by Edward the Dean and the Chapter of Wells of William Gyan of North Curry 1264
653. Reference an unpublished paper by my friend Alan Denny of the Yatton Historical Society, "*Robert Gyene 1290-1354: the ups and downs of life in the Middle Ages*". May 2008
654. Godden,M. (1990) *The Making of Piers Plowman* London: Longman
655. Zeldin, T. (1998), *An Intimate History of Humanity.* London: Vintage Books p63
656. Mukherjee, S. (2007) *Law and Representation in Early Modern Drama.* Cambridge: Cambridge University Press
657. Reay, B. (2004) *Rural Englands Basingstoke:* Palgrave Macmillan p 145
658. Pelling, H. (1963) *A History of British Trade Unionism.* Harmondsworth: Pelican. p41
659. Harrsison, J.F.C. (1984) *The Common People.* London: Fontana p265.

660. Arch. J. (1898) *Joseph Arch: the Story of his life*. Ed. Countess of Warwick. London. p22
661. Archer, M.S. (2000) *Being Human: The Problem of Agency*. Cambridge: Cambridge University Press p18
662. Giddens, A. (1984) *The Constitution of Society. Outline of the Theory of Structuration*. Cambridge : Polity
663. Giddens, A. (1991) *Modernity & Self-Identity. Self & Society in the Late Modern Age*. Cambridge: Polity p54
664. Hill, J.S. (1914) *The Place Names of Somerset*. P197
665. B. Record Society Vol 35.
666. Cf an article in the Bristol Times and Mirror, 23rd April 1927 by a Professor Fawcett, FRS.
667. J Anderson, 1742. *A Genealogical History of the House of Yvery*. Vol I Book V, Ch XIV p421
668. From photos and information supplied by Derek B. Lilly, 117 Kenn Road, Clevedon, BS21 6JE
669. Somerset and Dorset Notes and Queries 152 1894
670. Cecil Papers: November 1597, Calendar of the Cecil Papers in Hatfield House, Volume 14: Addenda (1923), pp. 25-29
671. www.stirnet.com/HTML/genie/british/ij/jennings01.htm
672. Rutter, J. (1829) *Delineations of the north western division of the county of Somerset*.

Index

A

Adelard 51, 52, 341
Agricultural depression 171, 174, 177
Agricultural labourers 176, 214, 241, 247, 248, 249, 252, 255, 256, 257, 260, 267, 270, 272, 319, 324, 325, 326
Algerian pirates 142
Alvaric 47
Avery, John 121

B

Barnard, Henry, Vicar of Yatton v, 171, 274, 293
Benzelin 46, 64, 66
Bible Christians 187, 190, 285, 286, 324
Bishop Ralph of Shrewsbury 67
Bishops of Bath and Wells 50, 64, 77, 93
Brougham, Lord- report into charity provision 159, 160, 254, 348
Bulbeck family 329

C

Church Ales 109, 124, 131
Church of England National School 217, 275
Claverham xii, xiii, 48, 49, 54, 55, 66, 67, 72, 77, 82, 86, 92, 101, 103, 104, 126, 147, 148, 149, 150, 161, 164, 181, 191, 194, 195, 196, 197, 199, 209, 212, 214, 221, 222, 235, 241, 248, 249, 250, 252, 254, 256, 258, 259, 261, 262, 285, 286, 288, 289, 294, 321, 322, 328, 337, 339, 348, 350
Claverham Manor 48, 49, 54, 66, 328
Cleeve xi, xvii, 17, 103, 123, 138, 195, 209, 211, 213, 214, 217, 219, 220, 222, 237, 248, 250, 254, 255, 259, 261, 269, 273, 275, 276, 279, 283, 284, 285, 286, 288, 289, 294, 339, 354, 356
Cleeve School 273, 279
Congresbury v, xi, xvi, xvii, 9, 10, 11, 15, 16, 17, 21, 23, 24, 25, 26, 27, 28, 35, 45, 46, 47, 62, 103, 109, 120, 163, 169, 222, 261, 266, 267, 279, 303, 333, 334, 337, 338, 339, 350, 352
Court de Wyck 77, 86, 92, 96, 137, 142, 328
Cranmer, Archbishop 124
Crosse, John (master craftsman) 104

D

Danes 38, 48, 110
David Clerk, Vicar of Yatton 274, 276, 289, 290, 293
Death Rates 71, 249, 272

361

Derham, William xii, 181, 182, 183, 184, 185, 186, 187, 188, 189, 194, 198, 267, 287, 308, 349
Deserving poor 160, 236
Despenser, Hugh 84
Disease 28, 71, 155, 202, 257, 271, 272, 273, 274, 313
Domesday book 35, 36, 38, 45, 46, 47, 49, 50, 58, 61, 252, 340, 341, 349
Domestic service 220, 259, 260, 261, 262, 354
Durban, Richard- legacy for school 161, 195, 196
Durocornovium Corinium 11, 14, 18

E

Edward IIIrd, King of England 84, 86, 344, 345
Edward IInd, King of England 65, 84, 85, 321, 322
Edward the Confessor 38, 45, 47, 136, 340
Egelina de Wyck 77, 83, 308, 322
Electorate, size of 267
Emigration 241, 243
Emmota Harvey (wife of Sir Richard Newton) 91

F

Fastrad (Fastrade) 46, 50, 51, 52

G

Geoffrey de Mowbray, Bishop of Coutances 48, 51, 308
Giso of Lorraine 38, 45
Gnomon 111
Great Bible 119, 124, 125, 126
Gregory, Eliza 181, 309

H

Hannah More 161, 162, 163, 287, 348
Henley Temple 16
Henry Knighton, Chronicler of Black Death 73
Hocktide 109
Holy Trinity Cleeve, grand opening 286
Horsecastle Chapel 186, 217, 219, 287, 288

I

Industrial revolution 164, 169, 170, 208, 212, 349, 353
Isabel de Cheddar (Lady Newton) 87, 91, 92, 93, 95, 96, 308

J

John Drokensford, Bishops of Bath and Wells 64
Joules, Isaac xii, 181, 199, 200, 201, 203, 204, 309
Joules, Merrily 201, 309, 351

K

Keene, David and Aquila 183, 184, 185, 186, 187, 188, 189, 190
Kenn xiii, xvi, 17, 48, 49, 54, 61, 62, 66, 72, 94, 96, 101, 102, 109, 112, 131, 136, 137, 138, 139, 141, 142, 164, 172, 181, 192, 194, 207, 208, 212, 213, 214, 215, 216, 219, 222, 237, 239, 240, 247, 248, 249, 250, 251, 253, 256, 260, 266, 273, 275, 283, 285, 286, 288, 289, 291, 293, 294, 295, 309, 327, 328, 329, 347, 351, 352, 359
Kenn, Christopher 96, 131, 136, 137, 327, 328, 347

Kenn hangings 194
Kingcott 145, 181, 190, 191, 192, 309, 350
Kingcott, James, 181, 190, 192, 309
Kingston Seymour 17, 47, 48, 61, 63, 64, 65, 66, 72, 101, 102, 112, 124, 137, 139, 141, 142, 146, 153, 154, 155, 156, 157, 158, 159, 160, 174, 190, 195, 196, 197, 209, 215, 218, 221, 229, 237, 239, 241, 242, 247, 248, 249, 251, 252, 260, 265, 266, 268, 270, 272, 279, 285, 286, 287, 291, 294, 295, 328, 329, 348
Knight's Fees 54, 55, 327

L

Leisure xvii, 17, 219, 278, 279
Le Sore 328
Lock-up, the village (jail) 146, 171, 193, 267
Luther, Martin 119, 120, 123
Lyson, Dr William 127, 131

M

Manor Courts 53, 157
Manor House, Kingston Seymour 82, 83, 93, 101, 102, 251, 293, 327, 328
Manor of Court de Wyck 77, 86, 92, 328
Manor of Kenn 137, 328
Manor of Kingston 137, 157, 327, 328
Manor of Wemberham 329
Manor of Yatton Rectory 54, 64, 182, 327
Mary, devotion to 107
Methodist chapels 287
Middle classes 252, 254, 255, 267, 272
Milo de Sancto Mauro 65, 327

N

Naylor, James 147
Norman conquest 11, 33, 38, 45, 54, 61, 64, 77, 341, 342

O

Orderic 48, 49, 341
Ordinance of Labourers 73, 74
Overseers of the Poor Rate 269

P

Palm Sunday procession 115
Peasant's Revolt 74, 316, 320, 321, 322, 343
Poor House 159, 238, 240, 250
Pope, the 23, 36, 63, 65, 66, 100, 123, 124, 284
Population of England 77, 169
Population of Yatton 175, 286
Poulett 137, 138, 139, 142, 144, 149, 171, 182, 194, 195, 249, 250, 251, 252, 328, 347
Prebendary of Yatton 66, 85, 135
Public Health 271, 273, 306

Q

Quakers 147, 148, 149, 150, 194, 195, 196, 197, 198, 285, 286
Queen Isabella (wife of Edward IInd) 78, 79, 85

R

Railways – arrival of xvii, 170, 171, 172, 173, 175, 177, 197, 218, 247, 269, 302, 314, 349, 352
Reeve 53, 56, 317
Reformation, the effects of, p119 95, 96, 100, 101, 103, 104, 106, 116,

119, 120, 122, 124, 127, 129, 139, 154, 303, 314, 346
Richard Trellick, Vicar of Yatton 66, 71, 72
Robert Fitzhamon 54
Robert Gyene, Mayor of Bristol 77, 78, 79, 80, 81, 83, 84, 85, 86, 92, 308, 322, 358
Rood Loft, Rood Screen 104, 112, 114, 115, 119, 124, 127, 128, 129, 130
Rowley, James and John 181, 192, 193
Rural Rides 1845, Joseph Leech 289, 290, 293, 356

S

Saxon influence 27, 34
Secularisation 304, 357
Serfs 49, 55, 56, 57, 74, 316, 317, 320, 321
Sir John de Wyck, husband to Egelina 77, 78
Sir John Newton 91, 93, 94, 110, 308, 328
Sir Richard Newton 91, 92, 93
Smyth-Pigot, John Hugh 102, 170, 175, 193, 242, 243, 250, 251, 276, 277, 329
Smyth-Pigott, George Octavius (G.O.) 291
Spirit-road 15, 16, 17
Stalling, Lady Florence 136, 347

T

The Green Man 100, 101, 111, 346
Thomas Cromwell 124
Tithe map, 1841 171, 189

V

Vespasian 7, 8, 10, 11
Vikings, influence of 37, 38, 45
Villeins 46, 49, 53, 55, 56, 57, 317, 321

W

Waimora 36, 47
Wansdyke 23, 24, 33, 339, 340
Wemberham Villa 13, 14, 15, 22
William of Yatton 66
William Worcestre 91
Women's work 346, 354
Workhouse 181, 201, 214, 215, 237, 238, 239, 240, 274, 353

Y

Yatton v, xi, xii, xiii, xvi, xvii, xviii, 17, 23, 33, 34, 35, 36, 37, 38, 45, 46, 47, 48, 50, 52, 53, 54, 56, 61, 62, 63, 64, 65, 66, 67, 71, 72, 73, 77, 78, 83, 85, 91, 92, 94, 95, 99, 100, 101, 102, 103, 104, 105, 106, 108, 109, 111, 112, 115, 116, 119, 120, 121, 122, 123, 125, 126, 129, 130, 131, 135, 136, 143, 144, 145, 146, 147, 148, 149, 154, 156, 159, 160, 162, 163, 166, 169, 170, 171, 172, 173, 174, 175, 176, 177, 179, 181, 182, 183, 184, 185, 186, 187, 188, 189, 190, 191, 193, 195, 196, 197, 198, 199, 200, 201, 203, 204, 207, 208, 209, 210, 211, 212, 213, 214, 215, 216, 217, 218, 219, 220, 221, 222, 223, 227, 229, 230, 235, 236, 237, 238, 239, 240, 241, 242, 247, 248, 249, 250, 251, 253, 254, 255, 259, 262, 265, 266, 267, 268, 269, 272, 273, 274, 275, 277, 278, 279, 283, 284, 285, 286, 287, 288, 289, 290, 291, 292, 293, 294, 301, 302, 305, 308, 309, 313, 321, 322, 324, 327, 328, 329, 331, 333, 335, 337, 338, 339, 342, 343, 345, 346, 348, 349,

350, 351, 352, 353, 354, 355, 356, 357, 358

Yatton- meaning of v, xi, xii, xiii, xvi, xvii, xviii, 17, 23, 33, 34, 35, 36, 37, 38, 45, 46, 47, 48, 50, 52, 53, 54, 56, 61, 62, 63, 64, 65, 66, 67, 71, 72, 73, 77, 78, 83, 85, 91, 92, 94, 95, 99, 100, 101, 102, 103, 104, 105, 106, 108, 109, 111, 112, 115, 116, 119, 120, 121, 122, 123, 125, 126, 129, 130, 131, 135, 136, 143, 144, 145, 146, 147, 148, 149, 154, 156, 159, 160, 162, 163, 166, 169, 170, 171, 172, 173, 174, 175, 176, 177, 179, 181, 182, 183, 184, 185, 186, 187, 188, 189, 190, 191, 193, 195, 196, 197, 198, 199, 200, 201, 203, 204, 207, 208, 209, 210, 211, 212, 213, 214, 215, 216, 217, 218, 219, 220, 221, 222, 223, 227, 229, 230, 235, 236, 237, 238, 239, 240, 241, 242, 247, 248, 249, 250, 251, 253, 254, 255, 259, 262, 265, 266, 267, 268, 269, 272, 273, 274, 275, 277, 278, 279, 283, 284, 285, 286, 287, 288, 289, 290, 291, 292, 293, 294, 301, 302, 305, 308, 309, 313, 321, 322, 324, 327, 328, 329, 331, 333, 335, 337, 338, 339, 342, 343, 345, 346, 348, 349, 350, 351, 352, 353, 354, 355, 356, 357, 358

Yersinia Pestis (Black Death) 28, 66, 67, 71, 72, 77, 81, 83, 99, 207, 305, 308, 316, 343, 344

Lightning Source UK Ltd.
Milton Keynes UK
174932UK00001B/25/P